C0-AUI-715

CITY SON

CITY SON

WAYNE DAWKINS

Andrew W. Cooper's Impact on Modern-Day Brooklyn

University Press of Mississippi / Jackson

Margaret Walker Alexander Series
in African American Studies

www.upress.state.ms.us

The University Press of Mississippi is a member
of the Association of American University Presses.

Manufactured in the United States of America

First printing 2012
∞
Library of Congress Cataloging-in-Publication Data

Dawkins, Wayne.
City son : Andrew W. Cooper's impact on modern-day Brooklyn / Wayne Dawkins.
p. cm. — (Margaret Walker Alexander series in African American studies.)
Includes bibliographical references and index.
ISBN 978-1-61703-258-5 (cloth : alk. paper) —
ISBN 978-1-61703-259-2 (ebook) 1. Cooper, Andrew W., 1927–2002. 2. Brooklyn (New York, N.Y.)—Politics and government—20th century. 3. Brooklyn (New York, N.Y.)—Social conditions—20th century. 4. New York (N.Y.)—Politics and government—20th century. 5. New York (N.Y.)—Social conditions—20th century. 6. African Americans—New York (State)—New York—Politics and government—20th century. 7. African Americans—New York (State)—New York—Social conditions—20th century. 8. African American journalists—New York (State)—New York—Biography. 9. Brooklyn (New York, N.Y.)—Biography. I. Title.
F129.B7D38 2012
070.92—dc23
[B] 2011043556

British Library Cataloging-in-Publication Data available

To Carmen and Allie

Contents

Acknowledgments

This journey began in the summer of 2005 when Jocelyn C. Cooper asked me to write a biography of her late husband. I accepted the challenge because Andy Cooper profoundly affected my career. He gave me a start in journalism at Trans Urban News Service in the late 1970s and was largely responsible for my acceptance to the Columbia University Graduate School of Journalism. In the 1980s and 1990s, I followed Cooper's crusading *City Sun* while working at daily newspapers away from New York.

Writing a book demands solitude; finishing one, however, requires many people. Jocelyn Clopton Cooper provided a comfortable place for me to work when I traveled from Virginia to Brooklyn. Whether it was Third Street in Park Slope, or Plaza Street East at Grand Army Plaza, both residences were launching pads where I could come and go as I pleased to meetings, interviews, and research trips; write at the computer; or listen carefully when Mrs. Cooper matter-of-factly dropped important facts or pearls of wisdom on me. I made sure to keep my pen and notebook nearby.

Thank you to oldest daughter Andrea Cooper Andrews, especially for a lengthy face-to-face interview in February 2007 in Harlem. Youngest daughter Jocelyn A. "Jo-An" Cooper trusted me with a cache of family photographs and, like her sister, provided valuable insights in several interviews. Robert Cooper, Andrew W.'s youngest brother and surviving sibling, and his wife, Dominga, invited me into their home near Las Vegas for a valuable face-to-face interview in August 2007.

Gloria Browne-Marshall, a friend of Jocelyn C. Cooper and a brilliant law professor who wrote a book in 2008 about the U.S. Constitution from a black perspective, cheered on my work and pampered me. I will remember the fried chicken and cake and several rides to La Guardia that saved me the usual ninety-minute rides to the airport on two subway trains and a bus.

Hugh Hamilton let me borrow copies of his *City Sun* investigative reports "Hidden Exiles No More," "Cheap Street," and "Uptown Eco Blues," the latter a special report on environmental racism. Hamilton has been waiting enthusiastically for the finished manuscript.

Basil Paterson graciously and promptly sent documents that described the gerrymandered Brooklyn political boundaries that Andy Cooper successfully rearranged.

About one and a half years into the journey, the Cooper project got a boost when in fall 2006 I won an Eyes on the Prize challenge grant from the National Black Programming Consortium. The grant allowed me to produce a multimedia project at Hampton University, where I teach. With my colleague Van Dora Williams and a handful of students, in 2007 I created "Voting Rights Northern Style," a Web-based project that focused on Andy Cooper's landmark voting-rights activism in the 1960s. Williams was a *City Sun* intern and advocate of my work. Thanks to Donald Carr for assisting with Web design and for designing the cover art. Kissette Bundy, a colleague at Hampton University, provided a big assist: her 1987 oral history of Wilbert A. Tatum, Andy Cooper's newspaper rival, was available at Columbia University. Earl Caldwell, who was a *New York Daily News* columnist during the *City Sun* era, was a valuable source and sounding board.

Hampton University students Austin Bogues, Ashley Ash, Melinda Skinner, Naima Gethers, Sheri Dennis, Antonio Hawthorne, Azania Jenkins, and Crystal Peters did valuable work as research and production assistants. Student Amelia Jones followed them and made contributions as part of her independent study project.

Noreen Malcolm of Queens, whom I have never met in person, was an incredible shadow researcher. After some e-mail exchanges, she cheerfully traveled to libraries in the New York area and photocopied articles for me, for example, Cooper's "One Man's Opinion" columns in the *New York Amsterdam News*.

Editors Ernie Suggs, Carolyn Butts, and Troy Johnson provided opportunities to write about Andy Cooper and the *City Sun* respectively in the *NABJ Journal*, *African Voices* magazine, and the African American Literature Book Club Web site.

A big thank-you to friend and editor Angela Dodson for repeatedly reminding me to get in touch with agent Regina Brooks at Serendipity Literary Agency. Regina Brooks and I connected; she is my agent. Craig Gill of the University Press of Mississippi expressed interest in publishing *City Son* when I pitched the project, and he earnestly embraced the manuscript.

Todd Steven Burroughs and Cheryl Devall blew powerful winds into my sails. Their reading, editing, and enthusiasm guided me to the finish line. Annette Walker and C. Gerald Fraser were other valuable readers of the manuscript chapters.

Betty Winston Baye lent her copy of Shirley Chisholm's *Unbought and Unbossed*, and was an important sounding board and devil's advocate.

Kevin Dunn was an invaluable source. In a closet of his Bronx apartment, he had a full set of *City Sun*s dating from 1990 to 1996. This cache was significant because the last six years of the *City Sun* were lost by a major library during a failed attempt to digitally transfer the content. I visited Dunn three times to take inventory, writing as much as possible into my notebooks.

Thank you to other people who provided documents, tips, and advice and helped me in ways both great and small: A. Peter Bailey, Ericka Blount Danois, A'Lelia Bundles, Constance Carter, Vernon Courtney, Clinton Cox, Jerry Craft, Anna French, Fern E. Gillespie, David Hardy, Clarence Irving, Simone Joye, Paul Kerrigan, Charles Isaacs, Joan Bacchus Maynard, Morris McKoy, Reginald Mitchell, Anthony Carter Paige, Vinette Pryce, Eleanor Rollins, Malik Russell, and N. Christian Ugbode.

I interviewed about a hundred people for *City Son*; my apologies to anyone I have missed in these acknowledgments.

Last but not least, generous thanks to my wife Allie and daughter Carmen. I know my work was mystifying: never-ending predawn writing and reading in my cluttered home office, dozens of road trips to research the biography, most of that time with no assurance of a book contract. I took the journey in search of Andrew W. Cooper on faith, and my family let me do the work. I am eternally grateful.

CITY SON

1. BOY TO MAN

Palmer Cooper, twenty-two, a World War I army veteran, married Irma Cathlee Robinson, twenty-four, of Charleston, South Carolina, on June 17, 1920, in New York City. They lived on 133rd Street in Harlem and attended St. Mark's United Methodist Church.[1]

The Coopers were black, and as Harlem residents they lived in the center of black America. They were married at the time of the Harlem Renaissance. Langston Hughes, Claude McKay, and Zora Neale Hurston lived and worked there during the twenties.[2] Duke Ellington and his orchestra entertained white customers at the Cotton Club.[3] W. E. B. Du Bois lived uptown, too, and he edited the *Crisis* magazine, then the militant and literary journal of the NAACP. The *Crisis*'s journalistic rival was *Opportunity* magazine, published by the National Urban League.[4] The Coopers lived in a community that was the home base of the 369th Harlem Hell Fighters, the World War I heroes who were celebrated for their bravery by the French government but shunned by the United States during an era of Jim Crow segregation.[5]

The Harlem that the Coopers lived in was a ghetto. Most blacks in New York City were packed into apartment houses and brownstones in a neighborhood that had originally been intended to be an upper-middle-class white suburb of Manhattan.[6] When the Coopers settled uptown, Harlem was evolving into a slum. During the 1920s, New York City's black population increased 115 percent, from 152,467 to 327,706 residents. The overwhelming share of those new arrivals were packed in Harlem. Meanwhile, for the first time since the Dutch settlers claimed Manhattan in the 1600s, the population of the island declined. First- and second-generation white immigrants left to live in the city's outer boroughs—Brooklyn, Queens, the Bronx, and Staten Island.[7]

The year that the Coopers were married, 1920, was a momentous one in the city. Mamie Smith became the first black woman to perform on a record when she sang "You Can't Keep a Good Man Down" for New York's Okeh label. Also that year, Marcus M. Garvey held the first convention of his Universal Negro Improvement Association, addressing twenty-five thousand of his followers in Madison Square Garden. James Weldon Johnson, one of the most prominent writers of the Harlem Renaissance, became executive secretary of the NAACP, the first black to hold that position.

Palmer and Irma began making babies. Their first child, Palma, was born on April 30, 1921. The Coopers intended to name their son Palmer; however, city officials misspelled the boy's name on the birth certificate. The Bureau of Records refused to correct the misspelling despite several requests by the mother and father, so Palma, the modified name, stuck.[8] Milton was born on February 12, 1923.

Early in 1927, Irma was with child again. The family was already crammed into their small apartment. In addition to husband, wife, and two sons, Palmer's mother, Louise Marie Schofield, was a member of the household.[9] The anticipated child would grow the family to six members. It was time to move to more open space. It was time to move thirteen miles south to Brooklyn.[10]

When the Coopers moved to 350 Grand Avenue in the Clinton Hill neighborhood, they were among the black arrivals to Brooklyn who more than doubled the African American population between 1920 and 1930. At the start of the Roaring Twenties, 31,912 blacks represented 1.6 percent of the more than two million Brooklynites. By 1930, 68,921 blacks were living in Brooklyn and represented 2.7 percent of the population.[11]

Andrew Wells Cooper was born on August 21, 1927, at the house on Grand between Greene and Gates avenues. The baby shared the first name of Palmer's sibling, who lived on the block near the family.

Brooklyn, originally called Breuckelen by the Dutch settlers, was a rural village community across the East River from urban Manhattan. Even in the twenty-first century, some Brooklynites still describe their subway excursions to Manhattan as "going to the city."

Brooklyn was colonized by Dutch settlers in 1636, a dozen years after setting foot on Manhattan Island to trade furs with the Native Indians. For decades Dutch and British settlers invited by the Dutch West India Company coexisted in New Netherlands (Manhattan) and across the East River in what is now Brooklyn, then known as "Five Dutch Towns."[12] In 1664 King Charles II dispatched the Duke of York and a military force to claim most of the eastern seaboard south of Massachusetts and north of Virginia for England. That year, New Netherlands was renamed New York, and in 1683 the British renamed the five Dutch towns across the East River Kings County.[13]

Blacks lived in Brooklyn from the early 1600s, in small numbers and sprinkled throughout the borough. In the late 1700s, more blacks lived in

Brooklyn than on Manhattan; however, Brooklyn blacks were outnumbered two to one by whites.

Many of the blacks were slaves and worked the farming villages or toiled as servants.[14] Enslaving blacks or Africans ended in Brooklyn and New York in 1785, under certain conditions. The New York legislature ruled that children born to slave women after 1785 were free at birth, but other blacks endured gradual manumission. In 1788 the slave trade in New York was banned, but again with exceptions.[15] Africans, whether enslaved or free, had a tenuous existence. Black men had no voting rights, and few owned property or businesses. Their numbers were small—8 percent of the young state's population in the 1780s—so they did not pose a threat to the white majority.[16]

Brooklyn grew rapidly throughout the 1800s and transformed itself from a network of rural villages into a mighty industrial city. Factories and bustling docks sprang up. Before the Brooklyn Bridge connected Brooklyn with Manhattan in 1883, ferry boats carried passengers between the cities. By 1898, Brooklyn was America's third-most-populous city.[17]

That same year, Brooklyn, also known as Kings County, consolidated with Manhattan, Queens, the Bronx, and Staten Island to establish the nation's largest city. At the time of consolidation, Brooklyn's black population was 18,367, or 1.6 percent of that former city's 1.2 million residents.[18] At the time, two-thirds of the black population of consolidated New York lived in Manhattan, specifically Harlem.[19]

Andrew was born on the same day as the opening of the Fourth Pan-African Congress, which met in New York City from August 21 to 24, 1927. Three months later, on December 4, Duke Ellington opened at the Cotton Club in Harlem. Blacks performed for white audiences but were barred as customers.[20] In November 1928, when Andy was a year old, Herbert Hoover defeated New York governor Al Smith for the U.S. presidency. Also during this time, Oscar De Priest, the first black congressman from the North and the first black in Congress since the departure of George H. White in 1901, was elected to the Seventy-first Congress from the First Congressional District of Illinois.[21] Andrew was two years old when the stock market crashed in October 1929. Sixteen million shares are sold at reduced prices; $30 trillion in stock value was wiped out. The most catastrophic day on Wall Street, October 29, was the forerunner of the Great Depression.[22] By October 1930, at least 4.5 million Americans were unemployed; nevertheless President Hoover insisted he would "preserve the principles of individual and local responsibility."

Andrew and his family were among the 68,921 black residents who represented 2.7 percent of Brooklyn's total population in 1930. Although the black share of the population was small, their numbers doubled between 1920 and 1930, and the black growth spurt continued in succeeding decades.[23] Employment opportunities were extremely constricted for black adults because of up-north-style Jim Crow discrimination.

In 1929 only ninety black men and two black women were employed by the NYPD. Conditions at the New York Fire Department were worse, where only five black men were employed.[24] In 1930, only one out of twenty black laborers was organized compared to one out of five whites.

Black workers were less skilled in the trades because there were not unionized, and that disparity was deliberate. An exception was the Brooklyn docks. Because of the falloff in European immigration during World War I, in 1919 black workers were used as substitutes. In 1930, 1,000 of the 1,200 members of Local 968 were African American. In 1930, Brooklyn had ninety-four black-owned businesses with combined net sales of $500,000, forty-eight full-time employees, and two part-timers.[25]

Despite the limited employment and entrepreneurial prospects for blacks in Brooklyn and New York, migrating black families saw better opportunities than the oppression they endured in the South. Virginians and South Carolinians were among the largest groups coming north, but one of those arriving families was the Broyards of New Orleans, Louisiana. The family patriarch was a master carpenter; in New York, however, he was denied a union card to work because he was a man of color. Paul Anatole "Nat" Broyard, a light-skinned Creole, decided to pass as white to get accepted into the carpenters' union. The deception worked, and Broyard was able to support his family.[26]

On March 1, 1931, when Andy was four, the nineteen-month-old baby of Charles Lindbergh was kidnapped in New Jersey and later found dead in May. Bruno Hauptmann was charged with the crime, convicted, and executed. On March 25, nine black boys were arrested in Scottsboro, Alabama, and charged with raping two white women on a freight train. The boys were declared guilty in three trials, but the U.S. Supreme Court eventually overturned the convictions.[27]

In November 1932, Franklin Delano Roosevelt, a New York Democrat, defeated Republican incumbent Herbert Hoover in a landslide. Andy was five. In the early 1930s, sometime during the early days of the FDR administration, Palmer Cooper was hired as one of the first black U.S. customs officers in New York City.

The position gave Cooper a special status in his community: most black adults worked, but because of the tenuous nature of the Depression economy, laborers, chauffeurs, elevator operators, and other workers lived day to day, week to week, unsure whether they would make the next payday. Cooper had a salaried civil service job in which he could reliably expect his paycheck, and his job included benefits.[28]

Indeed, customs work was demanding law enforcement duty. Customs officers looked for shady characters attempting to enter the United States illegally or move goods in or out of the country unlawfully. Palmer developed a "guilty until proven innocent" attitude in sizing up individuals. He usually expected to find the worst in people because bad people were frequently his customers. Palmer Cooper was gruff and sarcastic at home, so that it comes as no surprise that Andy took on many of his father's traits when he grew up to become a civil rights activist, aspiring politician, then newsman: he was skeptical on good days and cynical on bad ones, irreverent and sarcastic. Of the three sons, Andy probably tried hardest to win his father's approval, but he was rebuffed.[29] This was probably because Andy as a toddler reminded his father of his ne'er-do-well sibling.

Palmer's younger brother Andrew was so light complexioned that he passed for white and was hired to work on an oil cargo ship. When his true racial identity was detected, however, he was fired. Brother Andrew returned home and lived across the street from Palmer's family on Grand Avenue. Andrew drank heavily. He was unmarried and produced no offspring. He also brought disgrace on the family when he took Palmer's service revolver and attempted to rob someone in downtown Brooklyn.[30]

Despite his failures at work and bad choices, brother Andrew was favored by the boys' mother and family matriarch, Louise Schofield Cooper, who was living in Palmer's house. She fomented a Cain-and-Abel-like resentment between Palmer, the reliable yet overlooked older provider, and Andrew, the coddled loser. Did shadism and bitterness shape Louise Schofield Cooper's behavior? She was the whitish-looking offspring of a German Jewish father and black mother with Mohawk ancestry.

Louise's husband Osceola died in his early fifties, before the start of World War I, while working as a dining car server on the former New York Central Railroad.[31] Louise frustrated her older son. She was disrespectful to Palmer's wife Irma, a mahogany-skinned woman with a gentle temperament.[32] Louise sat up in the Grand Avenue house like the Queen Mum, expecting to be waited on by family members.

"Mother!" Palmer screamed a number of times, stamping his feet angrily during arguments with Louise. Palmer transferred his frustration over his mother's abusive behavior to one of his sons. One morning eleven-year-old Andrew walked by his parents' bedroom door and heard his father say, "No Andrew in this family ever amounted to anything." The overheard verbal jab cut the boy's psyche like a knife. The wound scarred him for decades.[33]

Young Andrew had a difficult childhood. He stuttered, and the speech disorder was aggravated because of a combination of Palmer's verbal brutality—Dad was a ruthless teaser—and Grandma's repressive behavior. Louise had a reputation as a teaser too, mean-spirited instead of good-natured. Also, as the baby of the family and youngest male of three, Andy endured roughhousing and hazing. He suffered a broken collarbone after his second-oldest brother, Milton, pushed him down the stairs.[34] Andy rarely if ever spoke lovingly or kindly about his oldest sibling, Palma.

Otherwise, Andy had a well-adjusted childhood. By the time he was old enough for school, he was living through the Great Depression, although he may not have been aware of the bad times. Andy and most of his childhood neighbors had at least three sets of clothes for church, school, and play. He played ball on the street with his neighbors. Saturdays were cleaning days for all children on the block. When the chores were done, many of them went to the Cumberland Theater at Fulton Street at Cumberland and Greene avenues and watched movies for ten cents.[35] Virtually everyone on Grand Avenue went to churches—Baptist, Methodist, Episcopalian, Catholic, Presbyterian, Brethren—and all the children went to the respective Sunday schools. The Coopers attended St. Mark's United Methodist in Harlem.[36]

The Depression continued to afflict Americans, and the stress on African Americans was compounded. W. E. B. Du Bois became a casualty; in January 1934 he was fired as editor in chief of the *Crisis*. Du Bois was so frustrated by urban, northern-style job discrimination by trade unions and other employers that he suggested in print that blacks should segregate themselves when it was in their best interests.[37] Though Du Bois qualified what he said, NAACP policy promoted unqualified integration. The magnificent social scientist, editor, and author was out of step with the association he had helped to found, and after a long internal and public debate in the pages of the magazine, he was pushed out of his post. The Du Bois editorial showed that the black press continued to engage in spirited debates over strategy and tactics—debates that began when the publishers of *Freedom's*

Journal, America's first black newspaper, founded in New York City 103 years before Andy's birth, split over the question of black colonization in Liberia.

On June 28, 1936, Robert, the fourth and last of the Cooper sons, was born. Andy was no longer the baby of the family; he was less than two months shy of his ninth birthday. In the summer of 1938, when Andy was ten, he was sent north to rural New England to work on an uncle's tobacco farm in the Connecticut Valley. Andy worked in the blazing heat for eight dollars a day and experienced or witnessed racial indignities.[38]

He attended PS 45 through June 1941, the year he turned thirteen.[39] World War II had been raging in Europe for nearly two years. The war was creeping closer to America. German U-boats blew up tankers and other freight ships in New York harbor.

The Brooklyn Navy Yard, where the battleships *Maine* (1890) and *Missouri* (1915) were built, was bustling.[40] The atmosphere was edgy and tense. Andy's life at home was tense, too. He felt the backlash from his father's frustrations at work. Palmer Cooper was passed over repeatedly for promotions because of the "one out of three" rule in civil service selections. Managers were not obliged to promote the top scorer on the list; they could select from every three candidates. Despite an outstanding record of arrests and confiscations, Palmer Cooper was rebuffed for promotion. He internalized the rejection at home and belittled Andy, the stutterer who would not amount to anything.[41]

The father did not notice that his third son was developing as a critical thinker. Palmer was a well-read man. He would send his youngest son, Robert, to the neighborhood newsstand to buy the *Saturday Evening Post*, *Colliers*, *Life*, *Redbook*, and *Cosmopolitan*. When his father was not reading the magazines, Andy slipped away with them and read them cover to cover. Deep reading compensated for his difficulty in articulating thoughts because of his speech impediment.[42] Andy read books away from home. His teenage friend Vincent Ragsdale recalled a day when Andy was walking toward him on 138th Street in Harlem dressed in a porkpie hat, brown corduroys, brown bomber jacket, and brogans, carrying a book that seemed as large as he. The book was *The Sun Is My Undoing*, by Margarite Steen, a British author.[43]

The more Andy read, the more confident he was at the dinner table to argue back at his father when he belittled or teased him. Andy not only challenged his father but began questioning the authority of his family's church. Andy told his mother once that the church was holding black people back. When Andy went to church and was told to hang in there because although he was oppressed on Earth, he would get his reward in heaven, he could no longer accept that.[44] He continued to read deeply and listen to mentors outside his home and grow as a critical thinker and critic.

When Japan bombed Pearl Harbor on December 7, 1941, and America entered World War II, Andy was fourteen and a ninth grader at George Westinghouse Vocational High School. He learned the plumbing trade. The black population of Brooklyn continued to grow rapidly to 107,263, triple the size of black Brooklyn two decades before. Despite the growth, blacks increased to merely 4 percent of Brooklyn's 2.7 million residents.[45] Two-thirds of the borough's black population was packed into Bedford-Stuyvesant, a central Brooklyn neighborhood that in a decade evolved into a ghetto, then a slum.

The hyphenated name did not stick until the 1930s, when the neighborhoods Bedford Corner and Stuyvesant Heights were merged.[46] Editorials in the daily *Brooklyn Eagle* in 1931 repeatedly used the hyphenated term, at times shortening the phrase to "Bed-Stuy," suggesting a "pig sty." The phrase became nasty code words for the mostly southern blacks moving in.

In the meantime, a public policy called redlining took hold. While tens of thousands of new housing units were built in South Brooklyn neighborhoods to attract ethnic whites, central and north Brooklyn residences deteriorated, and banks denied loans to customers who wanted to renovate their properties or buy new housing. The Home Owners Loan Corporation (HOLC), established during the Depression to minimize home foreclosures and bank failures, created a "Residential Security Map" of Brooklyn and assigned letter grades—A through D—for neighborhoods based on ethnicity. Neighborhoods with large numbers of Jews, Italians, or Irish Americans were marginalized with C- and B-minus ratings. Neighborhoods with concentrations of black and Puerto Rican residents were condemned with D ratings and were color-coded red on the HOLC map, leading to the infamous term "redlining."[47] Meanwhile local government denied services to residents in predominantly black Bedford-Stuyvesant. When Robert Moses was city parks commissioner, one playground each was built in Bed-Stuy and Harlem out of 255 playgrounds built citywide.[48] Adults protested that the lack of places for young people to play helped breed crime, but the appeals were ignored.

What criminal justice officials did not ignore were allegations that crime was rampant in Bedford-Stuyvesant. In August 1943, a grand jury was seated to investigate allegations. Instead of individuals, an entire community was scrutinized for alleged criminal conduct. An all-white grand jury listened to more than one hundred predominantly white witnesses who essentially claimed that an extreme state of lawlessness had festered for years: schoolchildren were robbed; churches curtailed or eliminated evening services because citizens considered it too dangerous to walk the streets at night; and gangs of hoodlums armed with knives and other weapons assaulted, robbed, and even murdered innocent people. People who testified also said the neighborhood was rife with prostitution, was a cesspool of filth and venereal disease, and many residents were on relief illegally. The last allegation was ironic because wartime employment and the draft virtually eliminated the need for welfare.[49]

The grand jury's report blamed mayor Fiorello LaGuardia and other city officials for neglecting the neighborhood and allowing crime and decay to spin out of control. LaGuardia dismissed the charge and suggested that Bedford-Stuyvesant's changing from white to black resulted in the lawlessness and filth: "Let's be more frank about it," said LaGuardia. "This is the [race] question we are talking about. When a neighborhood changes its composition that way there is bound to be trouble."[50] The all-white grand jury did not accept the mayor's answer. They recommended saturating the district with police and if necessary state troopers and National Guardsmen. In addition to calling for crime fighting, the grand jury concluded that Bedford-Stuyvesant was starved of recreational facilities for youth, and that condition aggravated crime and poverty. The grand jury went on record to criticize parks commissioner Robert Moses's park policies that exacerbated African American slum conditions.[51]

As for crime prevention, the mayor did next to nothing. LaGuardia won the battle for public opinion by dismissing people who accused the city of neglecting Bedford-Stuyvesant and central Brooklyn as liars and crackpots.[52] Moses meanwhile issued an eight-page release that said the grand jury report alleging neglect and racial discrimination was "without the slightest foundation."[53]

The same month that the Brooklyn grand jury sparred with LaGuardia and Moses, a race riot exploded uptown in Harlem. A white police officer shot and wounded a black soldier. The soldier objected to insulting language the officer was using toward a black woman during an argument. The soldier struck the cop and knocked him to the ground; the police officer retaliated and shot the GI. The woman began screaming that the soldier was killed, and rumors spread throughout the community. Rioting and looting occurred. Before order was restored, six people were killed, 185 people were injured, and hundreds of white-owned businesses were looted or destroyed (in August 1943, there were few black-owned businesses or even black employees in the stores). A combined 6,600-member force of city and military police plus civilian patrolmen was deployed, plus 8,000 state guardsmen and 1,500 civilian volunteers.[54]

The Savoy ballroom was an exciting place where blacks and whites danced and socialized without the strict segregationist codes. It was not unusual for white soldiers to leave the Savoy with black women. It was wartime, and many of the commissioned officers in New York were white southerners who were appalled by the mingling. These officers began spreading rumors that soldiers who frequented the Savoy were contracting venereal disease. The Savoy was shut down temporarily, adding to the tension that led to the riot.

After the violence and devastation, Harlem, which used to be the destination for nightclubbing, dancing, and drinking, now had the reputation as a dangerous ghetto where whites dare not tread. That stigma lasted through the end of the twentieth century.

In the same month in 1943, Bedford-Stuyvesant and Harlem were defined as dangerous places to travel to because of their high concentration of blacks. That month Andy Cooper celebrated his sixteenth birthday. He was about to begin the eleventh grade at Westinghouse High School. It is highly likely that he was working as a server at the Brooklyn Navy Yard. It was also likely that the cerebral teenager was reading and processing the negative news about Bedford-Stuyvesant and Harlem.

Palmer Cooper was a superb cook and frequently showed off his talent at home. Cooper cooked leg of lamb with mint jelly, young potatoes and Brussels sprouts, crown roast of pork with cauliflower and broccoli, roasted capon with corn stuffing and baby asparagus and white rice, and roast sirloin au jus with peas and baked potatoes.[55] It is probable that Palmer's knowledge of cuisine was passed down from his father, Osceola A. Cooper (1864–1915), a native of Louisiana, home of Creole and Cajun delicacies. Palmer's father also worked as a dining car server on the Pennsylvania Railroad. Andy observed his father's technique in the kitchen and presentation at the dining table.

In 1943, when Andy was sixteen, the United States was more than a year into fighting the war against Germany, Japan, and Italy. After a year of humiliating defeats on the battlefields, America was changing the momentum. Its advantage was factory production. American factories built tanks and ships faster than the enemies could destroy them. In prewar Detroit, a million cars rolled off the assembly lines every year; however, during wartime, factory production was so centered on the military that from 1942 to 1945, only 500 cars were built in the Motor City. Detroit assembly lines were in the war production business. In Brooklyn, the Navy Yard expanded wartime employment to 70,000 workers on the 300-plus-acre waterfront. The Hammerhead crane at Berth 12, Pier G, was the largest in the world at that time. The USS *Missouri* was launched from the Brooklyn yard in 1944.[56]

Andy became one of those Navy Yard workers. He was a message carrier and also worked as a dining server in the Officers' Club and officers' quarters. Family members suspect that Andy lied about his age and presented himself as an older teenager to be eligible to work. It is very likely that during the summer months of 1943 and 1944 Andy worked full-time hours at the yard. Andy served meals, delivered messages, and watched authority figures go about their work. Those observations surely informed his adult work decade later.[57]

In early 1944, Jocelyn Elaine Clopton, a teenager from Jersey City, New Jersey, moved in at 116 Gates Avenue and lived with her mother in a five-dollar-per-week rooming house. The Gates Avenue address was around the corner from the Grand Avenue block where Andy Cooper lived. In time, Jocelyn would become Mrs. Andrew Cooper.

Jocelyn Clopton was the only child of Lina Mildred Sullivan (1906–73), a native of Jamaica, and Robert Andrew Clopton (1906–75) of Jersey City. Jocelyn's parents met at Small's Paradise, the legendary Harlem nightclub on 135th Street and Seventh Avenue. In high school, Robert Clopton ranked in the top 10 percent of his class academically and enrolled at Howard University. He stayed for one year until he became Jocelyn's father. She was born on January 27, 1929, at the home on Orchard Street in Jersey City. Her parents separated when she was two.

Jocelyn did not grow up with her mother. Lina Mildred Sullivan Clopton lived a dual life. She worked as a waitress and passed for white. Lina kept two addresses and lived at 666 St. Nicholas Avenue off Edgecombe and later on Convent Avenue. As a child, Jocelyn saw her mother at least three times a year, on birthdays, at Easter and Christmas, and maybe for a week in the summer. Otherwise Jocelyn was raised by her father and paternal grandparents, especially Lucy Ann Reid (Clopton). The family moved from Orchard Street to 70 Jersey Avenue, and Jocelyn lived at that address for at least seven years.

Jocelyn's early childhood years seemed privileged. She wore silk dresses sewn by her grandmother, and the home was the first on the avenue to be connected to gas and electric service; other houses were heated with coal. But Jocelyn was born at the end of the Roaring Twenties and nine months before the start of the Great Depression. By the mid-1930s when she was a schoolgirl, her household stability collapsed. Her grandmother got arthritis and became obese and could not walk. Jocelyn became a street urchin, essentially homeless. She witnessed bread lines and experienced poverty. Jocelyn's father worked at odd jobs, on the Jersey docks, washing dishes, or shining shoes for thirty dollars a day on Saturdays at his father's barber shop. Compared to most black men, granddad was prosperous. His barbershop was near a railroad terminal and had an added bonus, a bathtub. Black male railroad workers could take baths and then dress for Saturday-night dates. In the 1930s, Grandpa Clopton made about $300 on Saturdays.[58] Robert's marginal employment had to be a huge letdown because his dream was to go to medical school and become a doctor.[59]

Jocelyn had a chilly relationship with her grandfather R. Alexander Clopton. She would ask him for lunch money and then go to school. When Jocelyn returned home, she prepared meals for grandma, who was sickly. Once Jocelyn asked her grandfather for money to buy two lamb chops from the market. He hemmed and hawed with the elementary-school-age child before giving her the money. Jocelyn resented the teasing. Grandpa Clopton died in 1936 at age sixty-one. Grandma Clopton, fifty-seven, died in 1943, on a Sunday and alone in the house.[60]

Jocelyn, at the time a fourteen-year-old ninth grader, moved in with a Mrs. Wiggins in Jersey City, who took care of a number of children.[61] Jocelyn stayed for eight months. That summer, she stayed in Asbury Park, New Jersey, and worked in a factory, where she stuffed cut rope into the sleeves of Marine Corps fatigues.

When it was time to return to Jersey City to get ready for school, Mrs. Wiggins told Jocelyn she could not come back. Her father had not paid the fifteen-dollar-per-week room and board for the two months Jocelyn was away, and the family was in default.

Jocelyn's mother, who had been distant, stepped in. While inside a corner store in Brooklyn, Lina Clopton told a fellow waitress that she was desperately looking for a room for herself and her daughter. The waitress friend said she operated a rooming house. In early 1944, Jocelyn moved to Brooklyn and for the first time lived with her mother. She also shared the rooming house space with her mother's sister Rose and Yvonne, a first cousin. Although Jocelyn lived in Brooklyn, she continued to go to Lincoln High School in Jersey City. To make the eight-mile journey, Jocelyn took the A train from Brooklyn to Chambers Street in lower Manhattan, then caught another train that traveled in a tube under the Hudson River to Jersey City. At Exchange Place she caught a public bus to school. The trips took at least an hour each way.[62]

Sometime in early 1944, Jocelyn and Andy met. She had just turned fifteen; he was two years older. One Sunday, the niece of the landlady brought Andy to the house to meet the aunt. Jocelyn was washing dishes in the kitchen. The niece introduced Andy to Jocelyn, and the teenagers exchanged pleasantries. Over time Andy kept an eye on Jocelyn. He watched her play at the Colored YWCA on Carlton Avenue in Fort Greene, and he watched her at work as a stock girl at the Abraham and Strauss department store on Fulton Street. Eventually Andy was able to manage his stuttering problem and find the nerve to ask Jocelyn out. Favorite dates were at dance halls, where both teenagers jitterbugged and did the Lindy Hop. After the fifth date, Jocelyn and Andy were seeing each other virtually all the time.[63]

As Andy's steady girlfriend, Jocelyn experienced Palmer Cooper's verbal brutality. On Easter, she showed up at the house wearing a green coat over a red, white, and blue dress. Jocelyn thought she looked cute. Andy's dad insisted she was countrified. "All of her taste," sneered Palmer, "was in her mouth." The teenage girl was reduced to tears.

Jocelyn and Andy had to notice the racial skirmishes exploding around them in Brooklyn like hand grenades on a battlefield. In June 1944, Lillian Oliver, a black trolley driver, was beaten in the face by two white men. Oliver exchanged words with a white woman who boarded her Flatbush Avenue car. Ninety witnesses saw Oliver's beat down. She fought back with a switch iron. When police arrived, Oliver was standing alone in the street. For refusing to surrender the iron she had used in her defense, Oliver was charged with disorderly conduct. Two weeks later, trolley driver Gadson Goodson was pulled from his car and beaten by passengers, and a retired white policeman beat Goodson again on the street. The same week, a man battered driver Mary Gaskin while the passengers held her.[64]

These attacks did not go unchallenged. Sixteen black women drivers pulled their trolleys off the street on June 6 and staged a wildcat strike. Representatives from the *New York Amsterdam News*, Harlem's top broadsheet, and the Women Voters Council met with the head of the board of transportation. The head insisted it was more efficient to replace black women drivers than provide them protection because the war emergency required that everyone cooperate.[65] The transportation head's attitude illustrated why many blacks along the East Coast promoted a "Double V" campaign. It was promoted by the *Pittsburgh Courier*, a crusading black newspaper that had editions in more than ten cities. The Double V reminded blacks they were fighting a two-front war, the war against America's enemies Germany and Japan, and the war at home against white supremacy that resulted in American apartheid in the South and restricted freedom for blacks in the North.[66]

Brooklyn and the rest of New York City were bewildered. Blacks continued to stream up from the South for freedom and opportunities, but they faced limits. They entered a land of limited democracy, fully dependent on the exploitation of the minority populations and a white-controlled social structure that stabilized their communities while destabilizing communities of color.[67]

Black workers were vulnerable, frequently excluded from good jobs, and exposed to racial animosity and violence when they appeared to be competing with whites for good work. When the black transit workers were assaulted, a white woman complained to Mayor LaGuardia and later to governor Thomas Dewey that the city was employing too many colored people in the subways. The Board of Transportation was told by a boss that nonwhite workers were "reasonably competent" but had poor attendance records and avoided weekend shifts. Yet the bosses' report stated that black laborers were disciplined in no greater proportion than white.[68]

Even freedom of movement for blacks on Brooklyn streets was limited. At night, Andy had to be mindful of where he walked in his neighborhood to return to his house off Grand Avenue. Private armed guards patrolled some streets and denied blacks passage through the neighborhood.[69] Defending his right to go home was humiliating for Andy, a native-born neighbor since 1927. Despite the hassles and humiliations, mostly southern blacks were pouring into New York, and the resulting dramatic demographic change would stir racial conflicts. A year before America entered World War II, two-thirds of New York City blacks lived in Manhattan, primarily in Harlem. By 1950, black Manhattan's population shrunk to 50 percent of all New York City blacks, and Brooklyn's black population grew to 28 percent, up from 2.7 percent of the borough twenty years earlier. In ten years, Brooklyn's black population nearly doubled from 108,263 to 208,478.[70]

Many people traveled hundreds of miles from southern hamlets, yet thousands jumped on the A train and moved a dozen miles south from Harlem to central Brooklyn. At the same time, whites were leaving the borough. A decline of 50,000 residents marked the first decrease in Brooklyn's population since the 1700s.[71]

In August 1945, America celebrated victory over Japan and the official end of World War II. That month Andy Cooper earned a plumbing diploma from George Westinghouse Vocational High School. He also celebrated his eighteenth birthday in August. Andy had a high school degree in hand but was far from finished with school. He enrolled at Boys High School and attended night classes to earn an academic diploma.[72]

Most black teenagers were steered to the vocational high schools to learn a trade, something constructive they could do with their hands. The career path was ironic and often cruel because trade unions in New York severely constricted black employment and saved the jobs for ethnic whites. Academic public high schools were for a select group of white students who were college bound. Plumbing was dirty yet well-paying work, but Andy was not interested. He had his sights on other careers that involved the life of the mind.[73]

2. JIM CROW BROOKLYN

By 1947, America was more than a year removed from World War II, and civilian society was transforming rapidly. One of the more dramatic changes occurred in sports, and the place was Brooklyn: Jackie Robinson joined the Brooklyn Dodgers and became the first black to break the Major League Baseball color line.[1] The single feat by Robinson and Dodgers management and the feel-good media story distracted from mass discrimination elsewhere in Brooklyn and New York City.[2]

Meanwhile many returning soldiers went to college courtesy of the GI Bill, and their educations would lead to good jobs that helped create tremendous wealth in the next decade. White flight from the cities to the suburbs began. Black flight from the South to northern cities accelerated.[3] By 1950, the Brooklyn's black population had nearly doubled in a decade to 208,478 residents and 7.6 percent of the borough's 2.7 million people. The majority were packed into the central Brooklyn ghetto that included Bedford-Stuyvesant. With the substantial and concentrated black population growth, Bert Baker became the first African American elected official in Brooklyn in 1948. Baker's win was preceded by a number of frustrating defeats by black candidates. His election to the state's Seventeenth Assembly District was largely orchestrated by white Democratic political leaders who wanted to stave off a rebellion of voters possibly electing a black Republican. The leaders were able to appease blacks with one seat and cater to a growing and potent Italian American voting bloc in the borough.[4]

The black population was growing with good reason: While the postwar retransformation was great for many white GIs, it was a nightmare for returning black veterans who expected to be treated like first-class citizens after risking their lives overseas. In 1947 the NAACP reported that the previous year was "one of the grimmest years in the history of the National Association for the Advancement of Colored People." A statement deplored "reports of blowtorch killing and eye gouging of Negro veterans freshly returned from a war to end torture and racial extermination" and said, "Negroes in America have been disillusioned over the wave of lynchings, brutality and official recession from all the flamboyant promises of postwar democracy and decency."[5] The GI Bill did improve the lives of many black veterans. About 1.3 million black and other warriors of color and 14.6 million white Americans participated in veteran benefit and education programs at similar rates, more than 73 percent. Yet despite the assistance, there was no greater instrument in widening an already huge racial gap in postwar America than the GI Bill. To get the legislation passed, the Roosevelt administration compromised with segregationist southern Democrats who chaired the key committees. The documents did not contain clauses that directly or indirectly excluded Negro soldiers. Instead implementation of the federal law was largely left to the discretion of the states, and in the South, its leaders were not about to upset the status quo. The American Legion even stated for the record that it was disinclined to challenge regional race relations to enforce equal treatment of blacks.[6] In 1948 GI benefits accounted for 15 percent of the federal budget, and from 1944 to 1971, $95 billion was spent on the universally praised welfare program. The GI bill was overwhelmingly affirmative action for whites that by 1955 produced results: 400,000 engineers, 200,000 teachers, 90,000 scientists, 60,000 doctors, and 22,000 dentists, as well as 5.6 million veterans pursing vocational and technical trades.[7]

One of the returned black GIs, Anatole Broyard of Brooklyn—who self-identified as white and attended the New School for Social Research on the GI bill—pursued a life as a writer of the Beat Generation. Broyard was among 150,000 blacks who passed into white society to dodge discrimination.[8] Jocelyn Clopton's mother Lina was among the people who passed.

In 1947, Andy Cooper was working with his older brothers Palma and Milton. Robert, the youngest of the siblings, was eleven. They ran a decorating service and painted houses. They also began selling vegetables and fruits to neighbors from the back of a truck.

That year Jocelyn's mother left the Gates Avenue home. Lina suffered from asthma, and she traveled faraway to Wenatchee, Washington, to breathe cleaner air. There she worked picking fruit in the self-proclaimed apple capital of the world. Jocelyn was seventeen when her mother left. She gained adult supervision from the Coopers: Andy's step-uncle, Joe Jefferson, a World War II veteran, and Aunt Lou Jefferson. The couple lived above Jocelyn, and Lou raised Jocelyn like a daughter.[9]

In 1948 the early rumblings of the modern civil rights era were evident. On July 26 president Harry S. Truman signed an executive order to desegregate the U.S. military.[10] A symbol of black pride was the confirmation of Ralph Bunche as United Nations mediator in Palestine. Bunche negotiated a cease-fire between Israel and Palestine.

Locally, the Urban League and NAACP waged a two-front battle to open up employment opportunities for blacks. The NAACP appeared militant because it sued in court for opportunity; the Urban League meanwhile needled businesses to open doors to qualified blacks. Andy Cooper walked through one of the doors. With help from the local Urban League, he was placed at Brevoort Savings Bank of Brooklyn as a clerk.[11]

Andy and Jocelyn, who had been boyfriend-girlfriend exclusively for five years, prepared to get married in fall 1949. They applied for a marriage license that cost two dollars. Andy and Jocelyn paid a dollar each to symbolize an equal partnership. When they wed on October 15, 1949, both sets of parents were present: Irma and Palmer Cooper and Lina and Robert Clopton. The ceremony was held at St. Philip's Episcopal Church on McDonough Street and Decatur Street between Lewis and Stuyvesant avenues.[12] Andy and Jocelyn were not regular churchgoers at the time, but because Jocelyn had received confirmation in a Jersey City Episcopal church at age twelve, she and her groom were granted a church wedding.[13]

Andy and Jocelyn moved out on their own, with help from the black press. Jocelyn placed a three-dollar classified advertisement in the Brooklyn edition of the *New York Amsterdam News*: "Couple desperately needs an apartment. Please call." Their call was answered. They moved into a two-room apartment at 768 Herkimer Street between Utica and Rochester avenues.

The Coopers' living arrangements were settled, but another inconvenience disturbed their marital bliss. After about a year of work as a clerk at Brevoort Savings Bank of Brooklyn, Andy was fired one week after he married Jocelyn.[14] He was not idle for long. With Jocelyn (and possibly dad Palmer and the other sons), he pooled enough money to lease a space at 2007 Seventh Avenue and 120th Street and open a restaurant called "Andy's Coop."

At that time black neighborhoods in Harlem and Brooklyn had few restaurants. There were bar-and-grill-type establishments, but few coffee shop–lunch counters or family-style restaurants. Blacks ate out at the benevolence of white proprietors. They were welcome to have a hot dog and an orange drink at a Nedick's counter or a cup of coffee and nutted cheese sandwich at Chock Full o' Nuts.[15] These establishments were along transportation corridors such as Fulton Street in Brooklyn, the path of the underground A train to Manhattan and numerous bus routes above ground, or Lenox Avenue in Harlem. These eateries gladly took black customers' money but did not hire blacks to cook or serve customers. Andy and his family introduced a black-owned family restaurant into the mix.[16]

In addition to running the restaurant, Andy began taking courses at Baruch College in Manhattan. That was the start of his twenty-seven-year on again, off again journey to a college degree. Work often got in the way of higher education. Jocelyn went to work, too. She was hired as a messenger at AT&T in Manhattan and in time was promoted to clerk. At the end of her shift, she would hop on a double-decker bus in lower Manhattan and ride uptown to help the Coopers at the restaurant.[17]

Andy's Coop in Harlem lasted about a year. The restaurant failed, in part because the hour commute every day taxed the men. The Coopers opened another eatery closer to home in Brooklyn. They occupied the former Bing's Luncheonette at 396 Gates Avenue at the corner of Nostrand Avenue.[18] Palmer Cooper occasionally cooked. Andy was a server. Milton also worked in the kitchen and at the counter. Robert worked near the ice cream stand, dispensed the soda, and served meals. Once Palmer was angered over something Robert did—or did not do—in the restaurant, and he physically attacked him. Andy wrestled his dad to protect Robert.[19]

F&M Schaefer Brewing Company was founded in 1838 on Manhattan by Frederick Schaefer, a German immigrant. The start-up distinguished Schaefer as the oldest lager brewery in America.[20] As the beer became increasingly popular with customers, Schaefer moved several times on Manhattan to expand his operations. In 1915 he sold his plant site at Park Avenue and East Fifty-first Street to St. Bartholomew's Church and moved the operation to Brooklyn, Kent Avenue at South Ninth and Tenth streets in Greenpoint, along the East River. Because of Prohibition in the late 1920s and early 1930s, Schaefer brewed "near beer" and manufactured dyes and artificial ice to make a living. When Prohibition was repealed in April 1933, president Rudolph Schaefer Jr. launched an extensive advertising campaign that placed his company in front of competitors.[21] By 1938, Schaefer was selling one million barrels a year and expanded to two million barrels yearly in 1944. With hundreds of workers, the brewery was one of the largest employers in Brooklyn.[22]

In 1950, Schaefer's racial makeup was not unlike most commercial companies in the borough; few if any blacks were hired. More than 208,470 African Americans lived in Brooklyn, plus an estimated 800,000 blacks in the entire city, with thousands more each year coming up from the South.[23] The Brooklyn Urban League waged a tenacious campaign in cajoling businesses to hire blacks at their operations. In 1948 the Urban League placed Andrew Cooper at the Brevoort Savings Bank.

Three years later, in 1951, the Urban League assisted again, and Andy was hired as a checker in the loading department at Schaefer. He was the second self-identified black employee hired.[24] Andy at the time was twenty-four. Before he took the night job, he had been attending night classes at Brooklyn College, trying to continue the course work he began at Baruch College in Manhattan. Now college was once again put on hold.

When Andy began working at Schaefer, America was about a year into the Korean War.[25] A draft was in effect, but he was exempted for two reasons: because of his stutter and, more importantly, because he was an expectant father. In early 1952, the Coopers left their Herkimer Street apartment and bought their first home, a three-story limestone house at 619 Decatur Street between Howard and Saratoga avenues. Twenty years later, in 1972, the Coopers sold the house to the parents of Chris Rock, the future superstar comedian.[26]

Andrea Suzanne Cooper was born on April 29, 1952. Her parents were cream-complexioned Negroes. As an infant, Andrea had wavy blonde hair and bluish eyes and looked like a white baby. Her looks fascinated the extended family and neighbors on Grand Street ("You gotta get down here and see this," said Jean Carnell, who was dating Andy's youngest brother, Robert). The baby's looks delighted Andy's mother-in-law, Louise Scofield, who was light complexioned enough to pass as a white person.[27] Andy resented his mother-in-law's heightened interest in his daughter's pale skin and resisted Louise's efforts to show off the baby to visitors. Andy continued to work overnight at the brewery. When Andrea was a toddler, she slept in her parents' bed and at dawn was awakened daily from a comfortable sleep to go back to her room. That was because Daddy came home eager to go to bed.[28]

While Andy Cooper settled into a work and family life routine, the black struggle locally for better representation and recognition continued and reported incremental progress. The New York City Council passed a bill that prohibited racial discrimination in city-assisted housing developments. This was a significant change, since many housing developments had public funding.[29] In June, Pfc. William Thompson of Brooklyn was awarded the Congressional Medal of Honor posthumously for heroism in Korea. This was the first grant of a Congressional Medal of Honor to an African American since the Spanish-American War.[30]

At the end of the year, Hulan Jack was sworn in as Manhattan borough president. He was the first African American elected to the position.[31] Jack's election reflected growing black political muscle in Harlem, where Manhattan's blacks were concentrated.

In Cooper's town, black central Brooklyn—mostly Bedford Stuyvesant—nearly matched Harlem in numbers but lacked any political representation of its own. Irish, Jewish, and Italian politicians called the shots for the black inhabitants. Also, at the end of the year, there was this fact about southern blacks flowing up to New York: 1952 was the first year in seventy-one years of tabulation that no lynchings in America were reported.[32]

Andy Cooper kept up his night work at the brewery through the 1950s. Sometime in the mid-1950s, he organized a strike among the checkers for better wages. Unlike the truck drivers, checkers were nonunion workers. Because Andy was the lone black on his shift, work was lonely with hints of danger. One night when he entered the men's room he found "Nigger go home" written on the mirror in red lipstick.[33] Jimmy Fox, Andy's supervisor, showed no such hostility, however, and encouraged the black employee. Cooper worked nights for eleven and a half years and was promoted to foreman.

The Seventeenth Assembly District in Brooklyn included Bedford-Stuyvesant, which at that time was about two-thirds black; yet an all-white and mostly Irish organization controlled the turf. The political organization elected the state senator, assemblyman, city councilman, and other local officeholders and by treaty with the similar clubs around it, picked the men for congressional seats, judgeships and other large-bore political jobs.[34]

In 1953, Shirley Chisholm, a college student, attended a few of the political club meetings whenever there was a speaker she was eager to hear. After the city councilman or commissioner had finished, there was a question-and-answer period. Hardly anyone ever asked questions. Chisholm did. Why wasn't trash picked up regularly in Bedford-Stuyvesant, as it was in the white neighborhoods? she asked the sanitation commissioner. Why hadn't the city councilmen delivered on their promises? Her questions were unwelcome, and after the meetings, organization people told her so. Chisholm feigned innocence: How do I know what kind of questions you're supposed to ask? But she knew very well, and so did the annoyed officials know that she was needling them to show how little they did or cared for the people who kept them in office.[35]

Wesley D. Mac Holder, another black resident, was fed up with white indifference and neglect and pushed for change. That year he formed a group called the Committee for the Election of Lewis S. Flagg Jr. Flagg was an outstanding black lawyer running for the district's seat on the municipal court bench. When the seat became vacant, the political machine had gone

one step too far. Not only had they passed over the qualified black nominees in the district, but they had also imported a white man to run for the job. The move outraged many of the blacks and some of the white neighbors. At that time there were forty-nine civil judges in Brooklyn, and not one of them was black. Mac Holder pointed out the whitewash in campaign mailings. He lined up heavy support for Flagg among the community's big names, both black and white. Chisholm and others in the ranks worked overtime canvassing and selling the candidate.[36]

They succeeded. Flagg was elected the first black judge in Brooklyn's history. At the campaign dinner in the town of Valhalla in Westchester County, Mac Holder made an emotional speech saying that he intended to live to see a black city councilman, a black assemblyman, and a black congressman representing Bedford-Stuyvesant. Holder did more than talk. He tried to hold the Flagg committee together by turning it into the Bedford-Stuyvesant Political League. The BSPL was, in effect, an insurgent political club. Chisholm was in it from the start and gradually became Holder's protégée and one of his chief lieutenants.[37]

Palmer Cooper died on August 20, 1953, at fifty-five. Andy was stoic during the arrangements and funeral. He did reflect on the measure of his father's life: World War I veteran, reliable husband, father and son (to his live-in mom Louise Schofield), U.S. Customs officer, but a black man who could have done much more if he had not been systematically denied opportunities because of his ethnicity. Andy kept his feelings to himself.[38]

Andy was twenty-six when the U.S. Supreme Court agreed in May 1954 to end racial integration in public schools "with all deliberate speed." Brooklyn's schools were actually segregating as more blacks from the South streamed into the borough, and Bedford-Stuyvesant each day became a concentrated ghetto.[39] Rev. Milton A. Galamison of Siloam Presbyterian Church noticed the segregating patterns. He led the Brooklyn NAACP education committee, then was elected president of the branch. In 1956, during a dispute over the integration of JHS 258 on Halsey Street, Galamison demanded the resignation of superintendent of schools William Jansen.[40]

In 1955, Andy and Jocelyn Cooper attended fourteen Dale Carnegie training sessions. Dale Carnegie training was self-improvement preparation to run businesses and manage people. The sessions helped Andy minimize his stutter and approach people with confidence. He still worked nights on the loading dock at Schaefer, but he had aspirations to advance. Jocelyn ended her office work because she was home with Andrea, a toddler, but Jocelyn anticipated reentering the workforce in time.[41]

As more blacks were populating Brooklyn, their environment was decaying. One in ten Brooklyn residents lived in Bedford-Stuyvesant; however, 86 percent of all blacks in the borough lived in that neighborhood.[42] Many blacks were herded into that neighborhood and barred from others.

By 1955, Brooklyn gained 200,000 units of private to-own housing, yet less than half of one percent of those houses—900—were purchased by blacks.[43] Employment prospects for blacks were grim. City government leaders fostered a segregated system that funneled blacks into low-paying clerical and service positions and saved the higher-paying skilled, white-collar, and managerial jobs for whites, even as the white population in Brooklyn and the rest of the city was declining.

Within the unions, locals came up with creative ways to bar blacks from skilled jobs and apprenticeships, which led a writer of an exposé to observe that Brooklyn had more Negro Ph.D.'s than plumbers or electricians. Overall blue-collar employment declined in Brooklyn in the late 1950s. The sugar refineries and breweries near the waterfront were collapsing.[44]

Another institution that had disappeared by 1955 was the *Brooklyn Eagle*, the borough's daily newspaper. Strikes killed the paper. The *Eagle* gave Brooklyn an identity. This was the newspaper that was once edited by Walt Whitman. In 1951 it won a Pulitzer Prize, journalism's highest honor, for stories exposing a bookmaking scandal.[45] The paper was not always noble, however. It had a hostile editorial posture toward the blacks populating Brooklyn. Only one black journalist worked at the *Brooklyn Eagle* in 1945.[46] The day Jackie Robinson was to play his first game as a Brooklyn Dodger, the team's hometown paper made no mention of him.[47] Nevertheless the death of any American newspaper is sad, and the community was diminished. The last flight of the *Eagle* was stark evidence of Brooklyn's economic decline.

In 1955 the Brooklyn Dodgers won the National League pennant, then beat the crosstown New York Yankees in the World Series. Jackie Robinson, who broke the baseball color barrier, Roy Campanella, Duke Snider, Gil Hodges, Pee Wee Reese, and company were immortalized in Roger Kahn's book *The Boys of Summer* (1972).

"Da bums" were lovable losers for decades and bridesmaids in the late 1940s and early 1950s. The team was always competitive but somehow would always find a way to come up short to their local rivals the National League New York Giants or the American League Yankees. But now the Dodgers had finally won the big one. They would have only a short window to savor their victory, because their hometown was declining and changing. Soon the Dodgers would have a new address, and Brooklyn would never recover from its loss.

The owners of the Dodgers announced they were leaving after the 1957 season. Was Crown Heights, the neighborhood home of Ebbets Field, really that unsafe as Dodgers owners and management suggested? Did New York politicians make a serious effort to keep the team? What was the team's economic value? Several hundred thousand white Brooklynites left the borough for the Long Island suburbs, Westchester, New Jersey, or Connecticut.

Meanwhile Los Angeles beckoned seductively and offered year-round warmth and an affluent lifestyle. L.A. and Southern California were booming in population and economic development. The Dodgers packed up and went West.[48]

In 1958, Andy Cooper worked nights as one of the few black employees at the Schaefer brewery. Jocelyn Cooper was a stay-at-home mom and cared for Andrea, who was now attending elementary school.[49] The Coopers' neighborhood, Bedford-Stuyvesant, was getting blacker because thousands of black southerners plus West Indians from the Caribbean were steered to that community and were barred from other neighborhoods through a combination overt and covert discrimination, school segregation, and redlining.

As the black population grew and became concentrated, social ills expanded. Bedford-Stuyvesant had extreme rates of welfare cases, infant mortality, venereal disease, and unemployment.[50] White leaders denied services to black Brooklyn but delivered them to the adjacent white neighborhoods. These same leaders blamed the decay and despair on the poorer, disadvantaged, and disenfranchised black citizens. Their social problems and miserable condition were a result of their nature, claimed the oppressors.[51]

As central Brooklyn became blacker and more segregated in the mid- to late-1950s, revolution stirred in the South: In 1955, fourteen-year-old Emmett Till of Chicago was kidnapped and lynched by white men in Money, Mississippi. The boy's crime was flirting with a white woman. Till's murder was a flash point in the civil rights revolution.

Also that year, seamstress Rosa Parks refused to give up her seat to a white passenger and move to the back of a bus in Montgomery, Alabama. Parks was arrested, and the community fought back with a yearlong boycott of the public bus system. The leader of the protest was a young minister named Martin Luther King Jr.

In 1957 nine black students attempted to desegregate Central High School in Little Rock, Arkansas. Northern-style segregation disenfranchisement was benign compared to the violent and suffocating oppression down South. The modern civil rights revolution was under way in the South, and northern cities would not be spectators. Andy and Jocelyn Cooper would soon get involved in making changes in their community.

3. POLITICAL AWAKENING

On December 5, 1957, New York became the first city in the United States to legislate against racial or religious discrimination in the housing market by adopting the Fair Housing Practices Law.[1] New York was becoming more racially segregated. Harlem was the black ghetto, and in little more than a decade, predominantly white yet integrated Bedford-Stuyvesant was manufactured into a black ghetto through discriminatory housing practices by banks and government officials.

In November 1958, Republican Nelson A. Rockefeller was elected governor in a surprise win, upsetting the Democratic incumbent W. Averell Harriman. Meanwhile another liberal Republican, Jacob Javits, won a U.S. Senate seat. In an article in *Esquire*, Javits made a bold prediction about race relations: In about fifty years, he said, America would elect its first black president.[2] November 1958 also saw the midterm congressional elections. Incumbent Republican Dwight Eisenhower had to share power with Democratic majorities in the Senate and House of Representatives. Fifteen newly elected senators gave the Democrats a 64–34 advantage and a veto-proof majority. Democrats also gained 64 seats in the House of Representatives and, now holding 283 of the seats, a decisive majority.[3] Many of these newcomers were conservative southerners who supported American apartheid in the South. That status quo, however, was under challenge by civil rights groups.

That fall in Brooklyn, Andy Cooper followed his routine of overnight work at the Schaefer brewery. Jocelyn was a homemaker, and the Coopers' daughter was attending the neighborhood elementary school. Jocelyn turned thirty in January 1959. She was restless. In the fall, she enrolled in Brooklyn College but soon dropped out because she could not afford the tuition. Jocelyn searched for ways to make additional money for the household. She tried to sell Vesta fire alarms as a home business, but the attempt failed: she was not able to sell a single alarm.

Jocelyn was aware that blacks were underrepresented politically in Bedford-Stuyvesant. Thomas Russell Jones, a black candidate, ran for the state assembly district seat and lost by 187 votes to incumbent Samuel I. Berman.

Jocelyn Cooper was remorseful about Jones's loss. "Why didn't I help him?" she asked herself.[4]

T. R. Jones was born in Brooklyn in 1913 and was the son of immigrants from Barbados. He attended public school and earned undergraduate and law degrees from St. John's University. Jones was admitted to the bar in 1938. At that time, many Americans stood anxiously on the sidelines and watched Hitler's Germany occupy one European nation at a time, while in Spain fascist Francisco Franco waged a civil war. As a young lawyer, Jones was elected chairman of the New York Youth Congress, an antifascist group supported by First Lady Eleanor Roosevelt. He joined the U.S. Army in 1941. In December 1942, Jones married Bertha Kantor, a Jewish woman who was involved with Jones in the youth congress. Jones was a first lieutenant when he took part in the Normandy invasion of 1944. Because he was a lawyer, Jones was placed on a courts martial board. Often he successfully represented black GIs who were falsely accused of rape and murder of white women.

When Jones came home from the war in the early 1950s, he visited the Democratic Party office on Kingston Avenue at St. Marks Place. He was told to go to the office of Sixth Assembly District member Bert Baker, the lone black state representative in Brooklyn. Jones found the instructions odd because he resided in the Seventeenth Assembly District, represented by Stan Steingut. The Seventeenth was getting blacker, and those new residents were virtually neglected by their white representatives. Jones challenged the status quo.

In 1955, Jones defended three Chinese workers who sent money home to relatives and friends and were thus convicted of aiding communist China.[5] When Jones made a 1958 run for state assembly, he partnered with Joseph K. Rowe, a Jewish resident and member of the Nostrand Democratic Club, who ran for committeeman.[6]

In 1958, Jacqueline McMickens moved with her family to New York City from Birmingham, Alabama. McMickens admired the black-owned *Birmingham World* newspaper because of its courageous editor, Emory O. Jackson.[7] Jackson turned fifty that year and had been with the newspaper for sixteen years, since 1942. Jackson was noteworthy because he confronted white segregationist authority in the pages of the *World*, deep in the heart of Dixie. His courage was remarkable because leading black newspapers of that time like the *Chicago Defender*, *Pittsburgh Courier*, *Baltimore Afro-American*, and *New York Amsterdam News* all thundered against the oppression of southern blacks, but it was a fact of geography that the editors often roared from a safe distance.[8] The *Birmingham World* came out twice a week and was owned by the Scott family, publishers of the *Atlanta Daily World*. The family's politics were conservative and gradualist regarding racial progress. Jackson often was at odds editorially with his employer.

During World War II, Jackson criticized J. Edgar Hoover's FBI for not hiring a significant number of Negroes in law enforcement positions and for holding a "Nazi-like racial philosophy." When segregationist Dixiecrats held their convention in Birmingham, Jackson tried to cover the proceedings from the balcony until Bull Connor's police removed him and ordered him to run. Jackson walked away, aware that running might give police an excuse to shoot him in the back. Another bold move was his scheme to help two Negro women try to desegregate the University of Alabama. In 1953, Pollie Anne Myers and Autherine Juanita Lucy both applied to the university. They did not reveal their race. Alabama accepted both students, and Jackson ran a front-page story announcing their acceptances. The university balked, and Myers's and Lucy's admissions were delayed. Both women and Jackson challenged the school in the courts. The effort to enroll failed.[9]

When Jackson was using the *Birmingham World* to challenge authority and get his community thinking and engaged, Andy Cooper was thirty-one years old and 980 miles away from where Jackson worked. Andy was focused on supporting his wife and daughter as a brewery employee. Two decades in the future, when Andy was fifty, he would be an editor and writer engaged in remarkably similar hell raising.

After his close election loss in 1960, T. R. Jones initiated a series of workshops on political organizing. Neighbors in Bedford-Stuyvesant learned how to fill out election petitions and complete them perfectly so they would not be disqualified. Neighbors also learned about the differences between election, assembly, and senate districts. Jocelyn Cooper met Ruth Brooks, one of Jones's volunteers. Brooks asked Jocelyn to help out with a mailing. She agreed. Brooks was a Vassar-educated white woman married to a black man. Her father was a judge, a Republican appointee named Benjamin.[10]

Jocelyn became a committed member of the neighborhood organizing effort and began recruiting new people, starting with her husband. Andy was recently involved in a one-day strike and walkout that ended cordially between Mr. Schaefer and the workers. "Maybe you can help," Jocelyn told her husband. Andy was not thrilled about going to the night meetings. He wanted that time to rest and relax before he went to work his overnight shift at the brewery.

Jocelyn would not be moved. The couple fussed a bit before Jocelyn put her foot down. Andy compromised, and the couple went to a meeting with Jones and other neighbors in the Seventeenth Assembly District.[11]

Jocelyn initiated the political activity in the home because her husband worked nights. But eventually he was drawn in. She recruited other neighbors. There was Enoch Williams. He worked late nights, too; when Jocelyn knocked on his door, he greeted her and daughter Andrea in his pajamas. Williams promised to get involved.[12] Then there was neighbor Earl Graves. Some arm twisting was necessary, but Graves agreed to participate and come to the club meetings.

In fall 1960, Jones challenged incumbent Berman for the Seventeenth Assembly District seat. Former First Lady Eleanor Roosevelt, now seventy-five and enjoying a decades-long reputation as a champion of the Negro, spoke at one of the Jones-Rowe rallies that drew four hundred people. Entertainer Harry Belafonte, growing in his activist efforts, was a sponsor, and the campaign received labor support.

Unity Democratic Club and the Nostrand Democratic Club partnered and formed a Committee for Full Registration and Adequate Representation to recruit and train canvassers. Canvassers agreed to be volunteer poll watchers on Election Day. Because they watched, they made regular election officials edgy and angry, and the officials threatened to call the police. The volunteers did not budge; they were briefed on the law and were not frightened. They told the election officials to go right ahead and call the law.[13] Jones lost to Berman, but having earned 42 percent of votes, he was motivated to run again in two years.

Tom Jones went to A. Philip Randolph's founding of the Negro American Labor Council in 1959. Randolph was the revered labor leader who had organized the Brotherhood of Sleeping Car Porters and in 1940 convinced President Roosevelt to desegregate the defense factories or face civil disobedience and plant closings. Two decades later, Randolph tasked people to go back and start projects.

Jones made Andy coordinator of Operation Unemployment, an anti-discrimination crusade with the motto "Buy where you can work."[14] Andy and his team met on Wednesday nights at the YMCA at Bedford Avenue and Monroe Street. He told club members that they would target Brooklyn businesses that continued to discriminate against Negroes and Puerto

Ricans. Operation Unemployment was a more militant employment initiative than the earnest Urban League efforts of the 1940s and 1950s. For years the Brooklyn Urban League had cajoled businesses to hire blacks in blue- and white-collar positions, yet black employment numbers were abysmal. Sheffield's dairy and other businesses that employed hundreds of people each—but no blacks—were challenged to desegregate, since they conducted business in what was now predominantly black neighborhoods. Sheffield's, which had a plant on Fulton Street in the heart of the Bedford-Stuyvesant shopping district, resisted.[15] Andy Cooper became more forceful and organized demonstrations. His daughter Andrea got in on the act. At age nine, she tagged along with her dad and walked picket lines, sometimes in the freezing cold.[16]

Operation Unemployment paid special attention to the hiring practices of Con Edison, Sealtest Milk, and Drake's Cake.[17] A six-month confrontation with Sealtest won eight jobs for Negro workers at the Sheffield Farms Fulton Street bottling plant. The change broke the company's whites-only hiring policy. Five additional jobs for residents of color were promised. The Ebinger Baking Company and Broadway Maintenance Company, Andy promised, would answer next for their exclusive hiring practices.[18]

That fall Cooper and colleagues tried to reason with Ebinger's management. Of forty-two stores in greater New York, eleven were located in Negro or mixed communities. Ebinger's had a loyal customer base, but they hired no Negro or Puerto Rican sales clerks. Cooper urged the bakery chain to integrate or Operation Unemployment would picket the stores. Ebinger's management was deaf to the demands, so Operation Unemployment members walked in front of stores in January 1962. "You'll never get a job here. Go to Chock Full o' Nuts where you belong," one store manager shouted to a Negro woman picketer.[19]

Several weeks of talking and picketing passed. Ebinger's responded with an offer: they would hire two sales clerks. Cooper and Operation Unemployment answered: Ebinger's had no Negro sales clerks, truck drivers, truck driver helpers, or office workers, so the offer to hire two sales clerks was an insult.

Because Negro and Puerto Rican residents spent thousands of dollars each week in the stores, Operation Unemployment's counterdemand was for Ebinger's to immediately hire thirty-three Negro and Puerto Rican sales clerks in eleven of the stores by February 3 or else picketing would continue. Ebinger's management was silent. A week later, on February 10, representatives from Operation Unemployment, Unity Democratic Club, Local 485 of IUE, NALC, the Hancock Block Association No. 4, Kappa Alpha Psi fraternity, and others picketed three stores. Demonstrators chanted, "Integrate both sides of the counter," and "Don't buy where you can't work."

Cooper wrote that "the pickets got enthusiastic response from would-be customers who bought their cakes elsewhere. Our Jewish neighbors told us that Ebingers discriminated against them too. We showed Ebingers that although their cake is good . . . most people in the community—Negro and white—have had enough of their un-American employment practices."[20]

Elsewhere in metropolitan New York, Negro citizens and sympathetic whites challenged the segregationist status quo. In New Rochelle, about twenty-five miles north of Brooklyn, judge Irving R. Kaufman of Federal District Court in Manhattan in May 1961 ordered the 94 percent black Lincoln Elementary School in that suburb closed. New Rochelle's school board resisted the desegregation order, and two years of racial tension followed. By 1963, an incoming school board ordered Lincoln Elementary razed, and busing proceeded without incident.[21]

In January 1962, black and Puerto Rican parents filed a suit in Federal District Court accusing the New York City Board of Education of using racial quotas to keep many school virtually segregated.[22] In early February, seven whites and four blacks were arrested at City Hall in Englewood, New Jersey, after an all-night sit-in. On February 5, a lawsuit seeking to bar Englewood from maintaining racially segregated schools was filed in Federal District Court.[23] Then on May 28, 360 miles north of Brooklyn in Rochester, New York, the NAACP filed a lawsuit alleging de facto school segregation.[24]

Civil rights protests by blacks with white supporters dominated the news coming out of the South. The region was where the right to vote was denied—often violently—and public facilities and commerce were still segregated by customs and statutes. Yet in New York and other northern communities where there was limited freedom for blacks, those residents said the limits were now unacceptable. They wanted first-class citizen rights.

A political cartoon showed boss (Carmine) DeSapio as a sausage maker with two female New York City residents, one black and one white, surveying his handiwork. The special that day was Tammany pottage. DeSapio pushed "gambling scandals," "police corruption," racial bias," "graft," and "Clearview lard" into the Tammany Grinding Co. machine. Out of it came "poor public transportation," "bad housing," "poor schools," and "low wages." DeSapio told the women, "It's really quite tasty ladies, once you get used to it!"[25]

The cartoon was the cover illustration for the *Unity Democrat* newsletter in which Andy Cooper announced that Operation Unemployment would launch attacks on Con Ed, Sealtest Milk, Drake's Cake, and other businesses that discriminated against Negroes and Puerto Ricans. Tom Jones told UDC members that the club and other citizens of the Seventeenth Assembly District had voted overwhelming for incumbent mayor Robert Wagner in the September primary. Wagner, said Jones, pledged to fight for the interests of ordinary people, and give the Democratic Party back to the voters.[26]

In November 1961 at a special session, the Republican-controlled New York State legislature "struck a low blow to the body of Negro voters in Brooklyn," wrote Jones. "Gov. Rockefeller signed into law a bill drawing new Congressional lines in a crazy-quilt pattern. The Republican arranged this gerrymander to bar the election of a Negro Congressman from Brooklyn for the next 10 years."[27] Bedford-Stuyvesant, with its 371,000 Negro citizens and several thousand whites, was carved into four different congressional districts, the tenth, twelfth, fourteenth, and fifteenth districts. This plot was hatched at a secret meeting, alleged Jones, because political bosses knew that the Negro masses and white citizens were ready to elect a qualified Negro representative to Congress. Jews, Italians, Irish, and other white ethnics represented their neighbors in Congress. What fair-minded person would not agree that it was time for a Negro to represent that constituency in Brooklyn?

Joan Bacchus's illustration "A Tree Grows in Brooklyn" was published during Christmas season. The ten bulbs on the tree said:

> Wagner elected mayor 3 to 1 vote in 17th A.D.
> Operation Unemployment fight for jobs
> UDC joins reform movements
> The fight for Negro representation
> UDC an interracial club. Open membership.
> Political education. The workshop.
> Wagner primary, 60 percent of the 17th A.D.
> 1960 Tom Jones campaign
> A new library for Bedford and Crown Heights
> New voter registration campaign.

The glowing star at the top of the tree said, "A new deal for the 17th A.D."

Bacchus also drew a map of Brooklyn and labeled the many neighborhoods including Coney Island, Bensonhurst, Canarsie, Flatlands, and Greenpoint. A magnifying glass enlarged Bedford-Stuyvesant, the shaded area in the center of the borough. The caption read: "DO YOU KNOW THAT ... 320,000 out of the 370,000 Negroes in Brooklyn live here and are entitled to a Congressman, a state Senator, three Assemblymen, [and] 12 judges? At present, there is just one lone Assemblyman."[28]

Tom Jones's editorial that month, "We Declare for Democracy and Equal Representation," said in part:

> The Unity Democratic Club demands a halt to this highway robbery of the democratic rights of all the people of Brooklyn. We call upon the Legislature to reverse the gerrymander and draw new lines which show regard to the "natural community of groupings" which Assemblyman Bentley Kassell proposed in his bill. We demand equality of representation in the legislative body which rules our lives in New York State. The Negro people claim the right and honor to serve their white fellow citizens and themselves in all public offices. They believe, with the early patriots of America, that "taxation without representation is tyranny!"
>
> The people of New York know and our democratic system requires that the Negro people of Brooklyn are entitled to at least:
>
> One Congressman; one State Senator; three Assemblymen; one Federal Court Judge; 12 Judges on the Supreme, County, City Special Sessions Courts; two Magistrates; six Commissioners or Deputy Commissioners of City Departments; 12 Top Administrators [physicians and nurses] in Hospital and Health Departments and dozens of other policy making posts in Federal, State and City governments, create a State Senate District which takes in most of the heart of Bedford-Stuyvesant where the bulk of 371,000 Negroes live.
>
> Then the Democratic-controlled City Council will be duty bound to create three Assembly Districts within this Senate District to ensure equality for the Negro people of Brooklyn.[29]

With the Coopers and other Unity Democratic Club colleagues, Tom Jones continued to organize through 1962. In February, a new name was added to the Unity Democrat staff: Shirley Chisholm, who joined Mary Woods, Walter and Esther Linder, Elmeta Phillips, editor Lemuel Beckford, and art editor Bacchus. Chisholm walked away from another political club in 1958 after a dispute. She joined Unity in 1960.[30]

UDC was housed at 1103 Bergen Street, a building owned by Marcus Garvey's Universal Negro Improvement Association (UNIA). Jones's father was alive at that time and was an ardent Garveyite.[31]

Jones made his second run for the Seventeenth Assembly District seat. This time around he had additional, powerful teammates such as Pat Carter, owner of an insurance company, and his wife Constance. Like Jocelyn Cooper, Constance helped with mailings and other organizing and get-out-the-vote tasks. Pat, who quickly bonded with Andy, counseled Jones and others on political strategy. UDC members repeatedly said that the predominantly black district had a right to be represented by leaders of their own choice, not representatives hand-picked by the Democratic machine.

Jones was in a rematch with Berman, and UDC's Ruth Goring ran against Carrie Lark, a black woman who was put up by the regular Democratic organization.[32] On September Primary day, Jones beat Berman in a close race, 2,714 to 2,457. Jones also defeated Wesley McD Holder, Chisholm's mentor, for committeeman, 3,042 to 2,654. Goring won the committee co-leader seat over Lark.[33] The November 6 election was a formality. Jones joined Bert Baker of the neighboring Sixth Assembly District as Brooklyn's black legislators, and Jones and Goring, plus Baker and his co-leader meant four of the twenty-two members of the Kings County committee were black. African Americans were still woefully underrepresented in New York State's most populous county; nevertheless the progress achieved in fall 1962 was undeniable. On the other coast, in Los Angeles, Gus Hawkins made history as the first black congressman elected from the West.[34]

Two weeks later, on November 20, President Kennedy issued an executive order barring racial discrimination in federally financed housing. Kennedy's decision had profound implications for New York, since many of the multi-unit apartments under construction were government financed. Landlords would no longer have legal cover to discriminate and limit blacks to a few city neighborhoods.[35]

Indeed, there were breakthroughs in 1962. Black legislators won elections, like Jones in Brooklyn, and Hawkins of Los Angeles's Watts community. In addition U.S. representative Adam Clayton Powell Jr. of Harlem was elected chairman of the House Education and Labor Committee in January 1961, and Robert Weaver was sworn in as administrator of the Housing and Home Finance Agency, the highest federal post to date by an African American, in February of that year.[36] The black North that appeared passive compared to so much civil disobedience in the South was organizing and agitating. Something else was in the mix: a greater awareness of the African Diaspora. On October 9, 1962, the African nation Uganda gained independence and joined the former colonies Tanzania, Sierra Leone, Nigeria, Mali, Somalia, and Congo-Zaire as a sovereign nation.[37]

Closer to home in the Caribbean, Jamaica gained its independence on August 6, 1962, and weeks later so did Trinidad and Tobago on August 31. In Trinidad nine-year-old Utrice Leid was a schoolgirl destined to make noise in New York within two decades.

In the early 1960s, in New York City was a confluence of southern blacks, Caribbean people from newly independent islands, plus awareness from both constituencies of the revolution taking place in the South. If there, why not here?[38]

In 1963, Andy and Jocelyn Cooper and their eleven-year-old daughter Andrea witnessed one of the most politically violent and socially active years in U.S. history. On March 1, an Emancipation Proclamation centennial protest plus a voter registration campaign took place in Greenwood, Mississippi. On June 11, President Kennedy in a radio-TV address said that segregation was morally wrong and that it was "time to act in the Congress, in your state and local legislative body, and . . . in all our daily lives." The next day, June 12, Medgar Evers, thirty-seven, an NAACP leader, was assassinated in front of his home in Jackson, Mississippi.

On August 27, W. E. B. Du Bois, ninety-five, died peacefully in Accra, Ghana; on the next day, Andy and Jocelyn Cooper were among the 250,000 who participated in the March on Washington for jobs and freedom. They listened to the Rev. Martin Luther King's "I Have a Dream" speech.

On September 15, four little black girls were bombed to death during Sunday school at Sixteenth Street Baptist Church in Birmingham, Alabama; two months later, on November 22, President Kennedy was killed by sniper Lee Harvey Oswald in Dallas. Before Oswald could be prosecuted, he was shot dead by Jack Ruby. Kennedy's successor was vice president Lyndon B. Johnson, the first southern-based president since Andrew Johnson stepped in for Abraham Lincoln, who had been assassinated ninety-eight years before.[39]

Nineteen sixty-three was largely defined by violence and hardening attitudes between blacks and whites, yet there was hope, too: about one out of four participants at the March on Washington was white, evidence of a growing constituency of Americans who agreed with the martyred JFK's call to end racial segregation and discrimination. The Coopers participated in a racially integrated political club. The march and the assassination pushed them to greater social action.

4. CIVIL RIGHTS, BROOKLYN STYLE

Jocelyn and Andy Cooper attended the March on Washington in August 1963 and heard the Rev. Martin Luther King Jr. deliver his historic speech. Energized, Andy returned home, but Jocelyn and Pat Carter stayed in Washington for a meeting with representatives from the Democratic National Committee.[1]

DNC members remembered that Kennedy's margin of victory in 1960 was a thin 49.7 percent to Nixon's 49.5. Of 68 million votes cast, JFK won the popular vote by only 100,000. It was likely that a call of support to Coretta Scott King two weeks before the November 8 election attracted a decisive number of Negro votes to the Democratic side. Coretta's husband Martin Luther King led a sit-in protest and was jailed for violation of probation of a traffic offense. The DNC wanted to boost Negro voter support before the 1964 election.

During the meeting with black press journalist Ethel Payne and Tinsley Spraggins, Carter negotiated a contract to run a voter registration drive in Bedford-Stuyvesant. Jocelyn Cooper was named director of the registration drive. The strategy was guided by Payne and Spraggins, with Pat and Andy, Tom Jones, and Kings County Democratic Leader Stanley Steingut. In six weeks the workers registered at least five thousand Brooklyn residents and possibly as many as eleven thousand.[2]

In November 1963, the Coopers experienced the anguish of the assassination of president John F. Kennedy. The couple was impressed by the youthful Democrat. Now the Coopers pressed on with activity inside the Unity Democratic Club.

On February 23, 1964, Andy Cooper was invited to a church in the Mott Haven section of the Bronx to receive a certificate that recognized his community and civic work. The Rev. Carl Allen Thomas signed the certificate. At the church, Cooper had an inadvertent backstage meeting with U.S. representative John V. Lindsay, a liberal Republican representing Manhattan and a fellow honoree. As both men stood in a waiting area, Lindsay told Cooper that politics was the most important work anyone could be involved in and not to let anyone dissuade him from doing his work.[3]

Until 1964, Andy Cooper was a registered Republican. In his family, his father Palmer was a Democrat, while Andy's mother Irma was a Republican, and a poll worker. In 1964, Andy switched allegiances because of his activity in a political club.[4] One year later, Lindsay ran for mayor of New York, and Cooper passionately supported his candidacy.

On June 29, 1964, Jocelyn Andrea Cooper, the couple's second daughter, was born. Her name was a family affair, the first name from her mother, and the middle name from her older sister.

That summer, a race riot occurred in Harlem after a white policeman fatally shot James Powell, a fifteen-year-old black youth.[5] Eyewitnesses contradicted the police account that the officer gave a warning before shooting Powell. One witness said Powell and other boys were sprayed with water, and the boys scuffled with an apartment house superintendent, then chased the man into the building. When the boys came out of the building, the officer shot Powell and stood staring over the body for ten minutes. Student witnesses from the nearby junior high responded by throwing rocks and bottles. For days adults led marches on the local precinct. When the demonstrators got too close, the police pushed back; rioting ensued.[6]

In Brooklyn on July 18, the CORE chapter protested the Powell shooting. About a thousand onlookers remained on the corner of Fulton and Nostrand avenues and ignored the organizers' pleas to disperse and go home. Instead the people harassed police and ransacked stores. On July 21, violence and rioting erupted again. Two residents were shot, and sixty-five people were arrested. Ninety stores in a ten-block stretch of Bedford-Stuyvesant were damaged, and the estimated cost was $300,000.[7]

Local civil rights activism and awareness of the southern movement raised expectations for the black masses in New York City. The Board of Education was being pressured to integrate the schools. The Powell shooting during the summer inflamed the already tense masses. Mayor Robert Wagner was paralyzed. The New Dealer was sympathetic to black and Puerto Rican concerns, but he was not equipped to handle the new, aggressive civil rights activism.

Meanwhile the white ethnic groups of the city were annoyed by what they perceived as black "exceptionalism."[8] Jews, Italians, and other European ethnics did not insist on integrating with the Anglos, they complained. Why were blacks demanding special treatment? What the white ethnics did not acknowledge was that most of them assimilated into Anglo culture and toned down their ethnicity to get along. They achieved the melting-pot ideal.

However, for blacks and browns, even if they adopted the mainstream values, their complexion and hair texture denied them access to schools, jobs and other opportunities. The civil rights revolution locally and nationally challenged those old attitudes. Conflict between ethnic whites and blacks was inevitable.

In August 1964, Seven weeks after Jocelyn Andrea's birth, new dad Andy and Pat Carter were dispatched to Atlantic City, New Jersey, as delegates to the Democratic National Convention. The DNC faced many urgent issues. The presumptive nominee was Lyndon B. Johnson, who was finishing the last fourteen months of John F. Kennedy's term. On August 4, the bodies of civil rights workers James Chaney, Andrew Goodman, and Michael Schwerner were discovered, murdered and buried in an earthen dam on a farm near Philadelphia, Mississippi.[9] Cooper knew of the Schwerner family because his older daughter Andrea, attended the same Greenwich Village school as some Schwerner children.[10]

The segregationist Dixiecrat wing of the Democrats was challenged at the Atlantic City convention. The Freedom Democratic Party of Mississippi was the insurgent challenger to the status quo Mississippi delegation. The integrated Freedom Party's leaders were the Rev. Edwin King, a white man, and Aaron Henry, a black man. Yet a sharecropper's wife, Fannie Lou Hamer, was the figure who personified the delegation.[11]

Cooper and Carter were given clear instructions by the Brooklyn Democratic Party leaders: don't rock the boat, and cast your votes to seat the establishment Democrats. The instructions came from Unity Democratic Club leader Thomas Russell Jones, who was taking orders from his boss, Stanley Steingut.[12] Cooper and Carter balked, however, and cast their votes for the Mississippi insurgents. Both men were leaders of the Brooklyn Committee to Unseat the Mississippi Congressmen.[13] In June the duo staged a "Rally for Freedom" in Tompkins Park.[14] Cooper, Carter, and their Brooklyn supporters were won over by members of the MFDP. There were day and night meetings among the Mississippi crowd and Brooklyn people from Cooper's Bedford-Stuyvesant election district and Carter's Crown Heights' election district. Paul O'Dwyer, a Manhattan city councilman at large, was another supporter of the case to seat the MFDP.[15]

The Harlem Democrats, disciplined and structured, unlike the rowdies from Brooklyn, followed the party line. On August 25, the Credentials Committee of the Democratic Party seated an all-white Mississippi delegation and two members of the integrated Freedom Democratic Party as "delegates at-large." Both factions—Mississippi and Brooklyn—however, rejected the "peace" formula.[16]

That fall, LBJ won in a landslide over Barry Goldwater. The Republican candidate was perceived as too conservative, even extremist. It would take an additional sixteen years for Goldwater's philosophy to shift the American body politic.

Cooper and Carter were punished for their insubordination in Atlantic City. Their protest votes, however, did not harm the Democrats in November 1964. Both men and their spouses were persona non grata at local Democratic Party functions. At events the wives heard people say, "What are *they* doing here?"[17] They were Democratic Party loyalists, but outsiders because of their Unity Democratic Club affiliation. UDC needled the organization Democrats. That fall the UDC backed member Shirley Chisholm for the Seventeenth Assembly District seat held by T. R. Jones. He walked away from the legislative seat after one two-year term to fill an opening on the civil court bench in Brooklyn. The county organization showed a willingness to accommodate the black community. For Jones, a judge's pay was better, and he did not have to split his time and income between Albany and Brooklyn.[18] Also that season, William C. Thompson was elected state senator and made history as the first black from Brooklyn elected to that position.[19]

At that time, Mayor Robert Wagner, deep into his third term, repudiated the organization Tammany Hall Democrats. Wagner picked a bad time to disassociate himself, because the city had become a tougher place to govern.[20] "New York City in Crisis," a *Herald Tribune* exposé that began on January 25, 1965, and continued through the spring, chronicled the failures of the city government to provide a decent life for all its citizens. The newspaper cataloged the city's woes: narcotics, air pollution, poor education, welfare, ailing hospitals, one-party Democratic rule, business exodus, middle-class exodus, black and Puerto Rican poverty, elderly poverty, fear in the streets, and an inefficient city bureaucracy.[21] *Look* magazine also published an unflattering photo essay about New York City decay that winter.

In March 1965, Viola Liuzzo, a young white woman from Detroit, was shot to death in Alabama, day after a rally at the state capital that was the climax of the Selma-to-Montgomery march.[22] Liuzzo's slaying was a flash point of the civil rights movement. Killing blacks for demanding freedom was an unjust but a painful reality, but killing a sympathetic white woman added a new dimension to the struggle. In Brooklyn, the Coopers and

Carters continued to register black voters in their districts and assist voter registration in the South.

Early in 1965, Lindsay hinted that he was interested in running for mayor. In Chicago he gave a speech called "The Republican Challenge" and said that after the devastating defeat of Goldwater the past November, Republicans could not afford to ignore cities where 70 percent of the U.S. population was living at that time. Lindsay also stressed the importance of civil rights and protecting citizens from big business, big labor, big city-machine politicians, and big government.[23] For the next few months, Lindsay thought more intensely about running. When Lindsay declared his candidacy in May 1965, Democrats Cooper and sidekick Pat Carter did not miss a beat in supporting the maverick Republican. Cooper and others were impressed by Lindsay. He was liberal, Ivy League, and aristocratic. For liberal and moderate New York Republicans, Lindsay was their Kennedy at a time when JFK's Camelot legacy lived on.

"We're backing John Lindsay for Mayor," read an undated, four-page campaign promotion, "for the same reasons we: Stood in the picket lines in 'Operation Unemployment,' led the caucus to seat the Mississippi Freedom Democrats in last year's National Democratic Convention, ran the Urban League's voter registration drive, started a Democratic Reform Club in Bedford-Stuyvesant, led the Bedford-Stuyvesant campaign to elect John F. Kennedy, [and] led the Brooklyn Committee to unseat the Mississippi delegation."[24]

On the second page of the promotion, five black-and-white photos of Cooper and Carter engaging like-minded Democratic Party activists were followed by big type on page 3: "We're Democrats. Right to the bone. We've worked hard for and with the best in the party. Judge Thomas R. Jones, [state] Sen. William C. Thompson, Presidents Kennedy and Johnson, Sen. Robert Kennedy, Congressman William Ryan are just a few."

The next fourteen paragraphs of small type made the case for Republican John V. Lindsay. Cooper and Carter wrote that Lindsay would work for fair housing and employment, more funding for public schools, and a civilian review board that investigated alleged police misconduct. "In most elections we'd be saying all this about the Democratic candidate," wrote the authors. "Because in most elections, we believe the Democratic candidate will get more done. But not this time. We can't believe that this Democratic candidate is going to get any more done than the mayor we just had. How can he? He's part of the same crowd. And you know they've done nothing.

Even though they had 12 years to do it in. So we're backing John Lindsay for mayor. And we're going to vote for him. We hope you'll vote for him too."

On the back page, Lindsay shook the hand of a black woman with a beehive hairdo as four other black men and women looked on approvingly. The pamphlet encouraged citizens to come and say hello at Democrats for Lindsay headquarters at 809 Fulton Street.[25]

Meanwhile Wagner, weak and ineffective in his twelfth year as mayor, announced in June that he would not seek another term. Wagner was a widower, and he was about to remarry. As a newlywed, he would leave the problems of New York to someone else. Left behind would be Brooklyn and Bronx political bosses still furious that Wagner had repudiated the clubhouse system four years earlier. Also left behind would be the bosses from Manhattan and Queens who stood with the mayor but were left to answer for the spiraling urban woes of governing New York. Party bosses promoted Abe Beame of Brooklyn as the Democratic mayoral successor.[26]

Another candidate said that he could do better for New York. How about a Tory for mayor? William F. Buckley, publisher of the *National Review*, joined the race in June.[27] He ran as the conservative candidate in a liberal and Democratic Party city. Buckley was an unlikely spokesman for the majority white ethnic tribes of the city who had grown impatient about urban decay, higher taxes, street crime, and black and brown demands for equal opportunities and respect.

Buckley said that he eschewed ethnic politics and would not pander to the Catholic Irish, Italian, and Polish segments in the boroughs. He did raise eyebrows, however, when he gave a speech to six thousand mostly Irish American cops and emphasized law and order and minimized civil rights protest, even the murder of rights worker Viola Liuzzo in the Deep South.[28] Rapier-witted Buckley jabbed at black leaders and activists and suggested that they focus less on civil rights and more on controlling street crime and uncivil behavior among the masses.[29]

Buckley's campaign advanced four ideas: first, restore law and order because crime, not police brutality, was the problem; second, reduce taxes and government spending; third, reform welfare; and fourth, end school busing and return to neighborhood schools.[30]

Lindsay, the GOP underdog in the predominantly Democratic city, employed an unusual campaign strategy. He was handsome and photogenic, yet the Lindsay campaign at best used 30 percent of its funds for TV advertising. Instead his campaign used most of its budget to set up 122 storefronts operated by 25,000 volunteers. Lindsay walked the streets of all five boroughs and introduced himself to voters.

Yes, he was a Republican, different, yet one of them. In Brooklyn, he walked the neighborhoods, block by block, including the black ghettos.[31] Andy and Jocelyn Cooper were among those enthusiastic volunteers. They operated out of the storefront office at 809 Fulton Street.

Paul Kerrigan, thirty-two, a liberal Rockefeller, Javits, and Lindsay Republican, wanted to campaign for his new hero. He volunteered for the Lindsay-for-mayor effort and was dispatched to the neighborhood office serving Fort Greene–Clinton Hill. There Kerrigan met Andy Cooper and Pat Carter, leaders of the Lindsay movement. Kerrigan's day job was in retailing. Before that he was an army veteran who was based in Paris at NATO headquarters.

Cooper and Carter put him to work to press releases. Kerrigan also traveled to the black churches with Lindsay on Sundays. Andy wanted to show residents that they operated an integrated clubhouse. There was a black pastor who told his congregation with glee, "They say he [Lindsay] is a nigger lover, and they're right!" The election district office included Grand Army Plaza. Abraham Beame, Arthur Levitt (New York state comptroller for twenty-four years), and U.S. representative Emanuel Cellar were neighbors in this "gold coast" of the district.[32]

In August 1965, the Voting Rights Act became law. Its intent was to protect blacks in the South who were overtly denied the franchise.[33] But what about black citizens in the North, who voted but had no authentic voice or representation?

Proof of such impotence was an examination of the boundaries of Bedford-Stuyvesant. It was a compact rectangle with the approximate boundaries of Myrtle Avenue to the north and Prospect Place to the south, Bedford Avenue to the west and Stuyvesant Avenue to the east.[34] The inhabitants inside this rectangle were 80 percent black and Puerto Rican by the mid-1960s, yet the area was carved up by political hacks from the Brooklyn Democratic machine into at least five congressional districts represented by whites. Congressman John J. Rooney was essentially a Dixiecrat and Defense Department warmonger who had no relation to, or interest in, Bedford-Stuyvesant constituents. Hugh Carey was a benign representative; in a decade he would become New York governor.[35]

In August when the Voting Rights Act became federal law, a deadly riot became another flash point in the civil rights revolution: A confrontation between a black motorist and white police in the predominantly black

Watts section of South Central Los Angeles erupted into a devastating riot. In five days, 34 people were killed, 1,000 injured, and 4,000 arrested. There was $40 million in property damage.[36] Mayor Sam Yorty refused to accept any responsibility for the fiasco. Federal officials said that the mayor had ignored warning signs that trouble was brewing in the neglected neighborhood. Yorty complained that federal antipoverty programs that were brought in gave false hope to the poor.[37] In Los Angeles, the black poor and working class were contained by authorities in a sprawling ghetto. These citizens could vote, but their votes did not have much meaning. Small acts of oppression eventually boiled over into one big explosion. Similar occurrences would soon take place in other northern cities.

Andy Cooper and Unity Democratic Club colleagues engaged in voting rights activities. They registered local citizens and lent support to the black southern cause. Cooper, considered a renegade and persona non grata by the Brooklyn Democratic organization, soon turned his political activity elsewhere.[38]

Lindsay, the campaigner, began to de-emphasize his Republican affiliation and sell himself to voters as the "fusion" candidate who believed in nonpartisan government and would unite diverse interests to achieve good government.[39] Lindsay was walking in the footsteps of Fiorello LaGuardia, another Republican who had successful terms as a fusion leader in the 1930s and 1940s. Lindsay volunteers also worked on petition drives for Bronx County Democratic reform candidates who were running against machine-backed candidates.[40]

In September, the Lindsay camp was surprised when Abe Beame upset Paul Screvane in the Democratic primary. Beame won by almost 60,000 votes in his come-from-behind win.[41]

The mayoral campaign had circus charm. William F. Buckley, the voice of an emerging national ideological movement, offered himself as the Conservative Party candidate.[42] Lindsay's main opponent, however, was Democrat Abe Beame, a creature of the political machine culture. Writer Murray Kempton called out Beame with the dismissive line "He [Lindsay] is fresh and everyone else is tired."[43]

Lindsay, however, trailed Beame in the polls in early fall. An October 7 poll in the *New York Herald Tribune* projected Beame with 46 percent support, Lindsay with 36 percent, and Buckley with 10 percent.[44] Based on other polling data, however, Buckley appealed to about 20 percent of the electorate, especially white ethnic Catholic voters who liked his conservative, law-and-order stance. Lindsay, the handsome aristocrat, eschewed TV campaigning. He preferred walking New York neighborhoods, including the black and Puerto Rican streets, to shake hands. Buckley resisted ethnic campaigning on principle. "I'm not Irish or Catholic, I'm American," he declared. That was a tactical mistake.[45]

In the closing weeks of the campaign, Lindsay employed a counterintuitive strategy: he ignored front-runner Beame and went after competitive third-party opponent Buckley. Buckley, said Lindsay, appealed to ethnic whites' racial hatred and bigotry toward blacks. Furthermore, said Lindsay, Buckley's ideas about reducing crime were fascist. That accusation gave Jewish New Yorkers pause because Nazism was still fresh in many of their minds. Meanwhile many black New Yorkers who were transplants from Virginia and the Carolinas keenly remembered southern oppression and associated those bad times with Buckley.[46]

As Election Day approached, Beame the Democrat was endorsed by U.S. representative Adam Clayton Powell.[47] That approval appeared to lock up black votes. U.S. senator Robert F. Kennedy campaigned for Beame. RFK complained that Beame's handlers did not turn him loose in black sections of Brooklyn. That strategy was deliberate. The Beame people wanted to contain the popular Kennedy. RFK was used prominently in white ethnic neighborhoods to put in good words for Beame. Enthusiastic crowds often rushed to hear the charismatic senator and listened almost indifferently to the clerklike mayoral candidate.[48]

On Election Day, Lindsay earned 43 percent of all votes, Beame finished a close second with 40 percent, and Buckley picked up 13 percent. Eighty-one percent of the registered voters cast ballots in what was then the third-largest turnout in city history.

Lindsay the Republican liberal received 40 percent of black votes and 25 percent of Puerto Rican votes. Those numbers were substantial because Lindsay took a large share of voters of color that would have gone to Beame the Democrat. He also took 40 percent of traditionally Democratic Jewish votes. Beame carried working-class Jewish areas of Brooklyn, the Bronx, and lower Manhattan, while Lindsay gained wealthy Jewish areas such as Riverdale in the Bronx, Forest Hills and Rego Park in Queens, and Flatbush in Brooklyn.

The day after his victory, Lindsay did not go first to his Manhattan district or white sections in the outer boroughs to say thanks. His initial stops where to Harlem, Bedford-Stuyvesant, and Rego Park.[49] In the predominantly black Seventeenth Assembly District of Brooklyn where the Coopers lived, voters supported Lindsay 2–1.

The Coopers were rewarded for their support. Not long after the election, a Lindsay appointee hired Jocelyn Cooper as a consultant to do research for a social service agency. Andy Cooper was offered an assistant commissionership with the Sanitation Department.[50] That offer was significant because few blacks held managerial positions in city government.[51] At that time, Andy Cooper was a regional representative at the brewery. He was promoted sometime between 1964 and 1965 from night shift supervisor, a position he had held since 1960.

Cooper told his Schaefer bosses about the Lindsay administration offer. Oh no, one boss told him, we need you here. Cooper was promoted to a daytime, white-collar position in public affairs and promotions. The Schaefer executive was a Republican and Lindsay loyalist.

Cooper was well positioned to make the most of his promotion. His youth activity at St. Mark's made him knowledgeable about the performing arts. Talented singers, musicians, and actors performed inside the church in the 1930s and 1940s. Cooper was about to apply his knowledge and writing talent to work with leading black entertainers and promote the Schaefer brand.

Andy and Jocelyn remained focused on the gritty game of politics.[52] Andy Cooper evolved into a social animal, but dinner parties at home with his wife and several couples were more than social events. They were political strategy sessions or think tanks with food involved.[53] Andy's next mission was achieving voting rights, northern style. Bedford-Stuyvesant's political configuration could no longer stand, for example, a piece of that community stitched to a congressional district that was ten miles long and three hundred yards wide at the narrowest point.[54]

5. COOPER VERSUS POWER

On February 4, 1966, senator Robert F. Kennedy of New York walked some Bedford-Stuyvesant streets with local activists. With an estimated 450,000 residents, the Brooklyn neighborhood was a more populous black community than storied Harlem; 84 percent of its people were black, and 12 percent Puerto Rican. Bedford-Stuyvesant was a bigger ghetto than uptown, and it was comparable in size to Chicago's South Side, sometimes called the Black Metropolis.[1]

Central Brooklyn had its assets. Unlike Harlem, a land of tenements where only 2 percent of the occupants owned their homes, in Bedford-Stuyvesant, the land of brownstones, 15 percent of the neighbors were homeowners. The Coopers of Decatur Street were among those one in every seven central Brooklyn homeowners. Yet residents of the Brooklyn ghetto were more depressed and impaired than the uptown blacks in Harlem. There were fewer unified families, more unemployment, declining incomes, and less job history, a New York University study reported.[2] There was more misery in Brooklyn, yet less federal antipoverty aid compared to Harlem.[3] Activists who escorted Kennedy needled him about their suffering. "I'm weary of study, senator," Thomas Russell Jones, a judge, former assemblyman, and Unity Democratic Club leader, told Kennedy. "Weary of speeches, weary of promises that aren't kept. . . . The Negro people are angry[,] senator, and judge that I am, I'm angry too. No one is helping us."[4]

The activists' frustration and cynicism bruised Kennedy, but he rose effectively to their challenge.[5] Kennedy introduced legislation in Congress that allowed the creation of local development corporations. Kennedy's initiative was supported by Jacob Javits, the senior U.S. senator from New York. By the end of 1966, the federal government selected Bedford-Stuyvesant as the first slum area to participate in the new program. Two corporations were set up to work together, Bedford-Stuyvesant Renewal and Rehabilitation Corporation—a community group led by judge Tom Jones—plus the Development and Services Corporation, the business group that included William Paley of CBS, Thomas Watson of IBM, President Kennedy–era treasury secretary Douglas Dillon, and private capital experts.[6]

By April 1967, Jones stepped down, and the slum clearance effort picked up a new name: the Bedford-Stuyvesant Restoration Corporation.[7] New York

City deputy police commissioner Franklin A. Thomas, a Negro, resigned to become president of the new corporation. Between fiscal years 1968 and 1973, Restoration received one-third of $90 million the federal government dispensed for the national Special Impact Program, a public-private partnership. Restoration Corp. became the "largest and . . . most technically sophisticated" community development program.[8] Restoration established its headquarters at the former Sheffield Milk bottling site on Fulton Street, where years before, Andrew Cooper had led demonstrators who picketed for fair employment.[9]

In 1966, New York State prepared to hold a constitutional convention, a process by which the state's governing document could be amended. New York had adopted constitutions in 1777, 1821, 1846, 1894, and 1938. In 1915 voters rejected proposed amendments.[10] Warren Bunn, leader of the Brooklyn branch of the NAACP, and Andy Cooper were nominated by their peers to serve as convention delegates. Reginald Butts, a fellow UDC member and neighbor, enthusiastically supported Cooper's candidacy. At the time, Butts was teaching at New York University. He resigned his teaching position to head the operation. Butts also borrowed $25,000 to pay for the effort, but he did not confer with his wife Bobbye. Butts thought his spouse would hand his head to him, but she went along with the investment. The couple was committed to supporting a successful campaign.[11]

Bunn and Cooper were not representatives of the Brooklyn Democratic Party. Varying news accounts labeled Cooper a "reform" or "insurgent" delegate candidate.[12] By June, ten months had passed since the federal Voting Rights Act became law. The law could be assumed to be the antidote to overt tactics in southern states that prevented blacks from voting, whether the methods were violent in Mississippi, Alabama, and Georgia or arcane in Virginia and Maryland through the use of poll taxes and literacy tests. Did the enforcement of voting rights for all citizens apply in northern states too? Cooper and several friends decided it was time to test the new law.

On June 23, 1966, Andrew W. Cooper sued New York political leaders in U.S. District Court (Eastern) in Brooklyn. This was to prevent an election in black Brooklyn until the congressional district lines were redrawn. Cooper was "an insurgent Democratic candidate to the state constitutional convention," said a *New York Times* article on June 24 with the headline "Bedford-Stuyvesant Is Called a Victim of Gerrymandering."

Cooper made his move a year after the federal Voting Rights Act liberated millions of southern blacks. He alleged that New York State leaders had disenfranchised African Americans. Unlike the South, where black citizens were rebuffed through threats of violence, intimidation, or chicanery like poll taxes and "intelligence tests" (how many jelly beans are in this jar?), northern power brokers diluted black New Yorker's voting power.[13]

Cooper said in his complaint that Bedford-Stuyvesant, home of 370,000 Negroes, was partitioned into five congressional districts in "so torturous, artificial and labyrinthine a manner" that the lines were "irrational and unrelated to any proper purpose." As a result, Negro and Puerto Rican residents were frustrated in their "natural desire to present a generally common and unitary point of view with respect to political issues."

Indeed, his Brooklyn neighborhood Bedford-Stuyvesant was a compact, quadrangle-shaped community where nearly 80 percent of the inhabitants were Negro or Puerto Rican. Its population was about the size of an average congressional district, 400,000.[14] Yet somehow Bedford-Stuyvesant was carved into five congressional districts, each led by white representatives. All of Brooklyn's seven congressional representatives were whites from predominantly white districts, although blacks represented 14 percent of the borough population, and about 88 percent of those residents were packed into Bedford-Stuyvesant.[15]

Cooper's lawsuit named the following defendants: governor Nelson Rockefeller; Stanley Steingut, Democratic leader of Brooklyn; John R. Crews, Republican leader of Brooklyn; and all incumbent representatives of the borough. Three federal court judges in Brooklyn were asked to rule that the existing apportionment in Bedford-Stuyvesant was unconstitutional and discriminatory and that the representatives chosen under it were elected illegally.[16]

Cooper's complaint included co-plaintiffs Joan Bacchus and Paul Kerrigan. Bacchus lived on Halsey Street and was a commercial artist. Kerrigan lived on Willoughby Avenue and served as a member of the Board of Trustees of the Brooklyn Public Library. He was registered as a Republican; Cooper and Bacchus were registered Democrats.[17] The trio asked the courts to restrain the political parties from conducting elections to the House of Representatives.[18]

The existing landscape, Cooper told the *New York Amsterdam News*, "is the result of a cozy collaboration between the Democratic and Republican machines. It is time for the federal court to put an end to racially discriminatory districting."

Bedford-Stuyvesant's population was carved up in the following manner: 40 percent lived in U.S. representative Emanuel Celler's district, 13 percent lived in Eugene J. Keogh's district, 23 percent lived in Edna F. Kelly's district, 16 percent lived in John J. Rooney's district, and 9 percent lived in Hugh L. Carey's district. In Celler's district, 70,000 residents from the Rockaway section of Queens were added during the 1961 census redistricting to ensure that the political boundaries would not end up predominantly black.[19]

"The tragedy," said Cooper, "is that no Brooklyn congressman has any need to consider the wishes of the people of Bedford-Stuyvesant, who are doomed to be an ineffective minority so long as present apportionment continues. Such racially biased districts should have no place in American political life." Celler's congressional district was eleven miles long and as narrow as one mile wide. Keogh's district was ten miles long and also a mile wide in some stretches. Kelly's district was indescribable in terms of length and width because its seventy-five boundary lines reached out in all directions and cut the borough into numerous slices. Rooney's district was ten miles long and three hundred yards wide at its narrowest point. No one lived in that sliver along the waterfront, so in essence, Rooney had two districts, one in Fort Hamilton on the bay in southern Brooklyn, and another near Newton Creek up north. Carey's district was nine miles long and as little as one-quarter mile wide.[20]

When Cooper filed the complaint in the U.S. District Court, he was well aware that he had launched a missile at the powerful political forces in the city and the state, Republican and Democratic. Clearly he was both bold and bodacious.[21]

Both the Coopers were. Jocelyn Cooper and her husband took out a third mortgage on their limestone house on Decatur Street to underwrite the legal assault. At that time, their youngest daughter was days shy of her second birthday, and their oldest daughter was fourteen.[22]

Jocelyn Cooper and Andy were so broke from investing in the lawsuit they could not afford to pay a process server, so they delivered the court papers themselves. The couple nervously traveled to Bay Ridge, the white ethnic enclave of one of the congressmen leading the Twelfth Congressional District. They walked up a flight of stairs, down a dark, narrow hallway, delivered the complaint at the office, and then ran.

In the case of Hugh Carey, the Coopers lived nearby, and Jocelyn felt safe enough to travel solo and deliver the court papers to Carey's office. After he accepted the documents, Carey said, "It's about time. What took you so long?"[23]

Lawyers for the state attorney general and the New York City Corporation Counsel moved to have Cooper's suit dismissed because "it does not present a substantial federal question warranting the convening of a three-judge court."[24]

Andy Cooper wrote to Seventeenth District state assemblywoman Chisholm to seek her support for his lawsuit when he filed in June 1966. Chisholm, one of two black assembly members, did not respond. She was a member of the machine party Democrats in addition to Unity Democratic Club.[25]

Cooper and allies picketed the homes of several white members of Congress. National leadership of the Urban League, NAACP, and CORE joined the protests and became parties to the voting-rights lawsuit. Unity Democratic Club, which Cooper left in 1965, stayed conspicuously silent. Indeed, it opposed him and others when they ran as reform delegates to the state Constitutional Convention.[26] The election was on June 28. Cooper and Bunn did not win the seats.

Also in late June, Cooper led pickets around the West Fifty-fifth Street office of governor Nelson Rockefeller. They demonstrated for a "fair share" of the proposed $138 million development of low- and middle-income housing to be built at the Battery in lower Manhattan. After two hours of picketing, the group was granted a meeting with baseball great Jackie Robinson, who was the governor's special assistant. Robinson discussed the demands with the demonstrators. Cooper and his Constitutional Convention running mate Bunn asked the governor, in writing, to divert some of the housing funds to Bedford-Stuyvesant. According to a newspaper account, Rockefeller answered that nothing but "low-income housing was required" in Bedford-Stuyvesant.[27]

The wheels turned slowly. On August 10, federal judge John F. Dooling Jr., sitting in Brooklyn in the Eastern District Court, ruled that Cooper's petition could not be pronounced "insubstantial."[28] Dooling sent the case to chief justice J. Edward Lumbard of the Circuit Court of Appeals for the Second Circuit, who would designate a three-judge panel to review the case.

On September 13, 1966, a two-hour afternoon pretrial conference occurred, and on February 7, 1967, the court battle resumed in U.S. (Eastern) District Court in Brooklyn. Pretrial conference case 66C-594 was now called *Andrew Cooper et al., plaintiffs, v. James M. Power et al., defendants.* Power was the lead defendant because he was president of the New York City Board of Elections, administrator of the complex machinery that decided who governed.[29] After redistricting in 1952, Power became Democratic leader of the Thirteenth Assembly District, territory that included the Brooklyn neighborhoods Brownsville and Brighton Beach. Also that year, when a vacancy occurred at the city Board of Elections, Power was designated for the position at a stormy meeting of the Kings County Democratic Committee. David B. Costima, a Manhattan Republican, thought he was entitled to the post, but the bosses of Brooklyn ruled the day.[30]

Milton H. Friedman of Friedman & Perlin was Cooper's lawyer. Additional defense counsel included Arthur Sheinberg for U.S. representative Celler, Ira Rubin for U.S. representative Kelly, Mr. McGroaty for U.S. representative Carey, and Stanley Steingut, Louis Lefkowitz, and George Zuckerman for Governor Rockefeller and L. Johnson, corporation counsel representing the City of New York. The three federal judges were Joseph C. Zavatt (the chief), Leonard P. Moore, and John P. Dooling.[31]

Moore asked if it would be possible to wait for the population numbers in the upcoming 1970 U.S. Census so that reapportionment, then redistricting, could occur in 1971 for a 1972 congressional election. Cooper's attorney Friedman argued against waiting for five years. He wanted a ruling on the constitutionality of fragmenting Negroes and Puerto Ricans under the 1961 census reapportionment because there was numerical inequality. Friedman showed the judges maps of two Brooklyn districts, the Fifteenth and Sixteenth, that violated the principal of compactness and contiguity. Friedman also showed similar conditions in the Twenty-fifth Congressional District in the Bronx and the Thirty-fifth District in upstate New York.[32]

Twenty-five years before, in the early 1940s, Friedman told the court, Bedford-Stuyvesant had been an entirely different community from what people knew of it in the late 1960s. People knew what discrimination meant, and what blockbusting meant, and as some Negroes moved to the outskirts, whites moved, and Bedford-Stuyvesant grew, said Friedman.[33]

Then the tide turned. The pretrial conference resumed on March 28. Mayor Lindsay supported the lawsuit with a "friend of the court" brief. Six weeks later, on May 11, 1967, the three-judge federal court unanimously ruled that the 1961 reapportionment violated the U.S. Constitution. The judges' decision said the existing plan, with its "seemingly bizarre structure of most districts," should be scrapped and the new plan should be drawn up by the legislature in time for the 1968 election.[34]

The judges agreed with Cooper, Bacchus, and Kerrigan and their legal counsel Friedman: waiting a few years for a new decade and head count was unacceptable; egregious disenfranchisement of voters needed to be repaired within a year. The court recommended that the new districts be drawn without consideration of race but with equal population and "reasonably compact and contiguous" bounds.[35] The Liberal Party of New York and D. I. Wells also joined the voting-rights lawsuit. They argued that Cooper's suit did not go far enough because other political boundaries were racially gerrymandered. Those additional arguments, however, did not move the court. Ruling for Cooper was already the political missile that exploded. The government plaintiffs, including James Power, appealed the ruling.

On December 19, 1967, the U.S. Supreme Court, in an 8–1 decision, upheld the lower court. Indeed, the dilution of five congressional districts violated the one-man, one-vote principle. The high court ordered the Brooklyn districts' reapportionment in time for the 1968 election. Liberal Party chairman Donald S. Harrington urged legislators to establish a nonpartisan citizen commission.[36]

Just before Christmas 1967, a citizens' committee was formed to interview candidates for the new seat. Shirley Chisholm—the only woman among a dozen contenders—won the committee's unanimous endorsement.[37] In anticipation of redistricting, the Committee for a Negro Congressman from Brooklyn designated the first-term state senator as the appropriate candidate. This move was intended to thwart white machine bosses from choosing for black people.[38]

The activist and political establishments were not happy. Chisholm expressed no enthusiasm for the voting rights lawsuit when Cooper and friends filed in 1966. A year later, after favorable court rulings, she was suddenly extremely interested in the anticipated congressional seat.[39] Chisholm was fast on her feet and, intrinsically and instinctively, behaved like an opportunist. Andy Cooper fought for the creation of revised political boundaries mostly on principle. Now Chisholm came along and picked up the pieces.[40]

In addition, one Kings County Democratic regular said: "If we couldn't control her in Albany, how are we going to in Washington?"[41] William C. Thompson, a city councilman and former state senator, was the organization's man. Bertram Baker also favored Thompson, and Baker was Chisholm's political foe. Thompson first assured Chisholm he was not going to run and would back her, but he changed his mind before the circulation of petitions.[42]

Meanwhile Tom Jones, Chisholm's former Unity Democratic Club mate, expressed interest in the congressional seat. Pat Cyrus, a UDC member and Jones surrogate, visited Chisholm and asked her to step aside and allow Jones to run for the seat. She refused. Chisholm told Cyrus that she was going to be the greatest woman on the eastern seaboard and was going to control boards. People would be wishing she would speak to them.[43]

In reality, Jones could not run for the new congressional seat. He had sealed his fate four years earlier with a change that started Chisholm's ascent. Jones was compelled economically to opt for the judgeship because he could not live on $10,000 a year. Tom and Bertha Kantor Jones were putting a son and a daughter though college. As an assemblyman, Jones had to maintain residences in Brooklyn and the state capital. The municipal judgeship that Kings County leaders proffered in 1964 brought relief to the Joneses' household budget.[44]

Chisholm meanwhile could run for the congressional seat because she kept her job at a day care center. That was her living. She had no children, and that made the difference. When Chisholm replaced Tom Jones in Albany, she supplemented her legislative salary with the child care job. Again in 1967, Chisholm was in a better position to go after the congressional seat expected to be available in 1968.[45]

Pat Carter, Cooper's political buddy, thought about running for the seat too. He was asked to run for the seat before Chisholm. Carter asked his wife Constance if she would support his run. She was distressed because of their family situation—heavy workloads, marital stress, and civic commitments. "You do what you want," said Constance.

Her husband recognized disapproval in his spouse's voice. Pat did not want to give up his insurance business. He made a good living as an insurance broker and was responsible for renting the space at Nostrand and Atlantic avenues used by the Unity Democratic Club. Pat Carter nixed the dream of running for the seat.[46]

Pat was put off by Jones's ambition. Jones gave up his assembly seat for a secure seat on the court bench. Now he pondered losing that position in exchange for a congressional seat. "What did you expect?" Constance told her husband. "I'm surprised you're so naive about this."[47]

Other local males were in the hunt for the seat: assemblyman Sam Wright, Rev. William Jones of Bethany Baptist Church, and Rev. Gardner C. Taylor of Concord Baptist Church.[48]

As pretenders faded away, Chisholm faced a three-way primary: Her, Thompson, and Dolly Robinson, a labor organizer. Unity Democratic Club, said Chisholm, supported her.[49] Andy Cooper would laugh at her claim because the members who believed she was a political fence sitter and opportunist were gone; a different constituency at UDC was backing her.

Chisholm got a call from Wesley McD Holder, her longtime mentor but recent political foe.[50] Two decades before, in 1948, McD Holder said he wanted to live to see a black person elected to Congress from Brooklyn. "You're the easiest product to sell, and I'm going to organize the campaign and sell you," McD Holder told Chisholm.[51] With McD Holder's help, she began campaigning for the congressional seat in February 1968.

As many black Brooklyn residents in 1967 imagined gaining a congressman who looked like them, the lone black congressman from the state of New York was under siege. Adam Clayton Powell Jr. of the Twenty-second Congressional District representing Harlem was once the leader of the largest church congregation in America, a political demagogue, a congressional rebel, a civil rights leader three decades before the 1955 Montgomery bus boycott, a wheeler-dealer, a rabble-rouser, a grandstander, a fugitive, a playboy, and the most effective chairman of the House Committee on Education and Labor despite a high absentee rate in Congress.[52]

On January 9, when the Ninetieth Congress returned to Washington, Powell was censured on charges of wrongfully appropriating congressional funds. He was stripped of his chairmanship by a committee chaired by Emanuel Celler, one of the representatives from the gerrymandered Brooklyn congressional districts. On March 1, the full Congress voted 307–116 to expel Powell. The eleven-term representative was unrepentant; he accused his colleagues of racism and hypocrisy.

Because of a lawsuit and settlement that Powell refused to pay, he lived on a houseboat in Bimini, Bahamas, and did not set foot in his district.[53] Nevertheless, when a special election was held on April 11, defiant voters chose Powell over a reluctant black Republican challenger by a 7–1 vote margin. Voters emphatically told Congress they were keeping the representative they had chosen in November 1966 to serve through 1968.

Because the U.S. Supreme Court affirmed that Brooklyn congressional lines had to be redrawn by the state before the 1968 congressional elections, the odds of a second black congressman joining Powell in Washington became likely. In late February, New York state legislative leaders changed the game and changed history. They agreed on a congressional reapportionment bill that virtually ensured the election of Brooklyn's first Negro member of the House of Representatives. Edna Kelly, who represented the old Twelfth Congressional District for nine terms—eighteen years—was expected to retire, and she did.[54] Kelly's horseshoe-shaped district was almost as weird a creation as the Massachusetts district drawn by Elbridge Gerry in the 1800s. The word "gerrymandering" was based on Gerry's creative political mapmaking.[55]

One month later, on March 26, the redistricting bill passed the assembly by a 126–19 vote and then passed the senate by a 51–5 vote. Ninety minutes after the senate vote, Governor Rockefeller signed the legislation, just in time to meet a Friday, March 30, court deadline.[56]

Some critics said the redrawn lines did not reach far enough. Black citizens in Queens and the Bronx expressed disenfranchisement similar to Bedford-Stuyvesant residents, but the courts rejected their cases. Also, a plaintiff in the *Cooper v. Power* case, Paul Kerrigan, contended in 2009 that the federal courts actually ruled against their team by not dealing aggressively with gerrymandering and instead accepted the argument of the Liberal Party, which favored two new congressional districts in which at least two-thirds of all constituent residents were black.[57]

Like Pat Carter months before, Andy Cooper was interested in running for the new congressional seat. But the question was moot because the Coopers lived just outside the new boundary lines for the revised Twelfth District. Still, Cooper had his mind on political office. Instead of the congressional seat that he was largely responsible for creating, he made a move for a state senate seat.[58]

Starting in February 1968 and for the next ten months, Chisholm tramped the streets of Williamsburg, Crown Heights, and Bedford-Stuyvesant, telling her story to the people.[59] She wrote a slogan that said it all: "Fighting Shirley Chisholm—Unbought and Unbossed." She hammered this message home. The weekends offered the best opportunity for campaigning. On Friday nights and through Sunday evenings, led by Thomas R. Fortune, her district leader, Chisholm traveled with a caravan of twenty to fifty cars staffed by volunteers—men, women, and children. On both sides of each car, they posted pictures of the candidate, plus the slogan VOTE CHISHOLM FOR CONGRESS—UNBOUGHT AND UNBOSSED. Chisholm and the rest of her organization-backed slate had used that slogan as early as 1964, but it began to mean something to her for the first time in the 1968 race.[60]

Elsewhere, political developments overheated the year 1968. The Vietnam War was costing taxpayers $25 billion a year, announced President Johnson during his State of the Union address. He asked citizens to accept a 10 percent income tax surcharge. At the end of January, communist guerrillas in Vietnam launched a major offensive on the eve of Tet, the lunar New Year, as a brief holiday truce was about to begin. The assault knocked U.S. forces back on their heels. In February, Richard M. Nixon declared his intention to run for the Republican presidential nomination.

Johnson was the presumed Democratic incumbent, but he faced challenges within his party. On March 12, U.S. senator Eugene McCarthy (D-Minn.), an antiwar activist, won the New Hampshire Democratic primary with 42 percent of the vote. Four days later, U.S. senator Robert Kennedy (D-N.Y.) announced that he too was a Democratic candidate for president. At the end of the month, LBJ announced that he would not seek or accept the nomination to run for reelection.[61]

Four days after LBJ's breathtaking surrender, tragedy struck. The Rev. Martin Luther King Jr. was shot dead by a sniper in Memphis on April 4. King was in Tennessee to support black sanitation workers on strike for fair treatment and fair wages. News of the civil rights leader's murder touched off looting and rioting in the Washington, D.C., ghetto. Chaos spread to within blocks of the Capitol.[62] Two months after King died, Robert F. Kennedy was assassinated on June 2 while campaigning in Los Angeles.

In June, Chisholm won the Democratic primary for Congress. Because of a light turnout, she won by 788 votes, 5,431–4,643, over William C. Thompson, her main opponent. Dolly Robinson, who earned 1,751 votes, did not prove to be a spoiler. Chisholm carried four predominantly white election districts within the newly drawn Twelfth Congressional District.[63]

Andy Cooper tasted defeat in his state senate run. In a three-way race, Cooper got 36 percent or 2,431 votes out of 6,813 cast, and finished second to Waldaba Stewart, who got 41 percent and 2,796 votes. V.L. Johnson finished third with 23 percent and 1,586 votes.[64]

Chisholm's next move was to battle James Farmer, an imported candidate from the Liberal Party with name recognition. He was former national chairman of CORE. Local Republicans put ideology aside and joined forces with the Liberals to support Farmer.[65] He did not live in Brooklyn and did not have to. He rented an apartment in the Twelfth Congressional District for appearance's sake.[66]

Farmer had a well-oiled campaign. He toured the district with sound trucks manned by young dudes with Afros who beat tom-toms. He drew the national television cameras like flies: he was big national figure, prepared to become New York City's second black congressman, ranked after Adam Clayton Powell Jr.[67]

During this phase of the campaign, Chisholm had trouble sleeping. Her husband Conrad pressed her to see a doctor. Either you're pregnant, said her spouse, or you have a tumor. Doctors did remove a large tumor from her pelvic basin.[68] Chisholm had lost so much weight that from the waist down she looked like the fashion model Twiggy.

Chisholm wrapped a beach towel around her hips so her clothes would not fall off and resumed campaigning in August. That month, Nixon won the GOP nomination for president. Two and a half weeks later, Hubert Humphrey received the Democratic nomination at a convention marred by fighting between police and antiwar demonstrators outside the hall in Chicago.

Farmer was confident that he would win. He had a well-financed campaign, name recognition, and a small degree of voter wariness about a bossy, domineering female candidate.[69] Yet Chisholm apparently enjoyed the home-field advantage over the imported star. In the November 6 election, she beat Farmer by a ratio of 2.5:1, 34,885 votes to 13,777. Ralph J. Carrane, a Conservative Party candidate, came in third with 3,771 votes. Chisholm made history as the first black woman elected to Congress and the first black representative from Brooklyn.

Andy Cooper, the man who was responsible for the majority-minority congressional district because of his 1966 lawsuit and two-year crusade, recovered from his political defeat and watched from the sidelines. Cooper was a white-collar manager with the Schaefer brewery. His wife was a researcher with an antipoverty agency. Their sixteen-year-old daughter was in high school, and their baby was four.

Chisholm became the second black representative from New York and joined Powell on Capitol Hill. But Powell, as ever, dominated the headlines. When the Ninety-first Congress convened on January 3, 1969, Powell was seated after his involuntary ten-month absence. In June 1969, the U.S. Supreme Court rebuked Congress and ruled that Powell's suspension had been unconstitutional.[70]

6. SCHAEFER SUDS

Andrew W. Stanfield was a two-time Olympian and a medalist in track and field. He became a public relations representative with the F&M Schaefer brewery in the early 1960s. Stanfield was promoted to manager of trade and consumer relations in 1964. A year later he advanced to community relations manager.[1] His wife, Gloria Bolden Stanfield of Jersey City, was a childhood friend of Jocelyn Cooper and matron of honor at the Coopers' wedding in 1949.[2]

Andy Cooper, the second Negro hired at the brewery, had worked his way up through the ranks since 1951 from checker to foreman, and in the early 1960s he traded his blue collar for a white one. By 1964, Cooper was working in sales. In 1965 he campaigned vigorously and successfully for the election of Mayor Lindsay. The mayor-elect tried to reward Cooper with an assistant commissioner appointment in his new administration. Cooper alerted his bosses about the opportunity, and they made a counteroffer. They promoted him to the brewery's public relations department.

Cooper earned a reputation as an effective public relations professional in large part because of his community organizing skills. He was rarely in the office.[3] Cooper's promotion of the Schaefer brand in black Brooklyn and metro New York occurred during the time he was politically active with the *Cooper v. Power* lawsuit and during his 1968 run for state senate.

Stanfield retired in 1968, and the Schaefer brewery appointed Cooper director of community affairs. Wilbur "Skippy" Holton, another black man and Brooklyn resident, was promoted to assistant to the director of public relations.[4]

Gloria Thomas was a modeling and fashion coordinator who had met Stanfield at an event in the 1960s. He hired the twenty-something woman as a public relations representative, and she was later promoted to manager of women's activities. When Cooper arrived as Stanfield's successor, Thomas ran the Schaefer Show of Stars, a fashion promotion that targeted Negro customers. It joined Johnson Publishing Company's Ebony Fashion Fair as a widely promoted traveling black fashion show in America.[5]

Cooper had developed his writing skill over time, crafting calls to action for the *Unity Democrat* newsletter and documents for his voting-rights lawsuit. That facility served him well as a promoter of the Schaefer brand. He became managing editor of the *Schaefer Scene* newsletter, launched in spring 1969, and he was a member of a four-person editorial board that included Thomas. Since the Schaefer Show of Stars was entertainment, Cooper drew inspiration from the many musical and theatrical performances he witnessed as a youth at St. Mark's United Methodist Church in Harlem.

Cooper also recalled the many social evenings he and Jocelyn spent with Carl Thomas, who played host at his red-draped, one-room home on West End Avenue in Manhattan. Thomas and his friends took part in the Beaux Arts ball at the Savoy ballroom and invited the Coopers to artistic and flamboyant overnight parties in Mystic, Connecticut, at which young men dressed as the mythical god Mercury or as Native Americans.[6]

Cooper drew inspiration from the fine arts, too. The cover of the inaugural *Schaefer Scene* depicted an untitled color painting of a cityscape drawn by Fred Moore, a student at Pratt Institute, an art college in Brooklyn. Moore was among three art students Schaefer commissioned to draw covers for editions of the newsletter.

Cooper and Thomas launched another promotion, the Schaefer Circle of Music. The shows traveled throughout the East Coast, to Philadelphia, Baltimore, and cites in New Jersey and Delaware.

The tour was a self-help partnership of the corporation and civic organizations. Schaefer supplied the orchestra for various community organizations that held charity fund-raisers. These dances and fashion shows could be staged both indoors and outdoors. The brewery offered the orchestras as long as the events were for charity. The clubs and associations sold Schaffer products, and the brewery provided the promotional advertising.[7] Participants included local chapters of the NAACP, the New York and Boston Urban League, Provident Hospital in Baltimore, Deborah Hospital in New York, and the Links.[8]

In 1968, Cooper delved deeper into promoting. Civil rights and other civic groups gave $75,650 to charity because of the Schaefer promotions Cooper had orchestrated.[9] Patti LaBelle and the Bluebells (Nona Hendrix and Sarah Dash) performed when the show came to Philadelphia. On Long Island, Cooper booked the Reflections, a "girl group" recommended by Clarence Irving, director of a performing arts organization.[10]

Andy Cooper and bandleader Ron Anderson put together shows with concert promoter Ron Delsener. In 1966, Delsener got $35,000 in sponsor support for the Rheingold summer concert series in Central Park's Wollman Memorial Skating Rink. Parks commissioner Thomas Hoving worked with

Rheingold and Delsener to stage rock and pop concerts that admitted thousands of fans for one dollar each.[11] Sponsorship switched to Schaefer in May 1968.[12] Cooper's Schaefer Circle of Music bookings merged with Delsener, and both men worked in tandem.

Anderson was tasked to handle the other Schaefer music programming. A family friend of the Andy and Jocelyn Cooper recommended that the bassist approach the Schaefer executive about work. Cooper and Thomas came out to hear the thirty-two-year-old and his eleven-member band and were impressed enough to hire them. They were booked to play the Kwanzaa Festival in the two-thousand-seat Stark Skating Arena in Coney Island, and also booked for Gloria Thomas's Schaefer Show of Stars fashion shows.[13]

Cooper and Thomas set Anderson up in an office at Park Avenue and Eighteenth Street to work on the non–Central Park—related Schaefer music.[14] These acts included the Chi-Lites, Patti LaBelle and the Bluebells, Lionel Hampton, and Thelonious Monk. Delsener's lineup for the summer of 1969 represented an eclectic mix of rock, pop, soul, and jazz:

Benny Goodman and Lionel Hampton
Tiny Tim and Sweetwater
Flip Wilson and the Modern Jazz Quartet
Hugh Masakela and Willie Bobo
Miles Davis and Thelonious Monk
Blood, Sweat, and Tears and Carolyn Hester
Herbie Mann and Eddie Harris
The Byrds, Chuck Berry, and John Lee Hooker
Jeff Beck and Orpheus
Fleetwood Mac and Ten Years After
Cannonball Adderley and the Sweet Inspirations
Led Zeppelin and B. B. King
Joni Mitchell and Tim Hardin
Mongo Santamaria, Cal Tjader, and Chucho Avellanet
Sly and the Family Stone and Slim Harpo
the Beach Boys and Neil Young
Buddy Rich and Procol Harum
Frank Zappa and Buddy Guy
Dizzy Gillespie and Carmen McRae
Little Richard and the Checkmates
Tom Paxton and Gordon Lightfoot
Herbie Mann (return engagement)

Roy Ayers and Sonny Sharrock
Arlo Guthrie and Melanie
Lou Rawls, Carl Holmes and the Commanders, and Ruth McFadden
Nina Simone and Montega Joe
Sam and Dave and Patti LaBelle and the Bluebells (last concert in 1969)

In 1969 there were sixty-four concerts; 275,000 young music lovers attended summer shows in New York. In Boston, 180,000 people attended Schaefer-sponsored shows.[15]

Cooper continued to book performances from 1969 through 1971. The music pairings, harmonious matches of the same genre or dissonant matches of rock with jazz, were in tune with the unpredictable pace of news in 1969: American astronauts landed on the moon that summer; Charles Manson went on a killing spree in California, and actress Sharon Tate was among the slain; the Woodstock concert in upstate New York epitomized sex, drugs, and rock and roll; the war dragged on in Vietnam, and the rift between young antiwar demonstrators and the older pro-war establishment widened; during the Stonewall riot in lower Manhattan, homosexuals fought back against police; and lovable losers the New York Mets made an improbable run for National League pennant. They won and then prevailed in the World Series in October.

In the springtime, Cooper spent $170,000 from his community affairs discretionary budget to sponsor three concerts at the Brooklyn Academy of Music. Thelonious Monk performed before a nearly sold-out audience. The eccentric jazz master played energetically, then would stop and nod for a spell, resume his exuberant playing only to stop and nod for spell, yet he was very well received.[16]

Why was Monk's show the best attended of the three at BAM? Although the popular appeal of jazz was falling off, many people realized Monk's singular genius. The jazz community was tighter than the R&B and pop constituencies. Three jazz radio stations got the word out about Monk at BAM, and fans responded.[17]

In the other shows, Patti LaBelle and the Bluebells and the Alvin Ailey Dance Company played to half-filled halls.[18] Both appearances were meaningful nevertheless. Patti LaBelle's signature song was "Over the Rainbow." The Alvin Ailey performance was the closing show of the troupe's 1969 season.[19]

In February 1969, Cooper was appointed to the Brooklyn Advisory Council of the New York State Division of Human Rights by commissioner Robert

J. Magnum. Cooper served on the council with Chairman Raymond R. Brown.[20]

On July 2, Louise Schofield Cooper, Andy Cooper's paternal grandmother, died at age ninety-six. She lived in her late son Palmer's house at 350 Grand Avenue, the house in which Andy was born and where he grew up.

That year, Utrice C. Leid, a fifteen-year-old girl, immigrated to the United States from Trinidad and Tobago. She was one of nine children, seven brothers and a sister. Utrice's mother operated a restaurant, and her father owned a variety of businesses including a grocery store, movie theater, and bar.[21]

Cooper, forty-one, did not know about the girl's arrival, but in less than a decade he would be profoundly affected by the assertive Trinidadian.[22] Meanwhile Andy's wife Jocelyn was busy raising preschooler Jo-An, five, and teenager Andrea, seventeen.

That November, John V. Lindsay, the liberal Republican mayor of New York, won an improbable reelection, defeating challengers in a five-candidate runoff. Although he was a registered Republican, Lindsay was not endorsed by the GOP, so he ran on the Liberal Party ballot.[23]

A few observers said that the embattled mayor received a last-minute boost from the amazing Mets, perennial losers who rallied that summer to win the National League pennant, then beat the heavily favored Baltimore Orioles to win the World Series. Tom Seaver, Jerry Koosman, and Tug McGraw led the outstanding pitching rotation; Cleon Jones, Tommie Agee, and Don Clendenon provided clutch hitting; and Bud Harrelson, Ron Swoboda, and Jerry Grote played with heart and made believers out of skeptics. For a moment, New Yorkers put aside strikes, racial strife, and urban decay and reveled in the Mets' victory, as seemingly improbable as Lindsay's reelection.

The F&M Schaefer Company opened its brewery in Manhattan in 1842. After seventy years, it moved from Park Avenue and Fifty-first Street to the Greenpoint section of Brooklyn on land fronting the East River. Schaefer competed with Ballentine, owned by Jack Rupert, the builder of Yankee Stadium, and the Rheingold and Piels breweries. Schaefer's market share dominated the thirteen-state East Coast region and Puerto Rico. The brewery employed 4,500 people.[24]

For nine years the brewery sponsored the Brooklyn Dodgers. When the baseball team left for Los Angeles in the late 1950s, the brewery sponsored the Mets, who arrived in 1962. They were the offspring of the departed Dodgers and baseball Giants, who had left New York too (155th Street in Harlem) for California.

Many New York baseball fans knew the jingle "Schaefer is the one beer to have . . . when you're having more than one." One TV commercial opened with two hands chiseling a block of ice into a beer mug. A hand then poured Schaefer into the vessel. Another commercial depicted a rookie blue-collar worker who faced initiation by experienced workers. "Okay, you, up on the barrel," said the foreman. The nervous young man hesitated. Off to the side, a black employee smiled encouragingly and in a resonant baritone commanded the rookie to sing. On cue the rookie sang the Schaefer jingle, and he was accepted by the brotherhood.[25]

In 1948, not long after Jackie Robinson joined the Dodgers, Rudy Schaefer III began his training to lead the family business in the future. Twenty years later, in April 1968, Schaefer became a publicly traded company, ending 106 years of private ownership.

In the short term, the company thrived. Schaefer was a regional beer that sold its product for less than premium-label Midwestern national brewers such as Anheuser-Busch, Miller Brewing Co., and Jos. Schlitz Brewing Co.[26] One-third of Schaefer's sales were concentrated in the New York and Philadelphia metropolitan areas.[27] The brewer was America's sixth largest. By March 1970, Schaefer stock was priced at $52 per share, double its price when the beer company began trading publicly in June 1968.

Yet Rudy Schaefer III was not prepared to run a publicly owned company caught in the throes of massive manufacturing job losses in metropolitan New York. Factory jobs, workers, and beer-drinking customers migrated to the new Sunbelt, the American South and West. The Brooklyn brewery was old and inefficient. Schaefer reduced operations at the plant and in 1971 built a brewery in the Lehigh Valley region of eastern Pennsylvania, near Philadelphia.

That year, Cooper left the company, ending twenty years of service as a loading dock checker, foreman, advertising salesman, and finally public relations executive. In a two-year period (1968–70) as a corporate executive, Cooper and his department initiated an apprenticeship training program in the skilled-trade area with an integrated work group, established training scholarships with the Electronic Computer Training Program Institute of New York in cooperation with the city Human Resources Administration manpower training unit, and assisted in fund-raising for Greenburgh Community Center in Westchester, New York, Brooklyn-Cumberland Medical Center, the Willa Hardgrow Mental Health Clinic, Brooklyn Urban League, Brooklyn Branch of the NAACP, History, Art, and Nature Den (HAND), the Community Gallery of the Brooklyn Museum, and Provident Hospital of Baltimore.[28]

Its cultural and community outreach earned Schaefer a Business and Arts Award from the New York Board of Trade. The Urban Affairs Department also consulted with the Brooklyn Arts and Culture Association, New York Head Start, the Brooklyn Tuberculosis and Respiratory Diseases Association, and the Brooklyn chapter of the American Cancer Society. In the late 1960s, Cooper synthesized on-the-job workmanship, teamwork, and brand loyalty with off-the-clock community organizing, activism, and agitation. All of that heart-and-soul effort at Schaefer came to an end in 1971.

Just shy of forty-four, Cooper supported his family by establishing Andrew W. Cooper Inc., a public relations consulting proprietorship, first working out of his home and later from a midtown Manhattan office. He had to make the transition: by 1976, Schaefer was the last brewery standing in Brooklyn. The company closed the plant that year, and 850 jobs disappeared.[29]

Early in 1970, state senator Waldaba Stewart hatched a plan to create an improvement authority for Atlantic Avenue, the busy but shabby thoroughfare that began at the East River waterfront and pushed five miles east through central Brooklyn into the borough of Queens. Atlantic Avenue was a rubble-strewn wilderness that had been so neglected, some of its streets had not been paved since 1911, when William Howard Taft was president.[30] Stewart's proposal would allow developers to condemn and demolish houses on streets a few blocks off Atlantic to widen the boulevard. With co-sponsor Thomas R. Fortune, an assemblyman representing Bedford-Stuyvesant, the plan sailed through the legislature with little discussion.

Andy Cooper lived just beyond the corridor on Decatur Street, north of Atlantic. He saw the proposed changes not as an improvement but as a crude land grab that would allow the state to toss a few thousand residents out of their homes and build a superhighway. Cooper quickly rallied people to reject the plan by his adversary from the June 1968 Democratic state senate primary. In April, Cooper distributed fliers with photocopied stories from the *Daily News*, *New York Times*, and *New York Post*. He added the warning "If Senator Stewart's Highway Bill Goes Through, YOU WILL LOSE YOUR HOME!" Another flier included a map of Brooklyn that showed the boundaries of the improvement district, which in Bedford-Stuyvesant dipped well south of Atlantic Avenue to Park Place, real estate at the edge of Crown Heights.[31]

Cooper and friends organized hundreds of residents to travel by buses or carpools to Albany to demonstrate at the capital when the improvement authority proposal came up for a vote. On April 7, between one and four thousand residents marched along State Street with signs that said "Homes, not highways" and "People make cities, highways don't."[32]

The demonstrators were a coalition of black and white, middle- and working-class homeowners united by group anger that they could lose their homes. Once the details of the improvement authority proposal surfaced, they were widely condemned in the press. Mayor Lindsay opposed the plan and noted that the city had a contract to make $3.6 million in improvements. Because of opposition from constituents, Stewart proposed amendments to the authority plan.

The changes drew criticism from U.S. representative Hugh Carey. "This would be less of a project than I was originally informed about during a meeting with Mr. Stewart [on March 21]," said Carey. "What I had understood was a really massive artery including clearance and removal of border housing and industrial property to be included in an overall arterial authority. It would link the Gowanus and Interboro Expressways and I promised to inquire as to the possibility of acquiring Federal highway funds as part of this project."[33]

On Cooper fliers, the instigator circled the congressman's quotation and drew an arrow from a handwritten headline that said "Rep. Carey spills the beans!" A *New York Times* editorial said of the proposal: "No one opposes help for Bedford-Stuyvesant, but this is not the way to give it. There is only one real issue here—an ill-conceived and potentially harmful bill that should not be passed."[34] Under siege, Stewart and Fortune withdrew the development authority bill and vowed to reintroduce it a year later. Fortune promised the new legislation would be drafted only after meetings in the affected communities.[35]

In the week that Cooper, along with hundreds of demonstrators, confronted and defeated the Atlantic Avenue development plan, Cooper announced he was running again for the Eighteenth Senatorial District seat occupied by Stewart. "The attempt by a small group of greedy politicians to destroy our homes by condemning them for the construction of a superhighway has helped me recognize the need for new political leadership," Cooper wrote in a letter to friends and neighbors.[36] He urged supporters to come to an April 16 organizing meeting at 768 Nostrand Avenue.

In May, Cooper turned up the heat on Stewart. Cooper said that the senator had purchased three houses in the development authority district Stewart created. Stewart had a conflict of interest, Cooper claimed, because the elected official had created an opportunity to profit from his legislation. Cooper asked the Brooklyn district attorney and state officials to investigate

Stewart.[37] After the accusation and media inquiries, the senator acknowledged that he had purchased three boarded-up houses on Rogers Avenue, five blocks south of Atlantic Avenue, for use as a residence, offices, and rental property.

Stewart dismissed Cooper's charges. "It's tragic Mr. Cooper has to indulge in slander," Stewart told the *Daily News*, and a month later he told the *New York Times*, "My life is an open book. He [Cooper] is trying to fabricate an issue because he can't match me for performance and character."[38] Yet Stewart never disclosed his property holdings during the discussion of the proposed improvement authority, and he specifically committed a sin of omission when the improvement area was amended to include land that could benefit his properties.

State senator A. Frederick Meyerson of Brooklyn, a co-sponsor of Stewart's bill, said, "I had no idea he owned property in the area. If I had known it, I might have taken a second look at the bill, although basically it was a wonderful concept. It was Stewart's baby." Indeed, had the bill passed in April, Stewart would have had a major voice in choosing the twenty-nine unelected authority members.

Stewart said after the June primary that he planned to sue Cooper for libel. Cooper did not back down; he said that Stewart had climbed to his present position by a cunning use of the "rhetoric of blackness."

> The liberal element of the white community is very guilty over the inherent racism of America. Political leadership in New York is willing to trade off the black area of central Brooklyn as the fiefdom of black politicians as long as they can maintain their bases in the remaining communities.
>
> Therefore, a black leader purporting to speak up for the black community immediately gains support. This same black leader can respond to criticism of his schemes by charging racism. This was the defense Mr. Stewart used in his attempt to stem community anger and protest over the Atlantic Avenue Authority.[39]

Just before the June 23 primary, Cooper believed he had another damaging piece of evidence against Stewart—that he did not live in the district he purported to represent. Cooper was counseled by manager Pat Carter to hold back on the knockout punch; they were positioned to win big.

That did not happen. Stewart, a 7–1 margin winner of the senate seat in the 1968 general election, squeaked by Cooper with fewer than 250 votes.[40]

Stewart cruised to an easy victory in the November general election, but without the Atlantic Avenue Development project that Cooper—the watchdog journalist in the making—had derailed.

In 1970 the U.S. Senate extended the Voting Rights Act to 1975, and president Richard M. Nixon signed the legislation; Charles Rangel defeated Adam Clayton Powell in the June Democratic primary. In August the City University of New York initiated an open admissions policy designed to increase the number of poor and minority students.[41]

In 1971, the year Cooper left Schaefer and began working independently as a public relations consultant, the twelve members of the Congressional Black Caucus (including Chisholm and Rangel of New York) boycotted President Nixon's State of the Union address because of his consistent refusal to respond to the petitions of black Americans. A month later, the president met with the CBC to discuss a list of sixty complaints the caucus had filed on behalf of African Americans. Three months later, Nixon rejected the demands and said his administration would continue to support "jobs, income and tangible benefits, the pledges that this society has made to the disadvantaged in the past decade."[42]

Whitney Young Jr., the forty-nine-year-old director of the National Urban League, drowned in Lagos, Nigeria in February. In June, Vernon Jordan succeeded Young. Culturally, Louis Armstrong, who had shaped jazz and American music for most of twentieth century, died in Queens at age seventy-one. Marvin Gaye's haunting "What's Goin' On" was the number one R&B hit.

In September, inmates seized Attica State Correctional Facility in upstate New York and held guards hostage. Inmates demanded coverage by the state minimum wage law, better food, and no reprisals. In response, 1,500 troopers and officers stormed the prison; thirty-two convicts and ten guards were killed. An investigation revealed that nine of the ten guards held hostage were killed by the storming party.[43]

In January 1972, Andrea Cooper married Robert Lee Andrews. A month later, Andy and Jocelyn moved into a new house. After twenty years a 619 Decatur Street, on February 7 they moved to 548 Third Street in Park Slope, an elegant neighborhood on the edge of Prospect Park. Julius and Rose Rock were the buyers of the limestone house. Their son Chris, who turned seven the day the Coopers moved in, would grow up to be a comedic superstar. Rock is a close friend of Jocelyn A. Cooper, who grew up to be a music publisher and entertainment power player.[44]

The Coopers tried to ignore digs from disapproving whites, including a neighbor who wondered out loud whether they would throw "rent parties" the way Harlem residents did during the Depression. But the Coopers owned their house. They joined another black couple on the block between Seventh and Eighth avenues.

The Coopers' oldest daughter had just married, and their younger daughter was seven. Andy's mother Irma, seventy-six, lived with them. On July 28, Damani Yotanka Andrews was born. His middle name was a tribute to Sitting Bull, the Indian chief.[45]

7. ONE MAN'S OPINION

By 1972 Andy's champion, mayor John Lindsay, had switched his political affiliation from Liberal Republican to Democrat and entered the presidential primaries. George McGovern of South Dakota eventually won the Democratic nomination that summer. In November, McGovern was trounced by Republican incumbent Richard M. Nixon, who won 61 percent of the popular vote and lost only Massachusetts in the Electoral College.[1]

After the election, black representation in Congress grew again. Sixteen men and women were elected, including Andrew Young of Georgia, the first black man from the South elected to Congress since Reconstruction, as well as Barbara Jordan of Texas and Yvonne Brathwaite Burke of California. U.S. senator Edward Burke of Massachusetts, a Republican, was reelected.[2]

Shirley Chisholm was elected to a third term as representative from the Twelfth Congressional District of Brooklyn, New York. The previous January, she began an audacious six-month run for president of the United States. Chisholm largely courted white women from the emerging feminist movement, and black women and men from around America who were drawn to her tireless demands for inclusion in the political process. "I am not the candidate of black America," said Chisholm in her announcement, "although I am black and proud. I am not the candidate of the women's movement of this country, although I am a woman and equally proud of that. I am the candidate of the people, and my presence before you now symbolizes a new era in American political history."[3]

She broke all kinds of political rules. Chisholm did not follow Democratic Party protocol and defer to the male elders. She had the nerve to run for president when most American women could not get credit cards in their own names; their husbands had to vouch for them. Insurance companies added surcharges to the policies of single women who owned cars because the companies assumed the women were only letting their reckless boyfriends drive.[4]

Chisholm fomented conflict inside the overwhelmingly male Congressional Black Caucus. Walter Fauntroy of the District of Columbia said that Chisholm's run drained energy from candidates who had a chance to defeat Nixon. U.S. representative Ron Dellums of California supported Chisholm and held on until a tense meeting at the Democratic National Convention at which he threw his support to the front runner. A political insider said Chisholm angered her peers because she grabbed for the brass ring while some of them pondered whether to pounce. Had Cooper been in the room, he would probably have admonished them not to fault Chisholm for her consistency. She had not hesitated years earlier to pursue the new congressional seat in Brooklyn, even as she expressed no interest in fighting for its creation.

Chisholm's presidential run was not pointless. She successfully challenged attempts to bar her from debating McGovern and Edmund Muskie on network television. And during the California primary, Chisholm successfully upended the winner-take-all delegate system in the Golden State. She was entitled to 12 of 271 delegates. The rest were split almost evenly between McGovern and Muskie.[5] All along, Chisholm told supporters, it did not matter that she had nearly no prospect of winning the election; she wanted their votes to earn delegates she could use to leverage policy changes in the Democratic Party platform. In all, Chisholm received 152 of more than 2,000 ballots on the first roll call for president at the July convention in Miami Beach.[6]

Andy Cooper was working at his sole proprietorship public relations consulting company. Jocelyn Cooper was attending classes at Adelphi University in New York and working for the city Community Development Agency. Both parents raised "Jo Ann," Jocelyn Andrea, who was seven and a second grader. The family settled into its new house on Third Street in Park Slope. Andrea Andrews, the newlywed, and husband Robert Lee Andrews cared for their newborn Damani. Before the birth, twenty-year-old Andrea taught high school students at the Satellite Academy in the Bronx. She had previously attended Macalester College in St. Paul, Minnesota, a school that informed observers called the Harvard of the Midwest.[7]

On January 26, 1973, *Local Level*, a four-page, tabloid-size newsletter, was published by the Council against Poverty–Citizenship Education Program. Andrew W. Cooper was listed as the editor. The self-employed public relations professional produced the newsletter at his office on East Forty-second Street in Manhattan.

"Harlem residents believe economic injustice causes street crime, study reveals," read the cover story by Frank McRae of Community News Service. CNS trained minority journalists for work in the white daily press.

The edition included Andy's column "One Man's Opinion." "The communications gap . . . media and the minority community," read the headline.

There was a photo of Emma Bowen, leader of Black Citizens for Fair Media. Bowen was a campaign manager for Lindsay who later became executive secretary to the city Department of Mental Health and Mental Retardation Services. She ran for state assembly as a Republican.[8]

By early 1973, Lindsay was in the final months of his second mayoral term. Lindsay barely won reelection in 1969, and he was the unpopular mayor of an ungovernable city. A white ethnic backlash against the growing black and brown population was gestating in the final years of the Ethnic Symmetry era, the period from 1932 to 1976 when Irish, Jews, and Italians dominated the city.[9] Lindsay was a wonderful man, but a catastrophic mayor, said Cooper's co-plaintiff Paul Kerrigan. Lindsay could have been Batman, the urban patrician by day, caped crusader of Gotham City at night, often facing doom from the villains who menaced the city. Although he was the champion of many of the city's black and brown people, many of them complained that Lindsay had not done enough for them. One notable Lindsay appointment was Major R. Owens to commissioner of the Community Development Agency (CDA). Owens was a former librarian, then city councilman.[10]

Lindsay did not seek a third term. There was a contentious June runoff election among Democrats. In November 1973, Abraham D. Beame, the Democratic machine party favorite whom Lindsay had edged out in a three-way race in 1965, won the election and made history as New York's first Jewish mayor. Beame defeated Republican state senator John J. Marchi and won about 60 percent of all votes. He inherited a city with growing poverty and declining population aggravated by an exodus of working- to middle-class taxpayers and jobs to the Sunbelt states.[11]

During the 1970s, Cooper's beloved Brooklyn experienced its first population decline of the century. Still, the borough was huge, with more than 2.5 million residents. But Kings County, at that time the nation's fourth most populous, was sickly.[12] It had no professional sports team, no major hotel, a declining downtown shopping district, and deteriorating residential housing in many of its north and central neighborhoods.[13] The county's population was shrinking.

Cooper was keenly aware of Brooklyn's woes. In the late 1960s and early 1970s, he was on the front lines in battles about political representation, fair housing, and appropriate redevelopment of the deteriorated commercial districts. His voting-rights co-plaintiffs were community activists in their own right by the early seventies. Joan Bacchus Maynard led the campaign to preserve and promote Weeksville, a Free African community in a corner of Bedford-Stuyvesant that was established in the early 1800s. Kerrigan and a community group developed low- to moderate-income co-op housing in central Brooklyn, near Atlantic and Flatbush avenues.

Lina Clopton, Jocelyn's Cooper's mother, died on June 29, 1973, at sixty-seven. Clopton's death coincided with granddaughter Jo-An's ninth birthday. Mrs. Cooper strained to keep the news from her child, since the baby of the family was about to leave for sleep-away summer camp.

Clopton had a difficult relationship with her daughter. Clopton's milky complexion had allowed her to pass into white society for employment. The former Lina M. Sullivan married Robert A. Clopton, a physically unambiguous Negro, and the couple produced Jocelyn Claire. The daughter spent two of her childhood years with her mother and most of the rest with her father and grandmother.

Hours before Lina Clopton's death, mother and daughter missed an opportunity to try to repair their strained relationship. After spending a few years in the Pacific Northwest to get relief for her asthma, Lina returned to New York in the 1950s and lived at 450 West 149th Street at Convent Avenue. She had little contact with her daughter.

On the day before Lina's death, Jocelyn spoke with her on the telephone. Lina was in the hospital. "I bet you thought I never loved you," said Lina to Jocelyn. Her daughter listened silently. Lina explained that she had been sickly all her life. Jocelyn did not respond, and Lina died without hearing an answer.

In September 1973, Jocelyn Cooper enrolled at Adelphi University in New York City because her husband Andy insisted. Jocelyn had withdrawn from classes at Brooklyn College in 1959. Fourteen years later, Andy persuaded her to return by saying, "Look, you're going, and I'm writing the check. You can do it." Andy's insistence boosted his wife's confidence. In addition to working at CDA and raising Jo-An, Jocelyn was going to finish college. By February 1974, she was a member of the junior class. She was scheduled for January 1975 graduation with a Bachelor of Science in Social Welfare.[14]

In the December 8, 1973, issue of the *New York Amsterdam News*, Cooper's head shot and forty-six more were packaged in a feature titled "Black Executives in White Firms 'Taking Care of Business.'" All the businesspeople were men except for Ruth Allen King, founder of the group called Edges. Established in 1969, Edges' intent was to facilitate entry and upward mobility of minorities into newly established managerial positions in the corporate world. Since 1929, King had worked at the New York Urban League and National Urban League as a secretary, administrative assistant, and assistant placement officer.[15]

In July 1974, Andy Cooper began writing a weekly column for the *Amsterdam News* that appeared on the front of the regional Brooklyn/Queens/Westchester/Long Island page.[16] A boxed two-column logo contained the heading "One Man's Opinion: Brooklyn Political Scene, by Andy Cooper."

On August 17, he told readers about a fund-raiser for Thaddeus E. Owens, a candidate for civil court. Cooper praised Owens for twenty years of law practice that included counsel to Berean Church and for helping build the Allied Federal Savings and Loan in the neighboring borough of Queens. Cooper then told readers of the fifteen-year struggle to elect the first black state legislator in 1948 and how about a quarter century later there was much more black political talent. But instead of expansion of political power, he wrote, competitors were committing fratricide, much to the delight of the county political bosses.[17]

In politics, Cooper wrote the following week, there's no such thing as a sure thing. The experienced Richard Nixon, an eight-year apprentice for the presidency, had seemed like a sure winner over the young and Catholic John F. Kennedy in 1960, but unpredictable events and fickle winds resulted in JFK's razor-thin upset win.

A similar fate had visited William (Bill) Thompson, the first black state senator from Brooklyn (1964) and presumed successor to the redrawn Twelfth Congressional District that was the result of Cooper's voting rights lawsuit. White district leaders in Kings County pledged their support to Thompson. Thompson's challenger, assemblywoman Shirley Chisholm, had promised her husband Conrad that if she lost, she was getting out of politics.

But in June, Robert F. Kennedy, the U.S. senator from New York who was running a spirited campaign for president, was murdered in California after he won the state primary. RFK, the sponsor of Bedford-Stuyvesant Restoration, was to return from the West Coast and put his arm around Thompson, ensuring the state legislator's ascent to Congress. However, Thompson's white political support evaporated, and the Chisholm era rose like a phoenix.[18]

In fall 1974, Cooper joined his wife and returned to college after he had taken time off from school since the early 1960s. He enrolled at Adelphi University in New York City.[19] Cooper joined the Adelphi-NYC Training

Institute that recruited accomplished and gifted people who already made contributions in human services but had not earned degrees. Some of these men and women were city commissioners and deputy commissioners or community organizers and people who ran community development agencies. The twenty-five-member student body was largely black and Hispanic yet was highly integrated with whites.[20]

At forty-four, Andy Cooper became a student during a heightened period of community organizing. The world beyond his neighborhood was rediscovering poverty. The Adelphi-NYC satellite campus at Spring and Lafayette streets offered a seminar program for credit, several times a week for several hours. The social policy classes counted toward a bachelor of arts or master of arts in social work. Philip Coltoff taught Cooper. The student was an outstanding performer, according to Coltoff, gifted and bright and respected by the other students and the professor. Cooper had a slight stutter as an adult, but he hid it well.[21]

What Cooper emphasized in class was a clear political and ideological point of view. He had opinions he was prepared to defend, and he made that clear in two semesters of classes with Coltoff. Cooper earned the respect of his professor and adult peers because he listened to other people's points of view. He respected scholarship.

Cooper was ideological without being an ideologue. He was fully prepared to defend and explicate his own positions, which tended to be left of the political center. He identified with exploited and oppressed people. He definitely was proud of being an African American and was hopeful and optimistic about changes that needed to occur in America, but he was skeptical of leadership. He also understood the nature of power to secure change.[22]

In class, Cooper honed the mind-set of an exceptional journalist. He accepted the responsibility of struggling for objectivity. Cooper had strong opinions, but he did not have a closed mind. He liked competing and contrary points of view, and he strove to be fair.

On December 14, 1974, Cooper's *New York Amsterdam News* column was about the Atlantic Terminal Group in Brooklyn and its alleged "Wall of Silence" regarding development at Atlantic and Flatbush avenues. Cooper's article attracted personal correspondence dated January 6, 1975, from Ernesta G. Procope, president of E. G. Bowman Co. insurance, located on Fulton Street. Indeed, Procope wrote, the wall of silence "is so high that we cannot begin to climb it. Can you assist us in this area?"

In a follow-up letter on January 21, Procope asked Cooper to put her in touch with leaders of First Atlantic Terminal Housing Corp. On January 24,

Procope wrote Paul Kerrigan, Cooper's voting rights suit co-plaintiff, who was now chairman of the Fort Greene Non-Profit Improvement Corporation.

Kerrigan successfully got hundreds of units of low- to moderate-income housing built in the Atlantic Terminal corridor. "Since your project is almost completed," wrote Procope, "it is timely to discuss the permanent insurance. We look forward to seeing you prior to the board of directors meeting."[23]

Richard Nixon did not finish his second term as president. He resigned in disgrace in August 1974 because of the Watergate scandal. The incident began as what Nixon insiders dismissively called a "third-rate burglary" of Democratic National Committee headquarters at the swank Watergate apartment and office complex, but was later revealed as political dirty tricks and obstruction of a Justice Department investigation that was traced back to the president and his men.

Vice president Gerald Ford succeeded Nixon. By fall 1975, the interim president heard cries of help from New York City leaders. The city was teetering on bankruptcy because of underfunded union contracts and the losses of several hundred thousand jobs that severely eroded the tax base. On October 17, $453 million in short-term debt was due. At the eleventh hour, the teachers union invested $150 million from its pension fund and purchased Municipal Assistance Corporation (MAC) bonds to stave off bankruptcy.[24]

Still, the city remained in economic trouble. Ford did not commit to bailing out New York and vowed to veto bills that sought relief. A front-page *Daily News* headline in late October that summarized the president's position: "Ford to City: Drop Dead." Ford softened his position in early 1976. During an overseas meeting with the prime ministers of France and Germany, those heads of state warned Ford that a bankrupt New York would trigger a global economic crisis. Ford approved billions of dollars of loans, and city officials had to live with suffocating federal oversight.[25]

In 1976, New Yorkers felt a different kind of journalistic jolt: Australian media mogul Rupert Murdoch purchased the *New York Post*, founded in 1801 by Alexander Hamilton. By the late 1970s, the *Post* was a liberal-leaning daily tabloid owned by Dorothy Schiff. Once he got the keys, Murdoch shifted the newspaper's tone to the conservative right and attracted new readers with racy headlines. Advertising, however, did not follow as enthusiastically. Murdoch became a formidable opponent of the *Daily News*, the working-class tabloid owned by Tribune Company of Chicago. The broadsheet *New York Times* remained above the fray.

In his column of January 17, the week of Martin Luther King Jr.'s birthday, in about 600 words Cooper admired the power of the press during the Watergate saga and also scolded network TV news shows for not including black journalists as interviewers and analysts.

"The nation's major networks," wrote Cooper in his closing paragraph, "are maintaining an authoritarian, repressive and exploitative policy toward the black community by denying information to the black public. The Black press by not insisting its reporters be included in the questioning of those who wield authority and power does a disservice to the community whose only voice is through its pages."[26]

In that edition, Cooper also wrote a bylined news analysis, "A Waldaba Stewart Election Could Upset Political Balance." Six head shots of the political players complemented the four-column story. Cooper had lost to Stewart for state senate in 1968. Nearly two years later, in 1970, Cooper led a citizen revolt against Stewart's proposal to create an Atlantic Avenue Improvement Authority, a nonelected authority pining to convert the avenue into an east–west superhighway. Cooper challenged Stewart again for state senate and lost again. Stewart lost his seat to Vander L. Beatty after one term.

Now Cooper was reporting on a power struggle among black political leaders. Stewart, wrote Cooper, made a play for the eighteenth state senatorial seat vacated by Chester Straub. Cooper walked readers through the complicated process of Kings County committee members who controlled votes to recommend candidates.

In the sprawling and racially mixed Eighteenth, Thomas Bartosiewicz of the white enclave Greenpoint was favored as the anointed candidate because he was from the political club of Frank Creta. That district leader controlled eighty-four member votes. Meanwhile Lucy Vega, a district co-leader, said she was backing Stewart and controlled thirty-nine votes. Her co-leader Victor Robles controlled sixty-two votes. Carl L. Butler and Thomas Fortune, district leaders too, said they were committing their committee votes to Stewart.

The bottom line, wrote Cooper, was that "if Stewart succeeds in his bid, he will become the third black member from Brooklyn in the senate chamber and might put Congresswoman Chisholm's delicately balanced political empire in danger."

Stewart was a Chisholm loyalist, but with pledges from four committee leaders, it was possible that he would also seek support from Chisholm foe Beatty (the same challenger who had vanquished him in 1972) to gain the seat. David Dinkins, chairman of the Council of Elected Officials of New York State, told Cooper, "We are concerned about representation statewide. The Council calls for the designation of a black candidate to fill the district vacancy." That wish did not come true. Bartosiewicz, who resided in Chisholm's Twelfth Congressional district, was appointed to the vacant state legislative seat.[27]

Cooper's next column, on January 24, closed with the sentence "That's one man's opinion," which become his familiar sign-off. His January 24 and 31 pieces were cryptic: he did not name names, yet he scolded politicians who worried more about their next elections than the constituents they were supposed to represent. Cooper challenged journalists to ask tough questions and bring details to light that could help citizens make informed decisions, even if the decisions were to throw the bums out of office.

On February 7, Cooper wrote a news story in addition to his commentary. He reported that former state assemblyman Calvin Williams had been acquitted of bribery charges. Williams was owner of Black Pearl Cab Service, one of the most successful black-owned businesses on the East Coast, according to Cooper. An estimated 150 cabs earned $90,000 a month. Williams was indicted in 1973 for allegedly offering money and a job to a cab driver if the driver dropped the charges filed against Williams's son. A year later, the two-term assemblyman lost his seat to Al Vann, and Williams also lost his district leadership post to Carl Butler. When Cooper asked, Williams declined to comment about his political future after the state supreme court threw out "compounding a crime" charges.

By February 14, Cooper named names in his column. Tito Velez, a former prize fighter and political activist, was variously called "a scoundrel, traitor, sellout artist and sincere advocate of representation for his people" in committing the deciding votes that got Bartosiewicz chosen over Stewart for the Eighteenth District state senate seat. Cooper also wrote that Sam Wright, a city councilman, maneuvered to challenge Chisholm for Congress, and a handful of Brooklyn politicians were about to accuse one another of a variety of double crosses.[28]

The next week, Cooper turned up the heat a little more and quoted an unnamed political insider who said that Arthur Eve, an upstate assemblyman from Buffalo and chairman of the state Black and Puerto Rican Caucus, "was always treated as a stepchild in the Assembly by the New York City black pols. He was never taken seriously by Percy, Basil or Charlie."

The three were Percy Sutton, Basil Paterson, and Charles Rangel, who with Dinkins were the biggest players in the Harlem political machine. Curiously, no "One Man's Opinion" column appeared the following week, February 28. The column resumed March 6.[29]

In 1976, Utrice Leid was hired as a receptionist at the *Amsterdam News.* She was an immigrant of Trinidad and Tobago. Leid had come to the United States in 1969 at about age fifteen. She returned to her native land in 1973 because her father Claude died of a heart attack.

Leid went home to be with her grieving mother in Trinidad. That year, the island was shakily recovering from a failed coup attempt, and at about that time, Leid's interest in journalism began. During her yearlong stay, Leid researched how people had reacted to the coup attempt, and believed the information would make a good book. One day, however, machine-gun-toting men appeared at Leid's home and confiscated her seven hundred pages of notes. The gunmen informed the teenager that her project was subversive. Leid returned to New York and took a job as a receptionist at the *Amsterdam News.*[30]

Leid was overqualified for her job. Back home, she represented her school in debating contests. On Saturday nights, she and her siblings stood before their father and answered his questions about grammar, literature, and history.[31] Leid worked in the family businesses and was constantly pressed by her father about what her purpose in life would be.

The great debater Leid quickly found a soul mate in Andy Cooper, the new *Amsterdam News* columnist. Leid witnessed the handful of times Cooper's column was "spiked," or rejected for publication because his political prose rankled powerful friends of the newspaper owners.

Cooper's March 6 column explained the political and voting power—or lack of power—in Chisholm's Twelfth Congressional District. "The 12th," Cooper wrote, "is an example of a delicately balanced political body whose outer shell is black, but whose controlling nerve center is white."

He explained that under normal conditions, the member of Congress would relate to the district leaders and give them access to federal appointments plus $250,000 in funds for staff and district offices. There were seven state legislative districts inside the Twelfth, held mostly by black representatives. Yet the lone predominantly white district in Greenpoint had stronger voter turnout than the combined strength—or anemia—of four black districts. "The fact remains," Cooper concluded, "that the body is black, but the controlling nerve center is white. Politicians respond to the nerve center."[32] No column was published the next week, March 13.

When Cooper returned on March 20, he continued the political power theme. Black politicians, he wrote, suffered from schizophrenia. They articulated black concerns and railed against white abuses of the political system, but they were forbidden by bosses to engage in voter registration, citizen activity that could curb the abuses. Cooper referenced congressman

Herman Badillo, a Puerto Rican, who ran against Mayor Beame in the 1973 Democratic Primary. Badillo lost, but he energized Puerto Rican voter turnout, and the numbers rattled the political bosses. Fearing formidable political opposition, wrote Cooper, party regulars reached out to Hispanics and made numerous appointments.

"When in recent memory has there been a black political revolt?" asked Cooper in his closing paragraph. "When has there ever been a black political leader who advised bolting the Democratic Party or backed a Third Party movement, or got solidly behind a black candidate that had the courage to buck the regulars—citywide?"[33]

In the March 27 column, Andy wondered what might happen if a major movement were started to register a large segment of blacks in the Republican Party. What might happen if that decision were carried out in Brooklyn? Would the Kings County Democratic machine remain complacent about black Brooklyn?

In a presidential election year, could candidates continue to ignore black concerns if it became clear that there was a major voting bloc that could swing to the candidate or party that offered more than lip service? "Is Republican political philosophy," asked Cooper in his closing paragraph, "so far removed from the philosophy of some blacks: Self-sufficiency, independence, self-help, the accumulation of capital, and establishing businesses? Fascinating, isn't it."[34]

In March, Cooper attended the National League of Cities conference in Washington, where he grilled elected officials about their personal choices for U.S. president and vice president. Many people favored a Hubert Humphrey–Jimmy Carter Democratic ticket for November. Humphrey, who had lost the 1968 election to Nixon, enjoyed an impeccable civil rights reputation among black voters. Carter, the governor of Georgia, was a newcomer to national politics but had made a strong showing in the primaries. Could Carter be good for blacks?

Carter told the *New York Times* that if he was elected president, his prime commitment would be the preservation of the nation of Israel. In his April 10 column, Cooper asked where Carter's clear-cut statement concerning the survival of blacks was. Where is the clear statement regarding unemployment and job programs for black youth? What about economic development in the black community? Cooper persisted. Where was the plan, the outline, the statement? It was nowhere to be found.

Carter the southern Democrat wowed a number of black Baptist preachers, but Cooper counseled that support was not enough: "Someone should begin the process of asking Mr. Carter hard questions about blacks and his commitment to black survival. Charisma is a great quality to be gifted with, but it is no substitute for a plan for black survival. Those who are confused by charm and in turn advocate electing a vice president because he possesses it are not doing us any favors."[35]

In his May 1 column, Cooper alerted readers about a closed-door May 5 meeting in Washington of NAACP and National Urban League leaders, plus black politicians from both parties. There was alarm that black voters were apathetic, and their indifference could negate economic progress of recent years and make future growth difficult. Cooper reported that fourteen million blacks were eligible to vote, but only about half of them were registered. Less than one-third of registered black voters bothered to cast ballots in the presidential primaries.

Closer to home, voter turnout was poor in the April New York primary. Voters were split among U.S. senator Henry Jackson of Washington, U.S. senator Morris Udall of Arizona, governor Jimmy Carter of Georgia, and U.S. senator Hubert Humphrey, who was not on the New York ballot.

Charles V. Hamilton told the *New York Times* there was general voter malaise, but the problem was acute among blacks, who had been so worn down by a series of ethnic and national crises that "they would neither vote nor revolt."

Cooper refused to accept any excuses. He wrote that black politicians were responsible for inspiring their constituents: "Is it too much to ask of a political leader that he or she be indefatigable in the cause of America's oppressed black minority? If the constituency has confidence in its leadership, it will display that confidence. Black political leaders do not inspire confidence to any great degree." Cooper alluded to a Queens school case that he would explain next time as an example of political apathy and malaise.[36]

Howard Hurwitz, principal of Long Island City High School, had expelled a seventeen-year-old black girl who was scheduled to graduate. Hurwitz built a reputation as a no-nonsense disciplinarian with an authoritarian administrative style. He did not tell the girl why she was suspended or offer any reasonable explanation for his actions.

What Hurwitz did do was ask the district school superintendent to suspend the student. However, the administrator refused after examining the girl's record. Instead Hurwitz was suspended by the board of education for his high-handed tactics.

Elected officials and parents from the white, working-class, largely Catholic community rushed to Hurwitz's defense. Parents and other supporters barricaded the principal in his office to prevent his removal.[37]

Where was the support for the black girl and her parents? Cooper scolded in his May 8 column. QUALICAP, an antipoverty agency, investigated the case, and lawyer Jane Stern represented the girl. Black elected officials were missing in action. City councilman Peter Vallone was visible, representing his Queens district as broker among Hurwitz, activist parents, and the board of education. The black family of the suspended girl had no political support, even as student rights advocates such as Elaine Keith and Stern, both white, fought for the girl.[38]

Cooper reminded readers of the anxiety among black elected officials and civil rights leaders about voter apathy and alienation. The Long Island City High School conflict was a symptom of the malaise: "Black political alienation can be traced directly to a lack of personal involvement by black elected officials in the lives of their constituency."[39]

In his column the following week, May 22, Cooper referenced Hurwitz and the Long Island City conflict. After weeks of bashing inattentive black elected officials, Cooper singled out one for praise, assemblyman Al Vann of the Fifty-sixth District serving Bedford-Stuyvesant for his legislative report about a summer lunch program. Vann made an attempt to keep his constituents in the loop.[40]

Soon Al Vann was in political trouble. In April he ran against Carl Butler, his district leader, and lost. The close defeat left Vann vulnerable in the primal arena of Brooklyn politics. Butler's camp looked for candidates to knock Vann from his assembly seat in case he tried to come after Butler again in 1978. A few of Vann's closest aides deserted him after the losing fight with Butler. Vann was superior to the wannabe Albany legislators eager to represent black Brooklyn. The last effective legislator was Thomas Russell Jones, but he gave up the post to accept a state supreme court judgeship. Jones's successor, Chisholm, without being named, was deemed loud but mostly ineffective in Albany. Her recognizable achievement was securing SEEK grants for low-income students.[41]

Vann's district was inside Chisholm's Twelfth Congressional District. If Butler followed through on taking out Vann, the possibility loomed of a three-way assembly race that could result in a Hassidic Jew from nearby Crown Heights or Williamsburg running and winning the largely Bedford-Stuyvesant district. That was a potentially embarrassing loss of political real estate for Butler and Vann. Could both men work out their differences for their constituents?[42]

In June, Maude B. Richardson died. She was a lifelong Republican and member of the local Urban League and NAACP. She ran for the assembly in

1946 when Brooklyn had no black representation, and lost a close three-way race. Winner John Walsh won by seventy-seven votes. Richardson led protests at Fulton Street and Nostrand Avenue when establishments like Woolworth and White Tower would not hire blacks.[43]

About the same time, Vander L. Beatty, a state senator, lost his second job of district leader to Max Clemmons in an April primary. Beatty accused Clemmons of voter fraud in the Fifty-third Assembly District. Eugene Gold, Kings County (Brooklyn) district attorney, investigated the charges and issued a terse "no comment" when Cooper probed for answers.[44]

Legislators Beatty and Vann had clashed, and their differences of opinion threatened to unravel the state Black and Puerto Rican Legislative Caucus. Furthermore, Beatty was an adversary of Chisholm, whose congressional district included Vann and the state senator's turf. Beatty backed Sam Wright, Chisholm's challenger for the Twelfth Congressional District.[45]

No Cooper column appeared in the *Amsterdam News* on June 12, the week after his analysis of political warfare in Brooklyn. The column returned on June 19, and Cooper wrote about the imminent defunding of child care centers (Colony House). The next week, June 26, Cooper's column did not run.

Cooper's July 3 column began thus:

> The September primary is crucial to Black Brooklyn. At least one congressional, one state Senate, and two assembly seats, now held by black elected officials, can be lost to either Hispanics or the white minority. Shirley Chisholm's 12th Congressional District, anchored Greenpoint with a large population of white ethnics, state Senator Vander Beatty's 23rd Senatorial District with a population of Hispanics and Hassidic Jews, can fall.
>
> In addition, Assemblyman Thomas R. Fortune's 55th, and Assemblyman Al Vann's 56th can also be taken over. Fortune has had opposition from the Puerto Rican community for several years and has just squeaked by because of poor black registration in the 55th. Vann, with determined opposition from Carl Butler and Evelyn Dixon combined with a possible third entry from Williamsburg, can be defeated by the vote that comes out of that politically sophisticated area easily.
>
> If Jewish leaders decide to support one of their own, the 56th will crumble. Sentiment within the white community suggests that no seat held by a non-white is sacred. Since Hispanics consider themselves white, a combination of Jewish-Hispanic forces could wipe out political gains made by Black Brooklyn in the last 15 years.[46]

Cooper's piece was published just days before the bicentennial celebration of the Declaration of Independence. On July 15 at the Democratic National Convention in New York, Jimmy Carter was nominated as the party's candidate for the November election. The first nominee from a Deep South state since 1848 received significant support from black leaders and labor unions.[47] Cooper was one of a seven-member *Amsterdam News* political team credentialed to cover the convention. His July 17 column was about Jimmy Carter and his black Atlanta connection. The following week, Cooper praised black politicians' sophistication at the DNC.

A week later, Cooper profiled Barbara Jordan, an opening-night speaker who woke up sleeping delegates with a rousing speech. How did the first black woman elected to Congress from the South manage such success? She was a curiosity, a thirty-year old and an HBCU graduate (with a Boston University law degree) who was part of the Texas political establishment, which meant millionaires and their oil money, recently diversified in computers, insurance, and petrochemicals. Cooper referenced Mal Goode of ABC News, who observed, "She's smart, knows the issues, is a political horse trader of the first order, and represents a black district [the Eighteenth] that is the most politically sophisticated of any in the United States." Cooper noted that before election to Congress, Jordan was president pro tempore of the Texas senate, which meant she served as acting governor when the governor and lieutenant governor were out of the Lone Star State. Cooper was impressed with the power of the possible for black elected officials and shared those insights with readers.[48]

Cooper's early July column that pointed out the vulnerability of Chisholm's congressional seat was mostly on target. In the September Democratic Primary, she beat back a serious challenge from Sam Wright, who characterized her as a politician who neglected her district to pursue national fame. Chisholm fired back that Wright was "a modern-day black Tammany politician."

With no serious GOP challenge, Chisholm cruised to reelection for a fifth term. Cooper's warning that the Twelfth could fall to a Hassidic or Puerto Rican candidate did not materialize, but he did predict correctly that the infighting by black leaders inside the district eroded the power black voters had fought to achieve in Brooklyn.[49]

For ten weeks, from September 25 to November 27, the *Amsterdam News* published no Cooper columns. He submitted and was paid for his work, but the management decided not to publish the copy.[50]

By fall 1976, Cooper, joined by Utrice Leid, quit the *Amsterdam News* out of frustration. Leid worked at the newspaper for six months in 1976.[51] Cooper and Leid began working to create a news service that would sell news stories to media clients, daily or weekly, including the *Amsterdam News*. Cooper borrowed liberally from Community News Service (CNS), established to train minorities for work in mainstream media newsrooms.

Cooper's column returned to the *Amsterdam News* on February 26, 1977. Its look was the same: "One Man's Opinion: The Brooklyn Political Scene." But this time around, Cooper sold his column to the newspaper as a contractor, not as an employee.

In the November presidential election, Carter was elected the thirty-ninth president after a close race with Ford. Out of eighty million votes cast, Carter won by two million votes, and the Electoral College tally was 297–241. The results in Congress were lopsided. Democrats held a filibuster-proof 61–38 advantage, and the House grew to a 2–1 Democrat versus Republican advantage. The Nixon-Watergate legacy still battered the Republicans.

Cooper and Leid watched the local and national political activity with great interest. They strategized on the launch of a black-owned media vehicle that would be driven from Brooklyn.

In June 1976, Andy Cooper earned his bachelor's degree from Adelphi University. The educational journey that had begun in 1949 at Baruch College and resumed after time off at Brooklyn College and repeated interruptions because of work, family, and civic obligations was completed. Ten months later, on April 1, 1977, Jocelyn's father, Robert A. Clopton, died at seventy-one.

8. TRANS URBAN NEWS SERVICE

In spring 1977, I applied to daily newspapers along the Atlantic Coast. I cast a wide net, fishing for work at papers big and small, from Boston to Atlanta, yet my net did not appear big enough to catch a job. I had just graduated from Long Island University in Brooklyn, so my résumé probably showed my inexperience. Second, at twenty-one, I did not have a driver's license, an essential tool outside New York City, as necessary as writing a snappy lead or coherent news story.

In early July, I got a call from a college friend, Morris McKoy. He had graduated from LIU the year before I did. McKoy suggested that I come downtown and meet Andrew W. Cooper. He had just opened a news service called Trans Urban News in a small office on the sixth floor of 186 Joralemon Street, off Court Street. I acted on McKoy's tip. I opened the door and entered a small room. Behind it was Cooper's office, which had a desk, telephone, and typewriter. That day I may have met Cooper's associate Utrice Leid.

Cooper did not have a paying job to offer. I was not desperate yet for work. Though eager to strike out on my own in journalism, I could continue to live on Bradford Street in East New York with my mother and my eighteen- and eleven-year-old siblings. I had an eight-week summer job as a day camp counselor. I agreed to write voluntarily for the start-up operation beginning in August, when the day camp job ended. I probably heard a conditional promise from Cooper of volunteer effort turning into paid work after a few months.

Trans Urban News opened its office during the "Summer of Sam."[1] New York City and its boroughs were in a state of chaos. Steve Berkowitz, a.k.a. the ".44 caliber killer" and the "Son of Sam," was fatally shooting late-night lovers at close range in ethnic neighborhoods.[2]

On one of the hottest nights that July, the power grid melted down because of the 102-degree heat and all the air conditioners in use. New York City plunged into darkness.[3] Spontaneously, looters took to the streets and attacked shops with the ferocity of the Watts, Newark, and Detroit riots of the 1960s. Unlike those rebellions, the triggers were not heavy-handed police tactics that made many put-upon blacks say "Hell no, we're not taking this anymore." This time the black rage appeared to be poor, working-class black and brown resentment toward new middle-class black merchants. Stores in the ghettos were trashed, unlike the 1960s when a brother might counsel another not to hurl a brick through the window of a black-owned business.

Upscale midtown Manhattan and downtown Brooklyn stores owned by white elites were well guarded and untouched; Harlem and central Brooklyn and the South Bronx were trashed. Police made 3,776 arrests, 1,037 fires were reported, and firefighters answered 1,700 false alarms.[4] The devastation was so bewildering that John Procope, publisher of the *Amsterdam News*, broke an unspoken rule and criticized black leaders publicly for allegedly creating the vacuum that allowed hoodlums to fill and do harm.[5]

Nineteen seventy-seven was also the summer of campaigns to elect a new mayor. New Yorkers were looking for a leader to guide them out of the chaos. In addition to the blackout and the Son of Sam mayhem, New York was reeling from the fiscal crisis of the year before. The city was about $1 billion in debt and, like Cleveland, was facing bankruptcy.[6] The federal government vowed it would not bail the city out. "Ford to New York: Drop Dead," screamed the front page of the *New York Daily News* in October 1975.[7] With jobs escaping from the city—New York lost 600,000 jobs in the 1960s—the lack of federal support sapped the city's strength and stoked the perception that the city was crime ridden, fiscally out of control, and morally hopeless.[8] Critics outside the city suggested that the five boroughs could crumble off the mainland United States and float out into the Atlantic Ocean and not be missed.

New York City lost respect, and respect had to be restored, and restoration had to start in the mayor's office. So who would lead? Abe Beame, the Democrat who succeeded two-term liberal Republican John Lindsay in 1973, was done. Beame presided over the fiscal mess. The city's first Jewish mayor was short in stature and uncharismatic.[9] A crowd of candidates stepped forward. There was Mario Cuomo of Queens, a borough activist who had the support of governor Hugh Carey. Cuomo was Italian American. There were several Jewish American candidates: Bella Abzug, the brash-talking feminist with the big hats, Edward I. Koch, a congressman who represented the liberal Upper East Side "Silk Stocking" district yet campaigned as a law-and-order fiscal conservative. He needled incumbent Beame for "running the city like a second-class candy store."[10]

Previously, Koch and Cuomo had battled in 1973 over proposed low-income housing in middle-class, white Forest Hills, Queens. Koch served as spokesman for the mostly Jewish residents who fought the housing and argued that the units would lower property values and create slum conditions. Cuomo, who mediated the dispute, said that the scatter-site housing would integrate needy and poor—essentially black and brown—residents into the community. A compromise was reached. Half the original housing project became low-income units, and the remaining half became luxury condominiums. Koch used the Forest Hills battle as his first run for mayor. He lost, but he would return in four years.[11]

Percy Sutton, perhaps the first black to make a serious run for mayor, entered the 1977 mayoral race. On paper he made a formidable candidate: Manhattan borough president and a successful businessman; Sutton owned urban radio stations WBLS-FM/WLIB-AM. The other candidate of color was Herman Badillo, a Puerto Rican and, like Koch, a congressman. He represented the Bronx.

Black political pundits assumed that three Jewish mayoral candidates would split white votes and clear a path for New York's first black mayor.[12] Those political pros miscalculated. Koch disassociated himself from liberal politics and rode the waves of neoconservatism that were gaining momentum nationally. Abzug was colorful, but not colorful enough to gain wider support. Beame was simply tired, synonymous with the public employee unions that nearly bankrupted the city. A harsh and sweeping statement, yes, but that would be the excuse used by the CEOs and other business leaders who moved their companies to other parts of the United States because New York had become too expensive.[13]

As for the candidates of color, Badillo believed he was a role model for future Hispanic candidates and took pride in his independent views, but he did not get much support—11 percent of votes—and was viewed by political pros as not ethnic enough.[14]

Percy Sutton's timing was bad. The black mayoral candidate was walking into a fiscal disaster. Sutton was not associated with the mess, but he was not going to convince working- and middle-class whites in the city that he was the savior.

Furthermore, all the racial calculations could not be placed solely on whites. Blacks who liked Sutton as their borough president were not enthusiastic about his run for mayor. Sutton was not well known in Brooklyn and Queens, where most of the city's black population now lived. He received 14 percent of votes in that crowded field, not enough to qualify for the runoff.

Neither Sutton nor Badillo received 90 percent of black or Hispanic votes in heavily minority precincts, the usual formula candidates of color must have to win.[15] Koch, however, led the crowded field with 20 percent of New Yorkers' votes and was slightly ahead of Cuomo, who had 19 percent.[16] Neither candidate had enough votes to win the Democratic nomination, so Koch and Cuomo squared off in a runoff election. Koch beat Cuomo handily, 55 to 45 percent in a head-to-head rematch on September 20.[17]

New York City at that time was a Democratic Party stronghold, so the nominee was supposed to be a shoo-in. That was not the case in the 1977 November election. Koch continued to battle Cuomo, who after the primary defeat continued to run on the Liberal Party ticket. Republican candidate Roy Goodman offered a token challenge, and Conservative candidate Barry Farber, a talk show host, made the four-way race a little more interesting. Nevertheless Koch prevailed.[18] Sutton, the former Manhattan borough president, and many other black voters supported Koch in the November general election.[19]

The mayor-elect would soon occupy Gracie Mansion. Koch, however, kept his rent-controlled apartment in lower Manhattan. Koch was unmarried, and there were whispers that he was gay. During the campaign, a campaign slogan was "Vote for Cuomo, not the Homo."[20] Koch was friendly and sympathetic to gay voters, probably recognizing that they were a potent economic force.

Andy Cooper turned fifty in August 1977. After many years of off-and-on study, he received his bachelor's degree from Adelphi University of Garden City, New York. His wife Jocelyn earned her B.A. degree in social work at the same Long Island school the previous year. She would earn her master's in 1978. Because of her husband's persistent, even nagging, support, Jocelyn said fondly years later that her husband gave her three M's: marriage, motherhood, and a master's degree.[21]

The Coopers had been in their Park Slope home on Third Street for five years, since 1972, after twenty years in the Decatur Street house that they sold to the parents of future comedian and actor Chris Rock.[22] Cooper was six years removed from Schaefer, where he worked for twenty years until the brewery downsized then moved to eastern Pennsylvania. After Schaefer, Cooper made his living in public relations consulting. The journalism bug bit him when he got the opportunity in January 1976 to write a political column for the *Amsterdam News*, but that experience lasted six months.

Oldest daughter Andrea Cooper Andrews was twenty-five during the harrowing 1977 Summer of Sam and was estranged from her dad. He still felt betrayed for sponsoring a very public wedding when in fact his oldest daughter wanted to marry because she was pregnant.[23] Andrea in 1977 was a young wife—probably separated from Robert Andrews—with her son Damani, who turned five just before the September mayoral primary. Youngest daughter Jocelyn Cooper was thirteen and in middle school, IS 88, which she requested after attending St. Ann's parochial. In September 1978 she would enter Dewey High School, the independent study school.

Cooper was perceived as pugnacious and overly critical of politicians, yet he was admired because of his involvement in civic organizations like 100 Black Men Inc. and the National Urban Affairs Council and his service as a trustee with Brooklyn Hospital Center, Caledonia campus; his membership in the Addiction Research and Treatment Corporation, run by his former Sunday school teacher Dr. Beny Primm; and his advisory role with the American Management Association.[24]

He was nosy and newsy. In the Trans Urban News office, Leid, McKoy, and myself all cackled when Cooper left for daily lunch breaks, claiming, "I'll be right back." When he returned two hours later, his staff was convinced that he had stopped on Court Street to hold court and gather intelligence from numerous lawyers, judges, elected officials, and civil servants. Or had he been holed up in a booth at Gage and Tollner restaurant at the end of downtown Fulton Street, interrogating a source, out of sight of others?[25] During his downtown Brooklyn trips, Cooper applied the networking lessons he had learned as a teenage servant and messenger at the Brooklyn Navy Yard officer's club during World War II.

In the fall of 1977, I traveled with Andy Cooper to a screening of Williams Miles's PBS documentary *Men of Bronze*, the story of the all-black 369th Infantry Regiment that fought in World War I. The American soldiers were shunned by their government, yet the French government celebrated them for helping to liberate their country. Cooper and I posed with one of the "men of bronze" who attended. Though in his seventies, the wavy-haired veteran looked fiftyish and athletic. [26]

That fall, Cooper and Utrice Leid submitted a grant application to fund TNS and hire staff. TNS was to operate like Community News Service, a training ground that from 1969 to 1975 reported black news and prepared minority journalists to enter the mainstream press.[27]

Cooper and Leid were committed to journalism, but for the purposes of getting the grant, their eventual staff would be identified not as reporters but as "researchers."[28] Through the end of 1977, McKoy and I came in daily to the Joralemon Street office and worked as volunteers, writing occasional stories. Most of the time, the LIU grads watched Cooper and Leid go about their work. I learned lessons about local politics and journalism in ways not taught in my political science or journalism classes. Once I tagged along with Cooper to an evening political meeting and was introduced to a New York state assemblyman who took pride in actually reading the dense legislative bills that landed on his desk in Albany.[29]

Weekly, Cooper and Leid sent hard-copy packages of stories reported by the TNS quartet to clients the *New York Times*, *New York Daily News*, CBS News Radio 88, and the *Amsterdam News*. The *Amsterdam News* was the client most likely to publish TNS work. *Times* editors used the TNS packages as tip sheets to put reporters on the stories. The *Daily News* sometimes ran TNS stories word for word with their staff writer's bylines above the copy. A grizzled New York newsman once explained that pride—foolish pride, perhaps—would not allow the *Daily News* to publish copy attributed to a training program.

During the Christmas shopping season, police officer Robert Torsney was acquitted of fatally shooting Randolph Evans, an unarmed fifteen-year-old black boy, who had asked the cop a question. Torsney's defense was "temporary insanity." Black residents were outraged. A group led by the Rev. Herbert Daughtry began boycotting downtown department stores on Fulton Street in protest. Merchants said they were not responsible for the boy's death or the reaction of the justice system. Daughtry and other activists said inconveniencing shoppers was their way to get the attention of unresponsive political leaders.[30]

Daughtry, forty-eight, had been a pastor for two decades, but his teenage years were similar to those of some black youths who had dangerous run-ins with police. As an adolescent in Brooklyn and Jersey City in the late 1940s and 1950s, young Herbert was a dope addict, numbers runner, and was convicted of armed robbery and forgery. In prison, he began to read voraciously, whether the books available were the Bible or works by J. A. Rodgers, W. E. B. Du Bois, and E. Franklin Frazier. In 1959, Daughtry became an ordained minister and led a storefront church with nine members.

He grew the congregation, then moved from Fulton Street in Ocean Hill-Brownsville to a bigger church on Dean Street in Bedford-Stuyvesant, then again in 1970 to the sanctuary on Atlantic Avenue near downtown Brooklyn. In 1977, from the Christmas season protest downtown led by Daughtry and others, the Black United Front of Brooklyn took form.

In January 1978, Morris McKoy and I ended our volunteer service and became payroll workers with Trans Urban News Service. According to the terms of the eighteen-month Comprehensive Employment and Training Act (CETA) grant, we were both "researchers," but in reality, we went about our daily work like reporters. We were each paid $327 every two weeks. We were joined by about five other CETA researchers, two women and three men. At times the seven researchers, Utrice Leid, and Andy Cooper were packed in the two-room office on Joralemon Street. To fulfill the requirements of the job-training grant, the researchers were dispatched to survey residents about social conditions in Central Brooklyn.

Cooper gave me a key so that I could open the office at 9 a.m. after my daily twenty-minute subway ride from my apartment in Crown Heights. I answered the phones and monitored the newspapers. Leid and McKoy usually arrived about a half hour later after at least hourlong subway rides from their homes in the Bronx. Cooper would drive or take the subway from his house in Brooklyn's Park Slope. One day in early February, the staff all arrived late because of a blizzard that dropped nearly twenty inches of snow and virtually shut down metropolitan New York for several days.[31]

During the winter of 1978, Trans Urban News Service tried to establish news coverage routines. McKoy and I were sent to the Brooklyn and Manhattan state and federal courts to cover hearings and trials recommended by Leid and Cooper or to find stories on the dockets. There were periodic staff meetings at Colony South Brooklyn Houses, apparently for the government funder to monitor the performance of the employment training program.

Twice in the spring, on April 19 and May 25, Cooper, Leid, McKoy, and I met with editors at United Press International and received advice on journalistic writing.[32] Cooper collaborated with other news organizations, as well. He brought in former *Time* magazine reporter Sam Washington to work on investigative pieces. Washington often asked me to go for black coffee with two sugars. Washington committed suicide that winter of 1978; he died of carbon monoxide poisoning in the garage of his home.

Washington's funeral service was at Rev. Daughtry's House of the Lord Church. Another minister officiated. McKoy tapped me on the shoulder when Les Payne of *Newsday* slipped into the sanctuary. He was a revered black journalist among other black journalists because of his daring dispatches from apartheid South Africa.[33] Cooper also drew on the services of another senior writer, a white man named David Wise.[34]

That season, TNS staff members were introduced to Wayne Barrett, a political writer with the *Village Voice*, New York's alternative weekly newspaper. Founded by a group of writers including Norman Mailer after World War II, the *Voice* became one of the nation's top alternative newspapers, with a history of publishing award-winning long-form investigative and arts reporting. Barrett and Cooper began reporting an extensive article assessing the performance of the Koch administration in its initial months. McKoy and I stayed at the Joralemon Street office many nights and served as gofers, answering the phones or fetching coffee and Drake's cakes for Barrett and Cooper as they wrote drafts, argued about the tone and direction of their writing, and rewrote their copy. On May 29, the Wednesday after Memorial Day, the *Voice* published "Koch's War on the Poor," by Barrett and Cooper.

Edward Irving Koch was sworn in as mayor in January 1978. He inherited a city in fiscal distress; New York was $1 billion in debt.[35] A financial control board dictated how the five boroughs would stanch the fiscal bleeding and relearn budget discipline. Jobs and middle-class families continued to leave the city.[36]

Before Koch inherited control of New York City, Roger Starr, a Beame administration housing and development commissioner, proposed "planned shrinkage," a policy to neglect neighborhoods like the South Bronx because they were hopelessly devastated. The neighborhoods targeted for shrinkage were poor and inhabited by blacks and browns. Beame discredited the policy, but the idea lived on. The former commissioner later expressed the planned shrinkage vision as a neoconservative editorial writer for the *New York Times*.[37]

Koch, who campaigned as a fiscal conservative, called black elected officials and neighborhood leaders who controlled government funding "poverty pimps" and "poverticians."[38] Koch's broadsides played well with working-class whites convinced that an expanding welfare state had nearly bankrupted the city.[39] The welfare state drain was partially true. City workers' union corruption and political graft drained the city, too. However, the new mayor was not as feisty about recognizing those sacred cows.

Koch's verbal assaults were harmful because he had few blacks and Hispanics in his leadership circle. In May 1978, Barrett and Cooper visited City Hall to see if Koch made good on a campaign promise "to appoint more blacks in my administration than the combined administrations of [Robert] Wagner, [John] Lindsay and Beame." Barrett and Cooper's unofficial head count accounted for forty people on the mayoral end of the building, and the only blacks were four secretaries, two uniformed cleaning ladies, a couple of blacks answering telephones in the basement, and a custodian.[40]

The duo obtained documents from city agencies and from Koch's press aide Maureen Connelly. Connelly's list reported 25 minorities out of 121 appointments. A General Services Administration printout identified 113 top-level appointments that were not on Connelly's list. Fewer than ten of those people were minorities.[41]

Not one of Koch's personal staff and fourteen chairmen and heads of commissions was black. New York City, which demographically had nearly 50 percent residents of color, treated those residents like tourists based on the new mayor's appointment patterns. Black elected officials who supported Koch's election were chagrined. "I get the feeling," said U.S. representative Shirley Chisholm (D-N.Y.), "that Ed has written off blacks and he's saying 'I don't need you. There are just enough blacks in the administration to offset a charge of discrimination and I don't need you anymore.'"[42]

Koch appointed blacks and Hispanics to his administration without consulting politicians in the minority communities that would be affected. The new mayor's unilateral moves created a climate of distrust, and the blacks and browns who had titles and responsibilities—but often little authority—were perceived as rootless outsiders.

"Koch has broken specific campaign promises he made to me and others," fumed state senator H. Carl McCall, whose district represented Harlem. "Ed has always been successful with his arrogance," said U.S. representative Charles Rangel (D-N.Y.), a fourth-term member of Congress.[43]

Koch believed he spread equal-opportunity tough love to white ethnics as well as blacks and browns. In reality, the new mayor afflicted the already afflicted—poor New Yorkers of color. Koch sounded righteous when he attacked the "poverty pimps" mismanaging bloated social programs like Model Cities. City councilwoman Mary Pinkett of Brooklyn challenged Koch and his rhetoric: "If there are errors in a program," she said, "you deal with the errors. Where people are dishonest, indict them. But you don't throw away a program where people for the first time in their lives feel they can plan the future for themselves and their neighbors. You don't do that with a government agency."[44]

Koch ignored Pinkett's advice. Model Cities' administrative office and three neighborhood offices were closed, and 262 employees were replaced by 52 staffers who reported directly to Deputy Mayor Herman Badillo. Furthermore, $6.3 million in federal community development funds were taken from Model Cities.[45] In fairness, the new mayor had to slash government to deal with the city fiscal crisis. So where was Koch's cost-cutting zeal in dealing with city unions and civil service bureaucracy that was firmly controlled by the city's white ethnics? Koch muted his usual tough talk.

Koch personally loathed affirmative action, especially programs that imposed racial quotas to make up for past overt discrimination. The mayor's personal vision often clashed with established policies. The U.S. Department of Health and Human Services withdrew funds because the city Board of Education violated civil rights statutes.[46]

New York's head of the Commission on Human Rights resigned after she insisted on reviewing the city's record on affirmative action programs. "I couldn't justify going after any company in this city if the city didn't have its own house in order," Patria Nieto-Ortiz told Joe Conason of the *Village Voice*. A month after Nieto-Ortiz's departure in April 1978, only 21 of 90 city agencies filed affirmative action programs as required under federal guidelines.[47]

Koch's critique was somewhat valid. There were black leaders who used government antipoverty funds as their personal expense accounts, and the money did not get to the people in need. Andy Cooper railed against these rip-off artists. Cooper and his wife Jocelyn especially loathed the Harlem intelligentsia because they were seen as the most blatant offenders.[48]

The *Amsterdam News*, New York's leading black weekly and for generations one of America's top black newspapers, could no longer be relied on as a watchdog of African American politicians or Mayor Koch. John Procope, one of the paper's three co-publishers, had a $10 million insurance contract with the City of New York. This was a conflict of interest that cast doubt that the weekly was willing to tangle with Koch or risk losing the income. Procope vehemently denied there was a problem, but media critics were unconvinced.[49]

While critics alleged that the Koch administration neutered black leaders and their institutions and constituents in Harlem, blacks in the borough of Brooklyn, though oppressed, made lots of noise. The hot spot was Crown Heights, a working- to middle-class neighborhood just south of Bedford-Stuyvesant. Crown Heights in 1978 was about 80 percent black and 4 percent Hispanic, and specifically many of the blacks residing there were from the Caribbean.

The other significant ethnic bloc was orthodox Jews, specifically members of the Lubavitch sect. They represented 15 percent of the neighborhood. Combined, these 225,000 residents were packed into 200 city blocks. More than 75 percent of the residents were newcomers, having arrived within the last ten years.[50]

There were inevitable clashes. The orthodox Jews said they were mugged by black teenagers, and therefore some of their men had no choice but to organize security details to protect their families. Blacks complained that the Lubavitchers isolated themselves from the rest of the community and received preferential treatment from police and the Koch administration. Black residents also complained that police harassed them. In June, one of the police conflicts turned lethal. Arthur Miller, a thirty-five-year-old building contractor and black community activist, got into a scuffle with police officers. Miller tried to stop the arrest of Sam, his twenty-one-year-old brother, for driving a truck with a suspended license. Miller died of "asphyxiation," or a choke hold, during the dispute with at least sixteen police officers, four of them black. The Kings County district attorney investigated and concluded that the evidence was insufficient to indict any of the cops.[51]

Two days later, on June 16, Victor Rhodes, a sixteen-year-old black boy, was beaten unconscious on the street, then lapsed into a coma at the hospital. Rhodes had allegedly knocked a hat off an elderly rabbi.[52] About thirty orthodox Jewish males allegedly attacked Rhodes; however, only Louis Brennar and Jonathan Hackner, residents of Crown Heights, were charged with attempted murder and assault. Both men's cases were adjourned fourteen times.

On July 16, a month after the Arthur Miller and Victor Rhodes incidents, two thousand blacks demonstrated on Eastern Parkway, the tree-lined east–west boulevard that at the time defined the boundaries of the black and Jewish communities.[53] About five hundred police officers watched the crowd and several dozen Hasidic Jews also stood by. The tense standoff dissipated peacefully, yet the moment was emblematic of tension that would continue among the three factions.

Cooper, Leid, McKoy, and I covered those rallies and demonstrations and filed dispatches that ran weekly in the *Amsterdam News*. The emotional neighborhood coverage gave the TNS staff a focus. For months the reporters combed the court dockets in Brooklyn and Manhattan looking for stories. Some of the people or issues were in fact interesting, but the way in which TNS covered the courts with its small staff was hit or miss. The Crown Heights conflict, however, was a massive running story with many angles. Cooper and Leid felt comfortable mapping the assignments, and McKoy and I worked sources on the streets.

Predominantly black Central Brooklyn was tense because of Arthur Miller's killing by police in Crown Heights, as well as recent memories of the police acquittal in the slaying of an unarmed black teenager. Skirmishes between blacks and Jews in Crown Heights raised the tension level. Also, a sexual misconduct scandal involving a white congressman offered potential for anger to boil over. U.S. representative Fred Richmond of the Twelfth Congressional District was caught in Washington soliciting sex from a fifteen-year-old black boy. Richmond apologized for his "poor judgment." His Brooklyn district tiptoed through parts of a half-dozen neighborhoods from Greenpoint in the north to upscale Brooklyn Heights, Bedford-Stuyvesant, and Crown Heights. Richmond was skillful at bringing home federal funds for his patchwork quilt of constituents. Voters returned Richmond to office and apparently forgave his indiscretion, this time.[54]

On August 10, New York City's three daily newspapers, the *Times*, *Daily News*, and *Post*, went on strike, and the labor dispute lasted thirteen weeks, through November 5.[55] This meant that Trans Urban News Service's client base was cut in half. With the *Daily News* and *New York Times* out of service, the weekly *Amsterdam News* and WCBS News Radio 88 remained to receive and use TNS dispatches. Andy Cooper made at least one appearance on WNET-TV's *Special Edition*, where journalists from the striking dailies and journalists from the alternative and weekly press discussed the news on public television.

During the strike, New Yorkers could not read in their hometown papers about the Yankees versus Dodgers World Series, the pope's visit to the city, or the midterm House and Senate campaigns, among many news stories. The strike, which was combat between the non-news-gathering unions and management, weakened all three dailies, which were already coping with flat or declining circulation. The strike strengthened suburban dailies, including *Newsday* on Long Island, and Gannett's nine Westchester and Rockland newspapers just north of the city.

A week before the strike ended, Cooper and Barrett collaborated on their second *Village Voice* cover story, "Chisholm's Compromise: Politics and the Art of Self-Interest," on October 30. For this 8,300-word, 171-column-inch exposé, Cooper was the lead reporter, which was no surprise because of his personal knowledge of the five-term congresswoman.[56] They had belonged to the same political club, Unity Democratic, in the early 1960s, and both had been political candidates in 1968: Chisholm made history as the first black woman elected to Congress, and Cooper had lost a three-way race for a New York state senate seat. Cooper immediately acknowledged Chisholm's folk-hero reputation in much of Black America, then detailed her contradictory political behavior:

> Someone in the circulation department at the *Amsterdam News* told me that just the mention of Shirley Chisholm's name sold papers—lots of papers. Blacks in this town are sentimentally attached to her, still charged by the image of a spunky black woman with a fiery tongue and unpredictable spirit.

> But we have become—in some ways—a victim of our own imagination. We want that kind of indomitable hero so deeply that we create them—or worse, we let the media create them for us—and we go on stubbornly believing in them through decades of contrary realities.
>
> Those of us who know Shirley Chisholm's politics know that the woman who described herself as "unbought and unbossed" in a 1970 autobiography, has in fact, made a career of compromise. Since her election to Congress in 1968, she has sat out most of the critical and state races, refusing to back any of the leading black, female or reform candidates. In this year's Democratic primary, she backed organization candidates against every black independent in Brooklyn. In recent years, she supported white candidates for seats created by the courts to increase minority representation.
>
> Her district in central Brooklyn is populated by the largest concentration of black people in the country, a pivotal resource for the building of black political power. But Chisholm's brand of politics has divided and contained it.
>
> Her endorsements this September so provoked the *Amsterdam News*, that it departed from its usual, uncritical news approach to Chisholm and published an extraordinary pre-election editorial entitled: "The Shirley Chisholm issue." The *Amsterdam News* concluded: "One of the dissonant notes in the campaign has been the role played by Congresswoman Shirley Chisholm. . . . At some point we are all going to have to deal with the troublesome Mrs. Chisholm to make her accountable to a higher standard of political wisdom and loyalty, or to mount a serious effort to remove her. . . . She must lead at a level higher than the petty politics of a single district."

So what did the congresswoman do to stoke the anger of New York's black politicos? Chisholm refused to support black candidates for major political office. She refused to back Percy Sutton during his race for mayor the previous year. Sutton organized a fund-raiser for Chisholm during her historic 1968 congressional run, and he was her strongest supporter when Chisholm made a presidential run, against the wishes of Democratic Party leaders. Again in 1976, Sutton supported Chisholm for reelection against a formidable opponent, Sam Wright. Yet in 1977 Chisholm initially supported the doomed incumbent Beame and then threw in her support to Koch during his runoff race. "I believed I could count on her support," said Sutton. "I just don't understand Shirley Chisholm."[57]

Chisholm also declined to back Bella Abzug, who lost a close U.S. Senate primary race to Daniel Patrick Moynihan. Chisholm's neutrality was inexplicable when her behavior was weighed against her famous "unbought and unbossed" rhetoric. Indeed, in 1969 she crossed party lines and supported liberal Republican John V. Lindsay for mayor, but so did many blacks, like Cooper, who tired of the Democratic Party bosses.

Years earlier, in the 1970s, Chisholm high-stepped to the bosses' orders. For example, in Buffalo she campaigned against mayoral candidate Arthur O. Eve, a state assemblyman and chairman of the Black and Puerto Rican Caucus. Instead of supporting Eve, she campaigned for a white, conservative mayoral candidate. Her motivation? Chisholm had purchased a home near Buffalo and married a local assemblyman closely linked to Erie County Democratic boss Joseph Crangle. Like her allegiance to Kings County Democratic leader Meade Esposito, Chisholm was taking orders, too, from the upstate leader. Instead of being "unbossed," Chisholm was twice-bossed.[58]

Curiously, in 1976, she opposed Major R. Owens, a reform Democratic, and supported organization candidates fielded by Sam Wright, the man she had chastised for building a patronage empire out of antipoverty funds.[59] Chisholm had played no role in Brooklyn reform politics since 1972. Then she refused to support Allard Lowenstein, a national antiwar leader, and instead backed incumbent congressman John Rooney, a machine artifact whose votes on urban and race issues had an odious southern flavor.[60] Cooper and Barrett ended their exposé thus:

> In her two books—"Unbought and Unbossed" and "The Good Fight"—Chisholm portrays herself as an outspoken, independent force in politics *who makes no deals.* She's not. If she hadn't asked us to expect so much, maybe we wouldn't find it so difficult to accept her as she really is.
>
> She is not a venal woman. She's never ripped off community programs, never demanded a cut for herself in patronage or graft. That makes her an unusual politician—black or white. Her rhetoric and her votes on national issues are usually sound. She has the capacity to make poor people, women and blacks believe in themselves, at least when she isn't just trying to get them to believe in her.
>
> But she has based her political career on a fundamental compromise. She has disguised that compromise with the brilliance of her rhetoric. Only a careful examination of the consistency of her entire political life reveals that compromise. She has traded her independence for a secure

base at home and she believes that the only force that can guarantee her political security at home is the organization, not the people.

It's that choice that underlies every political decision she has made in this decade. Even her paranoia about enemies is calculated. She shares her enemies with the regular organization.

The saddest part of this compromise is that it is so unnecessary. Shirley Chisholm has underestimated herself. The organization could never beat her. The petty prizes she has won from them—her friend Lucille Rose as deputy mayor, Bill Howard at Metropolitan Savings [Bank] and Ed Towns as deputy borough president—were coming to blacks anyway and are such transient gains.

If she believed in her own rhetoric, the people would have taken care of her.

They still will.

9. TNS SHUTS DOWN

The eighteen-month grant that funded the payroll for TNS researchers—reporters, in fact—ended in July 1979. Cooper and Leid apparently worked for months without a staff. Two months later, in September 1979, I left for graduate school at Columbia. I occasionally wrote news stories for TNS that appeared in the *Amsterdam News* under my byline.[1] When I graduated in May 1980, Cooper offered me a job at $15,000, nearly double what I had made two years earlier, but I took another other offer, a $12,000-a-year reporter's position at the *Daily Argus* of Mount Vernon, New York. I believed that joining a daily newspaper was true to what TNS and graduate school had prepared me for.[2] Instead of returning home to Brooklyn, it was time to spread my wings and fly. That same year, Morris McKoy enrolled in law school. After he completed his studies, McKoy worked at Rodriguez and Leid law firm in the Bronx.[3]

In June, the TNS paused to celebrate. Reporters Utrice Leid, Morris McKoy, and I received the top award from the Public Relations Society of America for our four-part series on Crown Heights in May 1979.[4] In September, I collaborated with my fellow Columbia Journalism School graduate Betty Winston Baye on a three-part Trans Urban News Service series on the West Indian experience in New York. We based much of our reporting on interviews with elder immigrants who had settled in Harlem in the 1920s and, in many cases, migrated to Brooklyn to live in Bedford-Stuyvesant and Crown Heights. The pieces were published in the *Amsterdam News*.[5]

Cooper and Leid won another grant-funded contract from the New York State Department of Labor and the Comprehensive Employment and Training Act and opened the twenty-week TNS intensive writing and training workshop that summer.[6] Two dozen students put in twelve-hour days covering stories around the city and writing, on deadline, what they had learned. The students were highly motivated. Senior instructor Leid said they had to be, because "we're not in the business of running your basic anti-poverty program. If classes start at 9 a.m., we lock the doors at nine, and those who come late don't get paid. We don't do very much hand-holding. We stress that heavily that our students find their own way." Their ages ranged from twenty to forty-six, and many of them held undergraduate and advanced degrees.

There was Marlene Canty, twenty-seven, a Hunter College graduate who said she had "half of a master's degree from NYU." "This program," she said, "is not for the faint-hearted or the immature. A mature person won't have any problems dealing with the work."[7]

Another mature student was Vinette Pryce, who learned about the program after seeing an advertisement posted in local media by Colony South-Brooklyn Houses, a co-sponsor of the workshop. Pryce was a U.S. Army reservist, and she had learned broadcast journalism in the military. Pryce sought print experience from TNS. Qubilah Shabazz, a daughter of Malcolm X, was in the class, Pryce recalled, but she was kicked out.[8]

That summer was the season of the Atlanta child murders. Some mothers of the dead children visited Rev. Daughtry's church. Pryce reported on the mothers' visit and, independent of the workshop, sent stories to several newspapers. A community newspaper and several out-of-town papers picked the stories up.[9]

The students were each paid $108 a week to cover the cost of classroom time and long hours of street reporting. In November 1980, twenty-three workshop students graduated from the twenty-week program. Joan Roper, the program job developer, contacted one hundred employers. Unlike the Michelle Clark Program at Columbia University, TNS did not guarantee jobs to the students. It did promise job interviews.[10] Every student in the inaugural class pledged to Roper he or she would go beyond New York if jobs were offered. "They will go to Alaska if they have to," said Roper.

Sister Mary Hegarty of the Roman Catholic Diocese of Brooklyn convinced her institution to give the TNS program a $10,000 grant. That money helped to underwrite newsgathering costs. Guest lecturers who visited students in the classroom included journalists Wayne Barrett, Jack Newfield, and Thomas Johnson; judge William Booth; Paul Robeson Jr.; and the Rev. Herbert Daughtry and Rabbi Yisrael Rosenfeld.[11]

Many of the TNS students proved their mettle as research assistants for the third Wayne Barrett–Andrew W. Cooper *Village Voice* collaboration, "Koch's 99 Attacks against the Other New York," published on April 15, 1981.[12] Why was there so much black anguish about Ed Koch? In 12,860 words and 262 column inches, Barrett, Cooper, and associates inventoried statements, events and policies that were attacks on racial minorities and the poor of New York City. Both writers assessed the Koch administration in the third year of his first four-year-term. Their piece was the sequel to their critique of Koch about five months into his term in May 1978.[13] The next mayoral election was seven months away. Here is a sampling of bullet points from the "attacks" arsenal:

> **No. 1.** Despite a campaign pledge to appoint more minorities to top positions than his three predecessors combined, Koch runs the city without a single influential black or Latin adviser. All three of his minority deputy mayors have fled his administration, two in humiliation. Haskell Ward, Koch's last black deputy, was used as point man for the mayor's hospital closing plan. Ward walked away, described in the press as a "burnt-out case." Sighed one Koch source: "Ward really wasn't prepared to be called a traitor to blacks for being the mayor's 'upfront man' on the closings. He should have known, but he didn't."[14]
>
> **No. 14.** The mayor had to decline a campaign appearance with President Carter in Bedford-Stuyvesant because, he explained, his "presence in black communities was more likely to prompt disruptions than his appearances in other areas of the city." His initial town meeting in Bed-Stuy ended in an explosion of opposition. When he returned for a second try, he picked his own audience and the protestors marched outside.[15]
>
> A Harlem ministers group withdrew its invitation to him to appear as part of a Martin Luther King Day celebration. His town meeting in Harlem was another thunderous bust. Even Congressman Charles Rangel, who had introduced the mayor at the event, commented afterward: "It didn't work at all." Rangel questioned whether the mayor might have wanted a confrontation that would polarize ethnic communities. Koch had to flee his audience in the South Bronx and screen it, person-by-person, in Park Slope. To pave the way to some minority communities, he has had to resort to using the same sort of clubhouse dregs he'd once assailed as "poverty pimps" to sponsor and organize his constituent nights.[16]
>
> **Nos. 51 and 52.** The 1980 crime rate in public housing projects—where half a million poor people live—is out of control. Murder is up 24 percent; rape is up 43 percent, and assault is up 89 percent. The number of Housing Authority cops under Koch has plummeted so far that even Koch's management reports have conceded that it has had "a negative impact" on the anti-crime capability of the department. In the last two

years, the Housing Authority lost 115 cops or almost 16 percent of its force. The latest public figures state the authority had only 131 cops on night patrol, covering 263 housing projects.

The situations is so desperate that Koch has now proposed hiring 100 new officers by 1982, but he has expressed doubts about his fiscal ability to pay for them.[17] The same unprotected Housing Authority tenants have also experienced a skyrocketing escalation of the time they must wait before serious repairs are made. Maintenance complaints that took an average of 2.6 days to resolve a year ago now require 5.1 days. As with virtually every other city agency that has great impact on minority life, Koch broke with prior traditions and has not appointed a black to the Housing Authority board.[18]

No. 99 [the final bullet point]. "There are things Ed should not have done," [Haskell] Ward concluded. "He should not have tolerated the seizure of the police station in Brooklyn. I think it set a tone that led to belief that he was not even-handed. I counseled him, also, against attacking Bruce Wright as strongly as he did. I think that hurt him a good bit. . . .

"The only thing that blacks want is to sit down and talk with him and to know that he's listening and not just getting up his back about it . . . Blacks know as well as whites that there is a fiscal crisis . . . but they don't get the sense that [Koch] is sensitive to the pain they are experiencing. In fact, he's adopting policies that may increase the pain.

"The perception that it is a deliberate policy on the part of his administration to profit politically by measures which will be seen as reducing services and considerations to blacks and Hispanics. I don't think it's true, but that is the perception that he has to work with and I don't think he's done enough to allay that. I think in fact, he has probably . . . fueled the suspicion more than anything."[19]

Trans Urban News Service began publishing in 1981. *TNS Reports*, self-defined as "A Journal of Minority News and Politics Produced by the Staff of Trans Urban News," published eight-page newsletters on ivory-colored paper beginning that summer. Layouts were comparable to those of the leading mainstream newspapers of the day. The pages, 8 1/2 by 11 inches, were laid out in two- or three-column widths. Headlines were big, 24- to 30-points deep, to grab readers' attention, and the editors ran plenty of photos—nine images in one edition—to add movement and color to the text.[20]

There were no ceremonial, staged "grip and grin" photos. For example, with the cover story "Black and Blue: Transit Guardians v. TA Police Dept.," A cropped horizontal photo of a black Transit Authority cop hanging on to a subway strap complemented Dan Jacobson's story, which jumped from page 1 to pages 3, 4, 5, and 6.

On page 6, the photo of the black TA cop was published again, this time as a full-size vertical shot that revealed an empty subway car. To the left of the photo was a smaller picture of two white TA cops walking up from a subway station and into the street.

Why were these words and images significant for TNS? As a four-year-old news service, it distributed stories to mainstream and ethnic newspapers and electronic media. After distribution, TNS lost control over publication and presentation. Leid often complained in either accurate or embellished tirades that the predominantly white New York dailies suppressed many TNS stories because they were "too hot"; they told gritty truths about black New Yorkers that might alienate a large segment of middle- to working-class white readers and their advertisers.[21] Meanwhile Leid and Cooper, pleased that many TNS stories were published in the black weekly *Amsterdam News,* routinely held their collective breaths each week and prayed that the host publication would not diminish their package of stories with misspelled headlines or illogical and uninspired page layouts.[22]

TNS Reports, though published only four times that year, gave editor Leid and news service director Cooper control over content they wanted to display with pride to decision makers around town. Take, for example, Jacobson's exposé in the fourth and final edition of 1981. The Transit Guardians, an association of black police, sued the city transit authority in federal court, charging racial discrimination in hiring and promotion, and harassment of officers who questioned authority policies and tactics. The U.S. Treasury Department Office of Revenue Sharing concluded that black Transit Authority officers "received a disproportionate number of harsher punishments than white counterparts."[23] Blacks made up 22 percent of the TA force but made up 33 percent of all officers reported as derelict, 51 percent of all officers suspended, and 70 percent of all officers discharged.[24] They accounted for 17 percent of all officers in the minimum charge category of "Warned/Admonished." About 65 percent of all black officers reported as derelict were suspended from the force, compared to 29 percent of white officers subject to the same charges.[25]

Sergeant Walter Smith of the Guardians told Jacobson that the "Shoo-flies," a plainclothes unit of mostly white cops, were dispatched during the

1970s by former TA Police Chief Richard H. Rapp to monitor police on patrol. "They came up with an ingenious idea," Smith explained. "If we give all these [black] guys complaints they will lose points toward promotion. We could say they have bad records and we don't have to promote them, so they started the shooflies, who began coming out and giving complaints . . . harassing black officers." Curiously, the so-called shooflies were dispatched before the TA scheduled its exam for promotions, then disbanded when the exam was postponed. When the exam was rescheduled, the shooflies were back on the street.[26] Jacobson's 2,300-word report did not have a happy ending.[27]

Half of the six hundred blacks in the TA Police were Guardian members, and there was dissension within the association over how aggressively to press the discrimination case.[28] Furthermore, Smith wavered between confidence and skepticism. If the Guardians won their case, would the authority enforce the ruling, or would managers continue to harass black officers? Jacobson's reporting did succeed in exposing an entrenched problem in a corner of New York's vast civil service empire. The story was indeed "too hot" for the mainstream dailies.

In the same edition, Cooper's "One Man's Opinion" column returned. The copy maintained the bite of the *Amsterdam News* pieces of 1976 that Cooper claimed publishers had tended to spike because of its strong political content. In "The *New York Post* as Political Lynch Mob," Cooper criticized the daily tabloid—and specifically editorial writer Bruce Rothwell—for writing pieces that smeared black Manhattan borough president candidate David Dinkins as an anti-Semite. Alleged anti-Semitic statements by two black men, James Lawson and Fred Weaver, were tied to candidate Dinkins.[29] Cooper wrote:

> "The *Post* and its editorial writer, did a job for Andy Stein—an obvious, nasty, vicious job of negative propaganda—that the Jewish community let stand. The leaders of the Anti-Defamation League . . . did not raise their voice in defense of Dave Dinkins or protest the political murder committed on the editorial page of the *New York Post*. Where is the voice of the American Jewish Committee, the New York Board of Rabbis, the National Conference of Christians and Jews? All silent!
>
> Jewish leaders are well aware of Dave Dinkins' reputation, yet they sat silent, symbolically washed their hands, and gave a good man up to the bigots in this city who see every black as a militant and project the shortcomings of a few on the mass. The tactic comes out of another era and was perfected in another country.[30]

Volume 1, number 4, of TNS reports also included a story by Iris Berman announcing that the TNS College Internship Program was funded for a second year. A horizontal photo showed fifteen members of the 1980 Intensive Journalism Workshop listening earnestly and sitting in front of their manual typewriters. Intern Gordon Balkcom wrote the back page of news briefs headlined "Call for Mayoral Task Force," "Venereal Disease," "Court to Hear Bias Case," "Arts Budget," "Affirmative Action," and "Africa News." There was one photograph labeled "Solidarity Day, Sept. 19, 1981, Washington, D.C."

In November 1981, mayor Ed Koch, a lightning rod for TNS coverage *and* critical scrutiny by Cooper, Barrett, and other journalists in the *Village Voice*, cruised to reelection, beating two challengers, a black and a white liberal.[31] Koch won 41 percent of the black vote, although he sometimes exaggerated in print and falsely claimed that 70 percent of New York's black voters had backed him.[32] Koch did not have to embellish, because he was securely in the driver's seat. The mayor, a Democrat in title, aligned himself with president Ronald Reagan. Reagan the Republican, ten months into his first term, fired striking federal air traffic controllers, cut social programs, and also lowered federal taxes for upper-income Americans.[33]

Koch and Reagan had related missions; Koch had to reduce the municipal deficit that had nearly bankrupted the city, and Reagan moved to tame inflation and 20 percent consumer credit rates that created a sense of economic malaise. Koch and Reagan harbored equal disdain for affirmative action.[34] In Reagan, Koch had a president who wanted to dismantle programs that assisted blacks and browns victimized by overt discrimination. Koch clashed with the Carter administration, which had been committed to enforcing existing affirmative action policies.

With Reagan in the White House, 1981 was a new day for Koch. Cooper, Leid, and TNS would have to take a gut check and renew their resolve to act as watchdogs of the political maneuvers of the mayor and local political maneuvers, and the president's national *and* global ones.

Cooper and Leid grew their journalist training programs. The first class of writers' workshop graduates completed their twenty-week stints in fall 1980, then a new wave of students began their twenty-week cycle in February 1981 and studied and did street reporting through June. Of fifty aspiring minority journalists from low-income neighborhoods, the program placed forty-six trainees in media or media-related positions.[35] Then the College Intern Experience Project (CIEP) launched in September 1981 and continued through August 1982.

Trans Urban News Service received a $50,000 grant from the Greater New York Fund and United Way Special Allocations Committee to underwrite the project.[36] By September 1981, eighteen college students from thirteen metropolitan New York colleges received full field credit. CIEP exceeded its commitment to ten students. Underwriters took note of the overachieving news service. In October, TNS received a second Special Allocations Committee grant to train twenty-five students in 1981–82. The grant funded more students, but with less money ($36,000). Eleven interns were in the program as of December 31, 1981.[37]

As for the original TNS volunteers who became interns, in 1981 Morris McKoy was in his final year of study at Howard University Law School. He was interested in pursuing communications law.[38] In 1981, I was working as a police reporter at the *Daily Argus* of Mount Vernon, New York. That November, I shared an Associated Press award for spot news coverage.[39] I also worked as a part-time editor in the TNS Writers Workshop.

Furthermore, Charlie Alejandro of Brooklyn College, a former gang member who interned at TNS in 1980, completed graduate studies at Columbia University Graduate School of Journalism and embarked on an accelerated writing career.[40]

Stephanie Griffith of Wesleyan University interned at TNS for consecutive semesters in 1979 and 1980, then was accepted into a one-year program offered by her college and the University of Barcelona. Griffith was also a candidate for the Summer Program for Minority Journalists at the University of California, Berkeley.[41] Brenda Jimenez of City College of New York interned at TNS and immediately after graduation was hired as a business reporter-editor with a major international corporation. Jimenez produced a monthly bilingual corporate magazine.[42]

On the publishing side, Trans Urban News Service issued the monthly *TNS Reports* newsletter. In 1981 TNS received $7,890 in subscriptions, twenty-four corporate at $300 each and two $45 individual subscriptions, to underwrite newsgathering and production expenses. In addition, TNS received $24,000 from nine foundation or corporate sources to underwrite training programs or publishing.[43] Cooper and Leid began branching out into other media. They negotiated with Inner City Broadcasting Co. to establish a Brooklyn bureau of WLIB-AM at the offices of TNS.[44]

After five years of operating TNS, Cooper and his news service gained official recognition at least twice in 1982. On June 29, Brooklyn borough president Howard Golden hosted a reception in honor of TNS at Borough Hall. On that occasion, WLIB News also announced the opening of its Brooklyn bureau.[45] On October 7, Cooper received the D. Parke Gibson Journalism Award from the New York chapter of the Public Relations Society of America. The award was named after Gibson, a black marketing expert who encouraged African Americans to enter the public relations field. Cooper was the second winner of the award. The first winner was Clayton Riley, who wrote the script for the *I Remember Harlem* series on PBS.[46]

Despite the celebratory moment, Cooper felt acute financial distress. Corporate grants that had supported his training programs were in short supply, and federal CETA funds that underwrote the writers' workshops fell to the Reagan administration's budgetary ax.[47]

10. RISING SUN

By October 1982, although it ran an overachieving job training program that was one of the best in New York State, TNS struggled despite its reputation for excellence.[1] Federal cutbacks by the Reagan administration left the state Department of Labor no choice but to reduce its support of training programs, even the proven successes. The grant for the latest cycle of TNS writers' workshop students ran out on September 30. TNS was granted a six-week extension to do specialized training and place students, but by mid-November the well ran dry. Out of the job training business, Leid and Cooper turned their attention to another venture, a newspaper start-up.[2] In the waning days of 1982, Cooper expressed his desire to publish a weekly called the *Inner City Sun*. The paper would circulate in black communities of Metropolitan New York.[3]

TNS hired consultants to compile statistics, analyze census data, and construct a profile of the kind of reader who could interest advertisers.[4] Additionally, Cooper and Leid created a philosophy, rationale, and business plan for their prospective newspaper. Cooper liked the prospects for the start-up. Thirteen newspapers—mainstream and ethnic—served New York's black communities, and served them badly.[5] There was little firsthand or authoritative coverage or analysis of the news, issues, and events occurring in those communities or of the policy decisions that affected blacks' lives at the city, state, and national levels.[6]

Existing papers gave politics only a superficial and naive treatment. It was politically expedient for publishers to ignore what was happening. Furthermore, their reporters were unable to make connections that could lend their reporting useful perspective and depth.[7] For example, Cooper was sickened when most papers ignored massive voter fraud that occurred at the Board of Elections in the Thirteenth Congressional District race between incumbent Major R. Owens and challenger Vander L. Beatty, a state senator.[8] TNS reported the story, but other black publications chose not to report on the fraud. All the local press took a pass on follow-up stories about district attorney Elizabeth Holtzman's inability to make a case.[9]

Demographic research told Cooper that a critical mass of black New Yorkers had the financial means and aptitude to support an independent, aggressive, even irreverent black weekly. More than 700,000 city residents ages eighteen to fifty-five were potential readers and subscribers of the *Inner City Sun*.[10] Brooklyn would be the home base, and Kings County had the largest percentage of that target market. The borough of Queens ranked second. After decades of decline, Harlem no longer was the center of the black universe.[11] The two leading black newspapers, the *New York Amsterdam News* (circulation 41,000) and Brooklyn-based *Big Red* (circulation 38,000) seemed stagnant and ill-equipped to tap into the readership pool that Cooper and his consultants identified.

The *Amsterdam News* also appeared vulnerable. On February 1, nearly forty employees represented by the Newspaper Guild struck the city's oldest black weekly. Management asked for a four-day work week and 20 percent pay cut to ease operating losses that threatened the life of the seventy-five-year-old newspaper.[12] In the 1960s, circulation of the *Amsterdam News* had peaked at 80,000, and the paper bragged on its masthead that it was "America's Largest Weekly." By the time of the 1983 strike, the newspaper had lost nearly half that circulation.

Cooper's new paper promised an editorial environment that was compatible with advertisers' interests without allowing them to dictate tone or content. The *Inner City Sun* promised to emphasize unique approaches to reporting—original stories, investigative pieces, and news analysis. Editorially, the views of conservative Thomas Sowell could share space on a page with liberal Benjamin Hooks, and policy makers like Haskell Ward and Norman Podhoretz would be welcomed to weigh in. Said Cooper, "There is no question that The Inner City Sun will serve black interests. It will be frank and open, courageous and bold. But it will not be an apologist."[13]

Cooper and Leid knew where they wanted to take the paper. Now they had to design and build the vehicle and also find the fuel for its engine. By May, they had changed the newspaper's name from the *Inner City Sun* to simply the *City Sun*.[14] Cooper and Leid identified and hired staff members to head the editorial, advertising, and marketing/promotion and circulation departments. Michelle Robinson, a former TNS writers' workshop student who was working at Gannett Westchester-Rockland Newspapers, was being considered for religion editor. That job required the editor to work with writers and develop stories that highlighted religion as a vibrant part of people's everyday lives, and also to perform routine tasks such as assembling church calendars, directories, and direct beat coverage of churches and church events.[15] Dennis Warren, another workshop student who was also working at a Westchester daily, was about to be approached about doing freelance pieces in the forthcoming Caribbean section. The staff members went to work and formalized their operations and responsibilities.

Specifically, the editorial department assembled a pool of stringers, correspondents, feature writers, and columnists.[16] Former TNS freelancer Betty Winston Baye and I were asked to quietly seek out and develop a pool of writers that the new paper could tap for stringer, freelance, and feature stories.[17]

Cooper said that $50,000 worth of advertising was committed in spring 1983, and advertising contracts were being worked on with major supermarket chains, corporations, and governmental agencies. Executives of major news organizations and corporations volunteered their expertise to the *City Sun*. Cooper took advantage of the offers. He benefited from their knowledge, expertise, and experience of the business side of newspapering. It was essential that Cooper and Leid listen well because despite their essential missions, the newsgathering sides of newspapers were non-revenue-generating operations. Cooper envisioned a master plan that would ensure a thriving and profitable *City Sun*.[18]

Circulation projections were ambitious. A consultant's plan promised a minimum 65,000 newspapers circulating weekly in traditional major outlets like newsstands, yet the *City Sun* was to be uniquely tailored for distribution in neighborhoods via supermarkets, local small businesses, street hawkers, and community organizations. There was no mention of home delivery. In New York, daily and weekly newspapers counted on a high percentage of street sales. Accordingly, Cooper and Leid invested much energy and commissioned one of the city's top graphic designers to a draw up a dummy, due at the end of May, that they counted on to interest potential advertisers in the *City Sun* product.[19] Cooper and Leid believed that they would launch the *City Sun* in September 1983.[20]

That fall, the atmosphere in New York crackled with energy from black journalists challenging their mediums. *New York Daily News* columnist Earl Caldwell and reporter Dave Hardy explained that the paper resisted settling a lawsuit brought by black employees that alleged discrimination in hiring, salaries, and promotions of the employees. "They have total contempt for us," Hardy told members of the New York Association of Black Journalists. He explained that half of the *Daily News*'s citywide readership was black or brown, yet only 5 percent of the editorial staff was black. Caldwell meanwhile quashed rumors that he had been fired. His thrice-weekly column was missing from the paper for more than a month. "I was not fired," Caldwell explained, "I've been on strike for a month" because of a salary dispute and the paper's decision to push his column from page 4 to the back pages.[21]

In October the *Amsterdam News*'s management let go of its editor John Davis. Wilbert Tatum's dismissal letter said he had fired Davis because of the debilitating strike that year, plus lean economic times that required personnel cuts.

Davis claimed that he had been fired because of insubordination: Tatum had handed him an article by Koch plus the mayor's photo and told him to run the article verbatim. Davis obeyed. He also wrote a piece of his own that criticized Koch's defense of his relationship with blacks.

"I understood that I was writing my own resignation," said Davis, who had worked as editor since mid-1981.[22] Davis affirmed Cooper's conviction that black-owned and mainstream media did not serve black New York well: "One of the failures of black journalists is many have succumbed to buffoonery, accommodation and puffery. Most black newspapers are cautious, apologetic and less than direct about our status." Davis also said as inept as the *Amsterdam News* management was, the newspaper "is the best thing we have. I can't think of anything in New York City where black people get a black perspective." Cooper and Leid, of course, were eager to hatch their response to Davis's argument.

Errol Louis of New Rochelle, New York, graduated from Harvard University a semester early in February 1983. He spent that summer as an intern in the *Wall Street Journal*'s Boston bureau. Louis turned down a job offer from Dow Jones and chose to work for Andy Cooper and his start-up venture.[23] From March to June 1984, Louis worked on sales pitches, demographics, and lots of nonjournalistic tasks. He worked closely with Cooper, Leid, Dan Jacobsen, and Marty Heller. Louis believed he was going to start his own black newspaper some day, so his training was valuable. He valued the opportunity to observe the right and wrong ways to assemble such a business.[24]

Louis knew the Coopers before he signed up with the *City Sun*. Andy's oldest brother, Palma, had married Louis's godmother, Milagros. Palma, a handyman-contractor, met her at Louis's house. Louis left Westchester for Harvard in 1980. When he returned home on breaks, his mother told him about the Trans Urban News Service internship program.

In the summer of 1982, Louis was with Andy Cooper in a work-study arrangement. His first TNS dispatch, "Police Break Up Child Sex Ring in Brooklyn," was published on the front page of the *Amsterdam News*.[25]

During three intense spring months of 1984, Louis gathered demographic information for the *City Sun* advertiser kits. He kept seeing the flip side of affluent people's lives: the lives of the have-nots. Louis collected the data and used them for the *City Sun*'s inaugural cover story on June 6, 1984. The paper launched nearly six weeks later than the April date Cooper had announced in December. But the June start conveyed symbolism about its publisher's hopes. The pre-summer sun was getting warmer, and this new news organization was primed to turn up the heat.

"DEATH of a GENERATION," proclaimed the Wednesday, June 6, 1984, edition. A horizontal photo of a mass of young black men stretched across the page and complemented the bold headline.[26] Louis reported that in 1983, 54 percent of New York City's black males age sixteen to nineteen were unemployed. Seventy percent of them were not seeking employment. In addition, 14 percent of black men ages twenty or older were jobless too, and 28 percent of them had stopped looking for work. Furthermore, the city's 42 percent high school dropout rate was extreme at four high schools in predominantly black neighborhoods.[27]

Louis's story began thus:

> Young Denny Jones paced nervously in his cell, his eyes and nose burning from tear gas fumes.
>
> Seventeen years old, he was in jail for the first time and now found himself just yards from the roar of a Rikers Island riot.
>
> It was the winter of 1972.

The story jumped from the cover to pages eight and nine. It quoted Beny Primm, M.D., executive director of the Addiction Research Treatment Corporation: Odds were ten to one for a boy to make it out of those bleak conditions, said one pull quote.[28]

Cooper and Leid asked Louis to write the investigative piece and to pull no punches despite the grim data. The story, said Louis two decades later, "set the pace for what was at stake."

On page 14, an editorial offered an introduction to the new newspaper. In the two-column-width space, Cooper reprinted the *Freedom's Journal* editorial of March 1827, which had appeared nearly a century before he was born.[29]

The staff box on the lower right of the editorial page listed Cooper as publisher, Leid as managing editor, and Daniel Jacobson as assignment editor. It added nine writers: Gordon Balkcom, Van-Alden Ferguson, Madeline Davis, Errol T. Louis, Jacqueline Robinson, Joe Sexton, Sonja Williams, Clinton Cox (Albany, N.Y.), and Isaiah Poole (Washington, D.C.). Contributors were Charles R. Owens, Don Palmer, and Art Rust Jr. Stephen Critchlow was chief photographer. A three-member advertising department was listed, as well as a two-member production department. Mary A. Griffith was in charge of administration. The *City Sun* announced that its mailing address was P.O. Box 560, Brooklyn, NY 11202. The annual subscription price was $26.

Weekly editions of the *City Sun* for the most part lived up to the promise of the seventeen-page manifest and prototype of the *Inner City Sun*. The early formula included an oversize black flag (newspaper jargon for the publication's name) accessorized with a red streamer that mimicked those of New York City's bare-knuckle tabloids, the *Daily News* and *New York Post*. The *City Sun* was a tabloid, too, which made reading and folding the pages easier for the crowds who rode the subways and transit buses. There was liberal use of wide-angle action photos. *City Sun* photos always showed movement, unlike the reliably static photos in the *Amsterdam News* or even in the *Daily News* and *New York Post*.

The edgier sensibility of Cooper's paper resembled that of the weekly *Village Voice*—no surprise, since he had collaborated several times with its journalists. Each *City Sun* edition carried an eclectic mix of stories about black New York life, regular news pages covering the Caribbean and Africa, a copious arts and culture section led by critic Armond White and arts writer Fern Gillespie, and an out-of-the box sports section edited by Anthony "Tony" Carter Paige.[30]

By the third edition, the first letters to the editor appeared on the editorial page. In response to the inaugural cover "Death of a Generation," eighth grader Ellen Kountz of Kings Point wrote: "Death of a generation' brought me to tears. The black community needs a pat on the back, not a beating." John Chamble, a lawyer from Brooklyn, countered, "'Death of a generation' was an incisive account of a black American nightmare." And L. E. Wilson of Far Rockaway promised, "I shall share my copy with my family and encourage them to purchase the paper every week."[31]

By edition 6 in July, the paper received its first of many letters from Mayor Koch. He took offense to Cooper's editorial from edition 4, "Return of the Flack Man." Cooper drew blood with an editorial punch. His upstart newspaper was too potent to ignore, and the prickly Koch was a willing participant who wanted to argue. Cooper gladly gave the mayor space to disagree with his editorial position.

The publisher and his *City Sun* were winners because they drove home this point: a black-owned political watchdog was in operation. The days of press-release political coverage, of reporters and editors unable or afraid to trace connections in the moves of elected officials and their operatives, were over, at least at one black-owned media outlet in New York City. Cooper relished the editorial combat, and he used every opportunity to heap scorn on his former news service client-rival the *Amsterdam News*.[32]

True to Cooper's roots as a community activist in the 1960s, his *City Sun* broke a taboo of other black newspapers—it criticized black politicians whenever it became convinced their behavior was venal, lazy, or self-serving.[33] "Something is rotten in Brooklyn," blared the lead editorial in the second edition. It noted the lack of due process in punishing state senator Vander L. Beatty, a politician who Cooper suspected was corrupt. Cooper was annoyed by the capricious process that was used against Beatty. Cooper argued that there should not be one set of rules for black elected officials and another for the white ones in Brooklyn.[34]

The fourth edition's cover story was "Albany's Buffalo Soldier," a profile by Clinton Cox of deputy state legislative speaker Arthur O. Eve of Buffalo. The photo that dominated the cover showed Eve raising his arms, champion style, with Democratic presidential candidate Jesse Jackson. The profile was mostly flattering. The larger issue was that the *City Sun* would be investing a significant portion of its editorial resources to cover politics. Cox, based near the state capital Albany, kept an eye on the legislature. He did not write process stories about bills and budgets. Instead, to explain present-day realities, he crafted long-form profiles and essays rich with historical context.[35]

The new paper sent its staff beyond its circulation area to cover significant political gatherings. Washington correspondent Isaiah Poole was dispatched to San Francisco to report on the Democratic National Convention. There, senator Walter Mondale (D-Minn.), the party front-runner, had support from most black elected officials and leaders of the civil rights establishment. He might have faced a serious challenge from Jesse Jackson, positioned as the champion of the black poor and other disaffected Americans, but Jackson's quest for the White House had derailed the previous spring when news reports leaked that he had called Jewish Americans "hymies" and New York City "Hymietown." Nation of Islam leader Louis Farrakhan, whom Jackson personally registered to vote, symbolically threatened the life of the black *Washington Post* journalist who revealed Jackson's off color, off-the-record remark.[36]

Although Jackson's presidential campaign was scuttled, he and his supporters still competed for influence inside the Democratic Party. Poole was there to report the maneuvers especially for *City Sun* readers. "Frisco's Winners and Losers" was the banner headline of the July 25–31 edition, number 8. A dominant horizontal photo of Jackson, Joseph Lowery, Ron Dellums,

Andrew Young, Maxine Waters, and Walter Fauntroy filled the page.[37] Poole's dispatch filled pages 8 and 9 inside. On the editorial page, "The Pleasant Sound of Compromise" assessed the give-and-take between the Democratic National Committee and Jackson. Now, would Mondale, the liberal Democrat, have a chance in November against incumbent Reagan and his ascending conservative juggernaut?

Another venue where politicians made sure they were seen was the West Indian Day Parade along Brooklyn's Eastern Parkway on Labor Day. The first Monday of September was the superstore of vote shopping, when as many as one million people packed themselves along a three-mile strip. Cooper's editorial "Journalism's Curious Disease" mocked the inadequate or deliberately deceitful coverage of the event by the city's daily papers.

The *New York Times* noted the presence of 900,000 people on Eastern Parkway in paragraph 21 of its Labor Day roundup. The reporter wondered why other New York City Labor Day events were sparsely attended, yet those events got more ink. The *Daily News* did a slightly better job by focusing on one family's initiation to curried goat. Meanwhile the *New York Post* was predictably inane, reporting that along Eastern Parkway, "Cops shoot 4 at Jesse [Jackson] rally."[38]

The *City Sun* detected mendacity in the Bronx. Ramon Velez, power broker or *caudillo* of the South Bronx, openly declared his support for Reagan but denied that the administration had directed money to his programs. Since Reagan was starving New York City and other major cities of federal funding, a local leader getting federal largesse was noteworthy.

Also curious was the assertion that Bronx Democratic insiders such as county leader Stanley Friedman and borough president Stanley Simon received funds for their development corporation though both men had proclaimed their support for Mondale, a Democrat. The game was on.[39] Unfortunately, the *City Sun* reported the mendacity barely a week before the election, not soon enough to influence many swing voters. Still, that cover story was another example of the paper sticking with its promise to connect as many dots as it could about what politicians were doing in the dark.

Come Election Day in 1984, Reagan demolished Mondale. The incumbent carried 49 of 50 states, plus the District of Columbia, and 59 percent of the popular vote. A quarter of registered Democrats supported Reagan. Mondale earned nine of every ten black votes and two of every three Jewish votes. The Democrat's running mate was a woman, Geraldine Ferraro (D-N.Y). Pollsters said a gender gap had hurt Mondale; he had a bigger problem with male voters than Reagan had with females, who gave him more support than in 1980.[40]

New York's working poor and desperately poor were involuntarily signed up for another four years of hostile federal policies. Their mayor, three years into his first term, would be a Democrat in name only, parroting the hard-line economic and social policies of the feds. For the *City Sun*, this moment was not a time of despair but a challenge to fight harder against Reaganism and the reign of Koch.

11. BRIGHT, SHINING YEARS

On November 3, 1984, Eleanor Bumpurs, a sixty-seven-year-old grandmother, was served with a warrant for authorities to evict her from her Bronx apartment because she was behind on her $96.85 monthly rent. The city housing authority manager who signed the warrant had been on the job for one day. Bumpurs, imposing at three hundred pounds but physically disabled and barely mobile because she suffered from arthritis, diabetes, and high blood pressure, begged the police who banged on her door to go away. A SWAT team of six officers forced their way into the apartment at 1551 University Avenue. Bumpurs kept the intruders back with a kitchen knife. When Bumpurs continued to resist the police, they shot her multiple times with shotguns.[1]

An eyewitness watched the siege through the peephole from his apartment across the hall. After the shooting, at least fifty police descended on the Sedgwick Houses, a public housing complex. The show of force must have been for crowd control because of the shocking procedure that followed. Bumpurs's corpse was carried out of the apartment naked. No one had the decency to cover her up. Two cavities in her torso leaked blood, which required a city worker to sop up the liquid trail.[2]

Bumpurs's death was a replay of the Eula Love case in Los Angeles five years earlier in January 1979. There a thirty-nine-year-old black woman faced with a utility cutoff was shot dead by two police after she kept them at bay with a butcher knife. She died because of an overdue $22.09 gas bill. The *Los Angeles Times* reduced the news of Love's death to a single paragraph. But the underdog *Los Angeles Herald Examiner* played Love's shooting big on the front page, and her case received follow-up reporting in the *Herald Examiner* and *Los Angeles Times* about other suspicious police shootings, choke-hold deaths, and spying.[3]

Five years later in New York, the *City Sun* crusaded for the family of Eleanor Bumpurs. Her shooting occurred days after the weekly newspaper staff published the October 31–November 6 election preview edition. With the anticlimactic landslide election of President Reagan, Cooper and Leid devoted what would have been the November 7–13 postelection analysis edition exclusively to the Bumpurs slaying. "The shame of the city" was the cover headline of the sixteen-page edition. Above was a full-width photo of five Bumpurs grandchildren placing flowers on her grave at Frederick Douglass Memorial Cemetery in Staten Island. The normal page 3 "This Week in History" floated a caricature of a grim-faced Bumpurs in white space followed by twenty-one lines of oversize type that summarized how she died.

The full-page editorial "Pay or Die" appeared next on page 4. "The killing of Eleanor Bumpurs—an ailing 67-year-old woman who relatives and neighbors alike said could barely walk because of crippling arthritis, high blood pressure and diabetes—so infuriated us, it hit so close to home, we decided that the full force of the community should be expressed.... No one, no city or state or federal official, can now claim that the black community did not articulate its feelings on the Bumpurs killing. No one will be able to say they didn't know the full depth of the impact this callous killing has had on us all."[4]

The "full force of the community" that contributed to the special edition included Alton Waldron, a Queens assemblyman and a thirteen-year veteran of the NYPD; Juanita Howard, a sociology professor at Baruch College; Wendell Foster, the Bronx city councilman who organized Bumpurs's funeral arrangements; Victor Garcia, the eyewitness to the Bumpurs shooting; Jack Newfield and Wayne Barrett, *Village Voice* writers and colleagues of Cooper, who wrote two "Tales of the Other New York" for the centerfold; a statement from the New York Civil Liberties Union ("Seek special prosecutor in killing"); Charles E. Cobb, executive director of the United Church of Christ Commission on Racial Justice; the Rev. Dr. William Augustus Jones, founder of the Organization of African-American Clergy; David N. Dinkins; the Rev. Herbert Daughtry of House of the Lord Church; Michael Amon-Ra of the Black United Front, New York City chapter; and James Murphy, president of the Sedgwick Houses Tenants Association for twelve years. The back cover of the *City Sun* was filled with two horizontal six-by-nine-inch photos of scenes from the funeral. No type was used to label the content.[5]

On November 14–20, the lead story was "BRUTALITY: Whites File Grievances Too." A front-page photo showed Mayor Koch warily looking away from the podium at an animated police commissioner Benjamin Ward, who was gesturing with his hands.[6] Leid's reporting began on the cover and jumped inside to page 7. "A Second Reminder in the Bumpurs Killing" was the editorial on page 18.

The next week, November 21–27, the newspaper covered groups that demonstrated frequently to demand answers to questions about the justification for the fatal shooting. A page 18 editorial by Cooper asked if there was "a thorough report on the Bumpurs killing, or a whitewash?"[7] On op-ed page 19, a house advertisement, "A Petition to Stop Police Brutality Now," appeared. Readers were asked to clip the ad, gather five signatures (lined spaces were on the petition), and return the document to the *City Sun* office.

"Bumpurs Heirs to File Suit," by Phil Makotsi, was the November 28–December 4 lead story. "City Still Won't Address the Brutality Issue," read the page 18 editorial. Next to the opinion on the right began a three-column-deep letter from Koch headlined "The Mayor Cries Foul." Koch's 48-column-inch letter was a reply to guest writer Jack Newfield's "Tales of the Other New York" published on November 7–13.[8]

Koch claimed that Newfield had made inaccurate statements. According to the mayor, the city's economic resurgence was improving the lives of blacks; their employment had increased 24 percent since 1977. The number of jobs in all city boroughs increased for the first time since 1977 (the city had bled several hundred thousand jobs for at least a decade), and New York City was the only major U.S. city to experience a decline in resident unemployment. Thirty-six percent of all new city employees hired in 1983 were black, said Koch, though the total city black population was 26 percent.[9] Koch also challenged Newfield's criticisms of underperforming public schools and the decision to close municipal hospitals in black neighborhoods with numbers that suggested a rosier outlook. Newfield returned fire a few weeks later in the same editorial space.

Andy Cooper and Utrice Leid accepted Koch's lengthy written objection with glee and thrilled at the opportunity to print it. Cooper got what he wanted: the powerful came forward to speak their truth, and the masses could decide on the credibility of the message. Koch could have ignored the *City Sun* and dismissed the weekly as irrelevant. But it was a relevant and feisty little newspaper, and it was unafraid to publish perspectives—at length—that were unlike its own. The mayor answered the challenge.[10]

After four consecutive weeks of front-page Bumpurs coverage, the *City Sun* moved the story inside and led with something else: "Living with the New FBI" in the December 5–11 edition displayed a cover shot of a husband and wife each holding one of their small children. Makotsi reported that Omowale Clay of Brooklyn and seven other members of a so-called New York Eight were engaged in a national campaign of "legal terror," according to federal investigators. The defendants were suspected of conspiring to commit armed robberies, like a 1981 armored truck robbery in Nyack, New York, that resulted in three police officers shot and killed in an ambush.

Prosecutors conceded that none of the defendants had committed any crimes, but under provisions of a federal law that became effective a week before the New York Eight were arraigned, the accused men and women could be charged with conspiring to commit a crime.[11]

"A Response to the Mayor" was a letter from *Village Voice* writer Jack Newfield that began as two full columns to the right of the page 18 editorial and continued on the next page. In response to Koch's lengthy letter the previous week, Newfield wrote:

> The quality of life in New York during Koch's administration has improved—for suburban residents, for credit-card tourists, and for the elite who send their kids to private schools, who can afford co-ops and condos and who can get a private room in the best hospital. But for 921,000 people living on welfare and for 40 to 50,000 homeless, it has certainly deteriorated. And it has gotten worse for all of us who depend on the subways, as I do, and who send our children to public schools, as I do.
>
> Koch is in the habit of saying that his critics just don't like his "style." But what I object to, and what causes the unequal conditions of life, are Koch's policies and budget priorities. Koch does not deliver a fair share of services, capital investments and programs in poor neighborhoods.[12]

Newfield offered the following evidence: The city unemployment rate was 14 percent for blacks and Latinos, but 7 percent for whites; since 1981, city rents had risen 25 percent, while renters' income had increased 16 percent (Koch lived in a rent-controlled apartment). Total apartments had decreased by 36,000 since 1981. The vacancy rate was 2 percent—an "emergency," according to housing law. In the subways, the crime and fire rate increased in 1984. "What disturbs me about Koch's letter," Newfield wrote, "even more than the misleading claims . . . is the underlying attitude of complacency and defensiveness."

Koch had no complaints with the equally lengthy criticism from Wayne Barrett that chronicled black lives lost to deadly force during Koch's watch. Bumpurs was the 226th black person police had killed. Barrett reminded readers that the mayor had remained silent about the grandmother's killing until a *New York Times* editorial prodded him to acknowledge it. Koch did not attend Bumpurs's funeral. And Barrett wrote that the Police Benevolent Association was the only union that treated murder investigations of their members as if they were contractual disputes.[13] The Bumpurs story was off the front page, but it was not forgotten. The front-page skybox tease for a story that began on page 5 read "Says Eviction was 'Best' Way to Help Bumpurs."

The December 12–18 cover story was "On the Line vs. Apartheid." Black city leaders were among the demonstrators arrested at the South African consulate on Park Avenue in Manhattan. The leaders included David Dinkins; Basil Paterson; Hazel Dukes, state president of the NAACP; bishop Emerson Moore of St. Charles Borromeo Catholic Church; and Melvin Lowe, president of the City University of New York student senate. They demonstrated in response to South Africa's arrest of twenty-one black labor union leaders, plus the white-minority government policy of constitutionally mandated apartheid.[14]

December 19–25 was the last edition of the year. In the skybox, Andy and Utrice announced that the staff was taking a two-week break until January 9–15, 1985. "The Battle for a Block" was the cover story. A photo of a slum tenement jumped off the page. Q. Nadir Saafir's page 4 story was about a proposed Harlem Hospital multipurpose community center to be placed on Lenox Avenue between 137th and 138th streets. The front-page tease promised "some kind—and not so kind—words for a select group of New Yorkers who somehow will touch your life in '85." The pictorial on several pages was a year-in-review and preview. The select group included Cooper (for joining the arrested anti-apartheid protesters), Joan Maynard and Agnes Conway (the Weeksville women), a black Catholic order of nuns (Harlem's handmaidens), Al Vann (laying low and loving it), Vy Higginsen (producer of "Mama I Want to Sing"), Eddie Murphy ("No laughing matter," regarding his *Beverly Hills Cop* character Axel Foley), U.S. representatives Major R. Owens and Ed Towns (Brooklyn's two most worried men), Jesse Jackson (the year's best bet), Douglas White (the new head of the state Human Rights Commission, "But does he believe in EEO?"), and Denny Farrell (chairman of the assembly banking committee and "the bankers banker").[15]

The week after the *City Sun* resumed publication after its winter break, it ran a lengthy rebuttal letter from city police commissioner Benjamin Ward. The editors gave Ward plenty of space to air his disapproval of the paper's opinion regarding the police slaying of Bumpurs, but the editors did not let up on their crusade on her behalf.[16] By midwinter, several police officers were indicted in connection with the shooting. Bumpurs family members still expressed dissatisfaction with the indictments.[17] A *City Sun* editorial referenced a *New York Times* series about police brutality and suggested an insidious problem with the officers in blue. The newspaper covered the protest by thousands of off-duty cops who opposed the indictments of their brother officers.[18] A *City Sun* editorial pondered whether that alternative show of force unnerved the mayor and police commissioner.[19]

Nine months into weekly publication, the *City Sun* was in deep financial trouble that belied the power of its crusading headline stories and fist-pounding editorials. In early March, Andy Cooper's company filed for bankruptcy protection from creditors so that the paper could continue publishing.[20] In addition, he filed a voluntary petition for reorganization of the City Sun Publishing Company. On March 25, a reorganization plan was drafted, and a month later, on April 25, a Statement of Financial Affairs was filed with the U.S. Bankruptcy Court, Eastern District, in downtown Brooklyn.[21] Publishing the *City Sun* had been a tricky financial venture from its start in June 1984. The business plan called for the paper to start in the red.[22] Second, there was the probability of an accounting oversight by Cooper and company: in shifting Trans Urban News Service assets to the *City Sun* enterprise, had Cooper forgotten to change the tax status from nonprofit to for profit?[23]

Cooper's *City Sun* expressed strong dissatisfaction with the policies of mayor Ed Koch. The mayor's second term was up at the end of 1985, and he wanted a third. Another win would place him in the league of three-term New York mayors Fiorello LaGuardia and Bob Wagner. Who would take Koch on? His disdain for black New Yorkers and their leaders was unbearable. Koch fancied himself as an equal-opportunity insulter, yet the record revealed that he preferred to kick blacks harder. Koch told Ken Auletta in 1979, "I always like to tweak people if I can, especially if I don't like them. That is something really vicious in me."[24] Koch was convinced that blacks were inherently anti-Semitic, and he was a superloyalist when it came to his Jewish heritage. It was no surprise that he was outraged after Jesse Jackson called New York City "Hymietown" in 1984. Koch repeatedly denounced the presidential candidate Jackson as a racist. So why would Koch call U.S. representative Ron Dellums of California "the Watusi from Berkeley"? Koch insisted he was not insulting the fierce apartheid opponent; he was paying a "compliment." There were other examples of Koch-speak: he regarded his assumption that all blacks were anti-Semitic as "refreshing candor." When a jury acquitted a white vigilante, Koch called the decision "Solomonic," but a jury's decision to indict a white police officer was "terrible." For Koch, black people were enemies who had to be pursued, humiliated, and destroyed.[25]

At the start of 1985, the probable mayoral challengers were Basil Paterson, a deputy mayor in the Koch administration and a former assemblyman from Harlem; Carol Bellamy, the city council president; and Herman Badillo, the former congressman from the Bronx who had made a mayoral run in 1977. The Coalition for a Just New York organized to support a viable candidate against Koch after Paterson, the leading black challenger, decided that winter against making a run. The coalition shifted its support to Badillo, the Puerto Rican.

By midwinter a surprise mayoral candidate—Herman D. (Denny) Farrell, a black assemblyman from Manhattan—entered the field. He was endorsed by a second group, the Coalition for Community Empowerment, which included state legislators, members of Congress, and Democratic Party officials who represented largely black communities in Central Brooklyn. Many politicians were members of both coalitions. For example, assemblyman Al Vann of Brooklyn, who chaired the Coalition for a Just New York, supported Badillo. Vann gave up the leadership post after Farrell gained the endorsement of the Community Empowerment coalition, which Vann also chaired. Badillo believed Farrell usurped an endorsement that was rightfully his, and furthermore the newcomer surfaced as a candidate after bitter infighting inside the Coalition for Community Empowerment. The *City Sun* editorial page expressed doubts too that Farrell was tough enough to take on Koch. Rather than unifying the coalitions against a common enemy, Farrell's candidacy sparked a verbal civil war.[26]

Not long after Cooper through his *City Sun* editorial expressed strong doubts about the credibility of a Farrell mayoral run, on March 13 Cooper used the entire left column and nearly half of the right column usually reserved for letters to praise Bertram M. Baker, eighty-seven, who died on March 8. Cooper appreciated the black political pioneer. Baker had emigrated to Brooklyn from Nevis, the Caribbean birthplace of Alexander Hamilton. He had worked as a self-employed public accountant and had founded the United Action Democratic Association to empower a bloc of West Indian homeowners.

In 1948, Baker became the first black assemblyman elected from Brooklyn, and he served for twenty-two years until 1970. The first legislation drafted in the United States to forbid housing discrimination was Baker's bill. Baker was a can-do legislator: the first black assistant prosecutors to serve in a district attorney's office were those that he pushed; the first black judges appointed to serve in Brooklyn courthouses were candidates he fielded, supported, and mentored; the first black state senator elected from Brooklyn was sponsored and backed by Baker, and as majority whip in the assembly in 1968, he was the highest-ranking black Democrat in the state.[27]

Baker was a loyal Democrat, but he did not sacrifice his black constituents to the party machinery. At times he had to part company with the organization and operate independently. Even in his leisurely pursuits, Baker was an activist. For thirty years he was secretary of the American Tennis Association, an alternative organization that was formed to allow blacks to play competitively. Baker's work helped Althea Gibson win the 1957 tennis championship at Wimbledon and set the stage for Arthur Ashe's future greatness.[28] Baker gave Brooklyn and New York state four decades of political leadership and social action. Cooper counseled current politicians to follow Baker's example and expand his work.

By the spring it became clear to political pros that Farrell's organization and campaign were in trouble. His campaign people went to numerous organizations within city assembly districts to circulate petitions for support of his candidacy. Many people rejected Farrell's candidacy. Why then did Farrell seek the endorsement despite so much opposition at the ground level? He did not offer a satisfactory answer.[29]

Farrell entered the mayoral campaign naked, said an astute observer, and only had limited time to dress up his campaign. Farrell's bid to be a credible challenger to Koch was strained. By June, Brooklyn members of the coalition that endorsed Farrell withdrew their support. They made their decision at a closed-door meeting.

While most coalition members denied to speak to the *City Sun* for attribution, the Rev. Herbert Daughtry of House of the Lord Church in Brooklyn remained loyal to Farrell and said the coalition members had an obligation to pledge their support to the candidate they had originally endorsed. Daughtry's chief aide Charles Barron said this of the abandonment: "It fits the pattern of attacking the Farrell candidacy without helping it become viable. When they didn't get their way [in the Coalition for a Just New York vote] they didn't just pick up their marbles and run; they picked up their marbles and started throwing them at the campaign, which is an unprincipled thing to do."[30]

Farrell's candidacy burst into flames. Beyond its own pages, the *City Sun* took to the airwaves to explain what happened. Cooper and Leid appeared on Pacifica station WBAI-FM for an "In Search of the City" program called "The Farrell Candidacy . . . How Did It Really Happen?"[31] Meanwhile the incumbent Koch cruised. In July, he announced that he would seek a third term and promised to campaign only for a few weeks and so as not to burden voters.[32]

Carol Bellamy emerged as the last best challenge to Koch now that Farrell's quest appeared hopeless and Badillo and Paterson were out of the race. The *City Sun* posed questions to Bellamy. Black members of the city Transit Police pressed their five-year- old case that they were overtly discriminated against in non-job-related, biased tests, denials of promotions, repeated high-risk assignments, physical and psychological intimidation, on-the-job harassment, surveillance, unlawful suspensions, demerits, demotion, dismissal, and even alleged murder setups. The white supervisors inside the Transit Police, said past and present members of the Guardians (a black police association), engaged in a campaign of selective racially motivated triage.[33]

Damning evidence surfaced in the transit cops' federal complaint against the Metropolitan Transit Authority. In 1980, when Bellamy was a board member of the MTA, she brushed aside the Guardians' pleas to make the Transit Police adhere to civil rights laws and equal employment guidelines. The City Council president said she could not get involved; she could not exercise her authority as an appointed MTA member to insist on an investigation.[34] That was then. But because the black cops aired their plight in public at a nonjury trial in federal court in Brooklyn, what did she have to say as a mayoral candidate? Bellamy resisted the *City Sun*'s prodding and said as little as possible. She enjoyed prominent black political support for her mayoral candidacy—congressman Major R. Owens, state senator Velmanette Montgomery, and assemblywoman Cynthia Jenkins—but could they serve as adequate cover to shield Bellamy from these questions? Transit Police were under investigation for the mysterious death of Michael Stewart. The *City Sun* reminded readers that the Transit Police behaved like a semi-autonomous paramilitary force, accountable practically to no one.[35]

Farrell's mayoral candidacy was so inept that his campaign failed to gather the minimum ten thousand required signatures needed to place his name on the ballot.[36] Yet Farrell insisted he had a viable campaign and stayed in the race. Before the Democratic primary, an unidentified poll published by the *City Sun* projected that Koch would win with 54 percent of the vote and Farrell and Bellamy would split the remaining 46 percent. The poll also predicted low black voter turnout—about 30 percent—because the challengers did not elicit enthusiasm and confidence. The weak mayoral challengers to Koch could be a drag on other citywide races and meaningful borough races like president and district attorney.

On primary day, Farrell attracted 13 percent of citywide votes. He beat Koch 41–37 percent in predominantly black election districts, but Farrell's race for mayor was an unqualified disaster.[37] Koch won 64 percent of the vote and became the presumptive third-term mayor.

Just before the election, Cooper's editorial page declined to endorse any of the mayoral candidates. Koch's November victory by a 3:1 voter ratio over Republican Diane McGrath and Bellamy, who continued as a third-party candidate, was a mere formality.[38] Koch picked up significant support from a new stream of minority voters, Hispanics. Based on the overwhelming vote, Koch had a mandate to be more outrageous and dismissive toward black New Yorkers. Yet soon polarizing events would make even Koch supporters weary of his antics, and corruption by powerful surrogates would soon dog the mayor.

There were two bright spots in a dismal election. Former city clerk David Dinkins was elected Manhattan borough president. That meant a black person now joined the powerful Board of Estimate that included the mayor, borough presidents, comptroller, and city council president. The board became all male because Bellamy was no longer city council president. Andrew Stein, a Manhattan city councilman, replaced her.

On September 15, 1983, Michael Stewart, a graffiti artist, was arrested for allegedly defacing a subway station at Fourteenth Street and First Avenue. Transit Police brought the young black man to the hospital. He was in a comatose state and died a dozen days later. The Stewart family charged that police initially caused his death. Stewart had tried to run from police, but he was caught, handcuffed, and hogtied with wire gauze.[39] Authorities said the twenty-five-year-old man was drunk and had injured himself. For the next two years, the case was fraught with contradictions and allegations of misconduct by Transit Authority police, the office of the district attorney, and the medical examiner. In 1985 when Stewart's case went to trial, the *City Sun* stayed on the case week by week through the late summer and fall.

Louis Clayton Jones, one of the Stewart lawyers, said a Manhattan assistant district attorney was sabotaging the case. At the time, six Transit Police officers were on trial. The officers faced felony charges—criminally negligent homicide for three officers, and assault and perjury for the others—yet none of them was indicted or specifically charged with Stewart's death.[40] So, asked the *City Sun*, "Who killed Michael Stewart?" in a front-page editorial that jumped to the usual editorial position on page 18.

Cooper criticized assistant district attorney John W. Fried for a predictable, unimaginative, and ill-advised prosecution that would lead to the officers' acquittal. The editorial also criticized the behavior of chief medical examiner Elliot Gross. His theory about what killed Stewart kept changing. First he announced that the young man had died of cardiac arrest and there was no evidence of beating. Two months later, Gross revised the cause of death to a spinal cord injury that resulted in a heart attack (other experts said that the spinal cord was injured because of strangulation). A few months later, Gross said the evidence suggested Stewart's injuries were the result of a beating.[41] The state health department announced that it intended to bring medical misconduct charges against Gross in nine cases. About half those cases involved civilians' deaths while in police custody.[42]

Other medical experts who contradicted Gross's conclusions said that Stewart's autopsy revealed that hemorrhages in the man's eyes indicated he was strangled. Inexplicably, Gross removed Stewart's eyeballs and placed them in a formalin solution that bleached out evidence of the hemorrhages.[43]

Cooper's editorial page and the newspaper reporting staff had another reason to suspect that the fix was in at the Stewart trial. The defense attorneys for the Transit Police declined to call any witnesses. So why did the Manhattan district attorney grant immunity from prosecution to five Transit Authority cops who were also at the scene with the six officers on trial? Neither the prosecution nor the defense called any of those protected officers to testify.

In late November, after a five-and-one-half-month trial, a jury acquitted all six Transit Authority police officers of all charges in connection with Stewart's death. In an editorial, Cooper wrote that the verdict did not surprise his newspaper, yet the court decision did not mean that the case was over: "We call on all decent-minded citizens to adopt the struggle for justice in the Michael Stewart case as a personal commitment to our collective well-being and liberation. We urge all people of good conscience to protest by mouth, word and deed the obvious denial of justice here."[44]

The following week, an editorial said that the office of the Manhattan district attorney was incapable of acting in the interest of (black) people; therefore the *City Sun* filed petitions with Governor Cuomo and state attorney general Robert Abrams to investigate the office in connection with the Stewart case.[45]

Many New Yorkers were upset about what they viewed as the authorities' heavy-handed and dismissive treatment of the Michael Stewart case. At least two churches in Brooklyn assembled crowds of people who had often clashed before over political and personal differences. This time the factions were united in seeking justice after the Stewart verdict.[46]

Jocelyn and Andy Cooper, wedding photo, 1949. Courtesy of Jocelyn C. Cooper.

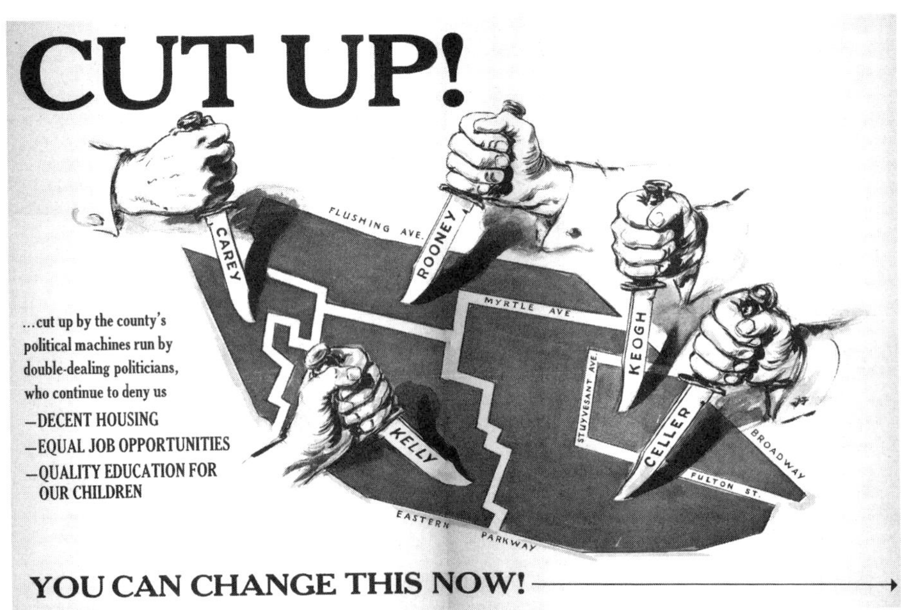

Cut up! 11" x 17" image of gerrymandered Bedford-Stuyvesant. Courtesy of Paul Kerrigan.

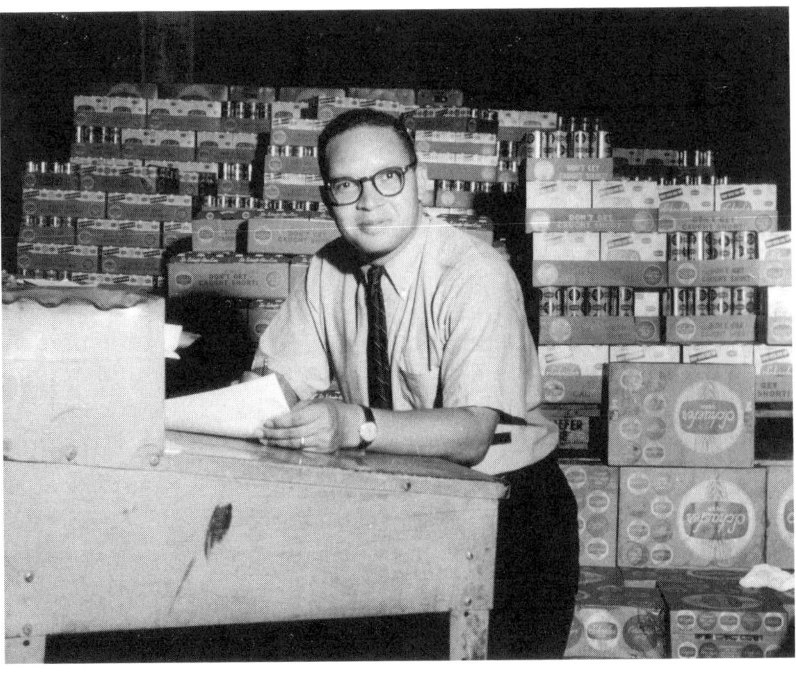
Andy Cooper at the Schaefer brewery, 1950s.

Jocelyn and Andy Cooper with Daphne Shepard, Brooklyn editor of the *New York Amsterdam News*, early 1960s. Photo by Cecil Layne.

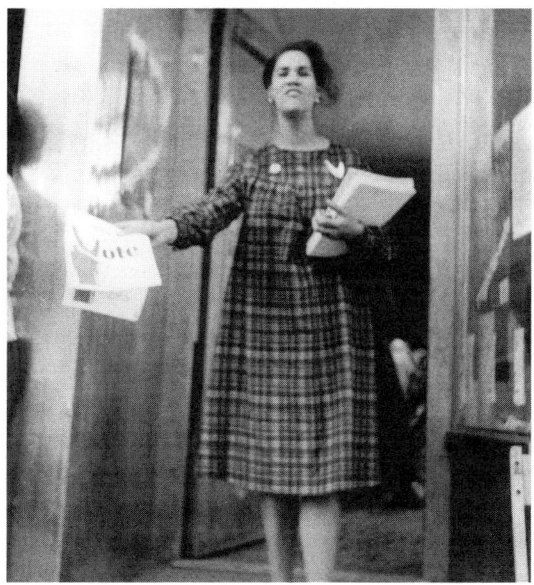

Jocelyn Cooper, pregnant, working at the voter registration office, 1964. Courtesy of Jocelyn C. Cooper.

Andy Cooper, mayor-elect John Lindsay, and Pat Carter, 1965. Courtesy of Jocelyn C. Cooper.

WHILE THE POLITICIANS TALK

ANDY COOPER FIGHTS FOR YOU!

BROOKLYN Amsterdam News EDITION

QUEENS

LONG ISLAND

SATURDAY, JUNE 25, 1966—B

Files Suit Against Rocky, Boro Leaders

ANDREW W. COOPER

Would Stop Elections

Andrew W. Cooper of 619 Decatur Street, Brooklyn, announced Thursday that he had filed suit in the Brooklyn Federal Court together with two other residents of Bedford-Stuyvesant against Governor Rockefeller, Stanley Steingut, the Democratic leader of Brooklyn, Robert Crews, Republican leader of Brooklyn, and against all of the incumbent Brooklyn congressmen.

The purpose of his suit he said is to upset the existing Brooklyn Congressional District lines.

Cooper, who is presently a candidate for Delegate to the State Constitutional Convention, said that his suit also seeks an injunction to restrain the November congressional election unless reapportionment takes place at once.

The other plaintiffs beside Cooper, are Mrs. Jaon Bacchus of 762 Halsey Street and Paul Kerrigan of 195 Willoughby Avenue.

Mrs. Bacchus, is an artist. She and Cooper are Democrats. Kerrigan, a member of the Board of Trustees of the Brooklyn Public Library, is a Republican.

All of the plaintiffs live in Bedford-Stuyvesant, where most of Brooklyn's Negroes and Puerto Ricans are concentrated. Milton H. Friedman of 36 West 44th Street, New York is their lawyer.

Cooper, spokesman for the plaintiffs, said: "Brooklyn - Stuyvesant is the biggest and most populous compact community in Brooklyn. Some 300,000 Negroes live there. But because of deliberate gerrymandering, the county is divided into seven serpentine, twisted congressional districts, and five of them snake into Bedford - Stuyvesant, thus

(Continued on Page 55)

(Continued from Page 29)

fragmenting the Negro vote so that it is helpless to elect or defeat any congressional candidate.

"This is the result of a cozy collaboration between the Democratic and Republican machines. It is time for the Federal Court to put an end to racially discriminatory districting."

Cooper presented figures from the 1960 census to support his thesis. He said that Bedford - Stuyvesant had a total population equal to that of the average congressional district — 400,000 —and that 75 per cent of the community was comprised of Negroes and Puerto Ricans. He added:

"But it is split up so that the Bedford - Stuyvesant population forms less than 40 per cent of Cellar's district; 13 per cent of Keogh's; 23 per cent of Mrs. Kelly's; 16 per cent of Rooney's; and 9 per cent of Carey's. Celler's district is beefed up with 70,000 Rockaway residents in Queens in order to be sure to keep the Bedford - Stuyvesant people in a minority.

"The tragedy is that no Brooklyn congressman has any need to consider the wishes of the people of Bedford - Stuyvesant, who are doomed to be an ineffectual minority so long as present apportionment continues. Such racially biased districts should have no place in American political life."

Cooper pointed out that:

"It is not only the Negro and Puerto Rican people who are disfranchised by the ridiculous gerrymandering policy followed in Brooklyn. Cellar's district, eleven miles long and as little as one mile in width, embraces people of divergent classes, interests, backgrounds, traditions and needs.

"It winds around and cuts in across various assembly districts and neighborhoods. It is governed by neither natural lines nor political lines. It is designed for one purpose: to Keep Celler in office and to inhibit organization of the electorate around a rival candidate.

The same may be said of Keogh's district which is ten miles long and as little as a mile wide. Mrs. Kelly's district is indescribable in terms of length or width, as its 75 separate boundary lines reach out in all direcions to cut the borough into numerous slices.

"Rooney's district is ten miles long and as little as 300 yards wide at its narrowest point. Nobody lives in the waterfront area of its narrowest width, so that Rooney really has two separate districts, from Fort Hamilton on the bay at the southern tip of Brooklyn to Newtown Creek in the north. Carey's district is almost nine miles long, and its width is as little as one-quarter of a mile.

"These are not truly congeessional districts. They disfranchise all voters including white voters. No one is in a position to gather his neighbors to discuss an approach to federal legislative problems, for his neighbors are a miniscule part of the district and they do not share the interests of other, distant communities," he said.

16 THE NEW YORK COURIER June 25, 1966

Protest Governor's Insult To Bedford-Stuyvesant

Andrew W. Cooper, an active leader in Bedford-Stuyvesant, and a candidate for the Constitutional Convention in the June 28th primaries, led pickets around the office of Governor Rockefeller, 22 West 55 Street for two hours, before winning a concession from Jackie Robinson, the Governor's special assistant, to meet and discuss the demands of the pickets.

According to Mr. Cooper, the pickets were demanding "a fiar share" of the huge development at the Battery, announced by the Governor During the announcement the Governor reportedly promised $138 million for low and middle income housing to be used for the huge development.

After the announcement Mr. Cooper and his running mate Warren Bunn, wrote the Governor seeking some of the funds for use in Bedford-Stuyvesant.

The Governor in turn answered their request stating that nothing but "low income housing was required" in Bedford-Stuyvesant.

The New York Times.

FRIDAY, JUNE 24, 1966.

Bedford-Stuyvesant Is Called a Victim Of Gerrymandering

Minority groups in the Bedford-Stuyvesant section of Brooklyn have been made politically impotent through gerrymandering, it was charged yesterday in a suit filed in United States District Court in Brooklyn.

The complaint, filed by Andrew W. Cooper, an insurgent Democratic candidate for delegate to the state constitutional convention, urges the court to direct the reapportionment of Brooklyn's Congressional Districts. It asks that meanwhile the political parties be restrained from "conducting an election" to the House of Representatives.

Bedford-Stuyvesant, described by Mr. Cooper as the home of 370,000 Negroes, has been partitioned among five Congressional Districts in "so tortuous, artificial and labyrinthine a manner" that the lines are "irrational and unrelated to any proper purpose," the complaint says.

As a result, it is contended, the Negro and Pueorto Rican residents are frustrated in their "natural desire to present a generally common and unitary point of view with respect to political issues." All seven of Brooklyn's Representatives are elected from predominantly white districts, according to the complaint.

"The economic and social needs of the people [in Bedford-Stuyvesant] need not be taken into account for political purposes by any member elected to the House of Representatives from Kings County or by any candidate for such office," the suit charges.

Discrimination against these minority groups was said to have been the sole purpose of the Legislature in its recent redrawing of district lines. Named in the complaint as defendants are Governor Rockefeller; Stanley Steingut, Democratic leader of Brooklyn; John R. Crews, the Republican leader, and all incumbent Representatives from the borough.

A three-judge Federal court is asked to find that the existing apportionment is unconstitutional and discriminatory and that representatives chosen under it were elected illegally.

ANDREW W.

COOPER

FOR STATE SENATOR

Citizens Committee
for the Election of
THOMPSON - COOPER
786 Nostrand Avenue
Telephone 467-7975

msterdam *News* front page and other headlines, designed as a political advertisement, 1966.

Andy Cooper, recipient of the JFK Award, kisses mother Irma Robinson, mid-1970s. Courtesy of Jocelyn C. Cooper.

Morris McKoy, Utrice C. Leid, and Andy Cooper, Trans Urban News Service, 1977. Photo by Wayne Dawkins.

Andy Cooper at his desk, Trans Urban News Service, 1977. Photo by Wayne Dawkins.

Andy Cooper and Thomas Russell Jones, Unity Democrats. Courtesy of the Cooper family and David R. Jones.

Jocelyn and journalist of the year Andy Cooper at NABJ-Miami, 1987. Photo by Durrell Hall Jr.

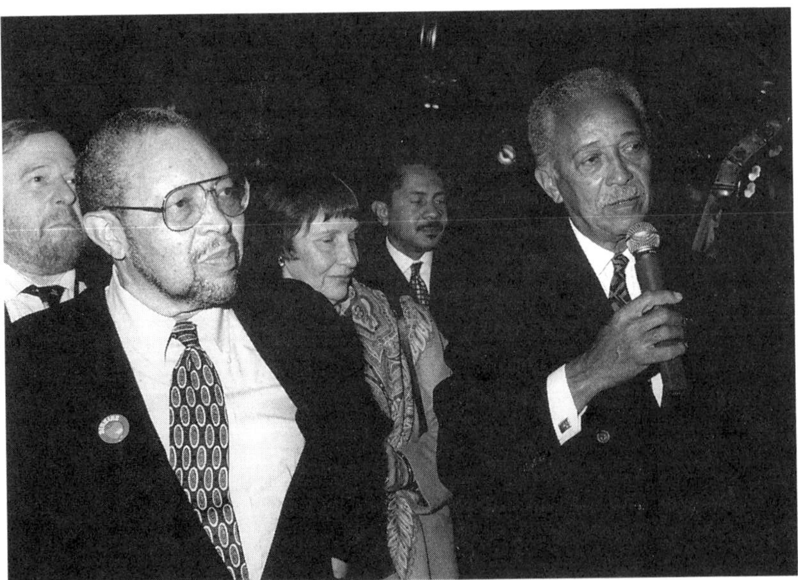

Andy Cooper and mayor-elect David N. Dinkins, November 1989. Courtesy of the Cooper family.

Adversaries Cooper and Mayor Koch in a playful moment. Courtesy of Jocelyn C. Cooper.

Jocelyn and Andy Cooper, August 2000. Photo by Ron West. Courtesy of Jocelyn A. Cooper.

Jocelyn A. Cooper with father Andy. Courtesy of Jocelyn A. Cooper.

12. NINETEEN EIGHTY-SIX

The Rev. Dr. Martin Luther King Jr. called Hospital and Health Care Workers Local 1199 "his favorite union." And why not? The predominantly black and Hispanic union of bedpan orderlies, sanitation workers, and others symbolized the underdogs. In the 1960s and 1970s, the union's leaders scored a string of victories for worker dignity. The leadership was mostly white, Jewish, and socialist. By the 1980s, Leon Davis and other white leaders like Moe Foner realized it was time to pass the power to a black leader. In 1982 they supported Doris Turner, a behind-the-scenes worker.[1] The two placed Turner on virtually every committee, arranged awards for her, and scheduled her as the speaker at key events. Turner zoomed to the presidency even as the union leadership knew she was unqualified. She was a poor administrator and had no understanding of big issues and no apparent interest in learning about the local's big-picture challenges.

Since Turner was handed so much power, she carefully built a political machine—based on loyalty, not competence—to insulate herself.[2] The old leaders understood that by not confronting Turner about her weaknesses and excesses, they revealed their paternalism and condescension. It was only a matter of time for the Turner mess to rot, then explode.

The *City Sun* initially called attention to rumblings inside the union with a cover story at the start of 1985.[3] During 1984 the local was hurt by a forty-seven-day hospital strike. In two years, ten district vice presidents and twelve of fourteen guild organizers left 1199. Those twenty-two people were either purged by Turner, said observers, or deserted her administration, which was Turner's view. In July the New York union detached itself from the national union.[4]

High-profile *City Sun* coverage resumed a year later in February 1986. Turner was accused of rigging her own election and embezzling union funds. Managing editor Utrice Leid reported and wrote most of the 1199 stories. At a particularly combative news conference, when Leid asked a question, Turner responded, "Who are you?" When Leid said she was from the *City Sun*, Turner declared, "I don't talk to you."[5]

By June, the majority of Local 1199 members had rejected Turner's autocratic and secretive leadership style. They booted her out. A "Save Our

Union" faction nominated a black woman named Georgiana Johnson, and she won. The new administration promised a more democratically run union.[6]

The *City Sun* resumed publishing January 8 after a two-week winter holiday break. The newspaper's editors de-emphasized reports about Mayor Koch and invested more of their time that winter to covering local activists' involvement in Haiti and South Africa. Cooper and Leid made these editorial choices because Koch appeared invincible. He had vanquished two mayoral challengers in the previous November and won more than 75 percent of the votes. By picking up additional Puerto Rican voter support, Koch could ignore and further humiliate black citizens. Based on the opening editions of 1986, the *City Sun* chose to engage Koch a little less.

Inauguration Day, January 1, should have been a happy time for Koch, as he was to be sworn in for his third four-year term. Koch soon learned that his carefully crafted political empire would begin to crumble. Donald Manes, borough president of Queens, Democratic county leader, and self-described "King of Queens," reported that he had been injured with a knife during a kidnapping. Manes said that while he was driving on Union Turnpike in Queens, two men who had been hiding in the back of his car attacked him. After an investigation, chief of detectives Richard Nicastro went on live television and announced that the police did not believe the borough president's story. The cops had lost patience with the borough president. The authorities went public after five days of stonewalling by the family and Manes's aides. Manes was moved from one hospital to another without notifying the police. Manes soon admitted to news reporters that his kidnapping story was a hoax and the knife wound—a slashed wrist—was self-inflicted.

Why did Manes try to kill himself? He did not say.[7] After a three-week hospital stay, he returned home in late January to recuperate. On Super Bowl Sunday, near the end of that month, Koch went on TV and told reporter Gabe Pressman that Manes was a crook.

This was a major blow because Manes was one of Koch's most trusted associates. Manes was executor of Koch's estate, and as king of two million inhabitants in Queens, he also was Koch's handpicked successor as mayor.[8] On February 11, Manes resigned as borough president and county leader.[9] His associates were indicted for racketeering and taking bribes in parking meter and cable TV contracts.[10]

There was no suggestion that Koch was involved in the corruption; if anything, he appeared to be a victim of it and was doing all he could to wash off the stench. The mayor was guilty of being seduced by power. In aligning himself with powerful borough leaders to run the city, he overlooked their roguish behavior. In the first three months of 1986, a torrent of corruption charges sent city government into a tailspin. The chaos got the *City Sun* interested in the Koch administration again. "The fish always stinks from the head," declared an editorial on March 12, accompanied by a cartoon of Koch shaving in front of a mirror with Donald Manes as the reflection. "I have never been aware of ANY wrongdoing in MY administration," read the caption.[11]

On the night of March 13, Manes fatally stabbed himself in the heart with a kitchen knife at his home. Just before his death, his wife Marlene was trying to arrange psychiatric treatment, and she asked a daughter to keep an eye on her father because he was behaving oddly.[12] After his failed suicide attempt in January, Manes succeeded in killing himself two months later.

As indictments of associates piled up before spring, the *City Sun* in a March 26 editorial declared, "Where there's smoke, there's Don [Manes]."[13] The editors also said they would not shrink from speaking ill of the dead. Instead of grieving for Manes, they wrote, grieve for his black Queens constituents, those in South Jamaica who watched the neighborhood run into the ground because of neglect; middle-class blacks in St. Albans who paid disproportionally more in property taxes than white neighbors in Jamaica Estates, and children in Hollis who attended schools as segregated as those in the mid-1950s American South.[14]

Joseph P. Addabbo was elected to Congress in 1960. He represented the Sixth Congressional District, a predominantly Italian, Irish, and German American district in southwestern Queens. Before the 1980 census, the district had a substantial African American minority that grew to 35 percent. After 1980, when the boundaries were redrawn, Addabbo's once-safe white ethnic district became 65 percent black as the geographic lines shifted into Jamaica. Some of his former constituents went to congresswoman Geraldine Ferraro's Queens district, and the rest were shifted to James Scheuer's neighboring Queens district.[15]

Because of the change in demographics, Addabbo was challenged by Simeon Golar, a black man who happened to be housing commissioner during the combative low-income housing dispute in Forest Hills during the Lindsay years. At the time of the congressional campaign, Golar was a real estate developer. He gave Addabbo his first political scare during the 1982 primary, but lost. Golar challenged Addabbo again in 1984, this time with the backing of presidential candidate Jesse Jackson, who swept the district. But the incumbent won again, that time handily with two-thirds of the vote.[16] In Washington, Addabbo was chairman of the appropriations committee, and he battled with President Reagan over increases in military spending. Reagan got his way most of the time, but the congressman scored a few victories; he blocked spending for the MX and Pershing missile programs.

In March 1986, days before his sixty-first birthday, Addabbo lapsed into a coma. It was no surprise that the powerful congressman from Queens became gravely ill; he had been battling bladder cancer for six years. The timing of Addabbo's decline delivered added stress to constituents. It occurred at the time another powerful Queens figure, Manes, killed himself. A month later on April 10, Addabbo died.[17]

Someone needed to serve the final eight months of Addabbo's term. Several African American candidates and a few whites expressed their interest in the seat. Had Manes been alive, his choice would be Archie Spigner, a city councilman and black clubhouse loyalist. But with Manes gone, the Rev. Floyd Flake of Allen AME Church in St. Albans made an aggressive bid.

Flake believed he was entitled. A decade ago, he had assumed leadership of a 1,400-member congregation with a $250,000 annual budget. Allen AME expanded its ministry to community development and, in cooperation with city agencies, built senior citizen housing and senior center, a health center, and a school. In a decade, Allen AME grew to five thousand members, and its yearly budget was $12 million. Flake got a taste of politics as a Jackson delegate to the 1984 Democratic National Convention. In spring 1986, a group of ministers urged him to run for Addabbo's vacated seat.[18] By June, five candidates had lined up: state senator Andrew Jenkins, assemblyman Alton Waldron Jr., assemblywoman Gerdi Lipshutz, and Queens district attorney John Santucci. The *City Sun* endorsed Waldron, a former police officer who had contributed an essay to the special report on Eleanor Bumpurs late in 1984. Waldron was also the pick of the Queens Democratic organization, which unsuccessfully tried to knock Flake off the ballot.[19]

A struggle ensued to choose a replacement for the deceased U.S. representative Addabbo in the Sixth Congressional District that served Queens. The Rev. Floyd Flake wanted the seat, but Democratic organization people blocked him. There were attempts to prevent him from getting on the ballot.[20] In a five-candidate battle, Flake edged out Waldron by 192 votes. However, after absentee ballots were counted—which did not include Flake's name—Waldron won by a 278-vote margin, 12,654 to 12,376. Flake used technical maneuvers to prevent the seating of the winner.

"Flake continues to frustrate the process. Why engage in this ill-meaning exercise?" chided the *City Sun* in an editorial.[21] Flake stepped back, and Alton Waldron Jr., who had electoral experience as an assemblyman, was appointed to the vacant congressional seat for a month that summer. Flake did not go away. He contested Waldron in the September primary and won. Waldron said that Flake's raw power—his church-based support—gave the minister the edge in the election.[22] Did Waldron suggest that the Democrats did not work enthusiastically for him?

Back in Brooklyn, Roy Innis of the once-venerable CORE announced he was challenging Major R. Owens in the Twelfth Congressional District.[23] A photo showed Innis at a National Rifle Association conference. The challenger called the incumbent a "leftist radical" for supporting the African National Congress's anti-apartheid struggle. Owens said he was on the side of a truly democratic South Africa, so there was no need to shun Innis's label.[24]

Waverly Yates, an Innis adversary at CORE who tried unsuccessfully to have the leader removed, told the *City Sun* that Innis had ordered someone to kill him. Innis refused to answer any questions about his past from any media.[25] Then Innis did not show up for a head-to-head debate with Owens. By September, the Democratic primary was settled: Owens trounced Innis by a 3–1 margin.[26]

In state politics, a Brooklyn assemblyman made peace with the Kings County Democratic organization to save his seat.[27] What happened: the Brooklyn Democratic machine used technicalities to knock black incumbents Roger Green and Al Vann off the ballot. Green appealed to borough president Howard Golden for peace and the restoration of his name. Vann remained silent.[28] At a fifth annual black political conference, speaker of the legislature Arthur O. Eve said it was time for blacks to help themselves. Roger Green, the Brooklyn assemblyman, was in his first year as chairman of the Black and Puerto Rican legislative caucus. That year Eve held hearings around the state to call attention to minority student dropout rates. Eve's initiative resulted in the commission of a report, "Dropping Out of School in New York State: The Invisible People of Color," prepared by the African American Institute. It marked the first time educators of color and community leaders came together to offer analysis and solutions to the dropout crisis.[29]

Arthur Eve, a two-decade veteran of the state legislature, announced his interest in running for speaker because the powerful incumbent Stanley Fink was retiring. The upstate assemblyman had been the longtime head of the Black and Puerto Rican Caucus, so it was mystifying that the coalition showed no unity. Only three of two dozen caucus members stepped forward to support Eve. A united caucus provided half of the votes Eve needed to win the political post, but he came up way short.[30] Melvin Miller replaced Fink as speaker.

Another political indignity surfaced with felon Stanley Friedman. The Bronx borough president was allowed to name his successor to a party leadership post. Friedman passed over A. O. Evers, a black official who expressed interest. Black representatives did not record any opposition.[31]

Throughout 1986, the *City Sun* kept its readers focused on apartheid in South Africa and the regional war against the white minority regime by neighboring black states. Nelson Mandela was spending his twenty-third year at Robben Island prison. South Africa's government made it illegal to show the image of the African National Congress leader, so U.S. supporters had to recycle a 1963 image of the freedom fighter.[32] The U.S. Senate imposed economic sanctions on South Africa in response to the government's brutal and lethal treatment of the black majority. President Reagan vetoed the bill from Congress, but a two-thirds U.S. Senate majority overrode Reagan, and sanctions became law. In an editorial, the *City Sun* said the Senate still had not punished South Africa enough.[33]

City Sun coverage worked two ways. First, it published dispatches from the Inter Press Service (IPS) in a weekly Africa section of the newspaper. Second, Cooper's editorials also hammered away at the regime, and reporters covered the demonstrations of New York–based activists. The paper showed readers that the struggle in southern Africa was regional. Zimbabwe, freed from apartheid since 1980 when it shed its former name, Rhodesia, was a hostile neighbor.[34]

Southwest Africa, South Africa's colony, was mineral rich and bountiful with fish in deepwater Walvis Bay. Guerrillas fought South African soldiers to create an independent nation that the revolutionaries called Namibia. In September, the *City Sun* published an editorial of support and a page-width editorial cartoon about mining.[35]

In October, when Mozambique's president Samora Machel died in an airplane crash, the *City Sun* devoted its entire editorial space to the story and lamented the loss of the front-line state leader. Machel's death was suspicious, and skeptics said so.[36]

In November, the *City Sun* profiled Mangosuthu Buthelezi, Zulu leader and rival to Mandela and the ANC. He was a benign critic of apartheid.[37] A month later the *City Sun* reported that CORE leader Roy Innis had made a secret trip to South Africa.[38]

For readers who counted on continuing, in-depth coverage of South Africa and its neighbors, New Yorkers had two choices: the *New York Times* or the *City Sun*. The first choice was assumed. The *Times* maintained foreign bureaus and devoted abundant resources to cover the story. The *City Sun,* bankrupt for part of 1986, covered the same conflict with about as much ink, not to mention more passion and attitude.[39]

On October 10, the City Sun Publishing Co. received notice of the time for filing acceptances or rejection of its bankruptcy plan. Throughout 1986 the *City Sun* continued its scrutiny of criminal justice and police conduct on several fronts.

Phil Makotsi was in court to report on the sentencing of the New York Eight, black men and women who were suspected of conspiring to commit armed robberies similar to the spectacular 1981 Brinks armored car attack in Rockland County, New York.[40] On April 9, the paper got an exclusive interview with Brinks armored car mastermind Mutulu Shakur, who stated his own case.[41]

Edmund Perry, seventeen, a Harlem boy who had just graduated from private school and was bound for Stanford University, was shot to death in June 1985 by an off-duty police officer. Edmund's brother Jonah, nineteen, witnessed the slaying and was charged with trying to rob the police officer to get money to attend a movie. Neighbors were skeptical that the Cornell University student had committed such a crime. The following winter, a court dropped the robbery charges for lack of evidence. Perry's lawyer, Alton Maddox, said that the prosecution had tried to frame the older brother to prevent murder charges against Lee Van Houten, twenty-five, a white cop with an unblemished record.

Nevertheless, said Maddox, "The fact that you have a badge and a gun does not allow you to do everything under the sun, and somebody had better send that message to the New York Police Department."[42] Jonah Perry resumed his studies at Cornell. His mother Veronica vowed that someone must pay for the death of her son.

On April 30 the *City Sun* front page was dominated by a caricature of a police officer's arm holding a gun amid black men in various poses. The question "Who's next?" led to an editorial inside that bellowed, "Black life is not cheap! Enough is enough! Derrick Williams, twenty, had been shot "accidentally," the editorial explained. Nearly 250 people—mostly black and Latino—had lost their lives to New York's finest since Koch became mayor in 1978.[43] Among them was Michael Stewart, who died in the custody of the Transit Police. Police were acquitted of criminal charges, and the Stewart family's push for a federal investigation fizzled.[44] Newspaper reporting also continued to press for justice for Eleanor Bumpurs. The police officer who had shot Bumpurs to death was acquitted.

In editorials the *City Sun* strongly suggested that the tart-tongued Koch could not control the city's police force. In addition to words, a cartoon depicted a scolding police officer lecturing Police Commissioner Ward, Mayor Koch, and Phil Caruso, head of the Patrolmen's Benevolent Association, above the question "Who's in charge here?" Cooper's editorials accused the police of intimidating the Bronx and Kings County district attorneys.[45] The newspaper pointed to a scandal inside the Seventy-seventh Precinct in central Brooklyn as evidence of an out-of-control force.[46] The police union maintained a different perspective. Its leaders emphatically resisted calls for a civilian review board that could hear complaints.[47]

Nineteen eighty-six was a year that put everyone to the test.[48] The deaths within a week of two politicians in Queens substantially rearranged New York's political landscape. Queens elected its first black congressman. The suicide of Donald Manes exposed the rotting hulk of the once-invincible Koch juggernaut.

College students and organized labor kept up the pressure on universities and other institutions to divest themselves of billions of dollars of holdings in South Africa until its white minority regime ended apartheid. In Haiti, "Baby Doc" Duvalier was swept into foreign exile, but were Haitian expatriates in New York ready to lead? Through a handful of high-profile cases, the *City Sun* continued to raise allegations of police and prosecutorial misconduct. As the newspaper's staff tried to wind down for the traditional end-of-the-year, two-week holiday break when the *City Sun* did not publish, a new conflict was about to draw them back into battle.

13. HOWARD BEACH

On Saturday, December 20, 1986, three days after the *City Sun* published its final edition of the year and Andy Cooper and his staff began a two-week holiday break, Michael Griffith, Cedric Sandiford, and Timothy Grimes walked along a street in Howard Beach, Queens. Howard Beach is located at the Brooklyn border and fronts on Jamaica Bay. On the Brooklyn side, the community was East New York, a predominantly black neighborhood that had comprised mostly Italian and Irish three decades before, as depicted in the movie *Goodfellas* (1990). Many of those real-life residents of East New York slipped across the border to Howard Beach, a white middle- to working-class enclave.[1]

Queens rarely came up in most New Yorkers' conversations, and it was rarer to imagine that three black men would walk through such a neighborhood late at night. Yet Griffith, 23, Sandiford, 36, and Grimes, 20, did walk several miles through Howard Beach. Their travels began Friday night, December 19, from Griffith's home on Pacific Street in Bedford-Stuyvesant. Curtis Sylvester, Griffith's cousin, was the owner and driver of a blue 1976 Buick. The foursome drove to St. Albans in southern Queens so that Grimes could visit a woman.[2] During the return trip to Brooklyn, the travelers, who were driving west on the Southern Parkway, became confused. They wanted to get off at the Rockaway Parkway exit in Brooklyn, but instead they exited at the sign that said "Rockaways," the barrier islands in Queens five miles south. So they traveled on the Cross Bay Parkway.

At about 10:30 p.m., the men entered Howard Beach and crossed the North Channel Bridge. The car broke down a quarter mile before the town of Broad Channel, located on an island in Jamaica Bay. Griffith, Sandiford, Grimes, and Sylvester were inside Gateway National Park wildlife refuge, an area patrolled by U.S. Park Police. Griffith and Grimes got out of the car and walked one and a half miles to a Tri-Borough Bridge and Tunnel Authority tollbooth and asked a worker for water for the disabled car. One of the men filled an antifreeze container, and they left.[3]

Adding water to the radiator did not start the car. A park police officer stopped by and promised to arrange for a tow. The four men waited until after 11 p.m. and shivered as the temperatures dropped into the thirties.

Three of them decided they had to move. Sylvester, twenty, a college student in Florida, said, "I never leave my car," and stayed behind, curled up in the backseat. Minutes before midnight, Griffith, Sandiford, and Grimes walked north in the southbound lane of Cross Bay Boulevard. They reached the southern foot of the North Channel Bridge at Howard Beach. At a traffic light, the men spotted two girls in a car and asked for a lift. The men were refused, and insults were exchanged.[4]

Griffith, Sandiford, and Grimes continued walking and were two and a half miles away from Sylvester's blue Buick. They reached an area of all-night gas stations and late-night eateries. At one of the gas stations, the men asked for a tow and was told none was available. They also asked for directions to the subway and were instructed to walk north on Cross Bay to the A train stop in Ozone Park. As the trio passed a restaurant, a black man cautioned them about lingering in the predominantly white neighborhood. At Cross Bay and 157th Street, a car with four white youths, three males and a female, approached. The passengers shouted racial epithets, and the three men shouted back. Jon L. Lester, one of the passengers, said, "Let me out of here, let me at them," but his friends restrained him. The carload of people was returning to a birthday party, where they dropped off the girl.[5]

Griffith, Sandiford, and Grimes stopped in the New Park Pizzeria at the corner and asked to use a phone. They were told no phone service was available. So the three men ordered pizza and sat down to eat. The carload of white male teenagers they had encountered earlier drove by the shop and saw the black men through the window. When they arrived at the party, Lester said, "There's some niggers in the pizza parlor—let's go kill them." At that time, Lester was fueled or "whacked out" on beer and Southern Comfort, as he later told authorities. At 12:39 a.m. on December 20, a female called the 911 emergency number and reported that three "suspicious" black males were in the pizza shop. Two police officers from the 106th Precinct arrived in a sector car, plus two additional officers in a "conditions" car.[6] When the cops observed that an alleged menace was unfounded, they left the scene.[7]

The pizza counterman assured the police there was "no problem," but seeing the cops, the trio finished eating and left. Outside, Griffith, Sandiford, and Grimes were confronted by ten to a dozen white teenagers who pulled up in maroon, blue, and white cars. Everyone got out except a girl and a boy who stayed behind because of a bad leg. Some of the people on foot held at least one baseball bat, and others carried tree branches. Grimes pulled out a knife. In response, one of the white teens tapped a baseball bat on the pavement and told his friends, "Get the nigger."

Grimes took off and ran north on Cross Bay Boulevard, then went over an overpass and ran west on the side of Shore Parkway. No one chased him. Griffith and Sandiford fled across Cross Bay and turned left on 156th Avenue with some of the white teens on foot and the others in two of the cars in hot, close pursuit. The third car did not start. Griffith got ahead of his stepfather Sandiford and had a two-block lead. The gang caught up with Sandiford outside 86-14 156th Avenue. Sandiford was on the ground. Lester tugged the baseball bat away from a companion and struck Sandiford across the arms and head. Scott Kern, 17, and Jason Ladone, 16, pummeled Sandiford with their fists and a tree limb. Sandiford was able to get up and run but was beaten again on the lawn of 156-17 Shore Parkway. He feigned unconsciousness and lay bleeding on the pavement.

Griffith meanwhile unsuccessfully tried to scale a six-foot chain-link fence, then saw a hole in the fence and ran through it. The attackers in pursuit tried to hit him, but it was uncertain whether they connected. Griffith crossed a three-foot concrete barrier onto the westbound lanes of the six-lane Belt Parkway. One of the whites who gave up the chase heard a loud impact, then saw Griffith's body fly twenty feet in the air. Griffith had been struck by a blue Dodge Aspen driven by Dominic Blum. Griffith was killed in the collision, 265 yards east of the hole in the fence.[8] Blum, twenty-four, a family court officer, left the scene of the accident.

Grimes, the family friend, did not see the accident. But as he was running he noticed that cars were swerving away from the parkway accident. A motorist picked him up and gave him a lift to a Brooklyn-bound subway.[9]

At 12:55 a.m., an anonymous female caller alerted police that whites were beating a black man. The location the caller gave was inaccurate; it was on the other side of Shore Parkway. The same sector car that had arrived at the pizzeria fifteen minutes earlier responded. Despite the wrong address, the cops took a route that put them at the scene of the beating. No one was there. At 1:03 a.m., the sector car went to the inaccurate location and radioed back that the call was "unfounded." Then two calls to 911 reported a man was lying unconscious on the Belt Parkway. That was Griffith.

Sandiford picked himself up from the lawn and staggered through the hole in the fence that his son-in-law had used to briefly escape. He ran across the Belt Parkway and walked west to Brooklyn. At the next exit, Pennsylvania Avenue in Brooklyn, Sandiford was greeted by a big blue sign that celebrated the tenth anniversary of Starrett City housing co-op. "We Live Together," read the sign.[10]

Sandiford continued running and threw debris in the street to get a driver to stop. Highway police noticed him and stopped to pick him up. They took him back to the scene of Griffith's death.[11]

Sandiford, beaten and dazed, was treated by police as a suspect rather than a victim. "Michael's lying there on the street, his head smashed right in front of me, and all the cops wanted to do was question me about a murder committed somewhere in the area," he complained to activist Sonny Carson and journalist Peter Noel at sunrise. "Then when we tried to find the guys, they're more concerned about the football game than the death of Michael."[12]

A similar account got back to Benjamin Ward. It agitated the police commissioner. Ward was committed to the fight against crime, and he also felt a duty to prevent the department from appearing inept, stupid, or racist in the eyes of the public. The *City Sun* excoriated police for using lethal force in two high-profile incidents—those of Eleanor Bumpurs and Michael Stewart. In both cases, the courts relieved the police of criminal culpability. Griffith's death could not be blamed on police violence this time, but their insensitive treatment of the victims could send a seething black New York community over the edge. As a black man leading an overwhelmingly white (and blue) cop culture, Ward was conflicted.[13]

Ward exploded at precinct commander Dillion: "Sandiford was treated like a goddamn perp. Those white uniforms laughed in his face at his story. The man was bleeding from the head, his body was all busted up, and he was made to sit in a patrol car, next to the body of his dead stepson for nearly four hours! Who went to look for the white kids? How did the patrol car miss them at the pizza parlor? Just what the hell is going on? Why the hell wasn't anything done about Blum? The papers are going to have a field day with this."[14]

Sandiford was a construction worker and a Guyanese immigrant who had served two years in the U.S. Army. He said that the police had frisked him, questioned him about another incident, and left him in a patrol car for two hours as he bled from wounds inflicted during the mob assault.[15]

Sylvester stayed in his disabled blue Buick until morning and was given a tow to the Rockaways that was apparently arranged by the National Park Police. The transmission was repaired for $500.[16]

Police continued their investigation. Two days later, on December 22, Jon Lester, 17, Jason Ladone, 16, and Scott Kern, 17, were arrested and charged with second-degree murder, and second-degree manslaughter in connection with Griffith's death. Lester, Ladone, and Kern were also charged with second-degree assault for the attacks on survivors Sandiford and Grimes.[17]

The next day, Jeffrey McCarthy, a white teenager waiting for a bus on Hillside Avenue in Jamaica, Queens, was assaulted by a mob of black teenagers who shouted, "Howard Beach, Howard Beach!" Police arrested three teenagers within a week.

Sandiford's fiancée, Jean Griffith, grieved for her son, the construction worker. Sandiford retained a lawyer, Alton Maddox, counsel in recent cases that involved racial violence or alleged police misconduct (Jonah Perry and the Harlem shooting, and Michael Stewart's shooting by the Transit Police, among others). The office of the Queens district attorney investigated the Howard Beach assault.

Seven hours after Sandiford was taken to the police precinct for questioning, around 8 a.m. on December 20, Alton Maddox showed up at the precinct to represent the beating victim. Michael Griffith's brother, Christopher, had called on Maddox for his services. Brooklyn community activist Sonny Carson also intervened and counseled Sandiford. Carson observed the police interviews with Sandiford and concluded that official accounts that were fed to the media contradicted facts and evidence.

On Sunday afternoon, December 21, the Rev. Al Sharpton led twenty demonstrators to picket New York Pizzeria. "We come not with hate or anger," said Sharpton, "but to let the people of Howard Beach know we are not going to run again, that we are not going to allow them to beat us into the ground." The countermen watched with bewilderment. Shortly before the attacks by neighborhood teenagers, they had served the three men pizza, not beaten them with their crusts. Sharpton's demonstration fizzled.[18] A few days later, Sharpton rallied his followers for a protest march outside Benjamin Ward's home in Queens. It was a very cold pre-Christmas day, and the protest leaders did not have Ward's address. The group wandered aimlessly through the backstreets of the borough, then dissipated.[19]

The sputtering protests were revealing. Sharpton was a Pentecostal preacher without a pulpit. For a dozen years he had led the National Youth Movement, an antidrug advocacy organization he had founded. He claimed NYM was thirty thousand members strong in sixteen cities, but Victor Genecin, a New York State prosecutor, said the group was "never anything more than a one-room office in Brooklyn with a telephone and an ever-changing handful of staffers who took Al Sharpton's messages and ran his errands."[20]

Sharpton may or may not have used deception, but he did have a flair for showmanship. He was the boy wonder, ordained as a preacher at age thirteen. A year later, the Rev. Jesse Jackson of Chicago named the teenage Sharpton youth director of Operation Breadbasket.

Sharpton toured with gospel great Mahalia Jackson. He also connected with soul superstar James Brown, who hired the young man as a bodyguard, then introduced him to his business agents. The Godfather of Soul adopted Sharpton as his godson. Brown had lost a son, and Sharpton was drawn to a series of father figures. His biological dad, Al Sr., a prosperous contractor, had abandoned the family, and Sharpton's mother supported the children as a cleaning woman and with welfare. At Samuel Tilden High School, Sharpton was a classmate of Willie Randolph, a future New York Yankees star and manager of the New York Mets. Sharpton attended Brooklyn College but dropped out.

By the mid-1970s, when Sharpton was in his early twenties, he engaged in acts of civil disobedience to call attention to alleged police misconduct and other mistreatment of black New Yorkers. While touring with Brown in 1974, Sharpton met the boxing promoter Don King. The young man began turning up at ringside of major title fights, like Muhammad Ali versus George Foreman.

C. Vernon Mason joined the case several days later to represent Timothy Grimes. Mason also teamed with Maddox to represent his fellow lawyer. "It began, I guess, almost as if I was representing Alton," said Mason, "because it was very, very clear that the district attorney and the police department—and this was prior to Ward's or Santucci's statements, which became very, very vicious over a period of days. When we found out what the real case was from Sandiford's viewpoint—that they were trying to cover it up and blame Alton for their cover-up—that's when I became involved."[21]

Maddox did engage in tactics that infuriated the authorities. He declared that his client Sandiford would not cooperate with prosecution unless Dominic Blum, driver of the car that had struck and killed Griffith, was arrested. Maddox said that Blum, 24, was part of the teen gang. Queens County district attorney John Santucci said that Blum's involvement was accidental. Maddox countered that Santucci and police were involved in a cover-up partly because Blum was the son of a police officer.[22] Could it have been coincidence rather than conspiracy that a car driven by a cop's son collided with Griffith as he ran onto a busy six-lane highway after midnight?

On the other hand, Blum had left the scene of a fatal accident but was not charged with that offense, which was peculiar. Six days after the bat attacks and the vehicular homicide, Maddox would not budge. He stated that his client was not cooperating and that "Sandiford will do what I tell him."[23]

That day, December 26, several hundred mourners attended funeral services for Griffith at Our Lady of Charity Catholic Church in Crown Heights. The following day, Griffith was buried in Evergreen Cemetery in Bushwick. On December 27, the day of the burial, 1,200 mostly black protesters marched though Howard Beach. They were heckled by about a hundred white neighbors who followed the demonstrators nearly two miles from John Adams High School on Rockaway Boulevard in Ozone Park to the New Park Pizzeria at 156-71 Cross Bay Boulevard. There were heated arguments and some shoving, but no serious violence.

Meanwhile Timothy Grimes was arrested in Brooklyn for allegedly stabbing his live-in girlfriend twice in the back with a knife. Cheryl Sandiford, a niece of Cedric Sandiford, had tried to flee from Grimes during an argument.[24]

On December 28, Mayor Koch visited Our Lady of Grace Catholic Church in Howard Beach and preached racial harmony to the all-white congregation. Heckling and boos greeted Koch's message. Later that day, the mayor took the message to Morningstar Missionary Baptist Church in St. Albans, Queens. The all-black congregation responded with applause and "amens."[25]

On Wednesday, January 7, eighteen days after the Howard Beach incident, the *City Sun* weighed in with a copyrighted cover story, "Lawyers Ask: Why So Many Missing Links?" Q&A interviews with Maddox and Mason began on page 4 and filled pages 5 through 7. In the introduction to the Q&A, *City Sun* editors said in part: "Theirs [Maddox and Mason] is a commitment to faith, they said, faith that this case will transform a judicial system that seems blindly faithful to the creed that 'no black man may have rights that a white man is bound to respect.'" The editors were citing Supreme Court justice Roger Taney's opinion from the 1857 Dred Scott decision that people of African descent were not citizens of the United States and were never intended by the framers to receive protection by the U.S. Constitution.[26]

The deaths of Eleanor Bumpurs, Michael Stewart, and now Michael Griffith at the hands of police with guns and badges or mobs with bats and tree limbs suggested that black New Yorkers had no rights that whites in charge should respect. The justice system was broken in New York, at least for black citizens, so Maddox and Mason were going to fight for their clients with a new set of rules by demanding an independent prosecutor from outside New York City.

This strategy was risky and outrageous. "Maddox and Mason," intoned the *City Sun* editors, "have been severely criticized for obstructing the official investigation of the case. Here in this wide-ranging, exclusive interview with the *City Sun*, they make their own case and plead their own cause." The last line invoked the words of the editors of *Freedom's Journal*, who began publishing America's first black newspaper in New York because the white editor of a leading newspaper published incendiary stories intended to incite the white majority against so-called Free Africans, blacks in America who were not enslaved but had no voting rights and limited property rights and as a minority group in the North lived in a constant state of peril. In the minds of Maddox and Mason, 1987 was as perilous for many New York blacks as 1827.

Maddox and Mason counseled Sandiford not to appear in Queens Criminal Court on December 29 to testify. The lawyers demanded that Blum, the driver who struck Griffith, be charged with murder. In court, the defendant was not Blum but three white teenage boys from Howard Beach. Criminal court justice Ernest Bianchi ruled there was insufficient evidence to charge the trio with second-degree murder because plaintiff witness Sandiford was missing. However, Scott Kern, Jason Landone, and Jon Lester were not off the hook; they were still each charged with reckless endangerment. (Had an assistant district attorney not included those charges, despite orders from his boss not to, all three youths would have walked away free, because the more serious felonies were dismissed.) Still, without Sandiford present, the prosecution, said the judge, failed to tie anyone to Griffith's death.

Kern and Landone were released on bond. Lester remained jailed at Rikers Island. After that hearing, Blum volunteered to testify before a grand jury without immunity from prosecution.[27]

Maddox and Mason called on Governor Cuomo to appoint a special state prosecutor to investigate the death, as well as alleged misconduct by law enforcement officials. The Black and Puerto Rican Legislative Caucus joined the chorus. They asked for the special prosecutor too to dispel "any perception of racial bias" in the case.[28] On New Year's Eve, the governor's spokesman suggested that the special prosecutor appointment was not going to happen. Maddox, said the spokesman, had "no credibility, zero credibility." (Maddox did exaggerate a number of times. He gave an erroneous or false description of Blum's car, and on the WABC-TV public affairs show *Like It Is* with Gil Noble, Maddox made exaggerated claims that the host allowed to go unchallenged.) Also on that day, dozens of black leaders accepted an invitation from Koch to meet and discuss the Howard Beach case. There was dialogue, but no conclusive outcome.[29]

Two days into the new year of 1987, there was a break. On January 2, state special prosecutor Charles J. Hynes asked Maddox and Mason to come forward with evidence that Queens County authorities were ignoring or covering up "vital elements of inquiry" in the Howard Beach case. The lawyers rejected the offer and repeated their demands for federal prosecutors or a special state prosecutor named by the governor to take the case away from Queens district attorney Santucci.

On January 3, Maddox and Mason held a news conference with their client at Abyssinian Baptist Church in Harlem. Sandiford repeated the explanation that he had stopped cooperating with authorities because they were conducting a "masquerade" and because the Queens district attorney and police were not taking his account of what happened on December 20 seriously. Police Department spokesmen disputed Sandiford's statements.

Commissioner Ward—who chastised the precinct commander because of the way Sandiford was treated on December 20—accused Maddox of exploiting the Howard Beach case for financial gain. Black groups expressed outrage toward the commissioner and even called for Ward's resignation. On January 5, Ward refused to retract what he had said.[30]

On January 6, Blum said he was being used as a "scapegoat" in the Howard Beach tragedy. He again denied he was part of a gang that chased Griffith to his death. Police that day announced that two people sought as witnesses of the Howard Beach attack had been found, but neither was able to identify the assailants. It was learned that police may have obtained Jon Lester's confession illegally, thus rendering it inadmissible in court. While inside the precinct, Lester became unnerved when someone walked by with a *New York Post* that carried a screaming lead story headline about Howard Beach. The boy volunteered that he had been "whacked out" on booze. Detective Peter Fiorillo did not solicit Lester's statement, but he took it down, since the teenager offered it.[31] Still, a potential problem remained because the detective recorded the words after the teenager had demanded to speak to his lawyer.

At Boys and Girls High School in Bedford-Stuyvesant, two thousand people met to discuss strategies in the wake of the Howard Beach case. The community meeting was closed to most of the press. Inside, a plate or cup was passed to raise money. At times, the speakers' rhetoric was inflammatory. "Dip into your wallets and pull out money," said one speaker, "but pretend it's a nine-millimeter that we're going put to Santucci's head."[32] Also that day, two black teenagers were charged with mugging a Latino youth outside a Bronx high school. The attackers chanted, "Howard Beach." The assault was logged in as the twenty-ninth race-related incident in New York since the Howard Beach mob attack.[33]

On Wednesday, January 7, the *City Sun* published its exclusive Q&A interview with Maddox and Mason. On pages 4 to 7, both lawyers criticized the official handling of the investigation and listed "missing links" in the case. Andrew Cooper headlined the editorial "Ours Is a Precious, Righteous Anger." The cartoon depicted a devil labeled "Howard Beach" holding a "racism" club. That day Cuomo announced he would establish a task force on bias-related violence to suggest how the state could deter racial violence and address its causes and effects. But the task force duplicated authority already vested in existing state agencies. Lester, the lone Howard Beach suspect in custody, was sentenced to up to three years in prison on a two-month-old weapons possession charge not related to the December 20 attack. Lester had illegally carried a loaded .32 caliber pistol. State supreme court justice Seymour Rotker said that Lester had violated the terms of a plea bargain by getting into trouble at Howard Beach before the weapons case sentencing.[34]

Still, the case against Lester and the accused homicidal Howard Beach attackers was hanging by threads because Sandiford, the key witness, on orders from his lawyer Alton Maddox, had refused to cooperate for weeks. An investigator urged Santucci to get aggressive and arrest Sandiford as a material witness. "Oh no," Santucci told the investigator. "I can't do that. The black community would crucify me."

The Queens district attorney wanted to wash his hands of the Howard Beach mess. Soon he got his wish. On Tuesday, January 13, a helicopter was sent for Santucci, and he was whisked to the governor's mansion in Albany, specifically to the second floor, the space where, in state capital-speak, "business of the highest importance" is conducted. A rumor spread among New York newspaper reporters on Sunday, January 11, that Santucci asked for a special prosecutor. He was accused of leaking a trial balloon to the media. Santucci denied any such act. Nevertheless he was summoned to the capital. Cuomo meanwhile consulted with David Dinkins, perhaps the most influential black elected leader in New York City, on how to proceed.

When Cuomo met with Santucci, the governor informed the elected prosecutor that he wanted Charles Hynes to take over the prosecution of the Howard Beach case. It was reported that Santucci was smiling as he walked out of the governor's office.[35] In the January 14 edition of the *City Sun*, the lead headline asked, "Will Cuomo Break the Impasse?" Negotiations continued. A week later, on January 21, the front page showed Mason and Maddox clasping hand outside Sylvia's, a Harlem restaurant, with the headline "Howard Beach: It Ain't Over Yet; The Fallout Continues." The editorial on page 18 was titled "Taking a Long, Hard Look at Ourselves," and an editorial cartoon at the top of the page caricatured Cuomo as engaging in the same old song and dance. The editorial words filled both columns, except for the staff box.

That Wednesday's *City Sun* coincided with the birthday of Martin Luther King Jr. On that frigid day, black elected, religious, and activist leaders including Sharpton staged a "Day of Outrage" demonstration along Fifth Avenue in Manhattan. Congressman Rangel led a delegation of officials to City Hall to express concerns. Koch dismissed the protests as "ridiculous."[36]

The *City Sun* recorded the demonstration in its January 28 edition. The editorial page was visual: three demonstration photographs and only ten lines of opinion. "We've gotten the picture, but have they?" read the headline. "Thousands demonstrated. . . . The big change ain't coming, it's already here!" The front page skybox teased readers to a page 4–5 story, "Inside the Negotiating Session with Cuomo."

On February 4, a report by Utrice Leid claimed that "black leaders turned down the heat on Cuomo," the last of a three-part series. There was a photo of the governor at the January 12 negotiating session.

The next week, February 11, horizontal front-page photos of Maddox and Mason were wrapped inside the headline "They've Got the RIGHT STUFF! Indictments Vindicate Lawyer's Tactics in Howard Beach Case." Leid's account began on page 4.[37] Also in that edition, a story asked whether Brooklyn assemblyman Roger Green had been the target of a political hit by Manhattan district attorney Robert Morgenthau. Green was among the participants in the January 21 "Day of Outrage" demonstration.

14. ARTS BEAT

In May 1986, the Coopers' youngest daughter, Jocelyn (Jo-An), graduated from Hampton University with a degree in mass communications arts. Formerly Hampton Institute, the college had recently upgraded to university status. After graduating from Thomas Dewey High School in 1982, Jo-An's other top college choices were Howard University in Washington, D.C., and Vassar College in upstate New York. Tony Brown, founding dean of Howard's School of Communications, urged the Coopers to send their daughter to Hampton. Jo-An loved her stay in Virginia. "Hampton was the best ever, the most amazing experience of my whole life," she said in an interview, projecting enthusiasm. Why? "I'm a Southern Belle at heart. I love the food, the formality, the warmth, the music, everything about it." She did not know what the South was like, despite knowing that her paternal grandmother, Irma Robinson, was from Charleston, South Carolina. How could Jo-An know? Robinson had moved north as a child and lost her southern accent.

"Wow, I love this," she recalled. "This is so amazing. People would speak in the morning. People were polite. There was a curfew for two weeks because McGrew Towers was being built. There was strong bonding with the young women. There were cliques of New Yorkers, southerners, and midwesterners, but we gravitated to a lot of the same things. There were cheerleader types and girlie-girls. Many of them were very happy. Fraternity and sorority culture was something I never saw before Hampton. My parents were very political and about solving problems, so socializing was like think tanks with food involved. At Hampton, socializing was light, about having fun with no agendas."

And at a historically black college or university, there was a layer of stuff she did not have to deal with, for example, constantly defining and defending her black identity, which could be a debilitating distraction on predominantly white campuses. By choosing to major in mass communication arts, Jo-An thought she was going to become a journalist like her dad. Arna Alexander Bontemps, son of the legendary Harlem Renaissance writer, was a memorable journalism and creative writing professor. Another professor taught nonverbal communications, one of the most amazing classes Jo-An took.[1]

After graduation, Jo-An moved to Nashville. Instead of journalism, she wanted to work in the music business. Her choice was not impulsive. She had interned at WLIB-AM while in high school, and the experience was pivotal in her life. She had internships in Los Angeles and then Washington, D.C., with U.S. representative Major R. Owens, Shirley Chisholm's successor and Andy's activist ally from the 1960s. Her boyfriend was from Los Angeles, and he graduated from Morehouse College in Atlanta, then enrolled at Meharry Medical School in Nashville. Jo-An decided to start in the music business. She worked at Zemwalt, Alman, and Hayes, a law firm that specialized in country and gospel music. To appease her parents, she applied to law schools. Nevertheless her career path was cast; Jo-An Cooper would make her media mark in the 1990s as a pioneering music publisher.

On August 6–12, 1986, an image of a young, stoic-faced black man wearing large eyeglasses appeared in the left-hand front-page tease box of the *City Sun.* "Do you know this man?" read the label under the picture. "Find out why he'll soon be a household name, why the movie business will never be the same." On page 10, Armond White explained. The man in the photograph was Spike Lee, a resident of Brooklyn's Fort Greene. He was a filmmaker, an NYU film school graduate, who produced *Joe's Bed-Stuy Barber Shop: We Cut Heads*, a short film that aired on PBS in 1983.

His first feature-length work, *She's Gotta Have It*, opened on August 8 in art house theaters. Instead of a headline, mug shots and labels invited readers to White's review: "Jamie . . . & Greer . . . & Mars . . . & Nola." Nola (Tracy Camilla Johns) was a graphic artist who lived in a loft in the shadow of the Brooklyn Bridge. She was in relationships with black men—working-class Jamie (Tommie Redmond Hooks), macho pretty boy Greer (John Canada Terrell) and impish Mars (Spike Lee). Nola dated three men who had components that combined into one ideal man. The gender-bending nature of the low-budget film surprised viewers.

Wrote White, "All the characteristic qualities of *She's Gotta Have It*—the story of a woman choosing a lover according to other than simple romantic rules, the frank sexuality, the colloquial humor of Nola's men and friends, the immediacy of the film's visual style, and the environs of black middle-class Brooklyn—reflect an influence and sensuality outside of mainstream moviemaking."

He continued, "Spike Lee makes an imaginative leap past the rectitude and 'worthiness' of most black independent filmmakers to obtain and define his own personal style. His characters in this serio-comedy are an assortment of egotists who each have synthesized the facts of everyday living into an acceptable, advantageous philosophy of survival. The plot is a sensuous, quasi-feminist sex farce that interweaves the different personalities in view creating a new, textured social satire."[2]

Lee produced the eighty-four-minute movie on a $175,000 budget and, except for one scene, shot the film in black and white. Hollywood took note of Lee's creativity. He was promised $2.5 million to produce his next feature film.[3]

On July 6, the paper set off a post–Fourth of July firecracker: movie and arts critic Armond White's blistering appraisal of Eddie Murphy's blockbuster comedy *Coming to America*. "Who's Coming Out of Africa? The Man Who Lost His Roots," read the headline on White's review.[4]

Now really, was it fair to level that kind of criticism on Eddie Murphy? Don't many blacks take perverse joy in laughing at their own foibles, out of sight or earshot of most whites? White's problem was that Murphy's references to African culture or African American social movements were consistently poisonous. Murphy's character Prince Akeem of the mythical African nation Zamunda rejected an arranged marriage to an African bride and traveled to America to find an independent-minded African American woman.

White noted a disturbing pattern in *Coming to America*: servants, concubines, and wannabe wives of Prince Akeem were dark-complexioned women, while his choice of a queen—from the borough of Queens—had light skin. These subtle and not-so-subtle messages were typical of Eddie Murphy's movies.[5]

White also took offense at a scene in which Prince Akeem sought a suitable woman on the stage of a tacky beauty pageant under a banner that read "BLACK AWARENESS RALLY." The critic wrote that Murphy handled satire and parody clumsily compared with his fellow black comics: "Indeed [the pageant] is the kind of thing Redd Foxx did on 'Sanford and Son,'" wrote White. "But Foxx, an artist from another generation and a different social-political perspective than Murphy's, might have called the contest what it is: A 'Miss Sepia Queen' or 'Miss Brown Sugar' pageant. Foxx wouldn't have called it a 'Black Awareness Rally.' He wouldn't have confused a political meeting with a sex show—either inadvertently or for ridicule. For Eddie Murphy, the very idea of black politics or the political expression of black pride is absurd."

The movie's Africa sequences, White wrote, handed Murphy another chance to showcase the roots hatred evident in his previous movie *Raw*, in which Murphy, in stand-up comic mode, played an obscene character called Umfufu and characterized an African woman as a "bush bitch." The critic added that Murphy pandered to the hip-hop audience by giving that culture's most conspicuous, tasteless fashions a pseudohistorical cultural legacy. "Like the least-enlightened rappers," White whispered in parentheses, "Murphy's just in it for the money."[6]

He did acknowledge Murphy's undeniable comic timing, wit, and talent for mimicry, but then referenced another experienced black comic with a better grasp of parody and satire: "Unlike Richard Pryor, Murphy does not make humor about how we are all foolish, ambitious, shy, neurotic, horny, greedy, and human. He confirms how black people really are the stereotypes their enemies have always claimed."

Four weeks later, on the cover of the August 3–9 *City Sun*, Murphy, in character as Axel Foley from *Beverly Hills Cop*, pointed a handgun and stared intensely at a target as he braced himself in front of a wall. "Murphy's Law: No Static" was the red-letter front-page headline below the photo, with the subhead "Aims at *City Sun* Critic: Point-Counterpoint, Pages 18–21." The shootout in ink was on.

The Murphy public relations machine bought its real estate—three full advertising pages—to battle film critic Armond White. Murphy bought 34 percent of that edition's ad space that week.[7] His ad appeared on page 18 with the letterhead "Eddie Murphy Productions, Television & Tours, Inc., of Los Angeles" and began, "Dear Readers of the *City Sun*: I have purchased this space because I value what you think of my work."

Murphy then complained by repeating White's critiques of *Coming to America* in his July 6 review: Murphy's film was "a menace plain to everyone" and "absurd"; the actor was interested only in "partying and sex," was traitor to "every instance of politics, history, sex and ethnic culture black people have ever known," was "just in it for the money," and was leading "a despicable career." Murphy responded:

> White attacked me in an unprecedented and uncalled for manner. . . . I found the lack of charity on the part of this black man for another black man's life and work to be puzzling, superficial, uniquely vicious and deserving of a public response.
>
> The subsequent wide public acceptance of "Coming to America" leads me to believe that Mr. White has some personal score he feels he needs to settle with me. The fact that the movie has sold $81.2 million in tickets as of July 25 indicates that I must have some understanding of the tastes,

> morals and values of the black community. I believe the reason large numbers of blacks have accepted the movie is that it urges them to bring the hidden and forgotten African part of us in touch with our American experience. Like a number of other critics, Mr. White makes this otherwise simple, beautiful, timely story needlessly complicated.

The second of the three ad pages said:

> Contrary to what Mr. White wrote, I do have political beliefs—I simply avoid pushing them down the public's throat. I was always careful to give people room to make up their own minds. . . . The secret to my success has been to find common ground between my audiences: to uphold the pride, dignity and intelligence of both black and white ticket buyers.
>
> I believe others who have attempted to copy "the Murphy Formula" have fallen short because they lacked the vision, clout, or credibility to keep black and white sensitivities in balance. What Jesse [Jackson] is trying to do on the political scene, Bill Cosby, Whitney Houston, Michael Jackson, Prince, Lionel Richie, Richard Pryor, myself and a few others have been doing in the entertainment business for a number of years. Success, Jesse says, is always found at the point of challenge. I have met the challenge again and again during my career. "Coming to America" is just the most recent example. God willing, and with your continued trust and understanding, I hope to continue to grow and broaden my appeal for years to come.

Murphy signed his letter and added a postscript: "I appreciate everyone's warm comments and generous support of 'Coming to America.'"

The third and final Murphy advertising page carried the "Eddie Murphy, Inc.," letterhead and mostly white space except for a dime-size smiley face with "Eddie Murphy" printed under it, and three lines above: "In case you missed it (or in case film critic Armond White tore it out), be sure to get another copy of the *City Sun* and read my response to his review of 'Coming to America.'"

On the next page, 21, the two-tier headline "Armond White Responds to Eddie Murphy" introduced a two-column, full-page reply in italic type. White returned Murphy's fire this way:

> The preceding advertisement may be the best work of Eddie Murphy's career so far. It is the most encouraging move he has yet made

> in the media wars that he and every other black artist, like it or not, are involved in—the presentation of black thought and language and the undertaking of black life through the principally white-dominated forms of film, television and journalism.
>
> By taking his "case" to the black community through this black medium, Murphy shows an encouraging recognition of the role black journalism and black communicators have in disseminating their own ideas and controlling their own affairs.
>
> Dependence on white media has stifled the intellectual growth of black artists and politicians and their public, just as it forestalled the development of an independent, regenerating black entertainment industry.
>
> This time the Murphy joke is, I think, on the white-media that has encouraged his rise as a casually abrasive, apolitical race comedian. Murphy's rebuttal suggests he understands that the essential meaning and effect of his work do not rely on white approval.
>
> Murphy, inadvertently perhaps, has taken the first step toward asserting the value and legitimacy of the black press by reacting to its impartiality—a stance I value *The City Sun* for allowing its writers. This should clarify the black press' role as a forum for the discussion of ideas and the investigation of truth—even in its entertainment pages which are generally perceived as a public relations dumping ground for ethnic artists. Murphy gets my respect for respecting [and supporting] black journalism.[8]

Five short, newspaper-style paragraphs damned Murphy with faint praise. Then, after a headline-size "However," White wrote:

> It isn't easy, or popular, to write criticism of Eddie Murphy, a comedy star who indeed understands the tastes, morals and values of the black community enough to make it enjoy its own humiliation. The trouble is, asking people to examine any item of pop culture that is presented for their pleasure is to risk being called an "attacker," or "uncharitable." (Charity for multi-millionaire Murphy!)
>
> Several lousy Eddie Murphy movies ago, I wrote a review in which I almost gave up and simply lamented "all that beautiful potential wasted." Since then, Murphy has proceeded to make more money off more films that reflect nothing serious or progressive about the experience of being a black person in the 1980s. The weak fantasy of "Coming to America"

> confuses African heritage and Hollywood pastiche without showing what distinguishes them from each other or what psychological or cultural conditioning compels them to merge in Murphy's mind.
>
> "The African part of us" has always been "hidden and forgotten" in Murphy's own movies (unless it could be used for a laugh, as in his obscene Umfufu routine in "Raw"). And bringing that heritage "in touch with our American experience" is not, despite what Murphy thinks, simple. In fact, it is a necessarily complicated process—unless one falsifies it, as "Coming to America does."

In the next four paragraphs, White wrote that Murphy's letter to readers refused to engage any of the points he made in the July 6 review. White reloaded, then fired again:

> This phony idea of brotherhood is the usual plea copped by scoundrel-entertainers who accept the ethical compromises of mainstream institutions like Hollywood for their personal benefit and then claim they are doing it for the good of the entire race.
>
> Unfortunately, it isn't only rascals like Murphy who suffer this delusion; many members of his audience are similarly misguided. Too many black people claim that anything Murphy does is all right because he is a black man "getting over" and winning in the white world. It's a neat switch on Malcolm X's phrase "by any means necessary."
>
> . . . Murphy's paid-for response is probably the closest I'll get to realizing the conversation I fantasized in my "Coming to America" review. Strange that the essence of his response is the same: "Because I'm RICH!" Wealth has made Murphy impervious to criticism. He doesn't deal with it; he deflects it.
>
> No matter how gladly banks and box offices accept Eddie Murphy, there is no way to get around the fact of difference that his race signifies. The white critics who like "Coming to America" don't display any special knack or insight; they simply like laughing at Eddie and his people. Eddie Murphy isn't important to them; they don't have a political or emotional stake in what he does. Every triviality he parades, every misconception he promotes, helps keep black people on the periphery of white consciousness. And since the film isn't about anything substantial, it is easily dismissed.
>
> The "common ground" Murphy thinks he has cleared for his audience is the same jungle of concealed hatred and misunderstanding in

> which the races continually condescend to each other, feigning fellowship while remaining emotionally and socially distant. Murphy's "innocuous" stereotype humor actually separates people. He has turned movie theaters into DMZ playgrounds for the expression and enjoyment of racist ideas. That's why he's a menace.[9]

The verbal shootout between Murphy and White shared the front page that week with courtroom drama about an authentic shootout—a gun battle between twenty-two-year-old Larry Davis and thirty police officers who botched a raid on Davis's sister's Bronx apartment in 1986, wrote Peter Noel. There was little dispute that Davis wounded six police officers and then eluded capture. What was in question, fumed the red, five-line headline to the left of the "Murphy's Law" story was the "focus of the Davis trial: who shot first?"[10]

Noel reported that sworn testimony by Melody Cecil Flood, Davis's estranged girlfriend, gnawed at the nerves of police and prosecutors trying to put Davis away for the attempted murder of cops. Noel's story jumped to a full page 27. Two-thirds of that jump page was a Q&A between Joel Blumfield, head of the Criminal Defense Division of the Legal Aid Society Bronx office, and Melody Cecil Flood. The story jumped again and ended on most of page 30 except for 3 by 4.5 inches of legal advertisements.

Davis's lawyer, William Kunstler, said he would prove cops went to the Davis sister's apartment to assassinate Davis, who sold cocaine and crack for a ring of corrupt Bronx cops who became worried about Davis after the September 1986 scandal at Brooklyn's Seventy-seventh Precinct that exposed a ring of dirty police officers. Davis, whom the police had recruited when he was fifteen, according to Kunstler, "might tell on them or would run away with their money."[11]

15. JOURNALIST OF THE YEAR

In the February 4 *City Sun*, staff writer Phil Farai Makotsi reported that jury selection was about to begin for a trial in which four black journalists from the *New York Daily News* sued the nation's largest-circulation metropolitan newspaper for racial discrimination. Through the end of the 1970s and into the 1980s, news outlets including the *New York Times*, ABC, *Newsweek*, and the Associated Press settled race and gender discrimination lawsuits out of court.[1]

The *Daily News* management offered a $500,000 settlement to the plaintiffs, but they rejected the deal. After that, the management was willing to wage a public fight in court. Observers speculated that the Tribune Company, owner of the *Daily News*, was gambling that the four black journalists would lose easily in the hostile, antiblack social climate of the Reagan era.[2]

Because of this unprecedented trial, the stakes for the newspaper industry were high. What was to follow in the next nine weeks was the legal equivalent of a bloody street brawl in which character flaws on both sides would be ripped open and exposed. Nevertheless plaintiffs David Hardy, a political reporter, Steven W. Duncan, an assistant news editor, Joan Shepard, Manhattan cultural affairs editor, and Causewell Vaughan, a copy editor, pressed on. They believed theirs was a compelling and righteous case.

The foursome began their battle in 1980 when they alleged that the newspaper's management discriminated against black journalists in salaries, promotions, and assignments and retaliated when the journalists complained.[3] At the nation's largest metropolitan newspaper (1.5 million circulation, and during its peak in the 1960s, 2.5 million) white editors casually referred to their employees of color as "niggers" and "spics."

Richard "Dick" Blood, a high-ranking editor, called Shepard a "streetwalker," or prostitute, when she returned from a walking tour with elected officials. Tony Marino, another white editor, routinely called black and Hispanic coworkers "banjos" and "bongos" and also called two women "nigger broads."

In other newsrooms, coworkers who trusted and respected each other sometimes accepted that kind of racial insult and crude humor. That was not the case at the *Daily News*. The coarse words were not comedic license; the newsroom was a hostile environment for blacks.

The black journalists were also seething because they found out during their research that the newspaper continued to employ a white editor who had killed a black teenager in a drunk-driving incident. In addition, economically, black and brown readers were a substantial piece of the *Daily News*' customer base—45 percent in New York City—yet the management allegedly practiced crude employment discrimination in newsgathering and dissemination and muted the majority-minority reality of New York in the late 1980s.[4]

Andy Cooper and Utrice Leid committed Makotsi to cover the trial in its entirety. The *Daily News* had been one of Cooper's four news clients when he operated Trans Urban News Service in late 1970s and early 1980s. The newspaper sometimes ran TNS stories almost word for word with *Daily News* reporters' bylines on top. (In 1979, when a TNS intern asked why that was done, a *Daily News* staff writer explained it was a matter of "pride" at the unionized paper.) Cooper and Leid often said they were training men and women who would eventually report for the *Daily News*. Makotsi's daily presence at the trial pleasantly surprised Daniel Alterman, the attorney for the *Daily News* four. It would be up to a judge and jury to determine whether the newspaper had caused egregious harm or the journalists' complaints had little or no merit. Alterman talked regularly with Makotsi and his managing editor Leid.[5]

Elsewhere, the *Amsterdam News*' coverage of the trial was indifferent compared to the *City Sun*'s fever-pitch interest. For weeks at a time during the nine-week trial, no mention appeared in the city's largest black-owned weekly. There was speculation that the *Amsterdam News* owners did not want to antagonize the Tribune Company, since it also distributed the *Amsterdam News*.[6] Other accounts in the trade journal *Editor and Publisher*, the *Village Voice*, and the *Washington Post* suggested sympathy toward the *Daily News* management's cause and excoriated the plaintiffs.

When the trial opened, lawyers for the *Daily News* attacked the professionalism and integrity of Duncan, Hardy, Shepard, and Vaughan. The foursome did not advance in their careers, said the respondents (this was a civil suit), because they were incompetent. Alterman challenged that assertion by introducing a letter from Rolfe Neill, an assistant managing editor, who wrote that Hardy had handled bigotry inside the newsroom well: "At the *News*, Dave's responsibilities have not given him a chance for leadership," wrote Neill. "But because he is black and bigotry has frequently come his way in the office, I have a number of times observed him under stress. He comes off well."[7] Neill left the paper to become editor of the *Philadelphia Daily News*, a tabloid-format paper like the *New York Daily News*. When Hardy joined the *Daily News* in 1966, an editor pulled him aside in confidence within a week of his hiring and told him that the New York paper wasn't "quite ready at this time to have any blacks in the sports department," after the high school and college track and field champion asked if he could be assigned to that beat.[8] Hardy left the *Daily News* to work at the *Washington Post* for a few years, then returned to the *Daily News* in 1972. He was assured by editor Michael O'Neill that the newsroom at that time was more tolerant of blacks.[9]

In that era of manual typewriters and carbon paper sandwiched between three canary-yellow copy sheets, writers and editors yelled to get the attention of copyboys to run their typed pages, or copy, to the appropriate desks. Bellowing "boy!" to a young black male employee in a virtually white, male environment had lightning-rod consequences. Roger Witherspoon, a news assistant in the early 1970s, recalled the time when a newly hired black copyboy, unfamiliar with the typical form of address, answered by punching out an editor who called him "boy." "As I understand it, [the copyboy] got canned," said Witherspoon, who stayed in journalism and later excelled at metropolitan newspapers in Atlanta and Dallas.[10]

In addition to Neill, Alterman's other expert witness was Les Payne, an assistant managing editor at *Newsday*, a Long Island tabloid that competed with the *Daily News* for suburban readers who included many Manhattan-bound commuters. Payne, a founding member of the National Association of Black Journalists and its fourth president (1981–83), testified that the plaintiffs were accomplished journalists straining under the yokes of racist practices at the *Daily News*. Before the trial, Payne was a paid consultant who briefed the plaintiffs' lawyers on how newsrooms conducted performance evaluations to rate employees for raises and promotions.[11]

U.S. District Court judge Miriam Goldman Cedarbaum and the jury of six—three white men, a white woman, a black woman, and an Asian man—heard *Daily News* management acknowledge in a public forum that there were instances in which white employees were selected for management positions and blacks and other minority staff were bypassed despite their seniority, lengthy experience, and deeper educational credentials. Such practices had cost the *Daily News* four and other colleagues raises and plum assignments. Hardy, for example, said that he had broken the Abscam story, the 1981 scandal in which four members of Congress took bribes from federal investigators posing as Arab sheiks in a sting operation. Hardy focused on U.S. senator Harrison Williams (D-N.J.). When Hardy brought his notes and documents to editors, however, he was told to turn them over to political reporter John McLaughlin, who got the byline and the credit.

Hardy, a hulking six foot five inches tall with an easy smile that just as easily turned to a scowl, protested. Editors called him a roguishly arrogant troublemaker and ringleader of the *Daily News* four. They accused Hardy of being a sloppy writer who turned in slanted stories, but when pressed in court, his editors could not recall any memos, warnings, or disciplinary action taken against the reporter. Hardy was criticized for fighting with a lawyer outside a courthouse, but the reporter explained that the altercation started during an exchange of racial insults and the lawyer threw the first punch. Under questioning, editors acknowledged that Hardy had been nominated twice for a prestigious Nieman Fellowship at Harvard University.

A letter the jury did not see was the *Daily News*' nomination of Hardy for a Pulitzer Prize for his reporting on David Friedland, a former New Jersey senator, who disappeared after he was convicted in a $20 million scam. While other media reported that Friedland died in a scuba diving accident in the Bahamas, Hardy went to the islands and concluded that the senator faked his death. Months later Friedland contacted Hardy, and the reporter scored a front-page story.[12]

At the time of the trial, Duncan had been a newspaperman for thirty-five years, since 1952. While on the staff of the *Baltimore Afro-American*, he covered the Emmett Till trial in a segregated courtroom. Years later Duncan attracted national attention for securing an exclusive interview with Fidel Castro when the new Cuban leader visited New York.

Duncan's first mainstream newspaper job was with the *World Telegram and Sun* of New York in the early 1960s, and he joined the *Daily News* staff in 1969. Duncan said that despite his experience, he was never considered for promotion, even as less-qualified whites, several of whom he had supervised, were promoted over him. In June 1980, Duncan filed a grievance with the federal Equal Employment Opportunity Commission. *Daily News* management then transferred him from his job as New Jersey section editor to the makeup room. Duncan said the *Daily News* had retaliated because he had complained.[13]

After Shepard complained about an editor calling her a "streetwalker," she was transferred to the captions department. Katherine Vanzi, a white reporter at the *Daily News* during the 1970s, testified that she had witnessed Blood disparage Shepard, and that the editor also told her that "blacks are not well suited for journalism. They didn't have the background and education." Vanzi added, "He would say we didn't have any qualified minorities. He would make snide comments about Afros and cornrows and dashikis." Shepard filed eight complaints against the paper. After she sued, Shepard was named cultural affairs editor.[14]

Causewell Vaughan began newspaper work in 1962 as a copyboy at the *New York Post*. A year later he was a stringer for the *Buffalo Evening News*. Vaughan became a copy editor at the *New York Times*, then worked six years as a newsman with the Associated Press in Newark, Atlanta, and Washington. Vaughan covered urban riots and the Black Panthers in the late 1960s, often when white reporters were shut out of those stories. Vaughan was hired by the *Daily News*.

At thirty, Vaughan made it clear that he wanted to be an editor. He reported for two years on the federal court beat, then was moved to general assignment reporting. On numerous occasions he filled in as an editor, including a six-month stint as acting night city editor. In 1977, Vaughan learned there was an opening for Manhattan regional editor. He expressed his interest in the position and was stunned when the management hired a reporter who did not want the job. Three years later, in 1980, Vaughan was named editor of the Brooklyn section. Then after a few months he was reassigned and told he would become editor of the Manhattan section, but again someone else was selected for the job. Vaughan filed discrimination complaints.

During the trial, Vaughan committed an ethical lapse that gave Morrison an opening to attack his competence and professionalism. While serving as Brooklyn editor, Vaughan allowed U.S. representative Fred Richmond (D-N.Y.) to co-sign his $2,400 personal loan. Vaughan said he had borrowed the money because he was broke as a result of the 1978 newspaper strike; at the time, he was supporting his ill father. The financial arrangement surfaced during a federal investigation of the Brooklyn congressman, who was later convicted of fraud. Vaughan defaulted on the loan after he had made several payments, and Richmond paid the $1,832 balance.

Vaughan said at least one of his superiors knew about the loan six months before it became public. *Daily News* editors suspended him for three weeks, then demoted him to copy editor when the *Amsterdam News* quoted him criticizing the *Daily News*' racial policies. Vaughan's editors scrutinized all his Brooklyn stories and could not find evidence that he had shown favorable bias toward the congressman. But Vaughan acknowledged that accepting help to secure a loan from a politician he covered was a mistake.[15]

Vaughan's lawyer Alterman drew blood by pointing out numerous ethical lapses by white employees. For example, two reporters, Phil Roura and Harry Slagle, were on the payrolls of elected officials. Roura had been promoted to editor while he worked for a state assemblyman from 1974 to 1979. Sam Roberts, who was city editor when Vaughan made his error in judgment, said the black journalist should have been fired, but in court he could not explain why no one had sacked the white journalists for their lapses.[16]

Alterman also put former metropolitan editor Richard Oliver on the witness stand and asked him to explain why he had the Fire Department illegally install—at taxpayer expense—a flashing light and siren on his personal car. Oliver claimed he never used the siren; Alterman produced a pretrial deposition in which Oliver said he "rarely" used the apparatus. The lawyer used Oliver's poor judgment to show that *Daily News* management treated its black employees more harshly for misconduct. Editor James Weighart insisted that there was no way to compare the Oliver and Vaughan incidents: "Vaughan never intended to pay back the loan. It was a shakedown." Oliver, however, said Weighart, "was a dumb cluck who had put a siren on his car like a jerk."

At what would later turn out to be the midway point of the trial, the *City Sun* edition of March 11 included a four-page pullout special report. It included lead reporting by Makotsi, along with his analysis, headlined "For Black Reporters at the *Daily News*, It's a Matter of Honor." Clinton Cox, a former *Daily News* reporter who had been writing for the *City Sun*, contributed "Life in the Belly of the Beast," a first-person essay about race, media, jurisprudence, and his former employer. Cox wrote that the *Daily News* management falsely tried to smear his former colleagues as troublemakers and incompetents. Then he recalled his own stormy tenure at the newspaper. Cox had pressed for a state capital assignment. The editor instead offered him the chance to open a bureau in Harlem, Bedford-Stuyvesant, or any black community if he would forget about Albany, but Cox refused to settle. In 1978 he became the first black reporter in the history of the newspaper assigned to the capital. "After an incredible amount of hassle [I] was transferred to Albany," Cox explained. "Once I was there, however, the *Daily News* took stories away from me, dropped my byline so many times I lost count, saw that I was excluded from social functions involving the job, and never gave me another raise. When I wrote to O'Neill, a self-professed fighter for liberal causes, detailing what was happening to me, he never answered my letter."[17]

Furthermore, in fourteen months upstate, Oliver, the paper's metropolitan editor, would not speak to him. "He had the *News*' operator make phone calls routinely to every other reporter assigned there during my tenure," wrote Cox. "Every time I answered the phone, however, Oliver would have the operator leave a message for one of the other reporters to call him back."[18] *City Sun* managing editor Utrice Leid wrote the other piece for the pullout, "Phone Home: An Opinionated View of the *Daily News* Trial."

A week later, Earl Caldwell, who in 1978 became the first black columnist for the *Daily News*, was asked by Makotsi of the *City Sun* if his newspaper discriminated as the four black plaintiffs alleged. Caldwell replied:

> I have seen management hire from top to bottom three times and they have never interviewed any blacks for any major jobs. One of the only blacks to hold a senior position was Bob Herbert, who briefly was city editor. But when the current regime took over [led by publisher James Hoge] they wanted their own city editor. They didn't believe in black city editors. They made Herbert a columnist.
>
> Now there are in New York City black people who are eminently qualified to be brilliant in any of these jobs. It's not that they are not qualified. Management just doesn't want blacks in these positions.[19]

Caldwell, co-founder of the Institute for Journalism Education in California, testified that he gave *Daily News* management a list of black prospects and learned later that those managers never called any of the candidates. "Part of the blame," Caldwell told Makotsi, "is on the black community because we accept it. No other community would accept that. The paper isn't going to change its attitude toward blacks unless the blacks demand that change."

> I don't think black people seriously think about this: they bring the paper into their homes, presenting it to their sons and daughters to inspire them to be better in reading and writing, despite the negative coverage. And yet they can't get jobs at the paper. We shouldn't accept it all but we do, though I think we're beginning to accept it less.
>
> For 50 years, the *News* has been getting fat checks from our people and they have never given up anything to get it. . . . If black and Latino communities were to involve themselves seriously in withholding the amount they spend buying the paper—$250,000 each day, Mondays through Saturdays and $1 million Sunday alone—I don't see how it can survive.[20]

Even as they admitted in open court that black journalists had plum assignments and promotions taken from them, *Daily News* managers countered that Hardy and company were "not as good as they think they are."[21] Thomas Morrison, attorney for the *Daily News*, called the plaintiffs "losers."

Losers? Duncan repeated the word in a rhetorical yet measured tone, unlike his blustery co-defendant Hardy. Their boss Mike O'Neill was the first editor in the history of American journalism to preside over a newspaper at which circulation dropped by one million copies. It happened on his watch from 1975 to 1982, Duncan reminded journalists at a 1987 conference.[22]

Granted, that was a tumultuous stretch in which New York City lost hundreds of thousands of jobs and residents to the Sunbelt or nearby suburbs, where growing daily newspapers flourished in North Jersey, Long Island, Westchester, and eastern Connecticut. But presented with such a dismal record of failure, could the counsel for the *Daily News* credibly call the opponents "losers?"

In court Alterman said that *Daily News* management had no interest adapting to the new demographic reality of the paper's market. "It is unbelievable that from the '60s to the late '70s, the *News* couldn't find a 'qualified' black; it has never hired a black as an executive in its entire history; [and] it has retaliated against plaintiffs for raising their [discrimination] claims. . . . This case is about four individual reporters who, though talented, qualified and committed, were not promoted and compensated like their white colleagues and as a result were unable to develop their craft; whose career and self-worth have been irreparably damaged solely due to their race."[23]

During Alterman's four-and-one-half-hour summation, he told the jury, "This is a simple case. The *News* broke the law and when the plaintiffs complained about it, they were retaliated against. We have neither the money nor staff, but we have the truth." Sue Singer, Alterman's associate who handled statistics for the case, told jurors, "I've heard some incredible things in this courtroom over the past couple of months, but one of the high points was hearing the *Daily News* lawyers tell you that the *Daily News* was a pioneer in moving people up the career ladder in the editorial department. The statistics you have heard are complicated and sometimes boring, but I do know there is one simple statistic . . . It's the number zero. The number of blacks who were promoted into management at the *Daily News* until this lawsuit was filed was zero."[24]

Over four days, the jury deliberated for twenty-three hours. The verdict: Out of twenty-three incidents of discrimination cited in the lawsuit, the jury agreed the *Daily News* was guilty in twelve of the counts. Jury foreman John Foley explained that after reviewing the facts, the plaintiffs were deemed "credible, professional journalists," despite the smears by *Daily News* management.

"VICTORY!" Proclaimed the front page of the April 22 *City Sun*. "*Daily News* staffers prove it's New York's homeland paper." The headline took a dig at *Daily News'* management and suggested a level of oppression similar to apartheid in South Africa. A special report began on page 8 and continued on pages 9 and 10.[25]

When the verdict was announced, Alterman shook the hand of legal adversary Morrison. Hardy, Duncan, Shepard, and Vaughan began vigorous hugging and embracing that began in the courtroom and continued as they walked briskly into the marble corridor. A grim-faced Morrison led his legal team out into the hallway and reluctantly fielded questions from two persistent reporters. As Morrison struggled to maintain a stiff upper lip, Alterman could not curb his enthusiasm. "Lights out! We got the suckers!" he shouted.

Jack Dunleavy, the *Daily News'* assistant publisher, said the newspaper would appeal the decision because it was still "unconvinced" he said that the newspaper had discriminated against its black employees.[26] Dunleavy was aware that five other black *Daily News* employees sued his newspaper for discrimination and their case was scheduled for trial. In June, days before the jury was to reconvene and decide on damages for the *Daily News* four, the newspaper agreed to pay an out-of-court settlement: $3.1 million in damages, plus $2 million in legal fees. By the summer, about ten black journalists joined the *Daily News* staff, boosting the minority reporting staff to 35 of 425 newsroom employees, who also included thirteen Latinos. The new editor was Gil Spencer, former editor of the *Philadelphia Daily News*, a spunky tabloid that employed Chuck Stone, founding president of NABJ, and a paper with a track record of employing blacks in editing and other management positions. Spencer said that managers linked to the lawsuit no longer worked at the *New York Daily News* or had been reassigned.[27]

After the settlement, Duncan, sixty-three, opted for early retirement (he went to a seminary and became a pastor); Vaughan was to be assigned to a better position; and Hardy and Shepard were to remain in their current posts. Hardy, Duncan, Shepard, and Vaughan had each paid about $12,000 in legal fees for a trial that seemed risky. They had won the bruising fight, but it took a personal and professional toll on each of them.

During the trial, Leid of the *City Sun* wrote a commentary that said the plaintiffs' emotional scars were not worth the cost: "The illusion of power, the empty promise of 'advancement,' the lure of big money, of travel, of starring in the three-ring circus were hard to resist," she wrote. "I just wish they'd really understand, that like E.T., they're extra-terrestrials in a world that does not, cannot and will not understand them, and like E.T., they'd do the logical thing and phone home. Or better yet, come home."

Leid's bravado was over the top. Her weekly did not have the financial resources to hire these experienced journalists. On May 4 at U.S. Bankruptcy Court in Westbury, Long Island, Cooper and Leid, principals of the City Sun Publishing Company, signed an agreement to convert their Chapter 11 bankruptcy to a Chapter 7 bankruptcy. Reorganization under Chapter 11 set no limits on the amount of debt, and the business was allowed to operate under the supervision of the court. With Chapter 7 reorganization, the newspaper owners could sell nonexempt assets—supervised by the court trustee—to pay off creditors and give their enterprise a fresh start.[28]

Second, journalists of color were obligated to challenge the *Daily News* to live up to its reputation as the metro area's hometown newspaper. The *New York Times* was still perceived as the newspaper for the elites in the city, in Washington, and in foreign capitals. At that time, it circulated more papers in Boston than in the Bronx. After a decade of ownership by Australian mogul Rupert Murdoch, the *New York Post* was hopelessly incorrigible. It employed few if any black journalists, and its managers laughed when critics pressed them to diversify their staff.[29] The *Daily News* was an institution worth changing, even it meant a fight.

The trial of the *Daily News* four sent shock waves across America. "It will trigger a more serious look at operations in newsrooms across the country," said Albert E. Fitzpatrick, president of NABJ and news executive with Knight Ridder Newspapers, corporate owner of newspapers that included the *Philadelphia Inquirer*, *Philadelphia Daily News*, *Miami Herald*, and *Detroit Free Press*.[30]

While Andy Cooper's *City Sun* was covering the *Daily News* four with gusto from February through April, rival publisher Wilbert A. Tatum of the *New York Amsterdam News* recorded his oral history with Columbia University journalism graduate student Kissette Bundy on three occasions, February 28, March 28, and May 3. Cooper's black weekly was young; it was approaching its third birthday in June. Tatum's *Amsterdam News* represented the establishment. It had been publishing since 1909—the same year the NAACP was established—and was based in Harlem, a place many African Americans still considered the capital of black America. Tatum's paper boasted twice the *City Sun*'s circulation and was at least seven decades older.

In forums and interviews, Tatum called the *City Sun* a competitor, but not a serious threat to the leading black newspaper in the city.

In the oral history interviews, Bundy asked Tatum about his recollections of the *Village Voice* writers who had written a series of articles between 1978 to 1983 that criticized him and partner John Procope for attempting to woo Mayor Koch with editorials in hopes of receiving city contracts for various business ventures.[31] During that time, Cooper had collaborated with *Village Voice* writer Wayne Barrett on exposés of the Koch administration. Cooper also was friendly with Jack Newfield, another writer with the alternative weekly.

Tatum answered Bundy's question with an obscure reply: "In terms of my own relationship with the sister newspaper, for which I have a great deal of respect, mind you, I countered with my truth." As for the *City Sun*, Tatum said, "It was my understanding that some of these same [*Village Voice*] political writers, some of them, were involved in the formation of another black newspaper called the *City Sun*. I cannot delve into that because I don't know, but if the *Amsterdam News* had died, the only logical successor to it would be the *City Sun*."[32]

The *Village Voice* writers did not help form the *City Sun*; Cooper and Leid did that. Tatum either was misinformed or was coyly trying to mislead the interviewer. In attempts to fend off his rival from Brooklyn, Tatum's comments over the years were wily and sly. He was a theatrical character, and his speaking style was clipped and declamatory. Sometimes, as he answered an interviewer, he suggested the punctuation for his quotes.[33]

Tatum's subordinates at the *Amsterdam News* said their boss was passionate about civil rights, but he was also stubborn and petty and at times prone to alienate people who agreed with him. Cooper was less kind: "He is egomaniacal, and more than anything, he likes to frequent those social affairs at which he can rub elbows with rich white people." Tatum, Cooper continued, "controls everything that goes into that newspaper. If you're talking about editorial integrity, it ain't there." Cooper apparently recalled his time as an *Amsterdam News* political columnist in the 1970s and the occasions editors spiked his column because he criticized political allies of Tatum and associates. "Cooper is unimportant," said Tatum in response to Cooper's assault. "He is making an effort to ride the reputation of the *Amsterdam News*, to make a place in the sun for himself. For all intents and purposes, he is without class."[34]

Tatum was fifty-four at the time of the interviews (Cooper was fifty-nine). Tatum was born January 23, 1933, in Atkinson, North Carolina. He was one of thirteen children. Tatum's father, Eugene, was a publisher, editor, and advertising salesman, and his mother Mittie Novesta Tatum was a schoolteacher. By the time he was ten, claimed Wilbert Tatum, he was managing editor of his dad's Carolina newspaper, the *Henderson Tribune*. His job was to clip the *Amsterdam News*.

Tatum attended Hillside High School in Durham. He won a scholastic journalism award at Columbia University in 1951 and earned a trip to New York City. After a stint in the Marine Corps from 1951 to 1954, he attended Lincoln University of Pennsylvania and earned a bachelor's degree. He moved permanently to New York City in 1956 when he was twenty-three. He said he had no money and slept in flophouses along the Bowery. He shoveled snow for $23 a month.

In the early 1960s, Tatum joined the Village Independent Democrat Club in lower Manhattan. There he met Susan Kohn, a Jewish woman who had fled Czechoslovakia at the start of the Holocaust. The two married. Inside the club, Tatum was a vocal advocate for civil rights. When he asked to record some of the meetings in 1962, he clashed with Stanley Geller, the president and a proponent of civil liberties. Geller did not want what he might say to be used selectively, so he squelched Tatum's request. Tatum criticized the club, and his interest waned.[35] A year later, in 1963, the Village Independent Democrats elected a new president: Ed Koch. He and Tatum would clash two decades later.

During a Harlem riot in 1964, Tatum said he was hit in the foot by a ricocheting bullet. For two years in the late 1960s, he was director of the Cooper Square Committee, which was founded in 1959 and prevented the demolition of affordable housing in the Cooper Square Urban Renewal Area. Tatum served as the paid director and ran the committee's office. Tatum and his wife lived at 65 Second Avenue until the late 1960s, when he purchased a brownstone on East Third Street with a loan from the Ukrainian Credit Union. Tatum took over three more buildings—burned-out shells—on East Second Street and Second Avenue. He worked with a group of men to renovate the buildings and then rented the apartments from the city. When Tatum proved that the buildings were viable, the city sold him the properties.[36]

Tatum joined the administration of mayor John V. Lindsay. In 1966 he became an assistant to the commissioner of the Department of Buildings, then associate director of community relations, and later director of community relations. His next move was to director of urban renewal for Central Harlem. In 1970, Tatum became deputy Manhattan borough president.

In the next administration of Abe Beame, Tatum was director of the mayor's office of Apparel Industry Planning and Development from 1973 to 1974.

In 1971, Tatum became a newspaper owner. While he was a Lindsay administration bureaucrat, Tatum bought the *Amsterdam News* from C. B. Powell—the paper's second owner—with partners Percy Sutton, Carl McCall, John L. Edmonds, John Procope, and Clarence B. Jones.[37] At that time, Sutton was borough president of Manhattan. McCall was pastor of Metropolitan United Methodist Church and was a commissioner of the New York City Council against Poverty; Procope was an insurance company executive; Edmonds was a lawyer; and Jones was a lawyer and a former speechwriter for Martin Luther King Jr. "None of us knew how to run a newspaper," Tatum told Bundy, "but it was available. . . . We had a belief it ought to be a more potent weapon."

In 1972, Tatum earned master of arts degrees from Yale University and Occidental College. After acquiring the *Amsterdam News*, he and his business partners made additional media acquisitions. They bought WLIB-AM and WBLS-FM, plus radio stations in Los Angeles, San Francisco, Detroit, and Texas.[38] Throughout the 1970s, Tatum grew his investment in the *Amsterdam News* and became the major stockholder in addition to vice chairman and secretary-treasurer of the newspaper.

In 1977, Ed Koch was elected mayor of New York, and he did not retain Tatum in his administration. Tatum joined Health Insurance Plan of Greater New York as senior vice president of marketing, public relations, and community relations and stayed until he became editor and chairman of the *Amsterdam News* shortly after 1980.

Tatum's newspaper was reformatted from a broadsheet into a tabloid thanks to a redesign by Ken Smikle, a features editor who managed to spread the changes he made in his section throughout the newspaper. In 1977, Smikle had his own business housed in the former McGraw Hill building on East Forty-second Street. He owned typesetting equipment that was used to produce newsletters for arts organizations. Jean Carey Bond, arts editor of the *Amsterdam News*, called Smikle to let him know she was leaving the paper. Smikle applied for the opening she had left and was hired in summer 1977 by executive editor Bryant Rollins.

Smikle immediately made layout changes. The arts and sports pages already were tabloid pullout sections inside the broadsheet. Smikle redesigned the arts section. He went about making the *Amsterdam News* look more like a *Village Voice*–style alternative newspaper instead of a broadsheet that published weekly.[39] Smikle borrowed graphics from the *Washington Post* weekend section and the *Village Voice* and converted news pages into single-topic tabloid pages. He created a template for a new front page and paid his wife Deborah to set type for the arts section copy. Smikle also moved his typesetting equipment to *Amsterdam News*' Harlem office to avoid farming out the weekly production to Mount Kisco.

In 1979, he left the *Amsterdam News*. Smikle said he was fired because he pushed for changes and improvements and over time was perceived as a gadfly. He returned to his business, which he never closed.[40]

During the union employees' strike in the winter 1983, Tatum, the editor in chief and principal owner, was locked in a power struggle with several partners. Partner John Edmonds had hired John Davis, the executive editor, but Tatum fired Davis for insubordination and also to save money because of financial losses incurred from the six-month strike.[41] Tatum said he borrowed $570,000 to cover losses from the strike. When the labor unrest ended, he cut the *Amsterdam News* staff by one-third.[42] Circulation that had stood at nearly 59,000 in 1977 when the paper published Cooper's columns declined to about 40,000 after the strike.

By the mid-1980s, Tatum's *Amsterdam News* had twice the circulation of the *City Sun*. The *Amsterdam News* was dominant, but not nearly as dominant a black-owned media force as it used to be. In addition to the *City Sun*, other competitors had entered the field: *Big Red News* of Brooklyn, a former numbers (gambling) sheet that evolved into a newspaper; the *New York Voice*, a Queens-based newspaper that catered to a moderate, middle-class readership; the *Daily Challenge* of Brooklyn, which published daily and offered readers syndicated and wire service news; and the *Black American*, which often published pinup photos on its front page.[43]

This crowded field of black newspapers competed for about 800,000 black readers aged 17 to 59 and living in metropolitan New York, according to market research Cooper commissioned. *City Sun* circulation was reported to be 18,500 by 1987, but pass-along readership was probably as much as 74,000, and in the case of the *Amsterdam News*, potentially 160,000.[44]

Still, rivals Cooper and Tatum had to face the bitter truth that the number one newspaper choice of black New Yorkers was the *Daily News*, the newspaper that four black journalists successfully sued for racial discrimination in spring 1987.

In February 1986, when Mayor Koch began his third four-year term and was immediately under siege because of corruption scandals involving his closest allies in the boroughs, Tatum began writing weekly front-page editorials that called for Koch to resign.

Tatum wrote that in addition to presiding over a corrupt, ineffective administration, the mayor ignored the needs of blacks and members of other minority groups. Tatum took a different approach than he had a few years before, when he ran Koch's upbeat Op-Ed defense of his administration. Then Tatum became annoyed when his editor ran a stinging rebuke of Koch in the same edition. By the time Tatum's front-page editorial series began in 1986, critiquing Koch was business as usual at the *City Sun*. Cooper's newspaper published editorials that ridiculed the mayor for professing ignorance of Queens borough president Donald Manes's corrupt governance. Manes committed suicide that winter.

The *City Sun*'s news menu was sparkling. There was the in-depth coverage of the *Daily News* four trial, copious coverage of the Howard Beach murder and the successful demands by militant attorneys for the special prosecutor, relentless coverage of the Local 1199 hospital workers' union political power struggle, and ongoing critiques of police brutality and misconduct.

A few weeks after the third anniversary of the *City Sun* in June, Cooper was informed that the National Association of Black Journalists had selected him as its Journalist of the Year. Cooper was the tenth person to win the award since 1979 and the first winner who represented black-owned media.

That year, for the first time in the twelve-year history of NABJ, both top award winners were representatives of black-owned media. The lifetime achievement award winner was John H. Johnson, founder of *Ebony* and *Jet* magazines. Johnson was the tenth winner since 1978 and the fifth from black-owned media to win.[45]

The August 19–25 *City Sun* carried a full page 2 house advertisement that read, "The National Association of Black Journalists has named the *City Sun* paper of the year and its publisher, Publisher of the Year. We are deeply honored by the NABJ and share it with our advertisers, supporters and readers of New York's most authoritative black weekly newspaper."

At the convention's Friday night awards program on August 21, Cooper's moment in the spotlight was uncomfortable—even awkward—for the award recipient and many NABJ members.[46] The co-hosts were black local TV journalists who apparently were not members. They were constantly mispronouncing the association initials.

British R&B singers Loose Ends ("Slow Down" and "Hanging' on a String") were to perform after Cooper and Johnson received their awards. But when they learned about an opportunity for a paid gig later that night, the singers Carl McIntosh and Steve Nichol told board members backstage that because the NABJ event was merely a benefit, they wanted to go onstage immediately, or they would leave. The board members yielded, and Loose Ends performed.

"People were dancing in their seats," recalled Yanick Rice of the *New York Times*, an officer in the NABJ New York affiliate chapter. "To honor one of our own, we didn't give him and the award the dignity he deserved. I cringed because I knew he [Cooper] was going to let us have it."[47]

Indeed, Cooper, a lion of a man who had battled with politicians, judges, union leaders, and business executives, socked it to NABJ: "I don't appreciate being upstaged by some variety act." His acceptance speech was more of a scold than a thank-you.[48]

Jocelyn Cooper sat with her husband in the front row. Decades later she said he had written an eloquent acceptance speech about journalism and public service. Being upstaged by Loose Ends kept him from delivering it. Rice said that immediately after the group performed and Cooper was brought to the stage, "I also feared we were going to miss out on his message."

Cooper returned to Brooklyn and with managing editor Utrice Leid resumed the *City Sun*'s bold, tough, and creative journalism. In July and August, they exposed a police undercover operation the *City Sun* called "Spy gate."

Activists Alton Maddox, C. Vernon Mason, and the Rev. Al Sharpton were targets of the police, reported the newspaper. The trio said Koch and police commissioner Ward must go. Three weeks later, in the July 29 edition, Esmeralda Simmons, director of the Brooklyn-based Center for Law and Social Justice, told the newspaper that the NYPD undercover operation had widened to her advocacy organization: "I'm convinced that the police are after us because of the work the center does for the community."[49]

"Exposed!" Screamed the editorial headline that said Koch and Ward were at a loss of words when questioned about the investigation of a so-called police department "black desk" that investigated activists. Maddox, Mason, and Sharpton had plenty to say to the newspaper and on WLIB-AM in protest. On television, *Like It Is* reran footage of a black spy for the FBI's counterintelligence program who mentioned a federal "black desk."

Another police-related conflict was the Larry Davis case in the Bronx. "Exclusive" was repeated twice in the skyboxes of the August 19 *City Sun*. Four text boxes surrounded a large cover photo of a muscular young man. "Who's trying to kill Larry Davis?" asked the headline. "Why do they want him dead?" Writer Peter Noel's narrative said that Davis was a drug dealer who also sold drugs for a band of rogue cops working out of a Bronx precinct.

Davis's pregnant girlfriend lost their baby. He learned that the fetus was poisoned with cocaine his girlfriend had received from one of the rogue police clients. Davis ended his business relationship with the drug-trafficking cops. The officers who feared Davis would expose their criminal enterprise reportedly tried to frame him for several alleged murders of rival dealers.

Police went to Davis's sister's home—where he was staying—to arrest him on murder charges. A fierce gun battle ensued. Davis shot six police officers. None of them were killed, but one lost an eye and took scores of shotgun pellets in his head. A follow-up story in the September 2 edition said Rudy Giuliani, crime-busting U.S. attorney, was reluctant to touch the Davis case. The *City Sun* ran an editorial that cataloged Giuliani's record of alleged selective prosecution.[50]

Meanwhile Cooper and Leid continued to needle Koch and police commissioner Ward. An editorial titled "Koch's Sublime Allegory" mocked the mayor for giving neckties with the city emblem to three unarmed black males who survived baseball bat attacks by twenty-five white teenagers in Brooklyn's Canarsie neighborhood. On Friday, September 11, a special messenger arrived at the *City Sun* office and hand-delivered a letter from Koch. In the September 16–22 edition, the paper published a 460-word front-page letter from the mayor that called the *City Sun* "vile" and "racist":

> I believe that what the decent people of all races want is equality and fairness. The *City Sun* believes that if a black person is assaulted by a white, a grand jury should be convened and special prosecutors appointed. If a white is acquitted, you denounce the decision as a symptom of racism.
>
> But when a white person is assaulted by a black, you suddenly develop a case of colorblindness. If the black is acquitted, you applaud. To the *City Sun*, Bernard Goetz is a racist monster because he shot and wounded four black men in the subway and was only found guilty of possessing a gun. Is that your opinion of Austin Weeks, a black subway rider who shot and killed a white who threatened him with racial invective? Weeks wasn't even convicted of gun charges. And what about the case of Andre Nichols, a young black man who shot and killed a white priest he claimed was sexually soliciting him? Andre Nichols was acquitted of murder and was not prosecuted on gun charges. Were these decisions racist? I doubt that you thought these questions through.

Managing editor Utrice Leid answered with a 1,360-word reply that faced off with Koch on the front page. She wrote:

> Frequent departures from linear reasoning are nothing new to Mayor Koch. He excels at it. With close to 250 people shot dead by New York City police—most of them black and Latino males killed by white males—since he took office, it is Koch who insists there is no police brutality problem in the Big Apple. A surfeit of boarded-up, city-owned housing does not sway him from believing that temporary shelters are the way to go. The unfolding corruption, bribery and sex scandals that continue to rock his administration in no way suggest he bears any responsibility. This is Koch's logic.
>
> The point of our editorials has been that the duality that exists in most areas of life for blacks—in education, employment, housing, delivery of city services, the law—in almost all cases is created, maintained and reinforced by the very systems of government that are supposed to root it out. The concepts of equality and fairness, therefore, are largely just that—*concepts*, not realities.

Then Leid answered Koch's criminal justice examples case by case. Goetz, Leid said, was treated as a special case by the justice system. The white suspect surrendered in New Hampshire nine days after shooting four black males in the subway, yet Manhattan district attorney Robert Morgenthau did not charge Goetz with leaving the scene of a crime, and Morgenthau "afforded [Goetz] something no black in similar circumstances would be afforded, bail."

As for the black shooting suspect Weeks, Leid said her newspaper did not applaud his actions. Weeks, however, was later found shot to death in his apartment, and police went to great pains to say his unsolved death was not related to the subway shooting. Neighbors and Weeks's family said that his death was a "revenge" killing.

As for Nichols, Leid said that an almost all-white jury believed his explanation that he was defending himself against the "illicit advances of a lustful pederast who happened to be a Catholic priest. It might interest the mayor," Leid wrote, "to know that even the judge and Catholic authorities congratulated Mr. [Alton] Maddox for handling the defense of his client with the utmost delicacy and professionalism."

"Psychologists and psychiatrists," said Leid's closing paragraph, "use a term called transference. It occurs when a person chooses not to deal with the harsh realities of the unsavory conditions he causes directly and is therefore responsible for so he affixes blame to someone else. This way he can assume a sense of righteous indignation because, after all, someone else caused the whole mess. Sorry Mayor Koch, if anyone has set loose the 'demons of racial hatred' it is you. But it is up to us to see to it that you and your minions don't surround us on all sides." In that edition, the *City Sun* reprinted the "Koch's Sublime Allegory" editorial on the Op-Ed page.[51]

In late September, the Howard Beach homicide case returned to the news. Charles Hynes, the special prosecutor for whom activists Maddox, Mason, and Sharpton had pressed Governor Cuomo the previous winter, put the defendants on trial. Jon Lester and Scott Kern, both eighteen years old, were charged with second-degree murder and other offenses. Michael Pirone, seventeen, and Jason Ladone, sixteen, were charged with manslaughter and other crimes.

Jury selection was completed October 1. The twelve members included one black woman, two Puerto Ricans, two Asian Americans, and a man from Guyana with Asian roots. Race mattered. The judge said that the defense tried to reject all black jurors, but he rebuffed the tactic, and the compromise was a jury that was half people of color, despite only one black representative.[52]

Defense attorneys tried to convince the jury that the December 1986 neighborhood confrontation that resulted in the death of Michael Griffith was an unfortunate accident and without racial overtones. Several weeks into the trial, while the jury was out of the courtroom, state supreme court justice Thomas A. Demakos declared that Claudia Calogero, one of two sixteen-year-old neighborhood girls, was a hostile prosecution witness because she appeared to give inconsistent testimony at the trial. Although Calogero and the other girl, Laura Castanga, were part of the crowd that had confronted Michael Griffith, Cedric Sandiford, and Timothy Grimes as the trio left the pizza parlor, the girl now said she did not see the baseball bat and tree limb used to batter the victims. Calogero was the former girlfriend of defendant Kern.[53]

Defense attorney Stephen Murphy also painted Grimes as a menacing troublemaker and said that the man had flashed a knife at the white youths. Grimes did not deny that; he said that when cornered, he had pulled out the knife in self-defense. Murphy's cross-examination of Grimes was bellicose and sarcastic. Murphy's statements were frequently ruled out of order by the judge, but the lawyer's tactics rattled Grimes. Twice he stormed out of the courtroom and vowed he would not continue to testify. In the hallway, Grimes cried in the arms of Christopher Griffith, a freelance photographer who was the older brother of Michael Griffith, who died that night in Howard Beach. Grimes's supporters convinced him to stand up to the verbal assault and finish testifying. He did.[54]

The daily metropolitan newspapers covered the trial, and the *City Sun* was there too. The weekly's October 14–20 edition included a pullout report on the trial.

On November 20, the prosecution rested after calling sixty-one witnesses. On November 25, Demakos barred television and photographic coverage of the trial. On December 2, the defense rested after calling thirteen witnesses. On December 5, an administrative judge reversed the ban on TV and photo coverage, and on December 11 Demakos allowed cameras to cover the verdict.[55]

On Monday, December 21, the jury found three of the four defendants—Lester, Kern and Ladone—guilty of second-degree manslaughter and acquitted the fourth youth on trial, Pirone.

The convicted teenagers' punishment was downgraded from the murder charges they had faced three and a half months before; still, the jury convicted them for killing someone. They faced prison terms of five to fifteen years for manslaughter, plus five to fifteen years for assault.

During morning rush hour—before the verdict was announced—sixty-nine people were arrested for a protest against racism that snarled subway service and resulted in a partial closing of the Brooklyn Bridge. The next day, hundreds of civil rights activists assembled in Brooklyn, and their leaders denounced Koch and Ward.[56] Many black citizens and officials praised the Howard Beach verdict. Many of these supporters qualified their praise by citing the undercurrent of racism during the trial.

The verdict cracked the criminal justice version of the glass ceiling: the perception that in New York a white law enforcement official or even a violent mob could never be punished for killing or maiming a black or other person of color. The Howard Beach trial, which ended a year and a day after the trouble began on a cold December night in 1986, was another milestone in city race relations. The previous spring, the city's leading newspaper had been convicted of racial discrimination against its black employees. The *Daily News* management promised to change its practices.

The *City Sun* was a brash agent of change. It aggressively covered racially sensitive cases such as Howard Beach and the *Daily News* four trial. When the establishment ridiculed Maddox and Mason's unorthodox and risky tactics in the Howard Beach case, the *City Sun* championed the lawyers, who prevailed. When the *Daily News* four employees looked like overmatched ragamuffins compared to the *Daily News*–Tribune Company juggernaut, the *City Sun* provided ample space and allowed the plaintiffs to plead their cause to readers. Cooper was recognized as NABJ Journalist of Year for his relentless and courageous work as publisher.

Yet at the same time the racial fever should have cooled, a bizarre new case kept New Yorkers on edge. This time the epicenter of the turmoil was not within city limits, but in Dutchess County, an exurb north of New York City.

16. TAWANA BRAWLEY

On Wednesday, November 25, the *City Sun* front page led with near-climatic developments in the Howard Beach trial. That issue's headline read: "Will Hynes' case Hold Up under Lawyer's Offensive?" Charles Hynes was the special prosecutor battling Stephen Murphy and other lawyers who represented the Howard Beach teenagers. On the day of the new edition, a fifteen-year-old black girl was reported missing in Wappingers Falls, New York, a village about seventy miles north of New York City. It was the day before Thanksgiving 1987. The girl's story would make the news on Sunday, November 29. For most of the next year, the saga of Tawana Brawley would tease, seduce, and vex the New York press, including the *City Sun*. In many ways, the teenage girl's case would become the weekly's Vietnam, with severe consequences for its journalists.

That Sunday in late November, Juanita Brawley called WCBS-TV 2 in Manhattan and told weekend assignment editor Tom Farkas a horrific story. Her niece had traveled to Newburgh and had been missing for days. When Tawana was found inside a plastic garbage bag, she was covered in feces. "KKK" and "nigger" were scrawled on her chest and stomach with a marker. Passersby took the incoherent girl to St. Francis Hospital in Poughkeepsie. When doctors examined Tawana, they reported that some of her hair had been chopped off, her face was bruised, and her body scratched. The girl may have been raped. She was treated for her injuries and for shock, then released to her mother Glenda and her aunt that morning.[1]

The story seemed too outrageous to be true, but WCBS received confirmation that the FBI was investigating, and the TV station assignment manager green-lighted the story.[2] Reporter Mary Murphy was dispatched to Dutchess County. Ralph King, Glenda Brawley's live-in boyfriend, greeted Murphy at a 7-Eleven store, and the reporter followed him by car to the home. Murphy's story was on the air at 11 p.m. before 1.2 million TV households. It included an on-camera interview with Tawana.[3] The girl said a white man dressed as a police officer forced her into a car near a gas station. The exchange with the reporter went like this:

Tawana: He told me to shut up.
Murphy: He told you to shut up?
Tawana: He was a cop.
Murphy: He was a police officer?
Tawana: Showed me a badge.
Murphy [narrating]: Tawana choked back tears, remembering how another man drove them to the woods, where she says she was surrounded by a group and raped and sodomized. Medical evidence shows her vaginal area was bruised. Lab tests will confirm the degree of sexual assault.

Murphy also interviewed Dutchess County sheriff Fred Skoralick. He was skeptical of the Brawleys' story. Glenda Brawley and Ralph King had had run-ins with the law, the sheriff said, but he did not elaborate. Less than two weeks before the attack, Brawley's family was evicted from an apartment complex for nonpayment of rent. When Tawana, a popular cheerleader at the local high school, was found disheveled in the woods, it was near her former home.[4] The sheriff made the following statement on camera: "We don't know whether someone put her in the garbage bag she was found in, or whether she got into the bag herself."[5]

A few days after the story aired, Murphy was shut off from the family for no clear reason. Tawana seemed believable, but her mother's demeanor was curious. Glenda Brawley did not express outrage during the Sunday interview and seemed disconnected from her daughter, never offering gestures of comfort or reassurance. In December and January, Chris Borgen of WCBS-TV2 continued reporting the story.[6]

On December 2, the Wednesday after WCBS broke the Brawley story, the *City Sun*'s lead stories were "Haiti Will Be Free!" and "Chicago after Harold Washington" (the city's first elected black mayor had died at sixty-five from a heart attack, shortly after his reelection to a second four-year term).

Also that day, four days after Tawana reappeared, Harry Crist, an IBM technician and part-time police officer from East Fishkill, a neighboring Hudson Valley town, committed suicide.

Crist, twenty-nine, lived in an apartment that was four blocks from the Brawley family's new home. Crist's looks—blond hair and a pale mustache—roughly matched the description of one of the assailants, according to the teenager's new advisers Alton Maddox, C. Vernon Mason, and Al Sharpton. Yet no evidence linked Crist to Tawana.[7] That same week, Tommy Masch, twenty-one, another young white man with blond hair and mustache, read news accounts that suggested he too was a possible suspect. Masch was a volunteer firefighter who drove a recycled state police cruiser. He reputedly flashed a police auxiliary badge when he arrived at the scenes of fires and accidents. Masch told *Daily News* columnist Bob Herbert that his life was turned upside down because of inferences based on flimsy circumstantial inferences.

Masch agreed to take a polygraph test, but on two occasions, logistical mix-ups prevented the test from taking place.[8] In the coming weeks, a chain reaction within the Hudson Valley community justice system would frustrate the search for truth in the Tawana Brawley case.

The following week, December 9, the *City Sun* led with "Upstate Race Case Is the 'Last Straw,' Say Activists."[9] On that note, the weekly began covering the Brawley story. Maddox, Mason, and Sharpton were on hand to comment. On December 14, the *New York Times* waded into the story with a piece by Esther Iverem, a reporter-trainee. In her account, the girl said she was sodomized by six white men, but Iverem's account added that local law enforcement officials questioned the truthfulness of Tawana's statements, and those statements had not been made in any substantive way to any local, state, or federal investigators assigned immediately to the case.[10]

The *Amsterdam News* weighed in a week after the incident and was quite reckless. Tawana Brawley, the newspaper reported without qualification, was "assaulted in the woods for four days by a wolf pack of Ku Klux Klansmen." KKK was written on Tawana's chest, but there was no proof that the domestic terrorists were involved. The paper also quoted Maddox, who said that a cop whom the teenager had identified was in trouble and could be fired. This reporting was curious because the three advisers kept Tawana away from investigators.

The Klan hyperbole resurfaced two weeks later on the *Amsterdam News* front page: "Klans Planning Big Queens Cross Burning Rally." The paper quoted one Hank Erich Schmidt, who called himself the "Exalted Cyclops of the National Klan" and vowed to lead the New York White Knights, carrying a seventy-foot electric cross, into Astoria, Queens, and to a black housing project. The threatened cross lighting did not occur, and Schmidt was not heard from again.[11]

On Wednesday, December 16, two days after Iverem's story, the *City Sun* cover was "Farrakhan Issues Warning on Upstate Race Case." The Chicago-based minister's apocalyptic words appeared in a left-hand vertical pull quote on the front page: "If you will not take the guilty parties and prosecute them and give them what the law demands, then we have no alternative but to prosecute them ourselves and bring justice to our breasts ourselves, regardless of the cost."[12]

This was edition number 50 and the last of 1987. The *City Sun* took its traditional holiday break and resumed publishing on January 6–12, 1988. The staff missed the chance to report the Howard Beach trial verdict, announced on the Monday after the final edition of 1987. "Fate has conspired against us," said an eight-line editorial.

That week on December 19, the Dutchess County grand jury was seated to hear evidence regarding Tawana Brawley's abduction and assault. About thirty witnesses from hundreds of people interviewed appeared before the panel. Newswise, the case stalled during the Christmas season through the 1988 New Year's holiday.

On January 21, Bill Grady, the second-term district attorney, abruptly quit the case and told supervising judge Judith Hillery that he had to withdraw because of a conflict of interest. Hillery agreed and sealed the minutes that contained Grady's explanation. The judge appointed David Sall and William Burke, both defense attorneys, as joint special prosecutors. Within twenty-four hours, Sall and Burke also withdrew, explaining that their investigation would likely be plagued by the conflict Grady had cited.[13] These setbacks occurred as Maddox, Mason, and Sharpton made daily denunciations and said that Tawana Brawley was the victim of a cover-up. Five days later, on January 26, Governor Cuomo stepped in and appointed attorney general Robert Abrams special prosecutor of the Tawana Brawley case.

For the second time in a less than a year, the prosecution of a violent offense against a black New Yorker was taken away from local authorities and handed to a special state prosecutor. And again the team of Maddox, Mason, and Sharpton represented the victims and demanded such customized justice. As before, the trio managed to shield their victim-clients from investigators and stage-manage the local press. The trio continued to appear on WLIB-AM to explain the case to a friendly, activist-oriented audience.

Though the legal patterns of the Griffith and Brawley cases were similar, something significant had changed. A year earlier, when the activist trio had managed the Michael Griffith case, the pecking order from the top was Maddox as the fiery lead, Mason as the smooth complementary counsel, and Sharpton was the newcomer who rounded out the team. Twelve months later, Sharpton moved to the head of the pack because of his ability to manipulate the local media, especially TV news. For weeks, Sharpton particularly engaged in a McCarthyesque smear campaign against real and perceived adversaries. He aired lurid and dubiously provable allegations of official misconduct. The minister without a congregation scolded certain journalists who resisted playing along with his farce. In one telling moment, an exasperated Sharpton asked investigative reporter Mike Taibbi of WCBS-TV, "Why are you [and producer Anna Sims-Phillips] trying to poke holes in our story?" Taibbi answered: "Because there *are* holes."[14] Gaps and contradictions included the following:

- Maddox, Mason, and Sharpton were not truthful when they kept saying that the family refused to cooperate with authorities. Actually, the legal team prevented the Brawleys from talking to investigators.[15]
- Some reporting led to doubts that Tawana Brawley was abducted by racist white men and sexually assaulted for four days. The girl was missing on Thanksgiving Day and Black Friday. Friends and acquaintances placed her in the Dutchess County communities of Poughkeepsie, Newburgh, Wappinger, and Wappingers Falls during the four days.[16]
- There was speculation that Tawana stayed away from home to avoid the wrath of her mother and violent stepfather after staying out too late with friends. During the media frenzy and stalemate with investigators, Tawana Brawley resided with her uncle, Matthew Strong, a cop who was (Tawana's aunt) Juanita Brawley's ex-husband.[17]
- One of Tawana Brawley's hangouts was the "crack street" in Newburgh. There were no suggestions that she was a substance abuser, but plenty of circumstantial evidence that Tawana's friends and acquaintances hung out on that strip.[18]
- There was a lack of proof of Tawana's sexual assault. The FBI crime lab and hospital rape kit did not detect an assault. WNBC-TV reporter David Diaz interviewed a seminaked Tawana Brawley at her hospital bed to try to verify there was an assault, but was unsuccessful. The advisers complained that the TV station took advantage of a minor.[19]
- A *New York Daily News* poll in early spring reported that after many months, 90 percent of respondents—white and black—believed Tawana Brawley should cooperate with authorities and testify. The poll also reported that there was strong biracial support for Governor Cuomo and Attorney General Abrams, top officials whom Maddox, Mason, and Sharpton routinely vilified.[20]
- The Brawley lawyers and spokesmen were bold enough to smear Stephen Pagones, a Dutchess County assistant district attorney, as

> one of Tawana Brawley's attackers. They offered no proof. A report by Taibbi said that Pagones was reluctant to talk because he was embarrassed about his handling of a restaurant liquor license case that was unrelated to the Tawana Brawley incident. Pagones's unrelated incident, however, did not stop Maddox, Mason, and Sharpton from tying the justice official criminally to their cause.[21]

On Wednesday, January 27, the day after the state attorney general was appointed special prosecutor, the *City Sun*'s cover story asked, "Who is trying to destroy this man?" It was the opening of a three-part series about Sharpton by Peter Noel. A near-life-sized head shot of the minister filled the front page, and Noel profiled Sharpton in a four-page centerfold pullout.

The previous week, *Newsday* reported on January 20 that for the past five years, Sharpton had been an FBI informant. The minister's confederates included known mob figures, and his targets were *other* blacks. On more than a dozen occasions, Sharpton wore a body wire when he met or sat for lunches with his targets. G-men listened through their earpieces.[22] The revelations should have meant that Sharpton was doomed in activist circles. A mass meeting at Harriet Tubman School in Harlem raised the question, "Can a black leader serve the community and be an agent of the state?" The consensus response was no.

Yet Sharpton survived his documented serial snitching. Instead of distancing themselves, Maddox and Mason stood with him as an adviser to Tawana Brawley.[23] Also, the majority of the New York media, eager for details about the lurid and mystifying case, ignored Sharpton's character flaw. As "the sound bite and the fury," journalists had to go through the minister, since he and his advisers muzzled the girl and the parents.

The reliably skeptical *City Sun* wore blinders on the Sharpton story. Reading the paper, it seemed sometimes that to Leid—who wrote some of the stories—Sharpton could do no wrong. In an interview with *New York* magazine, Cooper acknowledged that Sharpton was a "hustler" and a "media junkie," but called the *Newsday* exposé of the minister a case in which the newspaper was used by federal authorities to undermine black leadership as it was mobilizing public opinion.[24]

But did Cooper's newspaper momentarily forget its mission to cover black political figures critically and not ignore their faults because of their race or cause? When not speaking officially as publisher of the *City Sun*, Cooper posed as "Dan" and talked politics with Jim Sleeper for his book the *Closest of Strangers* (1990). Sleeper noted that during the Howard Beach case, Maddox and Mason played recklessly with facts, specifically about motorist Dominick Blum's role in Michael Griffith's death. As Sleeper listed his concerns over the phone, he heard a series of long, low chuckles. "Dan" did not deny the dishonesty of the lawyers and their supporters; he was enjoying their strategy because it was winning.

"This isn't about fairness and intellectual integrity," said "Dan," "It's about power—and sure, maybe it's the same morally bankrupt power whites have held over us through institutions like the Queens courts for years." Maddox and Mason, he continued, had been "naughty," but they had "gotten the system over a barrel."

In 1988, it looked as if Maddox, Mason, and Sharpton would repeat their mischief with their new client, Tawana Brawley. In time it would become clear that her cause was not as righteous as winning justice for Michael Griffith's death. Cooper, Utrice Leid, and the *City Sun*'s lapses in judgment would haunt the newspaper months later.

Meanwhile Sharpton was emboldened after surviving his informant scandal. He continued to inflame passions in the Tawana Brawley case and punish dissenters. In February, Brooklyn assemblyman Roger Green protested a new Sharpton verbal torching. The minister wanted Abrams ousted as special prosecutor. Sharpton said that asking the attorney general to continue was "like asking someone killed in the gas chamber to sit down with Mr. Hitler." Green, leader of the Black and Puerto Rican Legislative Caucus, said it was "intellectually dishonest" for Sharpton to make such a statement about Abrams, and furthermore, Green criticized Sharpton's "cavalier use of words like 'racism' and 'fascism'" and the use of "tactics that encourage race war." Green lobbied Governor Cuomo behind the scenes to find a resolution to the Tawana Brawley case.[25]

Green did not say that Tawana should cooperate with Abrams, nor did the legislator criticize lawyers Maddox and Mason. Green *did* challenge Sharpton to behave responsibly. Retribution against the legislator was swift. When media outlets called, the minister branded Green as an "Uncle Tom, a state pawn," and implausibly claimed that the elected official was "afraid the minister would challenge him for his Assembly seat." Not a single black elected leader rose to Green's defense. He almost lost his status as leader of the state caucus. Once again, Sharpton's unsubstantiated words were the last words.[26]

"Back to the Table on Brawley Case" was the lead story headline in the February 17 *City Sun*. Leid's story reported that Abrams and Tawana's attorneys Maddox and Mason tried to break the impasse in the case. On February 11 and in front of TV cameras, Cuomo, Maddox, Mason, and Sharpton described a three-and-one-half-hour meeting. Maddox promised that at an appropriate time Tawana Brawley would be a witness. A week later, the adviser trio announced that the deal was off, and the impasse was back in place.

Sharpton vowed that if the governor refused to replace Abrams, "We're gonna announce a day of civil disobedience like you've never seen before; we're gonna shut down the state capital."[27] On February 24, the cover headline for two-thirds of the *City Sun* front page was "The Brawley Case: Things Fall Apart—and Then Also Come Together." Tawana's lawyers said the break-off in talks was a blessing in disguise, reported Leid. On editorial page 24, a cartoon shouted, "Justice for Brawley now!"

On March 2, a process story appeared on page 5. "Grand jury hears Brawley case; teenager still won't cooperate," reported Chris Atwell and Utrice Leid. An editorial on page 18 asked, "So what's the point of a grand jury hearing?" An editorial cartoon depicted Cuomo as a puppet master who dangled Abrams and Tawana Brawley on his strings. On March 9, the lead story headline was "Grand Jury Is an Open Secret, Say Brawley's Lawyers." The editorial page was dominated by a cartoon that depicted Brawley's detractors cooking up a story. Letters to the editor completed the page. On March 16, a vertical left-hand head said: "Brawley's Lawyers Raise Questions about Grand Juries Probing the Case." A large photo of demonstrators appeared to the right of the headline. On March 23, a front-page editorial cartoon dominated the page and said "Tawana Brawley becomes a victim again."

By late March, one local TV station aired a hospital bedside interview of a seminaked Tawana Brawley. What she told interviewers then contradicted what her advisers claimed months later. The advisers said the footage exploited the girl; the station said it was necessary to show it to get closer to the truth.[28] Also, a skyline tease in the *City Sun* said, "What Every Black Person Must Know in order to Understand the Brawley Case." That headline led readers to Clinton Cox's essay "The RAPE of Us All: A Primer on White Mythology and the Media," a spread on pages 18 to 22 of the 24-page edition.

On March 30, "Brawley's Advisers Promise to Turn Albany and Poughkeepsie Upside Down" was the vertical left-cover headline. To the right was a photo of the state trooper arrest of Coolidge Miller, sixty-three, a blind Brawley protester. Inside on page 4, Leid's story was headlined "Prosecutor in Brawley Case Faces 'Arrest' on Assault Charges." The editorial pages carried two big Brawley cartoons related to the case, plus letters to the editor.

City Sun coverage offered a preview of the April Fools' farce in Albany that turned public opinion against the Brawley advisers. For weeks, Abrams kept cool despite the reckless statements and outrageous actions of Maddox, Mason, and Sharpton. He held his verbal fire. After negotiations collapsed, the advisers showed up unannounced at Abrams's New York City press room to attack the attorney general. Abrams shrugged off the trio's antics. Abrams's Brawley task force informed the grand jury that the girl would never tell her story under oath. Analysis of a hospital rape kit by the FBI crime lab in Washington, D.C., indicated no evidence of sexual contact. Witnesses who had said they saw a "troop car" of white men and also saw Tawana dumped from a car retracted their stories. Investigators said that after documenting the work and family routines of the men accused of attacking Tawana, there was no way they could have been involved in her abduction or a four-day orgy of rape and violence during the Thanksgiving break.[29]

But the attorney general and Brawley case special prosecutor blew his top when Sharpton claimed he was coming to the capital city to arrest Jack Ryan, the state trooper who arrested Coolidge Miller. Abrams promised severe consequences if Sharpton carried out his threat. The masses who the minister vowed would shut down Albany turned out to be a ragtag group of supporters outnumbered by law enforcement. Meanwhile news videotape that was broadcast suggested that Ryan had not physically jostled Coolidge Miller, the senior citizen. The Brawley advisers were routed in the capital, and they retreated.[30]

On April 6, the pages of the *City Sun* were Brawley free. The newspaper quickly transitioned to U.S. presidential politics. The Reagan era was about to end. The president was in the closing months of his second four-year term. Vice president George H. W. Bush was the GOP successor. For the Democrats, governor Michael Dukakis of Massachusetts was the front-runner, but he faced a credible challenge from Jesse Jackson, who made a second run for president and had a stronger base of white unionists and working poor, as well as black elected officials who were obliged to support the Democratic front-runner in 1984 but available to support Jackson in 1988. Jackson scored some notable primary wins in March—including his home state South Carolina—and the New York primary was in April. The April 13 *City Sun* primary edition included a surprise, a front-page editorial headlined "Jesse, Say It Ain't So," which jumped inside and filled the entire editorial page.

Despite a ringing endorsement four years before, this time the newspaper rejected Jackson. It said the candidate had abandoned the disenfranchised to be more acceptable to the establishment.

> The ideological maverick of 1984 has become a political hostage in 1988, trying to win white approval at the expense of the broader black imperatives that should have guided him—and us—all along. The emphatic shift from communal good to personal achievement has necessitated an equally emphatic shift from a badly needed systematic approach to effecting change to the easier alternative that demands of the black constituency that faithfully supports him an even greater sacrifice: We are to pretend that our problems are just as bad as everybody else so that Jesse Jackson can "win" white America. In the true spirit of brotherhood, we are to fuel the fire so it can warm everybody else—first.
>
> Jackson's political advisers and the network news may tell him he's doing well, and the scorecard may convince him of that, but it all depends on what one thinks winning is. If winning means having to yield on principles, having to toe the line, then being a loser is a far more honorable alternative.[31]

Since the *City Sun* was practically the only black newspaper in the United States to refuse to support Jackson's bid for the Democratic nomination, it was unknown whether the paper was just expressing its militant independence or throwing an editorial temper tantrum. Was it possible that the trauma from covering real or alleged racial violence in New York rendered a cynical assessment of Jackson's campaign? Did the *City Sun* feel obligated to position itself against him because its uptown nemesis the *Amsterdam News* was for Jackson?

In the weeks that followed, the *City Sun* returned to its true character and provided ample space for letter writers to praise, criticize, and condemn its editorial stance on Jackson. "The Jackson Fallout Continues," said the skyline tease on the April 27 front page. Two opinion pages were filled with ten letters and two op-ed essays in response to the Jackson editorial.

In Newark, New Jersey, a twenty-year-old black journalism student at Seton Hall University was a huge fan of the *City Sun*. Todd Steven Burroughs and another black Seton Hall student were so adamant about reading the paper every week that they gently petitioned a bodega near the university to carry the weekly tabloid. Clad in his African medallion and his Malcolm X T-shirts, and himself a cub reporter for the New Jersey edition of the Afro-American newspaper, Burroughs believed that the *City Sun* could do no wrong. He loved watching the paper's TV commercial on Sundays, which featured Imhotep Gary Byrd, a leading WLIB-AM host, as pitchman. Burroughs even made a wall collage featuring the paper's front pages in his room. The editorial dismissing Jackson's bid intrigued him so much, he decided to call the paper to register a gentle protest. "I couldn't believe I got Utrice Leid on the phone," he recalled years later. "From my view back then, it was like talking to God herself. I tried not to shake. I vainly tried to debate her for ten minutes on the paper's position on Jesse. She thought it was charming that a kid would actually call her up and challenge her. And I gotta admit; she did have a point."[32]

In 1986, Floyd Flake was elected to Congress, and the clergyman expanded black political representation as the first of his race to hail from the borough of Queens. On May 11, the *City Sun* cover was "Swaggart-Type Scandal Haunts Minister Congressman."[33]

Leid's story inside reported that Thelma Singleton-Scott had filed a sexual harassment complaint against the minister. She was a church aide who had worked for Flake and claimed that the two had an affair. When Singleton-Scott tried to end it, Flake retaliated by harassing her on the job until she quit. The following week a copyrighted story by Leid reported that Flake was the target of two federal probes for personal finance and business dealings. A former Allen AME church trustee also came forward with allegations of fiscal improprieties.[34] The story noted that his church board reappointed the minister.

The May 25 edition was the third consecutive week of front-page Flake coverage. Two large photos showed an embattled Flake walking a stairwell. He was leaving a private meeting with his accuser. "Flake Not Scot-Free of Misconduct Charges" was the headline. "Secret Tapes Tell a Different Story of Sex Scandal" was the headline on Leid's story on pages 4 and 5. In addition, "What This Newspaper Is About" was an editorial about the Flake scandal.

"Last week," the piece explained, "two black weeklies, the *Amsterdam News* and the New York *Voice*, ran editorials attacking the *City Sun* because of its stories on the Rev. Floyd Flake. The former called us 'morally corrupt,'—and that was when it was being complimentary. The latter 'warned' us that 'before [we] get to Rev. Flake we have to get Nat Singleton first'—whatever that means." Singleton was a veteran political activist who helped Flake get elected in 1986.[35]

"Even asiniaity has its purpose," the editorial continued, "and we thought we'd use these asinine actions to serve as a backdrop for a discussion on what a black newspaper is—or should be." In August 1990, a seventeen-count federal indictment charged Flake and his wife with diverting thousands of dollars in church funds for their personal use.[36]

The June 8 *City Sun* was the fourth-anniversary edition. In addition to the twenty-four-page newspaper was "Flare," a sixteen-page literary supplement. There was also an aggressive return to reporting and commentary on the Tawana Brawley case. "Taking Aim at the Wrong Target: The Travesty of the Brawley Case" was an editorial that referred to the *City Sun* news story "Glenda Brawley Goes on Wanted List," a Peter Noel account with a Poughkeepsie dateline.

Tawana's mother resisted the call to testify before the grand jury and was held in contempt of court. To avoid arrest, she fled to sanctuary, initially to a Queens church and then to Bethany Baptist Church in Brooklyn.[37] A week later, the June 15 *City Sun* scored an exclusive interview when Glenda Brawley spoke with reporter Phil Makotsi.

Brash claims by the Maddox, Mason, and Sharpton team that were usually displayed prominently in the weekly were temporarily muted. The trio was playing defense. Tawana had yet to tell her story publicly, and the insatiable local media machine grew weary of her advisers' antics. Black activists did not abandon Maddox, Mason, and Sharpton but realized they were hostages in an apparent hoax. The Rev. Herbert Daughtry summoned Maddox and Mason to his Brooklyn church to tell them they could not go on making wild gutter attacks on Cuomo and Abrams.[38]

Daughtry's earnestness contrasted with the gallows humor of other activists. At a Harlem meeting, when someone made reference to Maddox's ferocity, Mason's dishonesty, and Sharpton's FBI connections, the Rev. Lawrence Lucas said, "Oh, you mean Fire, Liar and Wire?"[39]

On June 22, a portrait of Maddox and a vertical headline filled the *City Sun*'s front page. "Brawley Family Lawyer Begins the Battle of His Life," read the headline of Noel's four-page copyrighted story, subtitled "The Trial of Alton Maddox: Inside the Stop-Maddox Movement."

Next week, June 29, the pre–Independence Day edition, the front page was as explosive as Fourth of July fireworks. "TAWANA WAS RAPED" the three-line headline screamed in red ink. "Evidence torpedoes Abrams', feds' handling of the case."

What was the *City Sun*'s evidence?

> Although state Attorney General Robert Abrams, Gov. Mario Cuomo and U.S. Attorney Rudolph Giuliani publicly have expressed doubts about the veracity of Tawana Brawley's accounts of her kidnapping and rape, documents obtained by the *City Sun* not only bear out major portions of her story but also point to a concerted attempt by law enforcement officials

> to cover up the crime, both in the initial stages of investigation and very possibly even now in the current grand jury probe.
>
> The documents also point up dramatic inconsistencies in the information being made available to the public by authorities and the press about key details about the case and the Wappingers Falls teenager who had disappeared without a trace for four days last Nov. 24 and was found in a disheveled, unconscious state behind an apartment complex where she used to live.

The documents were provided by Maddox, who with Mason and Sharpton for months had frustrated the criminal investigation and would have made senator Joe McCarthy proud with the way in which they manipulated the press corps and smeared adversaries by dangling accusations then pulling back the teasing details when pressed for proof.

Leid and her newspaper fell into the advisers' trap. Leid misinterpreted a handful of crucial facts extracted from the documents, thanks to Maddox's embellishments. She falsely reported that Tawana Brawley had been given a bath before the rape kit was administered and that the rape kit specimens had not been safeguarded.

It was also untrue that the Westchester County Medical Center, where the teenager was examined in December, "had come to believe Tawana was a rape victim," as Leid wrote. The document Leid cited was not a diagnosis or physician's report but a computerized billing form. There was no numeric code for the hospital's diagnosis of "alleged sexual abuse." A hospital clerk had entered an approximate term "rape" to satisfy World Health Organization guidelines.

Despite the distortions, Leid's story spread like wildfire in the black-owned media—as many harbored doubts that she had distorted key facts. Leid defended her story on WABC-TV's public affairs show *Like It Is* and insisted there could no longer be any doubt that Tawana Brawley had been attacked. Leid pointed to pile of documents on which she based her reporting and triumphantly told host Gil Noble, "This settles it."[40]

Leid's *City Sun* exclusive was tainted fruit, ripe and sweet at that moment, but still rotten. It would cause indigestion months later. In the short term, however, the story was a circulation windfall. At Edgar's, Ethelyn Smith's Brooklyn newsstand, she normally ordered forty copies of *the City Sun* and returned unsold copies to her distributor. But on June 29 she called and asked for another batch. Smith called again for more. By midafternoon, she sold three times her usual number of *City Suns*. At the end of the day, it was impossible to find a copy of the *City Sun* at Edgar's or any other news outlet in the city.[41]

Tawana Brawley's advisers staged demonstrations in an attempt to attract wider attention at the Democratic National Convention in Atlanta, but the media horde for the most part ignored them.[42] Jesse Jackson, whose second presidential run had faded by that July convention, distanced himself from the Brawley advisers.

Late summer saw a testy Brooklyn church rally for the Brawleys. *Newsday* reporters were singled out for alleged biased coverage by Maddox, Mason, and Sharpton. Tawana and Glenda Brawley's red-bow-tied security staff ordered the *Newsday* reporters to leave. An audience of three hundred people shouted "Put them out!" Within a minute, *New York Times* reporter Don Terry announced, "If Newsday leaves, everybody leaves." Nothing happened until a member of the security detail put his hands on a twenty-one-year-old female *Newsday* intern. The pack of journalists shut their notebooks, packed up their cameras, and filed out of the sanctuary.[43]

Sharpton demanded that each reporter apologize for disrupting the rally. "The press isn't supposed to show solidarity," he said. "They're supposed to be covering us."

Most of the reporters who walked out were black, like Lyle Harris of the *New York Daily News*, who said, "We've been held hostage on this story for months. We had taken enough abuse."[44]

In early October, the special grand jury reached its conclusion about the facts and evidence in the Tawana Brawley case. The ten-month saga of lurid, racially charged allegations and shadowboxing with no proof was an elaborate hoax concocted by the teenage girl and her mother and enabled by their advisers Maddox, Mason, and Sharpton, said the twenty-three-member panel. Tawana had lied. There was no physical evidence that she had been raped; she had faked evidence of physical abuse and then misled investigators at every turn.[45]

A *New York Times* investigative team reconstructed the hoax. In summary, it happened this way:

Tawana left her home dressed in denim jeans, but she also carried a change of clothes, a skirt and black stockings. She skipped school on that pre-Thanksgiving Tuesday to visit a young man, Todd Buxton, at the Orange County Jail. When she returned from the jail by bus, Tawana hung out with Todd's sister Sandra and their mother Geneva in Newburgh. Tawana wanted to stay overnight, but Geneva Buxton encouraged Tawana to go home. Tawana reluctantly returned to Wappingers Falls at 8:40 p.m. on a commuter bus. The driver suggested that the teenager call home to get a ride, but Tawana falsely told him that the phone in the new apartment was not hooked up. In fact, it had been for four days, and she had used it regularly.

Tawana did eventually call home from that public phone. Glenda answered and erupted with anger. Stepfather Ralph King's car soon arrived and he got out. He struck Tawana behind the left ear and left a small bruise. At the home on Carmine Drive, King demanded explanations of where Tawana had been and what she had done. In time King's interrogation ended, and Tawana's sobbing died down.

The next morning, the Wednesday before Thanksgiving, Tawana slipped out of the apartment again, this time with no intention of returning. She entered the vacant former apartment 19A at the Pavilion by climbing through a rear window with a broken latch. From there she called her mother and vowed not to come back because of her abusive stepdad.

To gain King's sympathy and get Tawana back home, the mother and daughter cooked up the story that authority figures had raped the girl. Glenda also planted seeds of deception. She called Tawana's friends and said her daughter was missing. Had they seen her? Next she called her older sister Juanita and said, "Nit, Tawana didn't come home. We're worried. Ralph's crying. We don't know what to do."

Glenda Brawley gathered a care package of food, a toothbrush and toiletries, and a radio and brought it to her daughter on Thanksgiving morning. Regarding the radio, Glenda counseled Tawana to play it quietly so that she would not tip off neighbors that she was squatting in the old apartment.[46]

Inside the vacant apartment, Glenda unraveled a weave in Tawana's hair to give the girl a disheveled look. The "KKK" and "nigger" that were scrawled on Tawana's chest were not done with an ink marker. The Brawleys burned the corner of a towel and wet it to create a charcoallike marker to write the slurs.[47] Tawana stuffed pieces of the cottonlike lining from a pair of boots into her nostrils to ward off infection and the stench of the dog feces smeared on her body to enhance the ruse of a spectacular hate crime.

The other victims of the hoax wanted closure. Stephen Pagones, the Hudson Valley assistant district attorney who had been accused repeatedly of being one of the rapists, filed an $890 million slander suit against the Brawley advisers.

Elsewhere, experts tried to assess the damage this case inflicted on race relations. Conrad J. Lynn, NAACP counsel for the Mid-Hudson region—ground zero of the Brawley case—told the *New York Times*, "Mason, Maddox and their group say I'm just doing a hatchet job for the white people.

But I'd say to anyone, I think their antics are terrible. As a black civil rights lawyer, in the past, it didn't bother me that I would go up to the Orange County jail and have an all-white jury. I could appeal to their sense of fairness. There wouldn't be the open hostility I'm seeing now. This has been the toughest year in my 56 years of practice, because white people have been so angry at Mason and Maddox, their abusive language, the accusations they make with no proof."[48]

Utrice Leid was unrepentant. She said, "Robert Abrams' statements condemning the victim of the crime—and by extension exonerating the people he should be targeting for prosecution—were proof positive of what the case is all about: The state, whenever it is deemed convenient, will abrogate its responsibility to protect the constitutional rights of certain members of society, depending on a number of variables such as race or political considerations."[49]

But make no mistake: The Tawana Brawley hoax damaged the *City Sun*. In championing the cause of the black girl who cried rape, Cooper and Leid either believed in the story too much and relaxed their usually reliable, skeptical news judgment or succumbed to cynicism.

As in the Michael Griffith slaying, two lawyers and a minister-activist sparked fear in the New York justice system that frequently treated its black citizens unjustly. This time, however, the trio abused the system and were exposed in a way that burned the militant weekly that at times acted as an editorial cheerleader for them.

Fortunately, Cooper, Leid, and their aggressive staff had little time to sulk about their embarrassing episode. There were more conflicts to cover, and a historic New York City election was on the horizon.

17. MAYORAL RACE

In winter 1989, political observers were looking ahead to September. Would Ed Koch run for a fourth term as mayor? He was still popular with ethnic whites in big boroughs like Brooklyn and Queens and in near-homogeneous Staten Island. But many liberal and progressive whites in Manhattan were weary of Koch's antagonistic relationship with the city's black and brown citizens. Most blacks were not weary; they had long wanted Koch out but were powerless or too disorganized to do anything.

Then a reluctant black candidate emerged, Manhattan borough president David N. Dinkins. In the early 1970s, Dinkins had been about to become deputy mayor, but the appointment was withdrawn after it was learned he had not filed income tax returns for years and owed $15,000.[1] After Dinkins cleaned up the mess, mayor Abe Beame appointed Dinkins city clerk in 1975, and he served for a decade. During that stretch, Dinkins ran for borough president in 1977, when fellow Harlemite Percy Sutton vacated the seat to run for mayor. Both men lost, and for the first time in twenty-four years there was no black representative on the powerful city Board of Estimate, where the mayor, borough presidents, comptroller, and city council president made decisions on land use and appointed key people to boards.[2]

Dinkins ran for borough president again in 1981 and lost, but he succeeded in his next try in 1985. Dinkins was New York City's highest-ranking black elected official. Governor Cuomo sought Dinkins's counsel during a pivotal moment in the racially tense Howard Beach case—just before he replaced the Queens district attorney with a special prosecutor. During the even hotter Tawana Brawley conflict in 1988, Dinkins chastised the Maddox, Mason, Sharpton team for belittling the governor and attorney general and for peddling accusations instead of proof.[3]

In national politics, in 1984 Dinkins supported Jesse Jackson for president when many black politicians were invested in Walter Mondale, the incumbent vice president. Dinkins stuck with Jackson in 1988 when he made a much more effective run for the office.

Jackson had another New York problem. In 1984 he called the city "Hymietown," a slur directed toward the powerful Jewish voting bloc. Would Jackson's behavior taint Dinkins? In the 1970s, Dinkins joined the

Black Americans in Support of Israel Committee, and he was well connected among liberal Jewish activists.[4] Dinkins was part of the Harlem "Gang of Four" with Sutton, Paterson, and Rangel, but he was not well known to blacks in the outer boroughs. He would not be an easy sell for mayor.

It wasn't clear that Dinkins even wanted the job. In the winter of 1989, he was not openly campaigning for it. Nevertheless, *New York* magazine assessed his chances: "There is a complacent quality to Dinkins; he lacks rigor. His unwillingness to confront the mayor—or anyone, for that matter—may seem statesmanlike but might just as easily be construed as an allergy to serious thought. . . . When asked a serious question—about anything—Dinkins will flee to the nearest platitude."[5]

Dinkins was among the black leaders who got arrested for protesting South African apartheid in December 1984. The *City Sun* rejoiced editorially when Dinkins was elected Manhattan borough president in November 1985 ("Dinkins Wins! Manhattan Gets a People's President," read the headline of the front-page story, and "Great Beginnings for Black Political Leadership" was the title of the editorial inside). His win was a bright spot during Koch's reelection landslide. Dinkins was a coalition politician who repeatedly said the city and nation were not a "melting pot" but a "mosaic." The latter term provided cognitive dissonance that irked members of the press in future years.[6]

Ruth Messinger, a Manhattan city councilwoman and coalition supporter, raised money in 1988 to campaign for citywide office. She wanted to run for borough president if Dinkins was motivated to make a move up to mayor. The Board of Estimate had been all-male for nearly four years because of former city council president Elizabeth Holtzman's failed mayoral run in 1985. In 1988, Dinkins repeatedly told Messinger there was "no way he was running for mayor" and also said "I have never had the ambition particularly to be the city's first black mayor." In the winter of 1989, however, Dinkins appeared to have changed his mind, but he held his cards close.[7]

In February, Dinkins announced that he was a candidate. "As things have evolved," he told his supporters, "I'm the best choice. I can get elected." Dinkins had heard the talk that he could be the black candidate who would break through, as black mayoral candidates had done in Detroit and Atlanta in the 1970s, and in Chicago and Philadelphia in 1983. At his announcement however, he said, "It's not a question of the city being ready for a black mayor."[8]

Dinkins did not intend to sell his candidacy by emphasizing his color. There was no question that Dinkins had a shot at the mayoralty because of black votes. During presidential candidate Jesse Jackson's New York campaign, more than 500,000 new voters were registered. Hulbert James, a Dinkins strategist who also worked on the Jackson campaign, believed that 250,000 additional voters needed to be registered for Dinkins to succeed in November.[9]

Governor Cuomo refused to make any endorsement, but without naming Dinkins, he favored him: "The person who is going to win is the leader who will say to the people of the city of New York: I will bring you together." By July, Dinkins was speaking confidently about why voters should reject the incumbent Koch: "We have to renew our sense of values—as citizens, as a city, as a society. It won't be easy, but we have to begin; and this is a battle we have to win. We have to put an end to this political era of cynical manipulation and divisiveness."[10]

The March 22, 1989, *City Sun* front page was mostly filled with the image of a black teenage boy earnestly tightening a bolt on a piece of circuitry. "Reversing the Science of Exclusion" was the headline below in white type on a red backdrop. Hugh Hamilton's special report began on page 6, jumped to three additional pages, and was complemented with big, bold environmental photos of minority teenagers in labs.

Hamilton's piece sounded a warning. Within a dozen years, 400,000 science-related jobs were projected to go begging for want of qualified people to fill them. In a dozen years, one of three Americans would be people of color, and white males who presently dominated science and tech fields would amount to 15 percent of new workforce entrants. In 1989, blacks made up 12 percent of the total population, but they accounted for only 2 percent of employed scientists and engineers. Blacks also represented only 1 percent of Ph.D.'s in science and engineering.

Whether the reason for the poor representations of Americans of color was conscious exclusion or accidents of poverty, the prospect of a shortage of qualified Americans to fill science and tech jobs posed a serious threat, sources such as physicist George Campbell of the New York–based National Action Council for Minorities in Education told Hamilton. Scientists and engineers representing AT&T, Exxon, IBM, Lockheed, and Ford Motor Co. agreed: "Unless we prepare the high-growth sector of our population for high-tech careers," said a letter to president George H. W. Bush, "the United States faces a decline in both its competitive edge and its standard of living."[11] When Ronald Reagan was president, he attempted to wipe out all affirmative action initiatives, even as corporate CEOs pushed back, recognizing the demographic change that was coming in the twenty-first century. Bush, Reagan's two-term vice president, promised a "kinder, gentler" administration after eight years of open hostility. Bush had credibility. He was a major supporter of the United Negro College Fund, and he lost a congressional race in part because he resisted taking extreme racial stands.[12] The new president could be receptive to the scientists' and engineers' calls for action on minority education.

Hamilton's special report on education recalled the *City Sun*'s inaugural edition nearly five years earlier, which had calculated abominable dropout rates at predominantly black high schools that contributed then to the death of a generation.[13]

A name was not given for it at the time, but the *City Sun* called for greater minority awareness and participation in what are known today as the STEM professions: science, technology, engineering, and math. Hayden Planetarium astronomer Neil Tyson, physicist Sylvester "Jim" Gates Jr., and chemical engineer Paula Hammond were among the future stars.[14]

April 1989 marked five months since a grand jury had concluded that Tawana Brawley's claim that she was abducted and repeatedly raped was a hoax. The Brawley family moved south to Virginia to escape the media glare.[15] The Rev. Al Sharpton still insisted that Brawley, now eighteen, had been violated, but his bluster amounted to the preacher who cried wolf. In the spring of 1989, a new sex assault would shock and divide city residents.

On the night of April 19, a twenty-eight-year-old white woman was jogging along a trail in Central Park. The Salomon Brothers investment banker was running near the northern edge of the park that touches Harlem. Police that evening received reports that gangs of youths—estimates of thirty to forty people—were menacing and robbing runners and bicyclists.

At 9 p.m., David Good told a cop on a scooter that he had been attacked. By 10 p.m., police cars were dispatched in response to multiple assault and robbery calls. At 10 p.m., John Loughlin was bludgeoned in the back of the head with what appeared to be a pipe. At 10:30 p.m., cops picked up five boys at 100th Street and Central Park West, including two of the suspects.[16]

At 1:30 a.m., as two construction workers walked through the park, they heard moaning and discovered the woman jogger writhing in a ravine. Police said she had been raped and her skull had been bashed with a large rock or metal pipe. The woman lost 80 percent of the blood in her head, and investigators believed she was going to die. She survived. When questioned, the woman had no recollection of what happened to her.

Police did make arrests. Six black and Hispanic teenagers were charged: Michael Briscoe, Steve Lopez, Antron McCay, Kevin Richardson, Yusef Salaam, and Kharey Wise. Police claimed that the boys engaged in a "wilding," slang for a rape and robbery spree. Local media picked up on the term and also dubbed the suspects a "wolf pack."[17]

In media accounts, the young, white blonde executive was a far more sympathetic figure than Tawana Brawley, the black teenager from a working-class family. Unlike the Brawleys, the woman cooperated with authorities, and because they had quickly obtained physical evidence, there was no doubt that she had been beaten unconscious and sexually assaulted. Mainstream media outlets honored an unwritten code not to name the victim of a sex crime, unless the victim self-identified, as was the case with Tawana Brawley, a minor. The *Amsterdam News*, however, broke the code and in its May 6 edition named the rape victim: she was Trisha Melli. Editor in Chief Wilbert Tatum said he was reciprocating the racist injustice of naming the black suspects but not the white victim.[18] the *City Sun* parodied sensational daily newspaper coverage with the April 26–May 2 front page headline "IT'S AN OUTRAGE!" Utrice Leid wrote:

> The same media that refused to print or say that Tawana Brawley was raped had no difficulty summarily in stating so in the case of the Central Park victim. The same media that demanded that Brawley "prove" her sexual assault made no such demands in the Central Park case. The same media that had no difficulty identifying the underage Wappinger Falls teenager by name, invading the sanctity of her home to show her face and even televising seminude pictures of her while she was in the hospital have been careful to avoid identifying the Central Park woman.

Leid's rant misstated several facts. A media outlet was called and invited into the Brawley home and did not "invade." Also, the teenager's family was indeed challenged to prove a rape had occurred *because* physical evidence was unavailable. That had to do with the family's decision to frustrate the investigation. Contrarily, in the Central Park case, gruesome physical evidence was easily obtained, and the victim almost died from the indisputable attack.

Leid tried to claim a moral equivalency between Brawley and the Central Park jogger when none existed. In response, Greg Tate of the *Village Voice* wrote, "When a woman as courageous and committed as *City Sun* editor Utrice Leid blazons the headline IT'S AN OUTRAGE! above a front page editorial that reads like a pathetic whine of sour grapes over Tawana Brawley, we witness how skewed political priorities can overcome the capacity for compassion."[19]

In mid-July, the mayoral campaign was relatively quiet. But the *City Sun* refused to behave passively about Dinkins the credible candidate. "It's Time to Show Your Face, Dave" commanded the headline in the July 12–18 edition. Above the headline was a full-width photo of what looked like the back of Dinkins's salt-and-pepper, medium-length Afro. The editorial inside goaded the candidate for playing it safe: "We're not dumping on Dinkins, but we are challenging him to show his face, to state his case, to articulate the black community stake in his candidacy. Or has he decided that we are to have a local version of [Jesse] Jackson's generic [1988 presidential] campaign—generic in the sense that black votes are to pump up a candidate that would serve 'broader' interests?"[20] Andy Cooper's editorial noted that there was no evidence of campaign supporters roaming Brooklyn or other boroughs for voter support, as in the 1960s when Cooper had campaigned passionately for John V. Lindsay, the liberal Republican. Dinkins was true to form, but the publisher was impatient with the low-key strategy.

The editorial nudge of Dinkins represented life. A movie review in that same edition represented art. Critic Armond White reviewed Spike Lee's *Do the Right Thing*, the Brooklyn director's third feature film, which pundits such as Joe Klein of *New York* magazine deemed incendiary with his prediction that the film about racial conflict on a steamy July evening would spark riots.[21]

The *City Sun* acknowledged the criticism because its tease to the review was "What They Fear Most about Spike Lee's Mind." In "Exiles in Catfish Row," White compared the new movie's characters to those in the Gershwin folk opera *Porgy and Bess*: "The other America—that one suppressed by mainstream popular culture and cut off from the social advantages of the monied and mobile classes—is 'Do the Right Thing's' subject. Black American habits, humor and interpersonal conflicts are relayed in a good-natured but cautionary microcosm."[22]

Two years had passed since the spring 1987 trial in which four black journalists successfully sued the *Daily News* for racial discrimination. *Daily News* management said that it had complied with the court settlement and made a number of improvements: it hired four additional black journalists within a year of the court decision; increased its commerce with women and minority vendors to $1.3 million, up from $293,000 in 1987; and hired a black editor, James "Hap" Hairston of rival *Newsday*, to lead the city desk. "We had an affirmative action program both before and after the lawsuit," said executive editor F. Gilman Spencer, "that made sense to us and was in line with other dailies of comparable size.[23]

David Hardy, the most militant of the four *Daily News* plaintiffs, maintained that his newspaper still wasn't doing enough. Until it hired Hairston, the newspaper, which was read by 40 percent of the city's African Americans, had no blacks in senior editorial positions. "There must be 100 top-ranking executives at the *Daily News*," said Hardy, "and they have one." Spencer's defense that the newspaper advanced minorities at a rate comparable to other metropolitan dailies did not impress DeWayne Wickham, president of the National Association of Black Journalists. Minority journalist employment at newspapers inched up to 7.5 percent in 1988 from 7 percent in 1987, while the American racial minority population was projected to reach about 30 percent by 2000. "While everyone publicly bemoans this slow pace of change," said the *USA Today* and Gannett News Service columnist, "few among the newspaper industry's leadership seem willing to chart new courses of action in pursuit of racial parity."[24]

NABJ, a thirteen-year-old association, had staged annual conventions in Washington, Chicago, Baltimore, and Atlanta, but not in New York, until 1989, when it was to arrive in August. The *City Sun* had generously covered Hardy and colleagues' successful 1987 case. That summer, when Andy Cooper received the NABJ's Journalist of the Year Award, he believed the organization treated him shabbily at the award ceremony. Months before the 1989 convention, Hardy led a protest against the NABJ's accepting $35,000 from the *Daily News* in co-sponsorship support for the New York convention.

The association board initially voted to reject the money, but after it investigated the *Daily News'* performance and was satisfied that the newspaper complied with the court settlement, the NABJ reconsidered. NABJ leadership—which included representatives from its New York affiliate chapter—contended that it was acceptable to receive underwriting from media companies it had criticized. Association members were committed to changing their institutions from within. Hardy was not pacified. The NABJ, he insisted, was "partying with racists."[25]

The 125-member New York ABJ convention committee wanted the first national gathering in their city to succeed spectacularly, but there were doubters. In 1987, New York lost a bid to host the 1988 meeting by one vote to St. Louis because skeptics believed New York hotels were too expensive for its visiting delegates. New York was pushed back a year, and the delay only increased the guaranteed hotel rates.[26] The visitors were eager to travel to the media capital of the world and the cosmopolitan city of art, fashion, intellect, and culture, yet many of them fretted about New York's notoriety for crime, high prices, and rude behavior. The fears evaporated once out-of-town visitors arrived at the Hilton Hotel in Manhattan. This convention was high-tech. Host organizers Linda (Waller) Nelson, Charles Moses, and Todd Beamon patrolled the convention floors with two-way radios, all on the lookout for overcrowding or problems with service. For the first time, participants used computers for writing and editing workshops.

"Shaping the World View" was the four-day convention theme, and for the first time, a foreign head of state addressed NABJ: Michael Manley, prime minister of Jamaica. He made a case for Third World debt relief: "A lot of you journalists are led to believe it's because of a lot of lazy people who don't work hard. . . . We're told it's our problem—but it's your problem too. Detroit can't sell enough tractors [to the Third World]." Manley said there needed to be a program that offered borrowing countries opportunities to breathe but respected lending countries. He expressed hope that such a program would end the existing state of economic paralysis.[27]

Another keynote speaker was a Bronx native and son of Jamaican immigrants, Colin L. Powell, a four-star army general whom President Bush had just nominated to be chairman of the U.S. Joint Chiefs of Staff, making him the first African American in the post. Powell paid tribute to black soldiers who had defended America for two centuries and made his achievement possible. Powell then veered into the conservative Cold War dogma of the Reagan and Bush administrations: "When you are beginning to see signs of victory and success, that's not the time to quit. . . . History has told us that many wars have been lost because the guard was let down." Powell's remarks came during the year when the Berlin Wall collapsed, unifying East and West Germany and sounding a death knell for the Soviet Union. That December, U.S. forces invaded Panama to take down General Manuel Noriega, who was under U.S. indictment for drug smuggling.

In another international first, black Briton Diane Abbott gave the W. E. B. Du Bois lecture at the Diaspora-inspired convention. A member of Parliament, in 1987 Abbott was among three Britons of African descent elected to the governing body for the first time. Immigrants had rebuilt London after World War II, she told a packed ballroom and added, "What does it mean to be a black journalist? Three components to a black world view:

A sense of history, international perspective and a degree of self-respect and self-love as black people."[28]

The NABJ Diaspora convention theme should have appealed to the influential staff members of the *City Sun*, a Trinidadian national managing editor (Leid), Guyanese national Caribbean beat writer (Hamilton), and narrative contributing writer of West Indian descent (Noel). They had covered an expanding Caribbean community. Instead the newspaper's editors and writers for the most part were unimpressed and even expressed hostility toward the visiting black journalists. The full-width, front-page cover photo for August 23–29 showed a floor sign that announced a convention workshop, "Facing Up to Racism." The sign on a post was positioned by the workshop door. No people were present in the photograph. "Black Journalists Miss Some of Their Own Cues" was the headline below, a reference to the editorial inside.

The brief editorial continued to scold NABJ for accepting sponsorship money from the *Daily News* and also sneered at the visitors for allowing the Central Intelligence Agency to briefly recruit talent inside the convention job fair (National office staff did in fact accept the CIA application and money; surprised and embarrassed board members returned the money and asked the recruiters to leave). *City Sun* management stubbornly implied that the NABJ was partying with the enemy, as primary source David Hardy of the *Daily News* insisted. The newspaper's militant posture clashed with the NABJ's mainstream philosophy: the organization would not shrink from critiquing employers' performance (or lack of performance) in coverage and hiring of blacks, but it would clearly and unapologetically work to change and improve the news media from within.

The first-ever convention in New York was an economic and networking success. The net profit was slightly less than the $183,000 reaped the previous summer in St. Louis, which did not have New York's union rates and other expenses. Final paid attendance was a record 1,991 people, up 30 percent from the 1,395 people who came to St. Louis. "NABJ realized that when it committed to New York City, the cost in such a major urban center was going to exceed other cities," said Nelson, "But the trade-off was an exciting program."[29] Excitement included a reception in dormant subway stop and a special A train that whisked 1,350 formally dressed guests from midtown to Harlem and the NABJ awards program at the Apollo Theater. The night before, Seventh Avenue runway models strutted their stuff at a fashion show.[30]

A few days after most NABJ delegates left town, a new racial attack—this time fatal, as in Howard Beach nearly three years ago—once again rattled the city. On August 23, Yusef Hawkins, a sixteen-year-old black teenager from East New York, watched a videotape of *Mississippi Burning* at a neighbor's house and told friends he couldn't believe people could be so cruel to one another for no other reason than the color of their skin.[31]

The boy and three black male friends then went to predominantly Italian American Bensonhurst to look at a used car. The visitors were confronted by thirty whites, some of them armed with baseball bats. Hawkins was shot to death. He was holding a Snickers bar in one hand and his eyes were wide open with uncomprehending fright.[32] Shooting suspect Joseph Fama, eighteen, fled and was picked up in upstate New York, and Keith Mondello, nineteen, was also charged with intentional murder. Four additional people were charged with murder for allegedly showing a depraved indifference to human life.[33]

Three days after the slaying, Al Sharpton and Alton Maddox led three hundred demonstrators on an eighteen-block march on Bensonhurst streets, many of them narrow and residential blocks packed with menacing white youths and sullen older residents. Scuffles broke out about ten times, but police broke up each incident, and no injuries were reported.

The adversaries traded grievances: "Whose streets? Our streets," chanted the visitors, who proclaimed a black person's visit to a white New York neighborhood should not constitute a death wish. Whites chanted "Central Park, Central Park," a reminder about rape and brutal beating of a white woman jogger by accused black and Hispanic teenagers. Black demonstrators changed their chants to "Yusef, Yusef," and the neighbors yelled back "We want Tawana."[34] At the end of the march, white youths taunted the demonstrators by shouting "Niggers go home," and some of them held up watermelons. "You couldn't get an uglier scene than this in Mississippi," said Sharpton, who compared the confrontation to those that civil rights workers had endured in the1960s.

"It's Howard Beach All Over Again," said the lead headline in the August 30–September 5 *City Sun*. The quote was from Cedric Sandiford, whose photo filled most of the cover. The skyline tease read, "Don't March against Racism? Is Koch Crazy?" It led readers to the editorial inside, "Sick and Tired of Being Sick and Tired," which criticized the venom directed at the Bensonhurst demonstrators.

That *City Sun* went to press several days before annual West Indian Day parade on Eastern Parkway in Brooklyn during Labor Day. That date kick-started the political season, and early September meant it was time for the final lap in the race for mayor of New York. A full-page advertisement from the Dinkins campaign appeared on page 2.

"Our vote is for Dinkins," read the skyline tease of the September 6–12 edition, which hit the stands days before the mayoral primary on Tuesday, September 12.

On Democratic primary day, Dinkins received 51 percent of more than one million votes cast and outpaced Ed Koch, who received 42 percent of the votes. The remaining 7 percent of votes was divided between Richard Ravitch, former Metropolitan Transit Authority chairman, and Harrison Golden, city comptroller. Dinkins won 29 percent of white New Yorkers' votes and 94 percent of the black vote. Dinkins competed against Jewish opponents yet earned 26 percent of the city's Jewish vote.[35] Koch's twelve-year reign was over. The brash, decisive leader during the fiscal crisis was rejected as a liability in racially volatile New York. A cross section of voters perceived Dinkins as a healer and unifier. "With the Dinkins victory there is hope," Utrice Leid told *Time* magazine, "But so much is desperately wrong."[36]

Indeed, the Democratic nominee had more persuading to do. Next was the November general election, a showdown with Rudy Giuliani, former federal prosecutor. To win, Dinkins needed to attract more white voters but not lose his black and Hispanic support. He needed to attract a strong black voter turnout but not suggest a black takeover of the city, which would alienate too many whites. Dinkins faced a tightrope walk to November.

Republican and Liberal ballots challenger Giuliani and his strategists were caught off guard. They had prepared for a battle with incumbent Koch. Dinkins's record as Manhattan borough president was not suited for attacks, so the Giuliani team chipped away at its opponent in other ways. They suggested financial misconduct from a questionable stock transfer deal by Dinkins to his son. Giuliani and this surrogates also attacked Dinkins's supporters such as Jitu Weusi (Les Campbell) and Sonny Carson.

Giuliani engaged in a forty-minute candidate interview with Utrice Leid at the *City Sun* office in late July. In an article headlined "Putting the Finger on Rappin' Rudy's Record," as well as an editorial titled Giuliani's "Field of Dreams," Leid questioned and challenged Giuliani's rapport with black and brown New Yorkers.[37]

Frank Macchiarola was chancellor of the New York City Board of Education during much of the 1980s. He served during much of Mayor Koch's administration. Macchiarola was a self-described education conservative. He favored standardized testing of students, and his attitude drew scorn from many liberal upper West Side Manhattan parents. In Queens at Andrew Jackson High School, he appointed a black woman principal and received praise from black middle-class parents. He also established the A. Philip Randolph School at City College and a medical sciences program at all-girls Clara Barton High School in Brooklyn.[38]

Late in 1989, Macchiarola stepped down as chancellor and ran as a Democratic candidate for city comptroller, the chief financial officer of New York. He visited the *New York Times*, *Daily News*, *New York Post*, and *Newsday* to seek editorial endorsements. Macchiarola also visited the *City Sun*. He enjoyed the discussion of public policy issues with Andy Cooper because the publisher's questions were relevant to how Macchiarola envisioned the job: the necessity of financial planning, being a fiscal watchdog. There was great depth to the conversation. Often, Macchiarola said, people wanted to talk about issues that are on their agenda. This was not the case with Cooper.[39]

Macchiarola did not win the Democratic nomination; former Kings County district attorney Elizabeth Holtzman was elected comptroller. Macchiarola returned to education continued having private conversations with Cooper.

The political race narrowed in a city in which the Democratic primary winner was the presumptive November winner. On Election Day, November 7, Dinkins lost 10 percent of his primary voters to Giuliani but still managed to squeak by, winning by only 47,080 votes, 51 to 48 percent. Dinkins won handily in Manhattan (58 percent), Brooklyn (53 percent), and the Bronx (62 percent) but was pummeled in Queens (39 percent) and Staten Island (19 percent).[40]

Dinkins eked out the closest New York City mayoral victory since 1905—a 3 percent margin—thanks to higher-than-expected black turnout (51 percent of his votes) and from union members who represented one in four eligible voters.

At the *City Sun*, Charles Isaacs, president of the research and marketing firm CSI Consultants, Inc., produced "The Hands That Didn't Reach Back," a front-page analysis explaining why votes had evaporated. Some polls claimed that the candidate was sitting on as much as a twenty-point lead. Just before the vote, margins of victory ranged from 5 to 12 percent, depending on the poll. Giuliani's attacks on Dinkins's surrogates, and the candidate's tardiness in answering the negative attacks, chipped away at his projected big lead.

Isaacs wrote that Dinkins was projected to get 33 percent of New York's white voters, but in fact he received only 27 percent. Once inside the voting booth, wrote Isaacs, many white voters did the reverse of what they had told pollsters: they voted three to one against Dinkins. Or they stayed home and voted for no one. Although one million white New Yorkers voted, their turnout was 100,000 votes short what polling experts had projected.[41]

Isaacs also singled out the 320,000-vote-strong Jewish voting bloc and suggested that leaders in that constituency had let Dinkins down during the election. Cooper's page 40 editorial, "The Jewish Leadership Must Restore Its Credibility," said that Dinkins had made a mammoth effort to appease progressive, moderate, and conservative Jewish leaders, often at the expense of offending his black and Hispanic political base. "This city," read the closing, "and particularly the man who has been elected to govern it, deserves some answers. Especially if it appears, Jewish leaders, and by extension their constituencies, intend to wield their influence in City Hall."

Dinkins won, but he had a fragile coalition and faced daunting challenges as the city's first African American mayor. Dinkins inherited a $27 billion budget and over 200,000 employees. The U.S. Census in the early 1990s would reveal that New York regained significant population it had lost, growing to 7.3 million from less than 7.1 million in 1980. In a decade, New York was a little blacker (25.4 percent, up from 24 percent). The Hispanic population grew to 24.4 percent, and "Hispanic" in New York was no longer synonymous with "Puerto Rican." Puerto Ricans represented half of the Spanish-oriented mix, and the rest was 19 percent Dominican, 4 percent Mexican, and 19 percent "other." Asians grew significantly from 4 percent to 7 percent of the population. Whites—famously the Irish, Jews, and Italians who competed for the levers of power in the twentieth century—had become a minority and constituted 43 percent of the city.[42]

18. DINKINS'S FIRST MONTHS

Mayor Dinkins was in office for only two weeks when his administration faced a new racial confrontation. On January 18, 1990, at Bong Jae Jang's Red Apple green grocer store in Brooklyn's Flatbush neighborhood, a Haitian immigrant woman accused Jang and two of his employees of assaulting her for allegedly stealing. The Korean merchants denied Giselaine Fetissainte's charge and countered that she became angry when they asked her to pay for three dollars worth of fruit.[1] Months before this skirmish, art imitated life. A scene in Spike Lee's *Do the Right Thing* depicted tense relations between Korean immigrant merchants and black customers. A language barrier caused misunderstandings, and a real one now occurred at Red Apple on Church Avenue. The argument spread like wildfire when activist Sonny Carson led a black boycott of Red Apple and the Korean-owned grocer across the street. Media reports at that time reminded consumers that Robert (Sonny) Carson was a former Dinkins campaign worker (and target of Giuliani campaign attacks) and a convicted kidnapper.[2]

Some black radio shows openly endorsed the boycott and urged listeners to participate. But the city's leading black newspapers kept a cautious distance. The *Amsterdam News* sought to convey the boycotter's point of view without engaging in cheerleading.[3] The June 9 lead headline, "Rallies Are Not Anti-Asian but for Justice, Organizers Say," tried to lend credibility to the activists' claims without openly endorsing them. The Harlem-based weekly also published guest editorials written by boycott leaders or advocates that included Carson and Alton Maddox.[4]

The *City Sun* used its pages to castigate the mainstream media for biased coverage of the boycott. The May 23–29 column "And So It Goes: Maintaining the Myths about Race" read in part:

> The Flatbush boycott story is being used as a counterweight to Bensonhurst (they've never shown as much emotion over Bensonhurst as over this boycott). The story takes some of the spotlight off Bensonhurst and, at the same time, lets the white media preachers say, "Look, there are black racists, too, not just the white ones. We've all got to work at brotherhood." . . . The New York City white media are a case study in the use

> of media power to define racial issues in a way that protects the status quo. Then they try to force the rest of us to live with their definitions.[5]

"Bensonhurst" referred to the Brooklyn neighborhood and the summer 1989 slaying of black teenager Yusef Hawkins by a white mob.

Washington Post media critic Howard Kurtz wrote that the Red Apple incident was a minor altercation that escalated. But the *New York Post* made a big deal of the clash. The tabloid played the story big for days and scolded its competitors for not doing the same. TV news cameras showed up at Church Avenue and Carson, and a few dozen demonstrators were able to act out before thousands of viewers.[6] The protesters denounced Dinkins on camera for failing to end the boycott. An element missing from the story frame was that many neighborhood blacks believed the Korean grocers were set up as scapegoats.

The *City Sun* remained more critical of the mainstream media coverage of the boycott than it was enthusiastic about the boycott itself. A few of its editorials mildly disparaged the boycotts. "More Heat than Light in East Flatbush," on May 16–22, lamented the boycott's "ineffective, confused leadership." Yet *City Sun* news coverage, like that of the *Amsterdam News*, treated the Red Apple boycott as legitimate political activity in pointed contrast to the mainstream media coverage.[7]

Dinkins behaved ineffectively, equivocally, and timidly during this demonstration. Both shop owners obtained civil court injunctions that ordered demonstrators to remain at least fifty feet away from the shop entrances. Police officials appealed the instructions and said that enforcing the fifty-foot rule would drive demonstrators across the street to gather in front of a church, where potentially they could incite violent confrontations. The mayor did not instruct police to enforce the order. Instead Dinkins appointed a commission to review his handling of the incident. The commission criticized the district attorney for not vigorously investigating and prosecuting the Haitian shopper's original complaint. A prominent newsweekly praised the mayor's conduct.[8]

As the boycott wore on for months, Korean American leaders saw their constituents as pawns caught between black demagogues on one end and a black mayor unwilling to criticize his own on the other.[9] In a letter dated January 24, Sung Soo-Kim urged Dinkins to get involved: "It is with great urgency that I call upon you as the supreme leader of this great city to intercede in a grave ethnic conflict currently taking place in Brooklyn. This current turmoil reminds us of how sharp and defined are the edges of the interlocking pieces of New York's 'gorgeous mosaic.' Your mayorship recognized and celebrated the beauty of different pieces of ethnic mosaic; we thus look to you to translate your vision of harmony to reality by engaging in this tragic confrontation."[10] As months passed and Dinkins still hesitated to personally engage, Korean American leaders focused less on the boycott and more on the administration's alleged discriminatory behavior toward their community. Those leaders were convinced that Dinkins had sold their community up the river to pander to black extremists.[11] The backstory to the boycott caused by a bungled three-dollar fruit transaction appeared to be black resentment and failure. Koreans were newly arrived immigrants, yet along with Arabs and Asian Indians, they owned 18,000 of 200,000 city businesses, and their numbers were projected to grow by 50 percent in a decade. Hispanics owned one of every five city businesses. Blacks owned fewer than 1,500 enterprises in the city.[12]

At 6:30 p.m., a group of mostly black Caribbean women began to cross the picket lines to patronize the grocers. Some boycotters denounced them as "Aunt Jemimas," and one of the women fired back, "Sonny Carson can't tell me how to be black!"[13] By September, the boycott was eight months old. Thousands of Koreans rallied outside city hall, and the crowd booed when Dinkins spoke. A few days after the rally, Dinkins demonstrated support for the merchants by visiting Red Apple to purchase ten dollars worth of fruits and vegetables.[14] His gesture deflated the boycotters and their action, but the mayor's equivocal handling of the conflict in Brooklyn hurt his credibility.

After midnight on Sunday, March 25, hundreds of young adults were dancing and romancing at Happy Land social club on Southern Boulevard in East Tremont in the Bronx. The clientele was largely working-class Honduran and Ecuadoran immigrants. Julio Gonzalez, an unemployed ex-convict and Cuban refugee, argued with his ex-girlfriend, who worked at the club as a ticket taker. Gonzalez stormed away, and partiers heard him promise, "I'll be back."

Gonzalez returned with a dollar worth of gasoline, splashed it on the club stairs, and lit a match. The fireball that erupted on second floor of the storefront killed eighty-seven people, most of them younger than twenty-five.[15] Mainstream media coverage focused on two angles: the vengeful ex-boyfriend who flew into a homicidal rage over the woman who rejected him, and evidence that Happy Land was an illegal and unsafe gathering place. There were no smoke alarms and inadequate emergency exits. The club owners had ignored city orders to close because of building and fire safety violations.

The *City Sun* found a third angle. "It Didn't Have to Happen," a front-page editorial that continued inside, declared: "This tragedy is not just the alleged criminal act of one man, it is also the end result of a series of interlocking interests in this town that rarely come in for the same kind of scrutiny and punitive action as people like Julio Gonzalez. Bronx District Attorney Robert Johnson believes he has an open-and-shut case against Gonzalez and already is talking about seeking a prison term of 2,000 years. What will the owners of the building that housed the social club get? What will Koch and Dinkins administration bureaucrats get? What will the Bronx Board of Realtors get?"[16]

City Sun Caribbean editor Hugh Hamilton wrote that a half-million Haitians were living in New York. The immigrants were there legally and illegally to work and send money home to their impoverished families or to flee the latest incarnation of their homeland's treacherous dictator. The Haitian immigrants were hidden exiles, massive in numbers but impotent in political clout. Few were U.S. citizens with voting rights, and many existed out of sight of law enforcement and at the mercy of exploitative employers.[17] The Haitians were misunderstood, like the woman who wrongly or rightly disputed a fruit purchase at a Korean grocery in Brooklyn and sparked a boycott. Haitians were stigmatized. During the less-than-a-decade-old AIDS epidemic, a U.S. government dictate prevented all Haitians from giving blood because they were a high-risk group for AIDS. That policy brought many Haitians out of the shadows in protest. On Friday, April 20, a hundred thousand Haitians, reported the *City Sun*, demonstrated in Lower Manhattan. Their show of demonstrative force caught police off guard and paralyzed traffic. Police had expected only two thousand demonstrators, and even the organizers had optimistically predicted thirty thousand.[18]

The organizers and police were not the only people the hidden exile explosion caught napping. Much of the political and media establishment made the rote assumptions: Harlem was called the locus of the black community, but that claim was based on reputation rather than fact. Black New York political conversations were based in Harlem and began with J. Raymond "Harlem Fox" Jones and the Gang of Four, Dinkins, Rangel, Paterson, and Sutton. Yet the assertion ignored political storms brewing in Brooklyn, Queens, and the Bronx. In 1990, Hugh Hamilton was living in Brooklyn's Brownsville and had been in America less than five years. With fresher eyes, he did not see why all establishment references about black life were about Harlem. The Haitian explosion, largely coming out of the most populous black community of central Brooklyn, affirmed that power and clout had already shifted within black New York.

Haitians occupied a unique and ambiguous position among New York–area blacks. Most Caribbean immigrants were Anglophones from Jamaica, Barbados, and Trinidad. Then there were the Haitians with their different language (Creole and some French), economy, and religion. The Haitian march on Lower Manhattan became a great hook for the *City Sun* to tell a bigger story.[19]

In three months, two incidents that individually or collectively involved Haitians—the Church Avenue grocery boycott and the AIDS-stigma demonstration—jolted many New Yorkers. The *City Sun* editors decided that the Haitian phenomenon was a big story worthy of an investigative report. The hidden exiles were even bigger than New York. The investigation would take writers and photographers to a geographic triangle: New York, South Florida, and Hispaniola, the island shared by Haiti and the Dominican Republic.

The modern sugar industry in Hispaniola emerged as a result of the U.S. occupation of the Dominican Republic from 1916 to 1924. Many Dominican natives were reluctant to cut cane, so they looked to former slaves in the Antilles to do the work. Dominicans maintained an uneasy relationship with their Haitian neighbors. Haitians had occupied the former Santo Domingo from 1822 to 1844. A century later, Dominican dictator Rafael Trujillo, professing commitment to European culture and Catholic values, ordered the massacre of twenty thousand Haitians during a three-day sweep in 1937. The migrants, who had fled destitution in their country to work in Dominican sugar cane plantations, were driven into stockyards and slaughtered with carbines and machetes. Haiti's president Sténio Vincent accepted a $750,000 indemnity for the families of the victims, though most of that amount was never paid.[20]

Fifteen years later, in 1952, a bilateral agreement between Haiti and the Dominican Republic meant the Haitian government was paid to provide workers to their island neighbors. The contract lasted until the fall of Jean Claude "Baby Doc" Duvalier in February 1986. The final payment was in excess of $2 million.[21]

When Essick shot photographs and reported from the island for the *City Sun*, 100,000 Haitians worked on Dominican *ingenios*, or plantations. When plantations such as El Batey, where Essick reported, were short of workers, the Dominican army rounded up Haitians from the 500,000 who lived in their country, explained a representative from the London-based Anti-Slavery Society.

In the Dominican Republic, Haitian sugar cane cutters, called braceros, labored seven days a week for sixteen hours each day on the *ingenios*, engaging in what amounted to slave labor. The laborers were paid $40 per month—$1.33 a day—for strenuous work.[22] Desperately poor Haitians needed that work, but many of them had bad deals and were coerced into this labor. Lead *City Sun* special report writer Hamilton did not travel to Hispaniola or Miami because his son was born in April. The new father decided he could not leave the infant and mother and go to the tropics. Hamilton did write the Miami story from New York by conducting telephone interviews. Photographer Essick's boots-on-the-ground observations also helped to shape his narrative.

Hamilton interviewed people in Miami's Little Haiti, the former southern black neighborhood Liberty City, fifteen minutes north of downtown, abutted by Interstate 95 and bisected by the main thoroughfare of Fifty-fourth Street.[23] Most of South Florida's 800,000 Haitians, Hamilton wrote, had settled in this community and were crammed into low-rise apartments and faded bungalows. Many of its residents left at dawn to work in factories and service centers outside their community. The immigrants' willingness to work long hours, plus their lack of education and the language barrier—Creole was their first language—was exploited routinely by employers who casually told employment agencies, "Send me a Haitian."[24] Some Haitians owned businesses, but the proprietors often exploited their countrymen, too. "The problem with Haitians," garment manufacturing owner Joe Celistan told Hamilton, "is that they lack respect for money."

Haitians tried to improve their condition by attending adult education classes at night after a day of labor in the factories or fields. ESL classes were in high demand, and the next step was preparing to take General Educational Development (GED) tests to prove high school-level knowledge.

By 1990, metro New York was home to 500,000 Haitians, wrote Hamilton. His reporting suggested that about one out of every twenty city inhabitants was Haitian, there legally or illegally. Among them was a small group of professionals who included doctors, nurses, lawyers, and teachers who were living the American dream. The majority lived on the margins and received the worst treatment of any immigrant group.[25]

Hamilton's special report told the story of Gerard Jean-Charles, a Hatian man who kissed his wife and children good-bye and hopped a plane from Haiti to New York to make money to send home. At first he worked in a factory and endured long hours and low pay (though for much better wages than he had received in his native land). After two years, with help from relatives and friends, Jean-Charles acquired a 1981 Oldsmobile and livery license plates. He declared his independence as a cab driver.

But freedom was a high-risk occupation. On an August night he picked up four males along Rockaway Avenue in Brownsville and was instructed to drive to St. Johns Place and Schenectady Avenue in Bedford-Stuyvesant. At the destination, instead of paying the fare, one of the youths took out a gun and ordered Jean-Charles to hand over his money. In broken English the cabbie pleaded that he had none. He flashed his empty wallet as proof. The angry gunman pointed the weapon at Jean-Charles's head and fired. The cabbie instinctively ducked. The bullet sliced a crease across his forehead. Jean-Charles survived a brush with death with merely a battle scar, and the armed robbers got away.[26]

At other times, customers refused to pay and ridiculed the driver's patois. Still, business was moderately good for Jean-Charles. He sent money home, and twice a year he visited his wife and four children. He lived in a small apartment in Flatbush. When he felt lonely, he dropped by his sister's house or hung out with her husband, Jean Cyrus, and reminisced about old times on the island.[27] Elsewhere in the special report, Essick's evocative photography depicted a mechanic, dancer, fashion designer, and businessman, all of them people whom Hamilton had interviewed.

Andy Cooper projected robust energy and rage on the editorial pages of the *City Sun*, yet his five-foot, eight-inch, 180-pound body was fragile because of several strokes, as well as hypertension and other ailments. Cooper drove his car less and less because of his unhealthy condition. Jocelyn used the family car much more to drive to Long Island to teach a class at Adelphi University.

In addition, on Tuesday newspaper production nights, Jocelyn drove her husband to the printing plant in the Greenpoint section of Brooklyn—the neighborhood of the former Schaefer brewery—to pick up one hundred copies of the newspaper, drop them off at the Brooklyn editorial office, and then take the other copies to the black-oriented radio stations WLIB-AM and WBLS-FM. That way the DJs could read the paper and chat up its headlines during Wednesday morning drive times. The radio stations were in midtown Manhattan and northern Queens.

Raymond Burrows found out about the early bird delivery routine and stepped in to assist. He wanted to ease Jocelyn's burden of teaching a night class and doing delivery driving for two hours. Burrows, a longtime NYNEX (New York Telephone) employee, met Andy Cooper about six months after the *City Sun* began publishing. Somebody brought Burrows the first edition of the newspaper. He remembered Cooper's political writing and commentary in the 1970s for the *Amsterdam News*. The articles always grabbed Burrows's attention because the analyses were smarter than the other knee-jerk articles in the Harlem-based paper. Cooper's writing made Burrows, then a young adult with militant opinions, think more deeply and expand his viewpoint. When the *City Sun* emerged in the 1980s, Burrows believed intelligent analysis of issues was the guiding editorial tone of the Brooklyn-based newspaper.

Within months, a "Friends of the *City Sun*" group formed, and Burrows attended a meeting. Participants included the Rev. Johnny Ray Youngblood, an activist minister with St. Paul Community Baptist Church. He and Burrows lived five blocks apart in Park Slope.[28]

Burrows was a forty-something man when the *City Sun* was publishing in the 1980s. A vegetarian and a runner, he often wore a red, black, and green Kufi or "crown" on his head. During his many years at New York Telephone, Burrows was a union activist. He was a self-described "sixties person," and when appropriate, he was with or against the company. *The Autobiography of Malcolm X* was his transformative book. At the telephone company, Local 1101 recruited Burrows to sit on the board of the North Star Foundation, which awarded grants to community organizations. In 1980 he successfully lobbied for funds that supported Cooper's Trans Urban News Writers Workshop. Years later, when Burrows moved to White Plains in suburban Westchester County, friends ribbed him because he lived on Main Street. They emphasized the "White" in White Plains.[29]

Burrows kept his Tuesday nights open. He became Andy Cooper's driver. That gave Burrows the opportunity to talk one-on-one with the publisher or simply to listen. Burrows would pick Cooper up at his Park Slope home at 8 p.m. The newspapers would be ready at about 9:00 or 9:30. Both men returned home about 11 p.m. Burrows took pleasure in the task. For him it was like enrolling in a top-flight school. Good publishers had access to all kinds of information and analysis, so the Tuesday night drives were pleasurable learning experiences. Raymond Burrows began driving Cooper in 1985 and continued the practice through 1990.

On July 28, 1990, Burrows married Barbara Rose. Barbara's father, Samuel Rose, died when she was five years old in her native South Carolina. She asked Andy Cooper to stand in, and he graciously agreed to give her away. Raymond and Barbara Burrows moved to Westchester County. Beginning in 1993, they hosted an annual "no meat" open house on New Year's Day. Andy and Jocelyn would show. Barbara and Raymond moved south to Memphis in 2000. By around 2005, Raymond Burrows joined an inventors' club.

When he lived in New York, Burrows tried to find a way to increase distribution of the *City Sun*, since the militant editorial content might limit advertising. He tried to use network marketing principles similar to those of Dick Gregory. Burrows thought his approach was highly appropriate because the circle is shaped like the sun. He used to buy more than one copy of the paper and have someone buy the other one back.

In late May, Alton Maddox, Tawana Brawley's attorney, was suspended from practicing law in New York State because he refused several times to respond to a grievance committee hearing complaints about his conduct in the case of the teenage girl. Maddox, who was forty-four in 1990, had practiced law in New York since 1976.

He alleged that the sanction against him was retribution by attorney general Robert Abrams, who had proved beyond a reasonable doubt that Brawley's claims were a hoax. Maddox was suspended but was also allowed to continue representing Rev. Al Sharpton at a trial in progress in Manhattan. The state of New York accused Sharpton of stealing $250,000 from a "phantom charity." Maddox's Brawley case co-counsel, C. Vernon Mason, had a misconduct complaint pending, too. William C. Thompson, the former Brooklyn state senator, was a member of the five-judge panel in the state supreme court appellate division that issued the order.[30]

In June, Nelson Mandela triumphantly arrived in New York City. In January, the seventy-one-year-old had walked out of Robben Island prison, where he had been held for twenty-seven years. That moment in January was the first time in decades that most people had seen Mandela's face. The ultra-right South African government banned images of the revolutionary, so that people relied on an image of Mandela from 1962, when he was forty-four. By June, Mandela was touring America like a rock star. Legal separation and oppression of the black majority in South African were being dismantled.

Mandela's visit was especially sweet for Mayor Dinkins and Andy Cooper. Both men had been arrested in the late 1980s during anti-apartheid demonstrations. The *City Sun* had kept the anti-apartheid and divestment movement fresh on the minds of readers too.

That June, the *City Sun* was not totally celebratory. Essayist Clinton Cox delivered a page 5 history lesson titled "Mandela's Visit and the 'Game of Nations.'" Cox's article opened: "Nelson Mandela has come to America, home of the Central Intelligence Agency that helped put him behind bars for 27 years because he threatened white control and U.S. interests in South Africa." President Bush, CIA director during 1976–77, was asked about the agency's role in the arrest of Mandela. His reply: "I haven't looked into it yet." Marlin Fitzwater, the president's press secretary, was asked if Mandela was owed an apology by the U.S. government for stealing nearly three decades of his life. Fitzwater answered, "We find no value in reviewing the 30-year-old history of this case. I don't like it when people question our motives in regard to blacks."[31] On two full pages of the fifty-two-page edition, the *City Sun* reprinted Mandela's letter from prison to president P. W. Botha, which read in part, "The ANC and the government must negotiate a political settlement."[32]

In August 1990, federal authorities indicted U.S. representative Floyd Flake (D-N.Y.) and his wife Margaret on embezzlement charges. In the late 1980s, Flake, the first black member of Congress from Queens, was scandalized in the *City Sun* because he allegedly seduced an office aide then harassed her into quitting the job after she ended the affair. The seventeen-count indictment in 1990 said that Flake and his spouse ad fraudulently obtained $66,700 from their church and embezzled $75,000 from a related housing complex for the elderly and evaded income taxes on both amounts.[33]

Flake denied the charges in a statement, and his lawyer said the accusations would fuel "a perception that minority politicians are being unfairly targeted for prosecution." Flake had been under investigation for two years, said the federal prosecutor.

The scorned church aide and a trustee of Allen AME cooperated with investigators. Dinkins said Flake's indictment "gives me great concern" and called the congressman "a caring and effective legislator." "I hope that is case is resolved quickly," Dinkins also said, "so that he may again give his full attention to his important work." Flake vowed to run for a third term in November.

In October, weeks before that election, someone killed the woman who had accused Flake of sexual harassment, thirty-seven-year-old Thelma Singleton-Scott, in a hit-and-run accident.[34] Singleton-Scott was sitting in the backseat of a Cadillac that was stopped on Rockaway Parkway. The car was struck from behind by a Chevrolet Camaro that was reported stolen. The driver of the stolen car fled on foot. Barbara Samson, thirty-five, a passenger with Singleton-Scott, also died. Their driver Genevieve Brookhouse, thirty-nine, was injured and hospitalized.

The August 29 *City Sun* front page expressed wariness about imminent war with Iraq. Its leader, Saddam Hussein, invaded neighbor Kuwait that month. The Bush administration, Western allies, and nervous nations of the Middle East assembled to respond with force and sanctions.

International crises called attention to the sharp-edged editorial cartooning of Abe Blashko. The East Village artist drew artistic critiques of the Bush administration's decisions regarding Panama, the Middle East, and the arms race in the post–Soviet Union world, for example, "I'm warning you Gorby . . . show extreme caution toward Lithuania," in the April 25–May 1 edition. Blashko had caught the eye of the *City Sun*'s editors in 1987 when they saw his caricatures of Supreme Court justices William Rehnquist and Antonin Scalia gripping a torn copy of the Bill of Rights. The illustration complemented an article by the radical attorney William Kuntsler in the *Guardian*, an independent left-leaning weekly founded by James Aronson in 1948. Blashko agreed to draw for the *City Sun*, too, and worked directly with Utrice Leid.[35]

In November 1990, a strike at the *New York Daily News* shuttered the tabloid for five months until March 1991. At the start, one union—the drivers—got into a fight with management, then eight of the nine other unions, including the Newspaper Guild that represented newsroom employees, sided with labor. Advertisers bailed out, and news dealers stopped selling the newspaper because of threats of bodily harm by union members and their allies. Someone firebombed a newsstand in Brooklyn to send a message.[36]

The *Daily News*' editor asked to purchase the NABJ's membership list to hire replacement workers. Critics immediately blasted the association for siding with management. NABJ leaders reversed their decision in twenty-four hours and denied management the list. Jesse Jackson came to town to show support for the unions, while the usually quotable Al Sharpton was curiously mute. The noneditorial craft unions were conspicuously white. The pressmen and mailers were predominantly Irish, and the drivers were Italian and Jewish.[37]

About 45 percent of *Daily News* readers in New York City were black and Hispanic, observed Earl Caldwell when black journalists successfully battled the owners in court. In 1987, Caldwell said black and brown customers brought the newspaper into their homes but they were disrespected by company. The virtual lockout from blue-collar work was damning evidence.

As the strike wore on into the winter, the *Daily News* laid off Richard G. Carter, a black editorial writer, and Pamela Moreland, a fellow editorial writer, left to become editorial page editor of the *Marin Independent Journal* in California. Carter and Moreland had been hired as a result of the 1987 discrimination suit won by four black journalists. An estimated three dozen black journalists struck the *Daily News*, but at least a dozen crossed the picket lines.

The Tribune Company of Chicago sold the newspaper to British publishing tycoon Robert Maxwell for $60 million. The price amounted to a fire sale. Joyce White, a nineteen-year veteran of the paper, said she left involuntarily because of "restructuring" by Maxwell.

Tribune decided to walk away from America's highest-circulation metropolitan paper because the company would no longer tolerate the filthy and inefficient printing plant and union rules that allowed overmanned presses and members who were paid for not working. Fifteen years before the strike, electronic typesetting had replaced the printers' traditional methods, so Tribune and the craft union agreed to $300 million in lifetime job guarantees to the displaced workers.

Elsewhere, sloth was so ingrained in the plant culture that the men who operated the presses at the Dean Street plant had three phrases for doing little or no work. Stage one was "beat out," meaning to beat it out of the plant and spend much of the shift in Freddy's, the corner bar, to drink beer. Stage two was the "buddy system" in which pairs of employees punched in, but one man beat out and the other covered both their job responsibilities. If a supervisor called roll, the worker in the plant explained that his buddy was in the bathroom or was running a work-related errant. If matters got serious, word got out that the guy better get back inside the plant. The third and most extreme stage was "marriage." Two pressmen worked half the days for which they were paid by permanently covering for each other on alternate shifts. Such arrangements were popular among pressmen who lived in Suffolk County, a three-hour round-trip commute for workers who knew they were not really needed.[38]

Before the strike, Tribune managers lost control of the plant floor. Threats of work stoppages unnerved the managers, and they blinked when the union bosses bluffed. Workers were immune to punishment for outrageous misconduct. In one instance, a worker brought loaded gun to work and threatened to kill a manager. A union supervisor convinced the worker to unload the gun. The manager told the worker he was fired. The worker shot back, "You can't fire me, you bastard, I emptied the gun!"[39] The employees held managers in utter contempt and discouraged them from coming into the plant.

In December 1990, the *City Sun* emerged from Chapter 11 bankruptcy. After six and a half years of uninterrupted weekly publication, the newspaper appeared healthier. The *City Sun* was heftier, fatter than the lean 24- to 28-page editions of the late 1980s. Editions in 1990 often contained 36 pages or more, especially when special reports like "Hidden Exiles No More" or "Uptown Eco Blues," about environmental racism in Harlem, commanded more space. In 1987 the *City Sun* was immersed in Chapter 11 bankruptcy, and the Long Island–based federal court converted the company's case in into a Chapter 7 issue. Its appearance in 1990 still masked flaws. Members of the young reporting staff were still paid erratically. Most of the staff members put up with the inconvenience because they were so young, impressionable, and eager to make names for themselves at the equally young, dynamic newspaper.[40]

Dinkins's first year of governing in the volatile city was the ideal environment for budding journalists to make their marks. Like the rest of the nation, New York was struggling through a recession. Dinkins inherited a $1.8 billion deficit, and he put the $28 billion budget in balance by raising taxes by $800 million and slashing city services by $200 million. About 1,100 new police officers were hired under Dinkins's watch, but the numbers amounted to one-fourth of the cops his commissioner Lee Brown said he needed to control crime. Despite the hires, the NYPD was 14 percent smaller than in 1975, when the force had numbered nearly 32,000 strong.[41]

Dinkins's administration complained that the U.S. Bureau of Census grossly undercounted the city and that faulty arithmetic would compound New York's economic and political woes. If the census had projected that the city had ended population decline and grown to 7.7 million, why did a September report put the count at only 7 million? Dinkins called the report "unadulterated nonsense."

City planners insisted that the feds had missed at least one million people. Evidence of missed inhabitants was everywhere, Luther Blake of the city districting commission told the *City Sun*'s Hugh Hamilton: "The Census Bureau figure is ridiculous. It would be laughable it not were so serious. . . . The city's birthrate is up, the school population is up, more drivers licenses are being issued, and surveys show that between 1983 and 1987 more than quarter of a million aliens settled in New York City. Where are these people?"

Dinkins and company did not want to wait until 1991 for the feds to adjust the numbers upward; they complained loudly and demanded immediate action because the city could lose $1 billion over the next decade, as well as seats in Congress and other representative offices.[42]

Between 1989 and 1990, New York City lost 370,000 jobs, representing an 8.7 percent decline.[43] Unions represented 237,000 of the 300,000 city workers. In a recession economy with a budget gap, Dinkins faced the daunting task of negotiating union contracts.

If the mayor showed weakness, he risked returning New York to the late 1960s, when unions ran roughshod over the Lindsay administration and contributed to nearly bankrupting the city by 1976. Dinkins settled with District 37 and the Teamsters. Stanley Hill of 140-member-strong District Council 37 was a major player in Dinkins's election, but during the mayor's first year in office, Hill said Dinkins lied to his members because he was balancing the budget on the backs of workers.[44] Hill also accused the mayor of running a chaotic government. Dinkins did not create the chaos; previous administrations had dealt him a chaotic hand. The way he played would determine whether he could manage the crises or succumb to them.

19. CROWN HEIGHTS RIOT

Leid and Cooper recognized a political change that would profoundly shape New York City politics for future decades. The duo's understanding of the city councilmanic phenomenon affirmed the Cooper-Leid genius. They saw that story and pursued it when the mainstream media missed or ignored it.

Big media institutions like the *New York Times* could not miss the obvious. In 1981, Beverly Morris of Brooklyn, with encouragement from the New York Civil Liberties Union, sued the city Board of Estimate in the local courts. Morris, a white woman and a union negotiator, said the board violated the equal protection clause of the U.S. Constitution because its representation was not proportionate to the population.[1] Brooklyn, the most populous borough with more than two million residents, had the same representation—one vote from its borough president—as Staten Island, the least populous borough with 400,000 residents and one vote from its borough president. The other board members were the mayor, whose choices were worth two votes, the city council president, comptroller, and borough presidents from Manhattan, Bronx, and Queens. The eight-member board, which had nine votes, awarded all city contracts, managed city property, and played the key role in formulating the city budget—at that time about $25 billion.

The trial court found in favor of Morris, and the court of appeals affirmed her case. The City of New York appealed to the U.S. Supreme Court in the case that was named *Board of Estimate of City of New York v. Morris*. In a six-to-three ruling, justice Byron White's majority opinion said the city board wielded substantial legislative power and was thus required to comply with the equal protection clause. Three of the justices in the minority concurred with the majority but differed with the results. The high court made New York City rewrite its city charter. That meant eliminating the Board of Estimate and transferring many of its powers to the mayor.[2]

Other powers and responsibilities were transferred to the city council and a Procurement Policy Board. Furthermore, the number of city council districts expanded from 35 to 51 members, and the new landscape was expected to reflect the profound demographic changes that had occurred in the five boroughs from 1980 to 1990. Cooper and Leid recognized that an expanded city council would be more than blacker and browner; the expanded council would foster intraracial and ethnic competition.

During the 1991 election, two blacks were elected to what were so-called Caribbean district seats. Una Clarke, an immigrant from Jamaica, won the Fortieth District seat in Brooklyn, and Lloyd Henry, a native of Belize, won in the Forty-fifth District. What was understood under the surface and not understood or reported by the mainstream press (or the leading minority press, for that matter) was the Haitian factor: when would that sizable community gain enough power to demand, then take, one of those seats? Their power became apparent in the 1990s when they demonstrated against U.S.-government AIDS stigmatization. Haitians protested as writers redistricted the boundaries of councilmanic districts with more representatives but less real estate.

Leid and Cooper had reporters such as Caribbean editor Hugh Hamilton relentlessly pursue the story.[3] The young writers (Atwell, Kenton Kirby, Farhan Haq, Matoski, and Hamilton, the "elder" of those reporters at age thirty) were eager to learn. That was part of what the *City Sun* was able to do: young people had opportunities to make their marks amid the energy in the newsroom.

The *City Sun* employed nonlinear processes to decide what to cover. Leid and Cooper provided leadership that led reporters to believe they could generate ideas that would lead to collaborative decision making. Traditional newspaper convention, with a 10 a.m. news meeting, or a boss telling a writer, "I have an assignment for you," was not the standard practice at the paper.[4]

For most of the young reporters, the *City Sun* was their first job in media. The dailies (the *Daily News*, the *Post*, the *Times*, and *Newsday*) generally required a minimum of five years' experience, and many reporters worked for at least two news outlets before they could compete for places at these metropolitan papers. At the rival weekly the *Amsterdam News*, the editorial staff was older and unionized like those at the dailies. *City Sun* reporters were younger and eager for opportunities to compete with the establishment media on big stories.

They also were ripe for exploitation by Leid and Cooper. Many of the young reporters did not lead independent or separate lives that included spouses, children, mortgages, or even rent payments. Money was tight at the *City Sun*, and there were no guarantee a reporter would be paid reliably. Payroll checks occasionally bounced. The paper sometimes paid writers in cash. The publisher likely made a conscious choice to do that. Cooper (and Leid) must have known they could not pay contributors who were not legally authorized to work, specifically foreign nationals in American on fellowship or still in the country with an expired visa.

Starting in 1986, a Reagan-era Immigration and Naturalization Service rule against hiring nonlegal residents cracked down hard on businesses that did not comply. The *City Sun* apparently—just barely—avoided breaking that rule.

The staff writers and freelance contributors put up with the inconveniences. They spent a lot of time in one another's company, putting the paper to bed, going out for drinks, or to the Zimbabwean embassy with Phil Makotsi. Leid took the reporters out to extended dinners. The socializing did not feel like work.[5]

Leid and Cooper had a collaborative and codependent work relationship comparable to that of pianist Duke Ellington and his arranger and songwriter Billy Strayhorn. The duo had worked together for fifteen years and shared a seamless vision of producing an aggressive, even militant, brand of journalism. Cooper and Leid very likely established a "good cop, bad cop" relationship with the staff; sometimes they played theatrical games.

Leid was the bad cop. She worked directly with the reporters and at times brutally edited their copy. With her red pen she bloodied stories she deemed to be weakly reported or poorly written. Writers left the office bruised by the managing editor's verbal jabs.

Cooper was distant to most of the reporters in the small newsroom on Court Street. To them he was the man behind the office door, who spent much of his time dealing with the advertising and circulation managers. Cooper wrote the editorials, but usually without input from reporters. He had his high- and low-level sources and his copilot Leid to assist him.

The "bad cop, good cop" routine extended to some paydays. Say a reporter received his check on Friday, and when he tried to cash it at the bank, it was rejected for insufficient funds. The reporter returned to the office incensed and stormed into Cooper's office to complain. Cooper expressed shock and indignation (or embarrassment) over what had happened to the employee. He quickly cut another check, which cleared when the reported cashed it. Years later, some reporters wondered whether the occasional bad-check incidents were a scheme to buy time because of cash flow problems.

In the winter of 1991, Mayor Dinkins traveled to Israel on a privately funded visit. Upon his return, a committee of Arab and Muslim organizations offered to sponsor a trip similar to the junket to Tel Aviv. At a news conference, Dinkins said he would decline the offer.

In response the *City Sun* tweaked the mayor. A front-page caricature by Abe Blashko depicted Dinkins leaping over Hispaniola, Liberia, South Africa, and bodies of water. Sweat trickled from Dinkins's brow as he looked over his shoulder to the Manhattan skyline. Smoke labeled "crime," "AIDS," "the homeless," "racism," and "drugs" belched from skyscrapers. Below the caricature was the two-line head: "A Foreign-Policy Agenda Dinkins Should Pursue."[6]

Hugh Hamilton's article began: "David N. Dinkins likes to think of himself as mayor of all the people. But when his willingness—or ability—to fulfill that mandate was tested last week, the mayor was found wanting." Hamilton's article on pages 4 and 11 recommended a Dinkins foreign policy agenda for 1992, visits to Haiti (where the Rev. Jean-Bertrand Aristide had just been sworn in as president), Dominican Republic (because of the estimated 500,000 Dominicans in New York), and South Africa (because of the goodwill from the Nelson Mandela visit to New York the previous June, the mayor's office could influence the dismantling of apartheid). The *City Sun* was sarcastic with its illustration, but constructive with its words.

On March 27, Hugh Hamilton and photographer Peter Essick teamed up to produce "Cheap Street," an investigative report on Fulton Street Mall, the shopping district a few blocks from the *City Sun* office. The $26 million public-private venture that opened in 1984 was supposed to revitalize downtown Fulton Street. Until the early 1970s, Fulton Street was the America's fifth-largest retail center. Abraham & Strauss, Mays, Korvette's, and Martin's department stores operated less than 1,000 feet of one another. Meanwhile 200,000 customers poured in daily from Bedford-Stuyvesant, Brooklyn Heights, Fort Greene, Park Slope, and beyond.[7] An elaborate network of subways and a dozen bus lines served customers. Often the buses crawled along the divided four-lane street.

In its new incarnation, Fulton Mall did not live up to the hype. It devolved into a dumping ground for shoddy goods and suspect services. For some shady store owners, every day was sale day. They rotated "going out of business" and "under new management" signs yet remained permanent fixtures. What was gone was every department store except A&S. When J. W. Mays's sixty-four-year-old flagship store left in 1988, a flea market replaced it the following year. The courts closed the bazaar after five months because of nonpayment of rent. Tacky fast-food joints hemmed in restaurant Gage and Tollner, an upscale fixture since 1889.

A decade of mall planning devolved into surrender, Hamilton's reporting and Essick's graphic photography suggested. The special report served as a wakeup call. Although the prosperous days were behind them, at least 80,000 people still visited the mall on weekdays, and the numbers swelled to 100,000 on Saturday. Hamilton conservatively estimated that if every person spent $10, the district generated $250 million a year.[8] Eight of every ten customers who visited the mall were black, but blacks owned none of the businesses on the strip. Jill Kelly, executive director of the Fulton Mall Improvement Association, told Hamilton, "Black managers, yes, but black-owned businesses? I don't think so."

Mall merchants complained that shoplifters and con artists hurt business. In a year, Kelly nearly doubled the mall security budget from $75,000 to $135,000. But the Fulton Mall Improvement Association did not independently measure criminal activity at the mall. When asked if the association looked up police department crime statistics, Kelly's answer was no. The improvement association accepted verbal reports from police officials, she explained, when they came to board meetings.

Management of Fulton Mall was sloppy, the reporting revealed, but the future of the shopping district was not hopeless. Peter Aschkenasy, the new owner of Gage and Tollner, rated the improvement association performance a 6.5 out 10 points, or a D grade. Kelly's self-assessment was 7.5 points out of 10, or a C. Economic development close to the mall suggested potential revitalization: One Pierrepont Plaza, a nineteen-story development, was completed in 1989, and Metro-Tech, a $1 billion commercial, academic, and research facility, was under construction. Could mall management seize the moment and elevate the Fulton district from a tacky "Cheap Street"? Hamilton and Essick's special report was a call to action.

The June 5–11, 1991, *City Sun* was the seventh anniversary edition, but unlike the previous June, Leid and Cooper did not fill the front page with a red numeral to mark the special occasion. This time they soberly recognized the milestone, yet offered bold, in-depth content.

The previous year the anniversary edition contained "Exiles No More," a special section on the Haitian Diaspora. For its seventh year, writer Hugh Hamilton and photographer Peter Essick collaborated again on "Uptown Eco Blues: Environmental Woes in Harlem," another twenty-four-page special report. A cover photo showed the skeletal remains of a car dumped alongside the wrought-iron fence of a city park.

Hamilton extracted data from an Emergency Planning and Community Right to Know Act (SARA Title III) and reported that two million pounds of toxic chemicals a year were discharged into New York City air. Within the city limits, 200 facilities handled chemicals that could cause death or serious injury if accidentally released. The 400,000 residents north of Central Park in Harlem—people such as Marjorie Moore, leader of the Community Environmental Health Center at Hunter College—began taking environmental activism into their own hands.[9]

Block-type headlines complemented by photographs of street scenes introduced the special section themes. Harlem was disproportionately influenced by asthma (the article reported an alarming rise among blacks; urban conditions increased the likelihood of attacks), noise (subway sounds exceeded 90 decibels; constant exposure probably caused hearing loss), particulates (invisible emissions from diesel buses and trucks were linked to several types of lung disease and cancer), water (raw sewage no longer was a major problem, but the Hudson River on the west side of Harlem was far from clean), and dumping (vacant lots and open spaces were prime disposal sites for household garbage and construction waste). Hamilton and Essick's special report also spotlighted mobilization (a new generation of black environmentalists confronting the status quo and redefining the issues) and enforcement (new laws created a system to monitor compliance and hunt down environmental outlaws).

By late summer, an intergenerational spat erupted between prominent African American artists when filmmaker Spike Lee announced his intention to make a biopic on the life of Malcolm X. The writer-activist Amiri Baraka in the *New York Times* challenged whether Lee should be the storyteller, because Baraka, 56, believed that Lee, 34, was an inauthentic messenger: "We will not let Malcolm X's life be trashed to make middle-class Negroes sleep easier." Baraka, who was shown the script, also concluded that Lee had never been part of the struggles of inner-city blacks and had made films that perpetuated negative stereotypes.[10]

The filmmaker from Fort Greene answered via the *Amsterdam News*: he had been eight when Malcolm X was gunned down and Baraka, at that time the former LeRoi Jones, who was living in Greenwich Village with a white woman, went running up to Harlem after the murder. Lee also asked, "Who appointed Baraka chairman of the African-American arts committee?"

About the time that Baraka and Lee clashed and exchanged words as hot as the August streets, Mayor Dinkins attempted cooperation and wanted to prove his accessibility to constituents to run what many assumed was an ungovernable city. Dinkins announced during a speech that on August 5 he would be in his office the whole day "to meet with New Yorkers who want to speak about how we can change our city." "Face to face, one on one," he added. Actually, he met face to face with relatively few of his constituents. The day after the speech, his office announced that most of the people interested in being helpful would be seen by commissioners, deputy mayors, and other members of Dinkins's staff. The mayor himself would talk only to those who had serious proposals. At the end of the open house, City Hall announced that 2,200 New Yorkers had come down to give advice. However, only about 1,000 stayed long enough to fill out forms and talk to Dinkins or his staff about their ideas, which included combating AIDS, homelessness, staging an international children's festival, and having poor people learn about, and participate in, the process of government budgeting and buying municipal bonds.[11]

Dinkins's open house got generally favorable reviews. The *New York Times* was especially laudatory about the day's helpfulness in giving ordinary citizens a sense of connecting with their government leaders. The mayor announced that he and his deputy mayors and commissioners and the rest of the staff might throw another open house soon.

Andy Cooper, Utrice Leid, and the *City Sun* were among the critics who suspected that Dinkins substituted open houses for governing. "Goofball government: Dinkins at the helm," was the heading of the editorial. It began: "Pardon us for asking, but isn't Dave Dinkins the mayor of this town? With what is going on at City Hall on Monday, we thought perhaps he was seriously considering a career change. Consensus taker? Pollster? . . . Dinkins suddenly decided he would like to get in touch with New Yorkers. . . . The dear, good mayor is confused: You don't first 'solve' a problem and then ask people to help you 'solve' what you already have 'solved.' . . . What this town needs is a decisive mayor who knows what leadership is." Meanwhile, the editorial concluded, the Dinkins administration, "marks time as the transition government between Koch and somebody much like him."[12]

The harsh *City Sun* review surprised a lot of media practitioners and political insiders on Manhattan Island. Why was a little black-owned paper in Brooklyn blasting the city's first black mayor? Shocked Manhattan elites were unfamiliar with Cooper's two decades of consistent watchdog coverage of black politicians—or they hadn't paid him much attention.

Future mainstream media stories expressed shock when Cooper and the *City Sun* served additional doses of tough love to Dinkins and his administration. The "Marking Time" editorial offered a warning Dinkins failed to heed.

"Around City Hall," a 3,900-word article in the *New Yorker* that referenced the *City Sun*'s harsh evaluation of Dinkins's open house, hit newsstands on August 19.[13] That night, two fatalities in Brooklyn crippled the remaining two and a half years of Dinkins's four-year mayoralty. At 8:20 p.m., just after dusk, a three-car motorcade moved briskly through Crown Heights. Rabbi Menachem Mendel Schneerson had visited the graves of his widow and father-in-law in Queens. He was returning to his home on Eastern Parkway, the world headquarters of the ultra-orthodox Lubavitch sect, Hasidic Jews with roots in Eastern Europe.

A police escort led the procession. Schneerson's chauffeured car was in the middle, and a third car driven by Yosef Lifsh protected the international leader's rear. At Utica Avenue and President Street, the traffic signal changed either to yellow or to red, according to witnesses' conflicting accounts. What was not disputed was that Lifsh continued through the intersection so that he would not break up the procession.

Shortly after crossing the intersection, Lifsh lost control of the car. Many neighbors were hanging outside their homes on the hot summer night. The driver tried to correct his error but worsened it by stepping on the accelerator instead of the brake pedal. The car plowed into the sidewalk, avoided a crowd of black adults, and struck a stone pillar. The pillar fell on two seven-year-olds, Gavin Cato and his first cousin Angela. A black neighbor pulled one of the Hasidic passengers out of the car and safely led him away from the angry crowd. Others pulled Lifsh from the car by and attacked him. Three minutes after the accident, Hatzolah, a volunteer Jewish-owned ambulance service, arrived and took the Hasidic passengers, including Lifsh, to Methodist Hospital in Park Slope. It did not transport the Cato children. A municipal ambulance arrived later for the children. Gavin Cato died from the crushing collapse of the stone pillar. His cousin was seriously injured, but she survived.

The vehicular homicide of a black boy was the match that torched the kindling of inter- and intraracial tensions in the city. That night a black mob stabbed and beat an orthodox Jewish rabbinical student, who died in the hospital hours later. Over three days, Crown Heights experienced a race riot that became the most lethal anti-Semitic event in American history and the most extensive racial unrest in New York City in over twenty years.[14]

An eerie combination of events offered kindling for the violent storm. As an angry crowd milled around accident scene at the President Street and Utica Avenue, hundreds of teenagers were returning from an outdoor

B. B. King concert at Wingate High School, one mile south of the accident. As young people returned to President Street, Charles Price was among several speakers who urged the crowd to retaliate for the child's death. "The Jews get everything they want," yelled Price, thirty-seven, a heroin addict and petty thief. "They're killing our children. We get no justice, we get no respect."

Another instigator said, "Let's go to Kingston Avenue and get the Jews." Kingston, three blocks west, was the main Lubavitch thoroughfare. A mob of young black males heard these calls to violence only weeks after Leonard Jeffries, chairman of the black studies program at City College, had delivered an anti-Jewish harangue that stunned many New Yorkers and moved critics to call for the professor's censure.[15] Near the accident scene, the young black men, urged on by the hate mongers, broke into bands and went on a neighborhood rampage. They assaulted and robbed Jews and threw stones, bottles, and debris at police cars, houses, and at bystanders.[16]

By 11:20 p.m., Yankel Rosenbaum approached the corner of President Street and Brooklyn Avenue. He was an orthodox Jew, but not a Hasidic Lubavitcher from Crown Heights. Rosenbaum was visiting America from Melbourne, Australia, to conduct academic research on pre–World War II Jewish life in Eastern Europe. Although he was a visitor, his beard and dark suit signaled to the mob that Rosenbaum was one of the neighbors. Just minutes away from where he was lodging, Rosenbaum was in the wrong place at the wrong time.

"Kill the Jew," "There's a Jew," "Let's get the Jew," said members of a mob of a dozen to twenty black youths, according to witnesses. The gang pummeled Rosenbaum, and he suffered a fractured skull. Most of the young thugs were satisfied with roughing up Rosenbaum, but someone in the crowd pulled out a folding knife and stabbed the rabbinical student several times. Two police officers rolled up to the scene and witnessed at least ten people beating Rosenbaum. The attackers fled when police sounded their car alarm. One suspect, sixteen-year-old Lemrick Nelson, was caught hiding behind a bush in front of a house one block from President and Brooklyn. The teenager had a bloody knife in his pants pocket and bloodstained pants. An investigation revealed that the stains were consistent with Rosenbaum's blood type, not Nelson's.[17]

Though seriously wounded, Rosenbaum was lucid, in stable condition, and appeared capable of recovering from the beating and knifing. Police presented him with a lineup of suspects, and Rosenbaum pointed out Nelson as the one who cut him. Mayor Dinkins visited Kings County

Hospital and spoke with the student. Dinkins held Rosenbaum's hand and comforted him.

Kings County was a notoriously bad municipal hospital. The facility was overworked and understaffed with minimally qualified doctors. Overnight on Tuesday, August 20, Rosenbaum's condition worsened, and he died.

A *City Sun* report suggested that hospital staff killed Yankel Rosenbaum, not the mob that included a stabbing suspect. Dr. Kildare I. Clarke, the black assistant medical director of emergency services at Kings County, told the *City Sun* that "Mr. Rosenbaum died of the same terrible standard of care that has been killing black and Hispanic patients here for years," and also said that emergency unit care at the hospital resembled "a colonial plantation run by absentee landlords." The paper used the incident to tell a history poor-to-fatal treatment of the hospital's predominantly poor black and Hispanic patients.[18] Jewish Crown Heights neighbors dismissed the account as a weak attempt to deflect the blame. They pointed to black male mob as Rosenbaum's killer.

However, in 2005, an apology by the city Health and Hospitals Corporation was part of a financial settlement with the Rosenbaum family: "Kings County Hospital recognizes that diagnostic and treatment errors made during the emergency room care provided to Yankel Rosenbaum in the hours after his stabbing played an important part in significant reforms that have enhanced and improved patient care at the hospital over the ensuing years," said a spokeswoman. "We extend our condolences to the Rosenbaum family."[19]

In six hours Crown Heights had seen two deaths—one accidental, one retaliatory—resulting from a traffic accident that went awry. Rebbe Schneerson did not apologize for indirectly causing the death of Gavin Cato; nor did he send condolences to the Guyanese family.

Some gesture could have cooled boiling tensions among the majority black neighbors. Instead Schneerson made a number of indirect and mystical statements that inflamed instead of calmed Afro-Caribbean and black neighbors. Some of Schneerson's supporters drew a flawed analogy to the U.S. president. The rebbe was an international leader, they said; the U.S. president is not expected to comment about a traffic accident in Washington. The fatal flaw in that analogy was that Schneerson had led the motorcade that resulted in the fatal accident and thus was unavoidably linked.[20] Maybe the rebbe's behavior was consistent. Crown Heights Lubavitchers were insular and avoided communication with Gentiles. Nevertheless the child's death cried out for a response from their community.

After two deaths and reports of assaults, robberies, and property damage, the Dinkins administration and its police department assumed that the spasm of anti-Semitic violence had cooled, and Crown Heights returned to a cooperative but tense multiethnic community. The authorities grossly miscalculated. Three hundred fifty additional police officers were dispatched to Crown Heights to restore order. Some black citizens walked the streets and pleaded for calm. Others complained that the influx of cops was an excessive show of force. The Lubavitchers complained to city hall that they had inadequate police protection. The city dispatched another round of police—1,200 additional cops.

Vinette Pryce, a graduate of Cooper and Leid's TNS writers' workshops during the 1980s, was arrested during the conflict. At that time, she was a "news service of one," she explained, freelancing primarily for the *Amsterdam News* and covering trials for the rival *City Sun*. On Tuesday August 20, she was on assignment for the *Amsterdam News* and was sitting in a courtroom to cover the St. John's University rape trial, the case of a handful of white college lacrosse players accused of assaulting a young black woman. The Rev. Herbert Daughtry entered the courtroom and informed her that street violence had erupted in Crown Heights. Daughtry said he was about to travel to the neighborhood. Pryce asked the minister if she could ride along.

That evening, Pryce tried to call in a story to the *Amsterdam News* about what she had witnessed. She was accompanied by news photographer Chris Griffith, whose brother Michael was killed at Howard Beach. At Utica Avenue and President Street, Pryce was speaking from a public phone when a cop told her and the photographer to leave. Pryce flashed her press pass at the police officer. The black female cop—Officer Taylor—pushed Pryce. Chris Griffith took a photograph. Officer Taylor grabbed his camera and slammed it to the ground.[21] Someone in a crowd who witnessed the commotion yelled, "They're trying to stop the *Amsterdam News* reporter."

Police arrested Pryce, Griffith, and eighty other people and charged them with resisting arrest and other offenses. Instead of the Seventy-first Precinct that served Crown Heights, Pryce was taken to a precinct in the Coney Island area. Personnel on duty ignored the reporter's requests to make a phone call. As hours wore on, Pryce began making her demands in a deliberate, officious tone: "It is 9:05," she announced, "This is my third request for a phone call." By the time Pryce announced, "This is my fiftieth request for a phone call," she was allowed to call her son.

Amsterdam News editor Wilbert Tatum and the president of the New York Association of Black Journalists called the NYPD, and authorities told them that Pryce had left the station when in fact Pryce remained in custody. She was not let go until 3 a.m., thanks to help from Sharpton and the renowned radical attorney William Kuntsler.[22]

Throughout the afternoon, hundreds of blacks and Hasidim threw rocks and bottles at one another. Sharpton and Lenora Fulani of the reputedly anti-Semitic New Alliance Party staged a rally, and afterward a crowd of black teenagers advanced on a line of police. They spit at officers and threw rocks and bottles. The advancing crowd grew.

Two hundred police stationed near Utica Avenue—the scene of young Gavin Cato's death—restrained themselves and retreated from a barrage of bottles, rocks, bricks, and gunshots fired from rooftops. Blacks in Central Brooklyn had long complained about police brutality, but this time they interpreted the officers' reticence as impotence, and that emboldened the mobs.

Rioting escalated and did not calm until midnight, when heavy rain drove people indoors. Police made twelve arrests, most of them for looting or assaulting cops. At least a dozen police officers and three journalists were injured that day, mostly by bricks and bottles.[23]

The violence and marching peaked on August 21, a Wednesday and the second full day of what would become three days of unrest. Sharpton and Alton Maddox stood on the steps of City Hall and warned that New York had seventy-two hours to arrest Yosef Lifsh or else they would make a citizen's arrest. On that day, eight police officers were wounded by shotgun pellets fired by snipers, Lubavitch men were pulled from cars by rioters and beaten, and another man was slashed. A group of rioters hurled stones and bottles at the Lubavitch world headquarters on Eastern Parkway while shouting "Heil Hitler." By early Thursday morning, Dinkins and police commissioner Lee Brown realized that lawlessness ruled the day in Crown Heights, and they had no choice but to crack down.[24] The police presence swelled to 1,800. That move averted the need to call in the National Guard. At a rally at the scene of the Cato accident, police outnumbered black demonstrators two to one. Quiet and order returned by Friday morning.

In context, the three days of violence was a shocking outburst of anti-Semitic acts, yet the level of injuries and property damage was minimal compared to devastating riots in Miami (1980, 1989) and Los Angeles a year later (1992). Violence and property damage in 1991 were more in proportion with rioting in Harlem and Bedford-Stuyvesant in July 1964 after a cop killed a black teenager for scuffling with a landlord.[25] Police made tactical mistakes at Crown Heights, but they contained the violence to a small area. There were only two deaths—Gavin Cato, crushed accidently, and Rosenbaum, who died in the hospital from an untreated knife wound after a mob singled him out and assaulted him.

For the remainder of Dinkins's term, Jewish leaders alleged that a "pogrom" enabled by an anti-Semitic mayor victimized Lubavitch residents. Pogrom was a lethal accusation because it suggested that the Hasidim experienced another Kristallnacht, or "Night of Broken Glass," when Adolf Hitler set his Nazi stormtroopers on the defenseless Jewish ghetto. The facts fifty years later did not support the inflammatory accusation. First, Dinkins was no anti-Semite; if that were the case, he could not have dreamed of becoming mayor in a city in which Jews controlled much of the power.[26]

Dinkins's black base believed the mayor had bent over backward to prove his allegiance to Jewish New Yorkers. Instead his effective deployment of the cops had minimized violence and property damage in Crown Heights. Hasidic leaders also blasted secular Jewish organizations—the so-called Manhattan and suburban elites—for abandoning them, but a contradictory undercurrent was that Hasidim in Crown Heights had initially rejected help, insisting they maintained cordial relations with blacks even as they avoided social contact with them.

The "pogrom" smear, Cooper wrote in the *New York Times*, was a tactic that Jewish groups used to scapegoat the mayor and to extract additional economic and political concessions from blacks. A *City Sun* editorial said a "quiet deal" was brokered to encourage mayoral hopeful Rudy Giuliani to use the word "pogrom" in his speeches. The smear proved to be the potent weapon that destroyed Dinkins's prospect for reelection in 1993.[27]

Al Sharpton delivered the eulogy for Gavin Cato August 26 at St. Anthony's Baptist Church before an overflow crowd of mourners, activists, and dignitaries that included the mayor and the press. The *City Sun* reprinted the minister's entire message in its August 28–September 3 edition on page 3, real estate normally reserved for "This Week in History." Sharpton said:

> The world will tell us [Gavin] was killed by accident. Yes, it was a social accident. It is an accident for one group of people to be treated better than another group of people. It's an accident to allow a minority to impose their will on a majority.
>
> It's an accident to allow an apartheid ambulance service in the middle of Crown Heights. It's an accident to think that we can keep crying, and never stand up and call for justice. That's the accident.[28]

Instead of healing, Sharpton chose demagoguery. His behavior during the eulogy was consistent with his antics during the racially tinged Tawana Brawley rape case discredited as a hoax two summers before. Sharpton's embellishments, like adding "apartheid" to the Jewish-owned ambulance service and identifying the Hasidim as "diamond merchants"—code words for capitalist oppressors—pandered to the conspiracy theorists in the crowd and provided colorful sound bites for the raw-meat-craving New York press.

It was highly unlikely that Sharpton knew about the reasons behind the formation of the so-called apartheid ambulance service. On New Year's Day 1977, ambulance attendants arrived drunk and unresponsive at the Crown Heights home of rabbi Sam Shrage, and he died of a heart attack. Hasidic Jews were outraged, and their response—insular and efficient—was to form a private ambulance service to protect their people.[29] Shrage had been blunt, honest, and unafraid. He earned the respect of black nationalists, scorned the Brooklyn Democratic machine, and backed liberal Republican reformer John Lindsay in the late 1960s. Had he been alive in 1991, Shrage would not have talked past his black neighbors; he would have engaged them.

Furthermore, the black rage and the perception of city hall's indifference toward them in favor of Hasidim was not imaginary. Many people in those pews recalled the 1978 police beating and choke-hold killing of Arthur Miller. Miller was a neighborhood improvement activist and a pillar of black Crown Heights.[30] Also that year, young Hasidics beat black teenager Victor Rhodes into a coma because the boy knocked a black hat off an elder's head. As for the patrol car that gave Schneerson 24/7 protection, it would surprise many African Americans that the car was stationed partially because of them but *primarily* to protect the international leader from rival Satmar Hasidics who lived two neighborhoods north in Williamsburg.

The rival sect rejected the Lubavitchers' pro-Zionist policies and had threatened on a number of occasions to harm the rebbe. When Mayor Koch, a Jew, took office in 1978, he suspended the patrol car stationed in front of 770 Eastern Parkway. The detail returned in 1981 after Satmar zealots made death threats on the rebbe.[31]

Gavin Cato was a seven-year-old boy who was being taught how to ride a bicycle by his seven-year-old first cousin, yet during the eulogy, Sharpton lionized the boy. He told the Cato parents that their son was in heaven with Malcolm X, the four little girls who had been firebombed in Birmingham, Alabama, and new homegrown martyrs Yusef Hawkins and Michael Griffith. Sharpton urged young people in the audience to continue demonstrating on the street. There was little evidence of the leader cautioning black teenagers to reject the robbing, assaulting—and homicide—of the Jewish minority that had occurred over three days. Instead Sharpton's embellished charge was: "Don't apologize. Don't be ashamed and don't back up. You come from a great people. In your blood runs the blood of Shaka Zulu. In your blood runs the blood of Imhotep, Moses, Jesus, Frederick Douglass and Marcus Garvey. In your blood runs the blood of Malcolm X and Fannie Lou Hamer. Stand by, don't ever sit down! Forward ever, backward never! We will win because we're right. We will win because we're strong. God is on our side."

Andy Cooper understood that Sharpton was a media hound, and he candidly said so to major media players in town. Yet the publisher also understood that the minister appealed to many of his customers who had activist or militant leanings. So Cooper and Leid prominently displayed Sharpton's bombast in their newspaper.

The minister was among "certain crazies, black and white," Cooper referred to in his 1993 *New York Times* op-ed article that said people on both sides exploited racial and religious tensions in Crown Heights.[32] Showcasing his institutional memory of Central Brooklyn, Cooper explained that Hasidic and black antagonism escalated in 1977 when Mayor Abe Beame and City Councilman Theodore Silverman successfully partitioned Crown Heights and created two local governing bodies—including community boards, school districts, and police liaisons—one for the blacks, one for the Hasidim, separate and unequal. The construct favored the orthodox Jewish minority. Crown Heights was the only bifurcated community in New York City. The decision by the city Board of Estimate, which awarded all contracts and was led by the mayor, was an affront to the middle-class black professionals who had lived in the urban oasis since the 1950s, and to the emerging waves of working-class Afro-Caribbean neighbors that included families like the Catos.

Eastern Parkway, the line of demarcation between the black and Hasidim communities, moved resident Anthony Morris to tell Cooper, "Eastern Parkway, no; Gaza strip, yes." If Morris appeared cynical to *New York Times* readers in January 1993, consider what Silverman said in 1977: "If we the City of New York were to partition Crown Heights, we would be acting in accord with American foreign policy because American foreign policy was created to assist emerging nations."[33]

When challenged, Crown Heights Jewish leaders insisted they received copious antipoverty, housing, and police support because they engaged the political system consistently and legally, unlike the blacks who cried sour grapes. The other side said the game had been rigged.

Ten days after Gavin Cato's funeral, a grand jury composed of eight blacks, five Latinos, and eight whites declined to indict driver Yosef Lifsh on charges of criminally negligent homicide or third-degree assault. New York courts traditionally ruled that the standard of negligence in a criminal case must be greater than in a civil negligence case. Grand juries were reluctant to impute criminal negligence to what began as a traffic accident. This Kings County grand jury was more impressed with the official police report and investigation than with slogans from black militants.[34]

A *City Sun* editorial a week later denounced the grand jury decision. Headlined "No Justice, No Peace!" it called the ruling "the most contemptible and contemptuous miscarriage of justice" since the state attorney general had refused to bring indictments in the Tawana Brawley case.[35] "The lives of people of color have no value," continued the editorial. It added that Hynes presided over a "two-tiered criminal justice system that continues to usurp their rights, their dignity and their humanity."

A year later, activist lawyer Colin Moore denounced Hynes in a *City Sun* op-ed piece. He said the prosecutor should have recused himself because he favored Hasidim over blacks and therefore had a conflict of interest. The *City Sun* gave Hynes op-ed space to respond in kind. The D.A. fired back that Moore was "a faker" who was a dubious player in the Tawana Brawley hoax. He noted that two years later as lawyer for the black woman shopper in the Korean grocery boycott, Moore suppressed a key piece of evidence.[36] the *City Sun* editorial and Moore conveniently forgot that Hynes had vigorously prosecuted the Howard Beach case, so suggestions that he was anti-black strained credibility.

On Saturday, September 7, two days after the grand jury decision, Sharpton led a march of 100 blacks on Hynes's summer home in a private beach community at Breezy Point, Queens, at the western end of the Rockaway peninsula. The minister proclaimed that the district attorney lived in "an apartheid village." Then demonstrators shattered the quiet of the remote beach community with shouts of "Hynes, Hynes have you heard? This is not Johannesburg!" Breezy Point was racially and ethnically integrated. Sixty percent of the houses were occupied year-round by Irish and some Jewish families, and Asian and Latino families lived in the neighborhood. It was hardly apartheid Johannesburg, but Sharpton was not there to have his beach theater contradicted by inconvenient facts.[37]

Three weeks after the riot, at the Democratic primary on Thursday, September 12, voters—and black elected officials, including congressman Charles Rangel of Harlem—rejected C. Vernon Mason, Colin Moore, and Pete Williams, a trio of riot fomenters who ran against Jewish candidates or blacks who maintained cordial relations with Jewish neighbors.[38]

After the grand jury decision the previous week, Yosef Lifsh left Crown Heights and returned home to Israel. Cooper wrote that blacks perceived Hasidic Crown Heights as a zone that Hasidic lawbreakers could use as an escape route to Israel because of their dual citizenship. Lifsh survived criminal prosecution but was still liable for heftier civil damages. On September 17, a day before Yom Kippur, Sharpton and Maddox flew to Israel to serve notice that he was about to be sued in civil court for wrongful death. The duo did not find Lifsh, and Jewish leaders in both Israel and New York denounced the trip as a publicity stunt.[39]

Sharpton embellished Gavin Cato's stature when he eulogized the child. Spokesmen for the Crown Heights Lubavitcher sect meanwhile misrepresented the identity of their adopted martyr Yankel Rosenbaum. He was neither a Lubavitcher—although his clothes made him look like one of them—nor a yeshiva student, as suggested to the media. Rosenbaum was an academic, and Hasidim Lubavitchers of Crown Heights for the most part did not attend college and scorned mainstream the academy. But to frame Rosenbaum as a visiting Jewish academician who died because he was in the wrong place at the wrong time would distract from the dramatic imagery of Crown Heights blacks and Jews in conflict.[40]

In late September, the Metropolitan Council of the American Jewish Congress issued a news release and statement about the Crown Heights upheaval that said the violence had occurred amid a vacuum in black leadership: "As the public leadership vacuum, for the most part, was filled by Sharptons, Carsons, Masons, Moores and Daughtrys and the *City Sun* and *Amsterdam News*, it was left to the Jewish community alone to assert that black racism is no less racist than white racism. Only the Jewish community rallied against the anti-Semitism of the hate mongers."

The *City Sun* fired back with a 1,500-word front-page editorial that concluded:

> The truth is that when organizations like the AJC say they are interested in a lasting peace, it comes with the proviso that blacks and Latinos will yield the very thing they seek: respect, power and equal access to the strategic resources of their communities. The AJC historically

has supported the efforts of Jews around the world, even by violent means, pursuing and protecting these precepts. The cudgel of moral authority that swings, however, historically has landed squarely on non-Jewish targets.

Which brings us to the old West Indian saying that sums up the status quo—but what should be the challenge—in Crown Heights: "Ya me? Ya you!"[41]

20. THE BREAKUP

Farhan Haq joined the *City Sun* staff in summer of 1991, the season of the Crown Heights riot. His reporting beat was international affairs. Haq was twenty-four and had previously reported for the *Amsterdam News* after earning his master's degree in English literature from Yale University. Haq earned his bachelor's degree at Williams College.[1]

International affairs at that moment dominated U.S. foreign policy. The Soviet Union collapsed in 1989, and out of the totalitarian rubble emerged Russia, Poland, several Baltic region countries that wanted to embrace Western-style capitalism and democracy, and the former Yugoslavia, which splintered into a handful of Balkan states with renewed hatreds among Serbs, Bosnians, and Croatians, and between Christians and Muslims. A continent away in South Africa, slow, painful steps to free the black majority from decades of white minority apartheid had begun. A U.S.-led coalition pummeled Iraq with a brief war in 1991 for invading oil-rich neighbor Kuwait the previous year. Tensions remained predictably high in the Middle East because of relations among Israelis, Palestinians, and a majority of Arabs in dictatorial nations that were hostile toward the democratic Jewish state, which had powerful allies in the United States and United Kingdom.

The *City Sun* made international news coverage an essential part of its weekly report. Haq wrote original stories informed by international sources based in New York, including people within the United Nations. The *City Sun* also filled its Caribbean and Africa pages with Inter Press Service dispatches. IPS was where Hugh Hamilton had worked as an overseas correspondent before joining the *City Sun* in the late 1980s as Caribbean editor. Among Haq's fall 1991 headlines were "'New World Order' Brings New Challenges to the Caribbean," "Palestinians Fear 'Autonomy' of Bantustans as Madrid Peace Talks Begin," and "An Egyptian (Boutros Boutros Gali) Is Named to Top UN Post."[2]

By February 1992, Haq's inside-page reporting shifted to the cover: about 2,500 Haitian demonstrators marched from the Dominican Republic consulate to the Haitian embassy in New York to demand the return of president Jean-Bertrand Aristide, who was toppled in a coup at the end of September.[3]

In addition to Haq's and Hamilton's global-centered local reporting and editing, political cartoonist Abe Blashko used a colorful palate to caricature president George H. W. Bush, secretary of state George Schultz, and major foreign players when Cooper and Leid penned editorials about foreign affairs. Bush was comfortable with foreign affairs and a so-called New World Order, established when the communist Soviet Union disintegrated. At home, a sluggish economy dogged him. America was in the early stages of an emerging postmodern world and a dying Industrial Revolution. Machines were replacing humans in factory jobs, and unemployment swelled. The *New York Daily News* strike of fall and winter 1990–91—the midpoint of Bush's first and only term—was a metaphor for the radical makeover of American labor and automation.[4]

As Bush took a political beating from the struggling U.S. economy, Democrats saw an opportunity to win back the White House in 1992 and thus end a twelve-year lockout. By spring 1992, the front-runner was Bill Clinton, the youthful governor of Arkansas. For years as leader of the Democratic Leadership Council, Clinton had pulled the party away from its left-leaning instincts and toward the political center to appeal to white southern and blue-collar voters who had dumped the Democrats since the late 1960s. Blacks were a reliable voting bloc. Although Bush had far more cordial relations with black America than his hostile predecessor Ronald Reagan, skeptical black poor and the middle-class civil rights establishment stayed overwhelmingly in the Democratic camp. A notable exception was a small number of young black professional "Buppies" who crossed over.

Editorially, the *City Sun* was wary of black GOP professionals. That was evident in its October 16–22 front-page editorial, "Clarence Thomas or Anita Hill? It's Bad News Either Way." The conservative Supreme Court justice nominee and the law professor who accused Thomas of sexually harassment when she was his subordinate at a government job were both "sheep" of white elitist sponsors who "shepherded" them, said the editorial, and neither showed any inclination to empower black masses.[5] Months later, the *City Sun* withheld editorial enthusiasm for Clinton. How could it be, when in 1988 the paper had rejected presidential candidate Jesse Jackson because the black progressive softened his sharper positions to position himself closer to the political center? During the 1992 campaign season, the *City Sun* did want to at least engage Clinton and other Democratic rivals and have them sell their polices to a black constituency the Democrats had historically taken for granted. That desire resulted in a clash with rival publisher Tatum and his *Amsterdam News*.

Tatum canceled an April 2 candidate debate between Clinton and former California governor Jerry Brown because Tatum did not feel he was sufficiently consulted about negotiations among campaign staffs and sponsors. Tatum's executive editor Don Rojas kept him in the loop, and Stephen E. Davis, a writer for the *Amsterdam News*, was liaison between the political staffs and sponsoring media outlets, which included WLIB-AM and Black Entertainment Television. A shaken Percy Sutton, owner of the Apollo Theater and CEO of Inner City Broadcasting, parent of WLIB, informed Davis that the candidate debate was canceled because Tatum objected and the publisher could flex his muscles as a substantial shareholder of Inner City Broadcasting.

Early in the negotiations, the *City Sun* was invited to be one of the media outlets to quiz the candidates. But Cooper said his newspaper would not participate if the *Amsterdam News* was involved. Rojas told Davis that Cooper's objection was based on a feud between him and Tatum that dated back to the late 1970s, when Cooper had worked as an *Amsterdam News* political columnist.

Tatum accused Davis of inappropriately speaking for *Amsterdam News* management during negotiations. Davis insisted that he did not speak for the newspaper or write any correspondence on the company's letterhead. Still, Tatum banished Davis from writing for his newspaper. Davis's 3,900-word anatomy of the aborted presidential debate was the lead story published in the rival *City Sun*.[6]

Cooper's charge that Tatum had sabotaged a presidential candidate debate because he did not play the role of kingmaker shed light on the narrowing competition between the black-owned weeklies. Robert McNatt of *Crain's New York Business*, a trade journal, profiled both publishers. Tatum reveled in his increased influence and access now that his Harlem crony David Dinkins was mayor. At Upper East Side soirees, the publisher loved to rub shoulders with the literati, including Jacqueline Kennedy Onassis and Theodore Sorenson. Or Tatum would take his limousine up and across town to Harlem for power meetings with so-called Gang of Four members Dinkins, Charles Rangel, Basil Paterson, and Sutton.[7]

Tatum occupied the catbird seat, yet the *Amsterdam News* took a beating during the recession of 1991–92. Paid circulation slipped below 30,000 in 1991, down 17 percent compared to 36,000 in 1987. Despite the circulation decline, the paper remained the leading black weekly in New York, as it had been since 1910. But not by much: Cooper's militant and visually bolder *City Sun* claimed it had narrowed the circulation gap and was poised to match the establishment leader and even overtake it. Audited circulation figures for the *City Sun* were not public, but its estimated paid circulation was about 18,000. Four years earlier, in 1988, the Audit Bureau of Circulation had reported that the *City Sun*'s paid circulation was 15,454. Journalistically, the *City Sun* was the stronger of the two. Several observers thought that product should attract more readers. "I don't think the *Amsterdam News* does as fine or full a job of covering New York as it could because the publisher's priority prevents that," said Phyllis T. Garland, a professor at Columbia University Graduate School of Journalism and a former black press writer for *Ebony* and the *Pittsburgh Courier*.

Thomas Morgan, who covered Brooklyn for the *New York Times* and was a recent president of the National Association of Black Journalists, said, "Tatum wants to be part of the political infrastructure while Andy Cooper wants nothing to do with it."

Said Garland, "The *City Sun* is more aggressively political, includes more commentary, and does more investigative work. It's sometimes irritating, but never boring."[8] Cooper tried to convince readers and advertisers to make his newspaper the top choice. He promised to increase the reach of the *City Sun* with fewer (but higher-quality) distributors. In a memo to prospective advertisers, Cooper wrote:

> **The Battle Is On**
> The eight-year-old *New York City Sun* and the eighty-year-old *Amsterdam News* are locked in battle for the minds and hearts of the city's two million African American and African Caribbean consumers. This market, worth more than $25 billion a year, can affect your bottom line. I submit this Crain's article for your information concerning that battle.

Cooper asserted that his younger, leaner *City Sun* was taking the fight to the older, declining *Amsterdam News*. Tatum maintained cordial relations with Dinkins, while Cooper said he was "working toward a civil understanding" with the mayor but reserved the right to stay an outsider. Cooper's weekly experienced two bankruptcies in its short life, and observers wondered whether the newspaper had the resources it needed to overtake the *Amsterdam News*.

During the U.S. presidential race, Ross Perot emerged as a third-party candidate, and the plain-talking Texas billionaire appealed to predominantly white independent voters who had tired of gridlock on the Republican right and Democratic left.

Across the country from New York, fourteen months after four LAPD officers were caught on an eighty-six-second home video beating an unarmed and prone drunk driver, Rodney King, an all-white Ventura County jury reached a verdict on April 29: the cops were innocent of criminal conduct despite having delivered an undeniable fifty-six baton blows to a man cowering on the ground. This incident fit into a long, bloody tradition of police brutality against blacks that started when posses would form to capture runaway slaves and later lynch mobs would hang free black men from trees who challenged the establishment. That Rodney King's attackers had been caught on videotape beating him like a slave finally showed a version of police interaction that was unfamiliar to most whites. Many black and Latino men in Los Angeles began to loot and burn property in protest. Several black men pulled Reginald Denny, a white truck driver, out of his vehicle and beat him. Another African American helped Denny to safety. The mobs targeted Korean American shopkeepers for looting.[9]

David Dinkins denounced the jury's verdict and the four police officers' use of excessive force. The mayor's protest renewed complaints from New York's orthodox Jewish community about the Crown Heights riot. Why didn't he express similar outrage when Hasidic Jews were under siege?

Furthermore, Dinkins's condemnation of the cops strained his difficult relationship with his own city's police union. Numerically, Crown Heights was a mild disturbance compared to the fury in Los Angeles, which killed fifty people over several days, prompted the governor to deploy the National Guard, and sparked the largest urban riot since the Civil War.[10]

Unlike a quarter century earlier, when people of color were virtually absent from mainstream newsrooms, April 1992 was dramatically different. Paula Walker Madison, a child of Harlem, Vassar graduate, and former member of the Nation of Islam, was a newsroom manager of WNBC-TV in New York. She watched the mayhem in L.A. via sister station KNBC-TV's satellite signal. Walker instructed her control room staff not to linger on images of violence any longer than necessary. She explained: "I told them you've got to show what's going on, but you don't have to show 30 seconds unedited of someone getting hit in the head with a brick 25 times."

Walker was concerned that the TV images could inflame passions in racially tense New York (the Crown Heights case was in its pretrial stage, and the Central Parker jogger rape trial was fresh on New Yorkers' minds). The acting news director called Los Angeles and advised reporters not to publicize the locations where looting was taking place without a police presence. "What I said to reporters is if you live in a neighborhood, are you going to tell people they can loot and there are no police around? They don't do it in Harlem [where she lived] and don't do it in South Central."[11] Madison advanced to news director in the mid-1990s.

Ironically, on the day after the riot began, *The Cosby Show* aired its final episode after a remarkable eight-season run. Bill Cosby and Phylicia Rashad portrayed the Huxtables, parents of an upper-middle-class African American family who lived in a townhouse in Brooklyn Heights, several blocks from the real-life *City Sun* newsroom. In one episode, paternal character Heathcliff Huxtable strolled down the staircase and conspicuously held an edition of the *City Sun*.[12]

In spring 1992, Utrice Leid promoted Farhan Haq, who had been international affairs reporter for nine months, to metro editor. Haq remembered the layout of the *City Sun* newsroom this way: Leid and Hugh Hamilton sat in the front row, Haq and arts editor Armond White sat in the second row, and sports editor Anthony Carter Paige and copy editor Angela Briggins sat behind them in the third row. When Briggins joined the newspaper, she was tasked with assembling the arts centerfold. Leid promoted her to chief copy editor because the managing editor trusted Briggins's line editing skills and command of grammar and punctuation. In the tradition of many great copy editors, Briggins's staff perceived her as spacey and eccentric. Such people worked intensely with words. Wrong or ungrammatical words on paper screeched, honked, and crashed in Briggins's head. As the new enforcer of grammar and style, Briggins's verbal approach was gentler than Leid's, but she wielded equally devastating results with her red pen.[13]

Other writers included Peter Noel and Clinton Cox, regulars who stopped by the office or filed remotely (in Cox's case, from upstate New York). Karen Juanita Carrillo also wrote frequently for the *City Sun*.

As a middle manager, Haq became familiar with the production routines: Cooper met with advertisers; Leid would determine the news hole space after the advertisements were placed on pages, and then she would convene the news meeting with the staff on Thursdays. The writers and editors put the newspaper to bed on Mondays and faxed layouts of the pages to the printer in New Jersey. The *City Sun* was printed on Tuesdays and distributed on Wednesdays.[14]

At times the unexpected occurred just before or after the newspapers were printed and bundled. Once Utrice Leid drove to the printing plant and fell asleep in her car as she waited for the printing to end. A banging against her driver's side window woke her. A police officer was pointing a gun against the glass and demanding to know what the hell she was doing there. Another time, bundles of *City Suns* were dropped at overnight locations for delivery on Wednesday morning. Leid followed a Hasidic man who picked up a bundle from the curb. Was he stealing or hiding the news? No, he was a *City Sun* deliverer.[15]

As metro editor, Haq gained insight into the weekly's finances. There was a problem with the *City Sun*'s tax status. It was operating as a nonprofit enterprise. Cooper's Trans Urban News Service of the late 1970s and early 1980s had been a nonprofit that evolved into the *City Sun* newspaper. At some point, however, the *City Sun* had become a for-profit enterprise and did not adjust its tax status. That oversight would mean trouble down the road.

Another notable newsroom promotion took place around this time at what was arguably the world's greatest newspaper. In late 1990, Gerald Boyd, an African American and former Washington correspondent, was promoted to metropolitan editor of the *New York Times*. Boyd, a St. Louis native who still rooted for the Cardinals, pumped life into an underperforming *Times* metro section. He hired talented women and minority journalists, including Felicia Lee and Brett Pulley, and motivated the veteran staffers he inherited. When necessary, he isolated and minimized veterans who tried to coast and resisted performing to his high standards.[16]

Boyd's arrival did not guarantee that black leaders thought *Times* coverage was always fair. In a letter, the Rev. Daughtry asked why was it necessary for a reporter to print his home address in suburban New Jersey in a story about demonstrators who marched on the residences of militant blacks like Leonard Jeffries.[17] Still, Boyd's promotion signaled a significant change at the *New York Times*. The *Times* was a vast bureaucracy, so managerial changes did not appear to shake the Gray Lady's foundations. Nevertheless Boyd was a blunt and probing editor who commanded the respect and adoration of the team of writers and editors he managed and animosity and jealousy from some rival editors.[18]

Among the rival tabloid dailies, a love-hate relationship continued between black reader-observers of the *Daily News*. There was grudging acceptance that the paper's management was not as racially hostile as it had been in the pre-1987 trial era. Briton Robert Maxwell, who bought the strike-battered tabloid in early 1991, pledged that his newspaper would welcome black New Yorkers more warmly than before, but his promise of happier days ahead evaporated. Maxwell died in a boating accident off the Canary

Islands on November 1991, and $1 billion was discovered missing from his publishing empire. A year later, the succeeding owner would be accused of ethnically cleansing the *Daily News* of experienced black journalists.[19]

The *New York Post* was deemed a lost cause. Rupert Murdoch's editors were unapologetic toward ignoring pleas that they hire journalists of color to cover racially diverse New York.[20]

Newsday of Long Island poured copious resources into its seven-year-old New York edition and was loaded with talented journalists of color, including Pamela Newkirk, a Trans Urban News Service trainee; Michael Cottman, whose investigative work debunked embellishments in the Tawana Brawley case; and Les Payne, a two-decade veteran editor who directed the foreign and national desks and wrote a weekly column that often dealt with local issues. Payne was a Pulitzer Prize winner and a founder of the National Association of Black Journalists.[21]

The legal proceedings in the Crown Heights case were at a sensitive stage. Lemrick Nelson was to be tried in the fall as the attacker whose stabbing contributed to Yankel Rosenbaum's death. The decision was rendered October 29, 1992, a week before the pivotal U.S. presidential election. A diverse juror mix—six blacks, four Hispanics, and two whites—acquitted Nelson, much to the horror of orthodox Jewish New Yorkers. The Jewish community pressed relentlessly until a federal court tried Nelson again five years later on a creatively conceived charge of violating Rosenbaum's civil rights in a public space.[22]

On September 17, ten thousand off-duty police officers and their supporters jammed lower Manhattan to protest Mayor Dinkins's proposal to create a civilian review board that would investigate citizen complaints of police misconduct. Many police officers in attendance were drunk and disorderly. There were isolated incidents of plainclothes cops referring to black elected officials, including Mayor Dinkins and city councilwoman Una Clarke, as "niggers." When *New York Newsday* columnist Jimmy Breslin, a longtime voice of white, blue-collar New Yorkers, wrote that he witnessed some off-duty police spouting racial epithets, he was roundly denounced as a liar. Breslin in turn called his critics "bindle stiffs," or bums.

The ugly police behavior spread to an M subway train. Yuwnas Muhammad, eighteen, got into a fight with three white men who turned out to be off-duty cops who had attended the rally. Muhammad was charged with punching and slashing one of the men after he stumbled on the train. But witnesses said one of men had tripped Muhammad, who retaliated in self-defense. The trio of white men pummeled the youth—breaking his jaw—and did not identify themselves as police officers. The officers later stood trial on assault charges. Muhammad told his story to the *City Sun*, and the paper published a full page with nine line drawings that illustrated his account of the beat down.[23]

The police union vigorously resisted the civilian review proposal and argued that an all-civilian board appointed by the mayor would politicize police decisions. In an essay, Clinton Cox wrote that the police crowd's rowdy and menacing behavior confirmed that they did not know the difference between democracy and mob rule. A front-page *City Sun* editorial also said: "So why weren't we shocked—as apparently so many people were—that former foot patrolman Phil Caruso still has illusions that he is something of a generalissimo in New York City, able to order his PBA squadristi to engage in acts of terrorism? Last Wednesday demonstrated, in fact, that was quintessential Caruso—thug tactics orchestrated by a thug who still insists neither he nor his union did anything wrong."[24]

The editorial, headlined "Mr. Mayor, Act Like It," made nine bulleted recommendations that included initiating civil and criminal actions against the PBA and Caruso and ending the "48-hour rule," a police contract work rule that said cops were not obligated to answer investigators questions—about anything—until forty-eight hours or two working days after the incident.

In early October, the *City Sun* filed for Chapter 11 bankruptcy protection. Twenty months before in December 1990, the paper had emerged from an earlier bankruptcy. By fall 1992, the weekly's finances were in disarray. Cooper had failed for years to pay withholding tax, and now he owed the IRS $750,000. Federal agents also froze Utrice Leid's bank account because legal documents listed her as a co-owner of the company.[25]

Furthermore, *City Sun* circulation figures did not add up. The paper's media kits and an account published on October 21–27 by Farhan Haq said that circulation was 53,000. Yet the newspaper's ownership statement printed in its November 11–17 edition reported that weekly paid circulation was 11,007 copies.

Cooper told the *Village Voice* that the substantially higher circulation number reflected unpaid readership. Still, "unpaid circulation" listed on the statement was 14,000 for a combined readership of 25,000 when added to paying customers. When Henry Rissmeyer of the Metropolitan Transportation Authority learned about the downward adjusted circulation numbers, the marketing and advertising official promised to alert the MTA's advertising agency to look into getting a rebate from the *City Sun*. With the *City Sun* under financial siege, Leid issued an ultimatum to Cooper: she demanded control of the newspaper.

At thirty-nine, Leid had built the weekly around herself, cultivating and protecting writers, banishing them when they did not get along, and placing defiant editorials on the front page.[26] Cooper's answer to Leid's demand was an unequivocal no. The managing editor and cofounder walked out of the Court Street office. On Monday morning, October 19, Leid was missing in action at the New Jersey plant that printed the newspaper. Cooper, sixty-five, came in and made sure the paper got out. The content lacked the usual editorial punch, and the product was bloated with wire copy, pumpkin soup recipes, and other filler that Cooper said amounted to an edition that was a "piece of shit."[27]

Among the perplexed staff, Leid's status was unclear. She said, "I have not tendered a letter of resignation nor have I been officially informed that I was fired." Cooper said he did not fire his managing editor, but he added that wasn't taking her back. "That page has been turned," he said, "and we're starting new with a blank page." Cooper packed up Leid's office materials in boxes for removal and changed the office door locks. Hugh Hamilton and Farhan Haq, Leid's prized hires, soon felt unwelcome. "Do you want to resign, or will I have to fire your?" Cooper told Hamilton, whose child was Leid's godchild. Both journalists understood that their boss suspected they were Leid loyalists.[28]

On Sunday, October 18, sports editor Anthony Carter Paige walked from the *City Sun* office to Leid's apartment in Brooklyn Heights and begged her not to quit. "We got a call on a Sunday," said Paige, who had been with the newspaper since 1984. "Utrice said she was resigning. She had 50 percent of the paper. Cooper was trying to dislodge her because of her controlling interest."[29] Paige's recollection that Leid was pressured to relinquish control contradicted Cooper's suggestion that Leid walked away after he rejected her demand for control.

State capital correspondent Clinton Cox, who called Leid the most talented editor he had ever worked with, resigned when the managing editor walked away. Cox, a writer for the paper since 1984, was a Leid loyalist who was convinced that the managing editor had tried to push the *City Sun* toward acceptable accounting methods, but Cooper, the publisher, resisted. "I told him, 'Andy, you gotta quit running the paper like a mom-and-pop operation,'" said Cox. "He wasn't about to let anyone see the books."[30]

A few weeks after she departed, Leid called the tumult at the weekly "a self-inflicted wound" and added, "The paper had extraordinary journalists and did not honor a covenant with them. There are serious structural problems." At that time, Cooper announced that he was looking for three journeymen reporters and a full-time copy editor. Leid said that filing vacant positions was the least of the *City Sun*'s problems. Reliably tart-tongued, she later said that her former paper had become a "pimper's paradise," quoting a song by the reggae superstar Bob Marley. Leid sued the newspaper for back pay. She claimed it owed her $250,000 to $300,000. Leid was unable to collect. Manhattan attorney Charles Simpson represented the Cooper family's interests.[31]

As the Cooper-Leid confrontation and breakup erupted, a number of big national stories were developing. After twelve years of wandering in the wilderness, Democrats won the White House in November 1992. African Americans cast 82 percent of their votes for the Democratic candidates, 11 percent for losing Republican incumbent George H. W. Bush, and 7 percent for third-party independent Ross Perot.

The election of southerners Bill Clinton and Al Gore also occurred as a record number of post–Reconstruction era black members were elected to Congress—eleven men and five women, including Earl Hilliard of Alabama; Corrine Brown, Carrie Meeks, and Alcee Hastings of Florida; Eva Clayton and Melvin Watt of North Carolina; Jim Clyburn of South Carolina; and Robert C. "Bobby" Scott of Virginia.[32]

Lost in the scuffle of the Cooper-Leid breakup was an investigative report that the newspaper never published. That fall, Leid had dispatched writer Hugh Hamilton and photographer Peter Essick to Metcalfe, Mississippi, a rural community near Greenville. The assignment was a story on poverty in the United States, and U.S. Census data identified Metcalfe as the poorest of the poor. Deep in the Delta, the nearly all-black community of 1,400 people was a generation removed from sharecropping. Welfare, unemployment, and hopelessness ravaged Metcalfe. To do the newsgathering, Hamilton and Essick flew from New York to Memphis, Tennessee, then drove to Greenville, where they slept and commuted six miles to work for days in Metcalfe. When the duo returned to Brooklyn to publish their findings, Cooper and Leid were engaged in their fight. The page proofs lay unpublished at Hamilton's home in Queens.[33]

The Leid-less *City Sun* limped along to the end of 1992. Clinton Cox's fiery political essays, rich with historical analysis, were gone. By late November news stories regained their muscle and became less of a capitulation to advertisers ("Retail Businesses Post Sales Gains," and "Caldor Makes a Competitive Bid for Alexanders," read one edition's headlines). Core weekly topics like political corruption and justice reappeared. Peter Noel, recently of the *Village Voice*, began to write for the *City Sun* again. Cooper stared at huge debts and the prospect of rebuilding a shorthanded staff.

Cecil Harris, a sports writer at the paper since 1989, left in 1992, not necessarily because of the breakup, but to accept an internship at Gannett Westchester Newspapers that jump-started his career in daily journalism. He said, "I admired the *City Sun* for its integrity, high journalistic standards, and literal interpretation of its front-page motto: 'Speaking Truth to Power.' The *City Sun* was the epitome of a fearless, truly independent, journalistically solid, and regrettably penurious African American weekly newspaper. I always wished the *City Sun* had more money, so I wouldn't have to wonder when my overdue checks would arrive, and most important, so the newspaper could expand on the unsurpassed coverage of New York's African American community—in breaking news, politics, social issues, sports and the arts."[34]

In December, the weekly affirmed Harris's praise of its unsurpassed coverage with its watchdog reporting of Interfaith Hospital of Crown Heights. Why, the December 2–8 report asked, was the facility losing millions under the direction of its $400,000-a-year director? Two weeks later, the front page published the mugs of Al Vann, Annette Robinson, Clarence Norman, and Edolphus Towns. "Who's Responsible for the Mess at Interfaith?" asked the headline. Hospital director Corbett A. Price was in the center of the cover, but a question mark replaced his image. True to form, Cooper confronted the political establishment, called them to account to answer questions, and his writers honored a fundamental rule of watchdog reporting: follow the money.[35]

In mid-December, the paper shut down for its traditional holiday break. Observers aware of the weekly's financial peril wondered whether it would reopen after the first full week of January. The *City Sun* did, and its staff had to scramble to keep up with several roaring local stories, including a terrorist bombing near the World Trade Center and the possible acquisition of a metropolitan daily by Cooper's most hated newspaper rival.

21. SETTING SUN

During the *City Sun*'s Christmas holiday hiatus, the *New York Times* published Andy Cooper's "Two Nations of Crown Heights" op-ed essay. Bankrupt again and without Utrice Leid, Cooper resumed publishing on January 12, 1993. Leid soon landed at left-leaning radio station WBAI-FM and thrived as the host of public affairs show *Talkback!* She encountered *City Sun* alumni and new recruits from time to time, and their off-air conversations were cordial. Leid spoke with Ericka Blount and Milton Allimadi with the confident air that said, yes, she was gone, but the weekly still mattered because she had largely built it. Cooper quickly recruited new bodies to restore energy to the enterprise. The new recruits generally shared these traits: they attended elite schools such as Columbia University, University of Pennsylvania, and Hunter College; they interned or freelanced at top news outlets like the *Wall Street Journal* and the *New York Times*; but they were seduced by the militancy, opportunity, and mission of the *City Sun* and were willing to work at the crusading weekly for meager pay.

During her senior year in 1991–92, Simone Joye met Cooper and Leid when the duo visited Hunter College. Leid encouraged students to apply for internships at the *City Sun*. Joye applied, but Leid sent a letter back that said, "You go to a community college. You can't work for us."[1] Joye replied with a scathing letter to Leid and Cooper. A year passed, and Joye was elected student representative to the NABJ board of directors. Cooper invited her to come in and talk about the rude letter she had received. By that time, Joye was with the *Wall Street Journal* Online in Princeton, New Jersey. Cooper hired her during Leid's last month at the weekly. The two women did not meet again.

Joye's newsroom boss was Tony Paige, the former sports editor who was moved into Leid's former managing editor slot. Joye's first cover story was "Unfriendly Fire," published January 27–February 3, 1993, about white police accidentally killing black plainclothes police. She wrote the article with Lucas Rivera, formerly of the *Daily News* and *New York Post* and probably the first Puerto Rican journalist at the *City Sun*. Joye's other memorable cover was her reporting that helped free Darryl King after eighteen years in prison after his wrongful conviction in a cop killing.[2]

Despite a seven-month stint of erratic paychecks that almost made her default on her rent, Simone Joye loved Andy Cooper. She explained: "To him, we were like family, like a father saying, 'Look, I know we gotta buy school clothes, but we have to keep the lights on.'" Cooper paid employees in cash whenever they confronted him about irregular payrolls. Paige said, "When there was no pay for two weeks, the staff rebelled and said we're not doing any work. 'OK,' said Cooper, 'You'll get paid Monday.' We walked into his office. It was like a Colombian drug dealer's. There was thousands of dollars of cash on the table. You signed for the checks in the office. Once he changed banks without telling his employees. Every Friday, Cooper bought ice cream and cake for the staff. I said, hey, checks are bouncing and we have no insurance."[3]

Joye said, "That seven months with him was life changing. He was a strong black man and a strong black role model at a time when many men of my generation were broken and didn't pass the batons from the civil rights era. He cared about the next generation. If you wanted to be a journalist, he'd help you. I studied the black press more and became a self-imposed scholar. I never knew the history before the *City Sun*." After three months of beat reporting at the paper, she was promoted to community affairs editor. She had just turned twenty-seven.

Others came and went. Hugh Hamilton, the Caribbean affairs editor, left in early 1993 to work as a legislative aide to City Councilwoman Una Clarke. Farhan Haq, the metro editor, left by April 1993. He became a spokesman at the United Nations.

In 1993, Ericka Blount of Baltimore was a student at the University of Pennsylvania. Her sister lived in New York City, and she read both the *City Sun* and *Amsterdam News*. When Blount visited from Philadelphia, she was most impressed with the *City Sun*. The newspaper's writing style grabbed her. Blount would get lost in Maitefa Angaza's stories because they read like literature. Andy Cooper's editorials—specifically his criticism of Rudy Giuliani's zero-tolerance policies—were spot-on. The *City Sun* was not afraid to attack anyone or any institution. Blount wondered, how do they do that?[4]

When she graduated from Penn in May 1994, she applied everywhere for jobs in media. She applied to New York University for a summer fellowship and applied to the *City Sun*, as well. The NYU program required a paid internship. The *City Sun* called. Blount became a paid intern in summer 1994, and NYU underwrote her salary. That summer, the *Washington Post* offered her a job as a copy aide or news assistant. The opportunity could have given Blount—a local kid from the *Post*'s circulation area—a foot in the door at an elite daily, but she wanted to be in New York, and she wanted to write.

When Blount got to the *City Sun*, she was sold. A huge downside was the newspaper's financial condition, which she did not know about until much later in her two-and-a-half-year stay. The NYU-financed internship protected her briefly from the inconsistent pay that other staff members endured. In fall 1994, the internship ended, and Blount became a reporter. She stayed until the newspaper's end. In the beginning, the pay was not as bad as it was toward the end in fall 1996. Sometimes Cooper paid Blount and her colleagues a week or two late. Toward the end in 1996, payments came a month late. "Andy Cooper would call us into his office one by one," Blount explained, "then he'd give us cash from his wallet. His secretary, Phyllis Caesar, had 11 kids. How did she function? I was single then, and I freelanced."

Blount was a general assignment reporter and the "City Scene" editor. Melody Wade preceded her. As a young reporter, Blount did whatever she was told. To produce the centerfold, Blount went out in the field and gathered cultural news items. Leaders and proprietors of arts and entertainment venues were excited about the way the section looked and the quality of the content. "City Scene" offered a broad view of what was going on in New York City. Arts and entertainment editor Armond White was the point man.

Blount was twenty-two when she joined the *City Sun* in 1994, but she looked much younger to a lot of people. One day during the first year of Mayor Giuliani's police sweeps and zero-tolerance policies, she was on her way to cover a press conference. Police randomly picked up high school-age truants, loaded them on buses, and took them to the precincts. A police officer stopped Blount and insisted she get on the bus even *after* she showed the woman her *City Sun* press pass to confirm she was adult. Blount argued with female cop and was given a ticket for disorderly conduct. Colleague Karen Carrillo wrote the story about the disagreement the next day—the headline was "Baby-Faced Blount Bagged." Blount's colleagues got a kick out of the story, but the police were not amused and a few made threatening phone calls to Carrillo.[5]

Milton Allimadi read the *City Sun* during his 1991–92 year at the Columbia University Graduate School of Journalism. "I was impressed," said Allimadi. "Wow, they did *real* reporting." In 1993, while interning at the *Wall Street Journal*, he began reporting freelance articles for the *City Sun*. By 1994, Allimadi became a *New York Times* metro section stringer. He did mostly crime reporting and soon grew tired of it. He quit the metro desk and aspired to work for the *City Sun* despite a significant cut in pay.

Allimadi recalled: "I walked into Andy Cooper's office, and he asked, 'Why would anyone affiliated with the *Wall Street Journal* want to do anything for us?' I said, 'Look, that's the problem.' We hit it off." Cooper may have been testing Allimadi. The *City Sun*'s first star reporter was Errol Louis, who in 1984 passed on an offer to work at the *Wall Street Journal* in favor of the start-up *City Sun*. When Allimadi arrived, Utrice Leid had been gone for more than a year, but he got to know her later. "We sort of became friends," he said. "She still loved the newspaper. Her legacy and influence still hung in the office."[6]

"Cooper was a true journalist," said Allimadi, "in the truest essence of reporting. He'd say, 'A story is a story. If the guy is a brother or a sister, we're going to go after them. I'm not into coddling.'"

Empowered by Cooper's crusading spirit, Allimadi reported aggressively, producing many noteworthy stories. First, Allimadi said, "A school janitor was accused of setting a locker room on fire. He was fired and became destitute and sold cans on the street. No investigation was done. The black man was fired by the principal based on the word of a white janitor. After I did a few articles, the man got his job back, plus his back pay. That man came to the *City Sun* office with his daughter. We did activist journalism, but it wasn't activism, it was reporting the mainstream papers were not doing. I listened to that man and believed him."

On another occasion, Allimadi said: "A white woman walked into the office. That was unusual. She said her Latino boyfriend was set up for a murder in Hazelton, Pennsylvania. The father of the cousin of her boyfriend was convicted of the same crime. He was a cop with the 53rd Precinct in Manhattan. When I called witnesses in Pennsylvania, they consistently told me the opposite of what they told authorities. The lead investigator in Hazelton called me and said I was harassing witnesses." Allimadi recalled that he was threatened with prosecution. "I asked him questions. He lost his temper."

"The local papers (the *Wilkes-Barre Times-Leader* and the *Scranton Times-Tribune*) began covering the case and reported 'according to the *City Sun*.' Both cousins (one was Juan Torres) got a new trial with the same jury pool. They were convicted again. I still believe they were convicted for a crime they did not commit. I gave my information to a CBS *60 Minutes* producer who was interested. The story was dropped when the producer got a book deal for another project."

Thomas Green rejoined the *City Sun* in 1994 at age twenty-eight. "I was seasoned," he said. "I did three to four articles a week. Cooper would say, 'We need another.' I'd knock it out." Green had graduated from DeWitt Clinton

High School in the Bronx in 1983. Soon afterward, he met Cooper and Leid when the start-up paper invited people to produce a youth pullout section. At first, Green felt a little intimidated by the college students who sounded as if they knew everything. "I was blown away," said Green. "The editors were the first to show me professional respect."

Young and eager, Green did a lot of sports work for Anthony Carter Paige. (Green's father, Thomas Sr., worked for the Federal Reserve Bank and was an unpublished writer.) Green left the *City Sun* in 1987 for the *New York Post* and worked as a copyboy and dictationist. He did his first writing there for the business section and was an agate clerk for the sports section. He moved on to a full-time reporter's job at the *Times-Leader* of Wilkes-Barre, Pennsylvania, then moved back to New York City to report at the *Staten Island Advance*.

Green said, "I broke the story about Con Ed overcharging black churches. The *New York Daily News* later claimed they had an 'exclusive.' Con Edison was charging many black churches the higher residential rate instead of the cheaper church rate." The *City Sun* ran Green's story big on the cover with a lightbulb illustration. Con Ed paid $1 million to one church but essentially ignored many other churches it had overcharged.

As for Cooper's demeanor, Green said, "He didn't care much for punks. During the bad times, he'd pay us out of his drawer. Some people got as little as fifty dollars. One of the girls was crying: 'What am I going to do with this?'

"When it was my turn to go in, I cursed him out. I said, 'You can't do this to people.' I thought I'd be fired. Instead Cooper put his arm around me. The next week he gave me a raise."[7]

A week before Valentine's Day, the *New Yorker* picked at a still-raw scab in the black public psyche from the Crown Heights riot: the magazine's cover depicted an illustration of a bearded Hassidic man dressed in black French-kissing an elegantly dressed black woman. Anticipating fireworks, the edition carried the following "Editor's Note":

> The painting on the cover of this issue of The New Yorker is by Art Spiegelman, whose "Maus," a two-volume narrative of the Holocaust in comic-book form, was awarded a special Pulitzer Prize in 1992. About the painting, which is Mr. Spiegelman's first work for the magazine's cover, the artist writes, "This metaphoric embrace is my Valentine's card to New York, a wish for the reconciliation of seemingly unbridgeable differences in the form of a symbolic kiss. It is a dream of course—in no way intended as any kind of programmatic solution. The rendering of

my dream is intentionally, knowingly naïve, as is, perhaps the underlying wish that people closed off from one another by anger and fear—Serbs and Croats, Hindus and Muslims, Arabs and Israelis, West Indians and Hasidic Jews—could somehow just 'kiss and make up?' Though I'm a maker of graven images by profession, I respect the fact that in the real world, the world beyond the borders of my picture, a Hasidic Jew is proscribed from embracing a woman outside his sect and his family. (I won't disingenuously attempt to claim that the woman in my painting is his wife, an Ethiopian Jew). I'm also painfully aware that the calamities facing black communities in New York cannot be kissed away. But once a year perhaps, it's permissible, even if just for a moment, to close one's eyes, see beyond the tragic complexities of modern living and imagine that it might really be true that 'all you need is love.'"[8]

The *City Sun* refused to accept the preemptive apology. In an editorial, Cooper responded:

> The February 15 issue of the *New Yorker* is an extreme study in sexism, racism and general bad taste. Mr. Spiegelman's painting of a Hasidic male embracing and kissing a barely clad black woman is perverse for several reasons. First, it is well known among African-American females and it is a general charge that Hasidic men on the whole indulge in sexual harassment toward them. Second, they are viewed as prostitutes and women of loose morals by the Hasidim. . . . The acceptance of this despicable, trashy piece of so-called art to be used as a front cover for the staid *New Yorker* speaks volumes about the new editor, Tina Brown, and organization's new scope and vision.

On the Op-Ed page, Carroll Carey Howard, who said she was the first black person the *New Yorker* had employed in 1960, rebuked the *New Yorker*'s illustration in a piece titled "Disrespect of the Black Woman," on February 17–23.[9]

At that time, the *City Sun* was waging a renewed battle with the *New York Daily News*. Mortimer Zuckerman, owner of *U.S. News and World Report*, the *Atlantic Monthly*, and now the *Daily News*, aggressively cut staff and effectively "cleansed" the experienced black reporters and editors from the staff. In an editorial, Cooper urged his readers to dump the daily:

> Since the *Daily News* has dismissed the majority of its black editorial staff, which covers our community, and has also handed out numerous

> insults over the years, they need to be taught a lesson. Writers like Les Payne of *New York Newsday* need attention. *New York Newsday*, if you must read a daily newspaper, and staff reporters like Merle English, Michael Cottman and Pam Newkirk (one of many reporters who were trained at pre–*City Sun* Trans Urban News Service) should be read. What else needs to be done? The *Daily News* needs to be completely ignored.[10]

On March 3, Cooper's wife Jocelyn had breast cancer surgery. That procedure would be among five major surgeries during her fifty-four years as an adult. They included open heart, two Caesarian sections, and a hysterectomy. Mrs. Cooper also had two minor surgeries, one of them a biopsy.[11]

The first World Trade Center bombing occurred on February 26, 1993. Managing editor Anthony Carter Paige reported from the scene and wrote the March 3–9 cover story "Hell at the World Trade Center."

Meanwhile the *City Sun*'s rival publisher had some news of his own. On March 12, 1993, the eccentric real estate developer Abe Hirschfeld named Wilbert Tatum of the *Amsterdam News* editor and co-publisher of the *New York Post*. Founded by Alexander Hamilton in 1801, the tabloid faced extinction. After a dozen years of ownership, Rupert Murdoch sold the paper in 1988 to acquire WNYW-TV 5 and launch his Fox television network. At that time, Federal Communications Commission rules prevented media owners from operating a major newspaper and television station in the same market. Murdoch's successor had no newspaper experience, and on his watch, the money loser bled red ink faster. Just before Hirschfeld, Steve Hoffenberg, a debt collection entrepreneur, published the paper for seven weeks; but Hoffenberg lost control of the paper after his assets were frozen and the Securities and Exchange Commission filed claims of investor fraud against Hoffenberg's Towers Financial Corp. Hoffenberg's editor was Pete Hamill, a veteran columnist and author.

When Hirschfeld acquired the *Post* after a court decision, he fired Hamill and inserted Tatum. There was a plan to insert copies of Tatum's *Amsterdam News* inside the *Post*. The decision, said Tatum, "will mean an opportunity for a newspaper that is not hostile to the aspirations of people of color and other ethnic groups." The *Post* newsroom staff rebelled after receiving the news that Tatum had become their boss. The paper did not publish for a day, and staff members vilified Hirschfeld and Tatum in print for the rest of the week. Some accounts accused Tatum of anti-Semitism.

Cooper jumped into the brawl. He loathed Tatum and was probably alarmed, jealous, or both that his black publishing rival could significantly expand his *Amsterdam News* brand if Hirschfeld's purchase worked out. Yet Cooper could not abide the scurrilous attacks on his adversary, whose wife was Jewish. In a March 17–23 editorial, "In Defense of Bill Tatum," Cooper spelled out why it was nonsense to suggest that Tatum was anti-Semitic. Turmoil continued at the *New York Post*. After a few weeks, Hirschfeld and Tatum were out, and Rupert Murdoch returned. He was allowed to run the paper for two months and work out terms for permanent ownership.[12]

In no time, Cooper and Tatum resumed trading insults. "He is egomaniacal and, more than anything, he likes to frequent those social affairs at which he can rub shoulders with rich white people," Cooper told the *New York Times*. Tatum, he added, "controls everything that goes in the paper. If you're talking about editorial integrity, it ain't there." Tatum responded in kind: "Cooper is unimportant. He is making an effort to ride the *Amsterdam News*, to make a place in the sun for himself. For all intents and purposes, he is without class."[13]

On March 24–30, the *City Sun* published "The Thorn in the *Amsterdam News*," a cover story about John L. Edmonds, lawyer-developer and 35 percent shareholder of the *Amsterdam News*, who was fighting in court to disarm Tatum of his majority shareholder status. Edmonds told the *City Sun* he was forced out as CEO in 1982 when co-owner John Procope sold his one-third share of the company to Tatum.[14]

By spring and summer, Tatum's Harlem buddy Mayor Dinkins prepared for a difficult reelection campaign. His clumsy management of the 1991 Crown Heights riot stuck to the mayor like Velcro. Rudy Giuliani was Dinkins's rematch candidate. In a May speech in Bay Ridge, a predominantly white Brooklyn enclave, Giuliani cavalierly described the riot as a "pogrom."

In an editorial, Cooper wrote that Giuliani and his like-minded allies had reached "a quiet deal" to pound the incumbent with that inflammatory term. The Girgenti Report, the investigation of the riot commissioned by Governor Cuomo, did not help Dinkins. The two-volume report landed just a few months before the November election and kept the two-year-old Crown Heights incident fresh on voters' minds.

When speculation of a Rudy Giuliani–Herman Badillo fusion ticket surfaced, the *City Sun* in an editorial characterized the pairing as an "unholy alliance."[15] During the mayoral campaign, Cooper's *City Sun* editorials hounded the mayor. Cooper's words were essentially tough love, calls to Dinkins to man up and get his act together. Dinkins stewed privately about Giuliani and company smearing him as a pogrom-fomenting anti-Semite. A handful of times in print, Cooper roared, "Spare us the self-pity and fight." In a front-page open letter to the mayor on August 25, Cooper counseled the self-identified tennis addict to "take off your tuxedo and white shorts and put on your sneakers and jogging suit. . . . When you attend the U.S. Open tennis tournament, take the No. 7 train, forget the helicopter . . . and don't attend every match." Cooper also advised that Dinkins buy a block of seats to the Open and take a crowd of disadvantaged kids with him.[16] Cooper, the public relations man in a previous life, took note that Giuliani had gone populist by showing up at Yankees games and also playing stickball and bocce with constituents.

The *New York Times* reported on Cooper's advice was and characterized him as a "staunch supporter" of the mayor. That would have been quite a surprise to Dinkins. The incumbent was in trouble. Voters perceived him as elitist, excessively polite in public (but surly in private), and—most damning—ineffectual as a public servant. Cooper continued to needle Dinkins in print. A front-page editorial in mid-September urged the mayor to shake off his reserve. It opened as follows:

> Dear Mayor Dinkins,
> There are citizens of New York, black, white, Latin, Asian and immigrants from all over the world, who love you and want to see you survive the coming election for mayor of New York City. They consider you a decent man and a good man, including this writer, who has known you for more than forty years. Their hearts ache at what seems to be the ineptness of your administration and what they are beginning to consider your weakness and inability to strongly govern. They WANT to vote for you but they also want to see you exhibit the courage that they know you have. *Frankly, you are beginning to look like a wimp* and they're wondering why you don't begin to govern with a strong hand.[17]

The "wimp" accusation played prominently in the *New York Times*, the *Washington Post*, and other major media. It was an unfortunate, prophetic assessment of what was soon to become of the first black mayor of New York City.

As the November mayoral and council elections approached, Cooper prepared his readers to go to the polls. Each edition ran a front-page banner that counted down the days to the election.

On November 2, Dinkins did not squeak by as he had in 1989 because blacks, Hispanics, and liberal whites came out while many white voters stayed home. This time, Giuliani edged out Dinkins the incumbent 51 to 48 percent. Superficially, Dinkins seemed to draw enough from his coalition to win: his votes came from 90 percent of blacks; 66 percent of Hispanics; 25 percent of whites, including four out of every ten Jewish voters. Seven out of ten registered Democrats voted for Dinkins. But a closer look at the numbers showed how Giuliani exploited Dinkins's flawed strategy, or lack thereof.[18]

Dinkins did not campaign in Brooklyn, the city's numerical center of black voting power, or in the Bronx. Many of those black and brown voters returned the favor and stayed home in response to the mayor's lack of energy.

Cooper, in a front-page editorial to the mayor-elect, told Giuliani that he should take little comfort from his victory. Dinkins did not lose, wrote Cooper; he took a dive.

Cooper also wrote that the deposed mayor was lazy, even as he was very good with math: At sixty-six, Cooper observed, Dinkins could calculate his imminent city pension, which could run as high as $100,000 a year, and add to that his twice-weekly radio show on WLIB-AM and a new position as a professor of urban affairs at Columbia University. Why resume the headache of serving a second term as mayor when he could cash out and relax? The deposed incumbent's decision not to campaign in the boroughs supported Cooper's critique of Dinkins as a hopelessly Manhattan-centric politician.[19]

Four days after the mayoral election, Andrew W. Cooper and Jocelyn Elaine Clopton's second and youngest daughter, Jocelyn Andrea Cooper, twenty-nine, married John J. Gilstrap during a sunset ceremony inside the Brooklyn Botanical Garden. At that time Jocelyn A. was a music publisher.

Midnight Music, which she named to honor the clandestine late-night reading classes run by slaves on plantations, was an informal, unpretentious midtown Manhattan destination where songwriters auditioned their material on old tape recorders, and the boss and her staff dressed in baseball caps, blue jeans, and Timberlands. Jocelyn A.'s marriage would not be so carefree, the parents ruled. Before proposing to Jocelyn A., Gilstrap formally and very nervously asked Andy Cooper for his daughter's hand in marriage.

"I told John he couldn't have her unless he asked me," Cooper explained. "That's the proper thing to do, and we're proper people. We had a meeting, and I asked him what his plans were. What were his ambitions? Why would I turn over this precious human being to somebody I did not know or was not satisfied with? That's the point. I had to be satisfied saying I am the person who gives this woman to John Gilstrap." In a scene straight out of a romance novel, the thirty-one-year-old groom, a marketing manager for Time Warner Music Group, proposed to Jocelyn A. on bended knee at the top of a mountain in Italy, despite his fear of heights.

Two days before the wedding, Andy Cooper suffered a stroke. He rebuffed pleas from his wife and daughter to go to a hospital. Cooper was present that Saturday evening to give his daughter away before 160 witnesses. Frail and ghostlike, he seemed barely to fill his tuxedo.

On that day, Jocelyn A. Cooper was transformed from the young woman who favored ball caps and jeans to a bride in a silk Vera Wang gown and long veil. After exchanging vows before the Rev. Calvin O. Butts, pastor of the Abyssinian Baptist Church in Harlem, the couple drank from crystal glasses that had been a fiftieth wedding anniversary gift to the bride's great-grandparents, who had been born to slaves.[20]

By February 25, 1994, Andy Cooper drafted a proposal for "The *City Sun* on the Air" and sent the plan to Rev. Ben Chavis of the NAACP, Fred Noriega of WNET-TV 13, Gil Noble of WABC-TV 7's *Like It Is*, publisher Jake Oliver of the *Afro-American* newspapers of Baltimore and Washington, Gus Heningburg of Newark (and more recently the WNBC-TV public affairs show *Positively Black*), Rochelle Evans of the *Times Mirror*, and Adriana Iglesias.

The proposal described a target audience 3.2 million strong—African Americans and Afro-Caribbeans residing in the tri-state New York metropolitan area, according to the 1990 U.S. Census. The public affairs show was to be broadcast Sundays from 5:30 to 6:30 p.m. on WWRL-AM 1600 and on Fridays from 5 to 6 p.m. on WNJR-AM 1430 in New Jersey with Kay Thompson Payne as Cooper's co-host. The Cooper Group reporters' roundtable lineup was Earl Caldwell, Les Payne, Peter Noel, and Joan Shepard.[21]

Transitions, personal and national, abounded. Pat Carter, Cooper's close friend and alter ego during the voter registration days of the 1960s, died in June 1994. Cooper served as master of ceremonies at the memorial service at the Brooklyn Academy of Music on June 18, 1994. Carter had contracted lung and prostate cancer and spent his final days in a hospice. That month in Los Angeles, the slain bodies of Nicole Brown Simpson and her male friend Ronald Goldman were found. Ex-husband O. J. Simpson, the football legend turned actor and commercial pitchman, led police on a slow-speed highway chase until he peacefully surrendered. Editorially, Cooper showed no sympathy for Simpson—unlike many people who called for black solidarity.

Cooper reasoned that Simpson was ambiguous, even indifferent, when it came to his blackness, so why did some leaders urge people to embrace Simpson because he was a prominent black man in trouble? Cooper's *City Sun* editorial that criticized O. J. Simpson and praised Jews for never forgetting where they came from attracted praise from *Jewish Week* on July 14, 1994.[22]

That summer, as Mario Cuomo prepared to seek a fourth term as governor, Cooper wrote letters to black state legislators seeking their ten reasons why Cuomo should be reelected. Cuomo called Cooper to complain about the resistance he was sensing from formerly reliable, malleable allies. Cooper listened patiently, then calmly asked, "So why should we reelect you?" He conducted his phone exchanges with leading politicians as civil conversations even when sharp disagreements surfaced. That November, Cuomo lost to Republican George Pataki. In Bill Clinton's America, New York City had become a Republican zone.

Sometime in late summer 1994, Jocelyn C. Cooper and Andy Cooper visited Jamestown, Virginia, for the 375th anniversary of the landing in 1619 of twenty Africans (eighteen men and two women), who were indentured servants. Jocelyn was fascinated with the story of Africans living in the first permanent English settlement in America, a twelve-year-old colony when the Angolans arrived on the captured former Dutch man-of-war. Mrs. Cooper had also become absorbed in the life and work of Harriet Tubman, who grew up as a slave on Maryland's eastern shore. It was Jocelyn who had first pushed her husband into political activism in the early 1960s. Recently retired from city Community Development Agency, she now nudged her husband the publisher to give more attention to literacy, family, and women's empowerment initiatives.[23]

Through 1995 and 1996, the *City Sun* operated as a bold and freewheeling weekly. The front-page formula was racism, police brutality, and political scandals. The *City Sun* confronted white hate talk radio, whether it was Bob Grant of WABC-AM or Beth Gilinsky, president of the Jewish Action Alliance, whom the paper sarcastically dubbed "the goddess" of white hate talk radio.[24] On March 20–26, in recognition of Women's History Month, the *City Sun* published an all-women's edition. The thirty-six-page issue was touted as a "collector's edition."

It included a national story on women prisoners and opinion pieces by the author Alice Walker and other contributors. The community arts section ran a feature on the author Barbara Chase-Riboud. The front-page skybox advertised a feature on Makaziwe Mandela, Ph.D., Nelson Mandela's daughter and a Fulbright scholar; Armond White profiled Echobelly lead singer

Sonya Aurora-Madan; and the sports pages carried a feature on Marsha Harris, who led New York University's Division III women's basketball team to a 27-4 record. In addition to the motto "New York's most authoritative black weekly newspaper," green coloring was added to the usual bold strokes of red and black. The all-women's issue was so popular with readers that the *City Sun* acquiesced and published an encore edition on May 8–14 for Mother's Day.

In 1995 the *City Sun* began publishing "The Last Plantation: Notes from the Federal City," a full page of political commentary from Washington, D.C., by correspondent Malik Russell, who had just left the *Washington Afro-American* weekly newspaper to publish a journal that focused on U.S. policy toward Africa. "The Last Plantation" critiqued the Clinton administration, the so-called Contract with America led by U.S. representative Newt Gingrich (R-Ga.), the GOP majority Congress that swept into power after the November 1994 elections, and the lessons learned from O. J. Simpson's "trial of the century": why many whites were visibly upset, why many blacks cheered the verdict, and why there were stubborn double standards and sins of omission and commission by leading media pundits.[25]

Throughout the summer, the paper published with no external appearance of distress. Internally, the opposite was going on. Cooper's enterprise in February had emerged from Chapter 11 bankruptcy, dating back to the fall 1992 trauma. The publisher was very ill. Matiefa Angaza, his executive editor, was writing most of the editorials in 1996 because strokes and other ailments had severely weakened Cooper. He could barely walk. "He was becoming more of a guest editorial writer," Angaza explained. "A lot was going on. It was window-ledge days, stress, high blood pressure. Some weeks he'd say, 'I want to do something on that.'"[26]

The September 25–October 1 front page led with an exclamation, "A Marvelous Idea!" Rev. Al Sharpton announced his intentions to run against Mayor Giuliani in 1997. A "From the Publisher's Desk" piece encouraged the activist minister's aspirations.

On October 21, as writers and editors were working on the October 24–30 edition, city marshals arrived at 44 Court Street and evicted the staff and its business from the third-floor offices. Rent had gone unpaid at the newsroom. Locks on the doors were changed. Kevin Quinn of the New York State Department of Taxation said the Sun Publishing Company owed New York $380,000 in back taxes. The *City Sun*'s printer was also owed money, although the proprietor declined to say how much.

The eviction was "very disillusioning," said Milton Allimadi, one of the journalists present when the marshals arrived. "I could see the potential of this institution. But there was hope. A major problem: the paper was Andy Cooper's baby. He would meet with investors, but when it was time to sign, he got cold feet. Cooper didn't want to lose control. I knew some of the investors, for example, an early producer of Public Enemy. He considered putting in a couple hundred thousand dollars, add color pages and more entertainment coverage." Cooper rejected that pitch and others and tried to convince a skeptical staff that the *City Sun* would resume publishing. Herb Boyd recalled that it was the same dedicated staff Cooper often paid in cash out of his desk drawer. Utrice Leid, established as executive producer and host of WBAI-FM *Talkback!*, scoffed at Cooper's claim that the paper would come back. If that were true, Leid said, "I am the queen of England." The estranged managing editor said she still had an active lawsuit against Cooper and Sun Publishing to recoup the $250,000 to $300,000 in income owed to her. Cooper insisted there had been no movement on that suit for years.[27]

Charles Simpson, Cooper's attorney, kept Leid at arm's length. As for his numerous creditors, Daniel Alterman, the attorney who had successfully represented the four plaintiffs suing the *Daily News* in 1987, was assisting Cooper. "I was trying to hold the line, Cooper's problems of borrowing from Peter to pay Paul," said Alterman. "I cleaned up, put out fires, and had to protect Cooper from himself and other people."[28] Alterman, who admired Cooper's crusading journalism, began assisting him in 1988 and was able to keep him publishing for much of the 1990s, but the fragile enterprise finally collapsed in October 1996. Cooper's adversary Tatum was conciliatory in print. His *Amsterdam News* was rid of its most nettlesome weekly competition. Furthermore, Tatum had complete control of his newspaper because in July he bought out the last partner.

Still, several parties tried to revive the flatlined *City Sun*. Son-in-law John Gilstrap promised that fall that the paper would reappear on the World Wide Web, which had recently become a mainstream phenomenon. Ten articles were to be up by December. A *City Sun* in cyberspace was intended not to replace the newspaper but to be an adjunct, Gilstrap told the *Village Voice*.

Bill Stephney, founder and CEO of Stepsun Records, had discussed buying the newspaper from Cooper. Stephney said he wanted to broaden the content and increase its coverage of hip-hop and New York's Latino community.

Alterman said the *City Sun* could be revived if Cooper could sell it for $1 million, use most of that revenue to retire the debts, and resume with an online or conventional newspaper edited by Les Payne. Randy Daniels would be the other partner and the money man who could work contacts and obtain needed revenue. Cooper, as editor emeritus, could write a column that would occupy prime real estate to the right of the masthead.

This rosy plan had several problems. Gilstrap, who was advising Cooper, was convinced that the bankrupt newspaper was worth more than $1 million, and his higher asking price drove investors away. Second, Payne, fifty-five, a top-level editor at *Newsday*, was not quite ready to give up a quarter century at the Long Island daily to take on this new labor of love.

Meanwhile Maitefa Angaza told the *New York Daily News* that she was working on a plan to revive the *City Sun*. Whether the promise was coming from Cooper, Stephney, Gilstrap, or Aganza, the reality was that after twelve years and four months of radiance and heat, the *City Sun* had set.

22. DUSK

By February 1997, four months after the closing of the *City Sun*, Maitefa Angaza, the newspaper's last executive editor, described the general state of the black press as "a medium in crisis." With her feisty former newspaper vanquished, the *Amsterdam News* stood at the top of the heap as the undisputed leader of New York City black weeklies, even as it had atrophied. Its circulation by 1997 had shrunk to 28,000, down from 37,500 in 1996 (even that number was down substantially compared to the pre-1983 strike circulation of 41,000). Other black-oriented papers—the *Daily Challenge*, *Carib News*, *Beacon*, and *Queens Voice*—listed much smaller circulation numbers and competed for crumbs from a shrinking pie.[1]

Angaza's outlook was gloomy because she was determined to revive the *City Sun*, but her dream would be daunting. The national monthly magazine *Emerge* published the kind of hard-hitting and irreverent stories that mirrored Angaza's local *City Sun*. *Emerge*'s circulation of 161,000 was fiercely loyal, but prospective advertisers considered it anemic. *Ebony* maintained a robust circulation—nearly two million monthly—and a healthy advertising-to-editorial ratio, but its content was notoriously cautious and bourgeois. Joel Dreyfuss, who was trying to convince investors to underwrite his *Our World News*, an online and print venture, was an admirer of the *City Sun*, and he indentified its problem: "I think the analysis of city politics in the *City Sun* was wonderful, and was really the only voice for that in the city. The problem is that I don't think that sells papers. It was like the *Nation* or the *New Republic*, which has solid analysis but never made any money." What those magazines had was underwriters with deep pockets who were willing to tolerate no profits or modest losses in exchange for must-read journals that catered to the political, decision-making elite. A lively, politically and culturally robust *City Sun* could not draw on those endless resources. "What happened to the black press," said Dreyfuss, a former *Black Enterprise* and *PC Magazine* editor, "is that the papers just became obsolete."

Dreyfuss's outlook was grim because sponsors quickly dumped quality black-oriented publications that did not pay for themselves. Youth magazine *YSB* (Young Sisters and Brothers), owned by Black Entertainment Television, shut down in the same month as the *City Sun* because of weak advertising support. The owners tried to appeal to twenty- and thirty-something *Vibe* magazine readers, but that demographic group did not respond with enthusiasm. BET turned its sights to another print vehicle, *BET Weekend*, an entertainment-oriented magazine that was inserted in a handful of big-city daily newspapers, including the *New York Daily News*. That magazine did not last long, either. Another publishing phenomenon was the free newspapers available to urban commuters via kiosks or from hawkers at subway entrances. Also, the venerable *Village Voice*, a longtime for-sale alternative weekly, became a free shopper with news and arts and entertainment content when its ownership changed.[2]

Meanwhile the *City Sun* had collapsed under a mountain of debt and bankruptcies. How could it rise again? That fall Angaza, Armond White, Milton Allimadi, former editor Rhea Mandulo, and Kevin Goldin formed the City Sun Employees Inc. and organized fund-raisers. Their initial event drew a light turnout but attracted supporters from Amnesty International and Manhattan city councilwoman Ruth Messinger. The event happened to coincide with the opening of Al Sharpton's new National Action Network headquarters. The City Sun employees raised $15,000 from an art auction at the Caribbean Cultural Center in Brooklyn and from another event in January. The group said it needed $500,000 to relaunch the newspaper. "We haven't raised the kind of money we hoped to raise," Angaza told the *New York Daily News*, "but enough to keep us going. The events that we have have shown that we have a lot of support."

Angaza projected that the group's SunRise Initiative needed to raise $1.2 million in capital to resume publication and then had to break even within seven months. Goldin said the new group would not be liable for any debts of the original *City Sun*, but the claim was debatable. Utrice Leid reminded them that her active lawsuit claimed the enterprise owed her $300,000: "It is a noble effort I suppose, but . . . there are other creditors who have to be satisfied."[3]

The employees' group sought Andy and Jocelyn Cooper's permission and blessing. Over dinner, Andy admitted that he was physically and financially unable to return and revive the paper, so he told his former employees to "go for it" if they wanted to try and resuscitate the *City Sun*.

By July 9, 1997, nine months after the *City Sun* newsroom doors were padlocked, there were promises of launching an online *Metro City Sun* editorial via Diaspora Africana. The climate was perfect for such a launch. Internet use had grown exponentially from ten thousand Web sites in 1994 to one million sites in 1997.[4] Most customers were using telephone dialup to access e-mail and the World Wide Web, a phenomenon that went mainstream when in 1993 the Netscape browser first integrated text with still and moving images. By the late 1990s there were warnings that a technological "digital divide" that would hinder black and poor customers and overwhelmingly benefit affluent whites with easy access to technology. However, middle-class blacks held their own when it came to using computer and wireless telephone technology. In some markets they overconsumed compared to white customers, and poor blacks and browns were resourceful about getting online even if they lacked personal computers at home. They obtained free e-mail accounts from work or school and used PCs in public spaces such as libraries to read, communicate, and hunt for jobs.[5]

Unfortunately, the talk of an online *City Sun* was merely talk. Andy Cooper wrote editorials, but they remained unseen, stored on floppy disks.[6] The City Sun Employees Inc. effort also fizzled. Allimadi, who grew impatient, broke away from the group. He convinced Bill Cosby to give him $20,000 to start a newspaper. In 1997 the Ugandan native launched the *Black Star News*, a weekly devoted to investigative journalism. Allimadi lavishly referenced the *City Sun* as inspiration and said the new paper's mission was "speaking truth to empower," a remix of the *City Sun*'s motto "Speaking truth to power."[7]

Angaza went on to edit *African Voices* magazine, an arts and literary quarterly that recalled the *City Sun*'s "City Scape" arts centerfold and hearty coverage of the performing arts. Carolyn Butts, founder of the magazine and a freelance writer during Angaza's *City Sun* editing days, sought advice from Cooper on how to launch her magazine, and she executed the plan.

On December 23, 1997, a decade after the Tawana Brawley story broke, Stephen Pagones sued Al Sharpton, Alton Maddox, and C. Vernon Mason for defamation. The Dutchess County prosecutor falsely accused of sexually assaulting the teenager by the trio sought more than $300 million in damages.

That month, E. R. Shipp and Utrice Leid were guests on Amy Goodman's "Democracy Now!" Pacifica Network radio show to discuss the development. Shipp was a member of the *New York Times* reporting team that had concluded the teenager's story was an elaborate hoax. Leid's Brawley reporting—which reached an opposite conclusion—was used as evidence in Pagones's defamation suit.[8] Also that month, Wilbert Tatum stepped down as *Amsterdam News* publisher and handed off the operation to his twenty-six-year-old daughter Elinor.[9]

In his post–*City Sun* life, Andy Cooper in 1999 tried one last time to participate in a media venture. He sent a six-page letter to Don Miller of *Our World News* regarding the start-up's business plan and a possible merger of efforts and skills. The idea failed to catch fire.

Cooper's health was fragile, yet his psyche was stubborn and immovable. Alterman, who admired Cooper so much that he answered his pleas for legal counsel to protect the paper from creditors, said Cooper could be maddening to serve. They would be in court to pay creditors. Give me the money, Alterman asked Cooper, after he had brokered a deal with a creditor. Cooper at times said no, emitted a low, gravelly laugh, and pulled out a bankroll of paper money, then stuffed it back into his pocket. The former publisher could be exasperating, but Alterman did not stay angry with Cooper for long. After a day in court, the lawyer took him to lunch at the Odeon restaurant in lower Manhattan.

Cooper could be just as passive-aggressive with his health. He knew he was supposed to stick to a restricted diet, but when Jocelyn or his daughters were out of sight, he would savor favorite foods like roast pork. If Cooper were out with Alterman or someone else at Gage and Tollner restaurant in downtown Brooklyn, he might indulge in the decadent chocolate soup. The excesses did not help Cooper's weakened body. Multiple strokes and hypertension robbed him of his ability to walk. When Alterman took Cooper to a Yankees game, Cooper refused to roll to the stadium box seat in a wheelchair. Alterman carried Cooper in his arms to the seat.[10] Jocelyn had health issues too, including diabetes, and she was a cancer survivor. She managed her health by adhering to her restricted diet and taking her medications.

At home, Cooper watched World War II–era movies and History Channel documentaries in excess. Jocelyn took her husband on a road trip to the civil rights museum in Memphis. Youngest daughter Jocelyn A. Cooper subsidized her parents' health care and living costs. Jocelyn A. at that time was head of artists and repertoire at Universal Records and senior vice president and special assistant to the chairman of Universal Music Group.[11]

Meanwhile oldest daughter Andrea Cooper Andrews taught film and TV production, creative writing and African American history in the public school system, including one school at which Alicia Keys was a student.[12]

Andy Cooper took time to advocate for and mentor teens and young adults to prepare for starring or leadership roles in fine arts, media, and public policy. Lynn Nottage, a primary school classmate of Jocelyn A., wanted to be a playwright but faced opposition from her parents who wanted her to pursue "safer careers" such as law or medicine. Cooper made a spirited case to the parents to let their daughter chase her real passion. In 2007, Nottage received a MacArthur "genius" grant. In 2009 she won the Pulitzer Prize for drama for *Ruined*, a haunting story about African women scarred by the civil war in the Congo. Also, Cheryl E. Chambers credited Cooper with motivating her to become a state Supreme Court justice in Brooklyn. She was with the Appellate Division, second judicial department.[13]

In June 1999, on the day that Cooper was to be initiated into Planned Parenthood, one of his wife's civic passions, he suffered another stroke. An ambulance was called, and he was carried out of the house and to the hospital.[14] On October 15 of that year, the Coopers' fiftieth wedding anniversary, Andy and Jocelyn renewed their vows. The Rev. Al Sharpton performed the ceremony at their home before dozens of witnesses.

On the day before his seventy-fourth birthday—August 21, 2001—Andrew W. Cooper suffered another stroke. He was kept on life support. The September 11 bombings of the World Trade Center towers and the Pentagon, and the U.S. invasion of Afghanistan to kill al-Qaeda terrorists and self-identified mastermind Osama bin Laden, occurred while Cooper was barely conscious.

At dusk on Monday, January 28, the day after Jocelyn's seventy-third birthday, Cooper died at Brooklyn Methodist Hospital. His sixth and final stroke was attributed as the cause of death. Cooper's immediate family was at his bedside. He did not leave a will, and the family could find no evidence that Cooper left them an estate plan.

The memorial service was held on February 15 at First Presbyterian Church at 124 Henry Street in Brooklyn Heights, a few blocks from the former *City Sun* office. News of Cooper's death was published in the *New York Times*, *Daily News*, and *Amsterdam News*. All the accounts led with his voting-rights suit as his epitaph. Ron Howell of New York Newsday.com demonstrated the best grasp of Cooper's recent impact on the city:

> The [*City*] *Sun* stood behind the Rev. Al Sharpton and activist lawyers C. Vernon Mason and Alton Maddox when they maintained a black teenager, Tawana Brawley, was sexually assaulted by a group of whites in upstate Wappingers Falls in 1987.
>
> Numerous investigations concluded that the charges were false. But dozens of incidents of racial discrimination and abuse became cause celebres and rallying cries in Cooper's *City Sun*, including the 1986 killing of black Brooklyn resident Michael Griffin by a crowd of whites in Howard Beach.

Jocelyn Cooper told Howell, "From the moment I met him 57 years ago he was so clear about the kind of world he wanted to live in, one that did not oppress people, and he was particularly concerned about the oppression of black people." As for his fierce love of his birthplace, she added, "He said if someone gave him a house in Manhattan, he wouldn't live in it. That's how much he loved Brooklyn."[15]

On the day of the memorial service, Brooklyn borough president Marty Moskowitz issued a proclamation recognizing Cooper's lifetime of work in voting rights, public affairs, and journalism. On June 22, 2006, Moskowitz issued a second proclamation declaring Andrew W. Cooper Memorial Day.

In March a former *Wall Street Journal* editor launched the daily *New York Sun* in lower Manhattan. Errol Louis, a *Wall Street Journal* intern and one of the original *City Sun* journalists, was among the staff members. He became a *Daily News* Op-Ed columnist in 2004.

That year, Andrea Cooper Andrews and her mother asked Frank Macchiarola, president of St. Francis College, to host an Andrew W. Cooper Young Journalists in Training Program at his institution on Remsen Street, one block between the *City Sun* and Trans Urban New Service offices. Macchiarola embraced the idea. "Why not?" he said in February 2006. "Anyone interested in leadership should learn what living a good life is all about. Andy Cooper is a heroic figure."

The young journalists' program had a welcome home at St. Francis, which called itself "the small college of big dreams." The Coopers were responsible for raising the money for the program. The initial goal was $200,000. Young Journalists in Training was open to St. Francis College students. It would not be a minority-only program, said Macchiarola, because that would lead to second-class citizenship. Like the A. Philip Randolph Campus High School uptown, it accepted everybody, although at the start the president anticipated that first class of trainees would be all students of color.[16] There were nine trainees in the inaugural 2006–7 class, and they were placed at WABC-TV, WNBC-TV, WCBS-TV, Lifetime, and *Esquire* magazine. Students also attended a series of lectures.[17]

In October 2005, the relatives of Mississippi summer voting rights martyrs Andrew Goodman, James Chaney, and Michael Schwerner took part in a forum at the college. Young Journalists coordinator Andrea Cooper Andrews had attended the same school with Schwerner's children in the early 1960s.

Andrew Wells Cooper's handiwork was etched all over Brooklyn and New York City's landscape. Before Cooper's voting-rights activism began in the early 1960s, only one black member of Congress hailed from the East Coast—Adam Clayton Powell Jr. of Harlem. Three decades later, in the 1990s, multiple black members of Congress represented Brooklyn: Major R. Owens, Shirley Chisholm's successor in the Eleventh District, and Edolphus Towns of the Tenth, whom Chisholm mentored and Cooper monitored. There was also Gregory W. Meeks of Queens's Sixth District. Charles Rangel, Powell's successor, represented upper Manhattan. Dozens of black and Hispanic state legislators and city council representatives served. When Andy began his political activism in the 1960 there were none, save for a few in Harlem and one black assemblyman for all of Brooklyn.

In the early twenty-first century, a stretch of Fulton Street in Clinton Hill, a few blocks from Cooper's Grand Avenue birthplace, had numerous restaurants, groceries, hair salons, and other small businesses owned by African immigrants and Caribbean Americans, a streetscape unlike that in the 1950s and early 1960s, when businesses took black consumers' money but resisted employing them.

Brooklyn and New York's other boroughs were no longer places that treated black residents crudely like strangers passing through town. Attitudes toward excessive and lethal police force changed profoundly after two decades of courageous, unyielding crusading by Cooper's news outlets, Trans Urban News Service and the *City Sun*. Post–*City Sun*, high-profile police outrages continued: the broomstick sodomizing of Haitian Abner Louima in 1997; the forty-one-bullet massacre of unarmed West African merchant Amidu Diallo in 1999, and the slaying in 2006 of Sean Bell at his bachelor party in Queens by plainclothes police.[18]

Unlike incidents in the 1970s and 1980s in which politicians and police routinely dismissed slain or maimed black and brown people as collateral damage, after the *City Sun*, victims' families were treated respectfully by the mayor and other authorities—including police brass—and there were credible investigations of what police did, wrong or right. Metropolitan New York was a more civil and safe area because of a dozen years of hell raising by the *City Sun*.

Travel just north to the crossroads of Atlantic and Flatbush avenues, the former blighted, abandoned site brightened after 2004 with big box stores such as Target, Old Navy, and OfficeMax and popular chain restaurants. The terminal shops rose four stories above the Long Island Railroad depot and city train nexus of nine subway lines.

Since the late 1950s, Brooklyn residents lamented the loss of their baseball team, the Dodgers. Bruce Ratner, developer of the $150 million Atlantic

Terminal, announced that the NBA's New Jersey Nets was vacating the Newark-area Meadowlands to occupy Flatbush and Atlantic in 2012.[19]

Cooper did not live to see a number of these economic development projects bloom, but he certainly was the determined planter who nourished the ground that produced these yields in his roles as publisher, civic leader, and public gadfly. Andrew W. Cooper was born in Brooklyn, he championed the borough, and he demanded that its citizens have first-class rights. He died on the land he had ferociously loved.

Cooper was Brooklyn's City Son.

Epilogue

Where are *City Sun* alumni now?

Harry Allen, a self-identified hip-hop activist and media assassin, wrote for magazines such as the *Source* ("The Unbearable Whiteness of Emceeing: What the Eminence of Eminem Says about Race," 2003) and was profiled in a 1995 *Wired* magazine article, "Rap Dot Com."

Maitefa Aganza co-founded a group of former employees who unsuccessfully attempted to restart the defunct *City Sun* in 1997. Aganza became managing editor of *African Voices* literary magazine, founded in 1995 by Carolyn A. Butts, who sought Cooper's counsel to start an art and literature quarterly.

Milton Allimadi left the shuttered *City Sun* and founded the *Black Star News* with a $20,000 gift from Bill Cosby. Allimadi said he was continuing the investigative reporting spirit of the *City Sun*. Since January 2010, Allimadi has been holding free weekly media literacy, basic reporting, and writing meetings that he calls "guerrilla journalism" at 492 Nostrand Avenue Brooklyn, between Halsey and Hancock streets, in a space that is a barbershop by day and a bookstore called True South by night.

Christopher Atwell founded Chris Atwell Communications to do public relations work, then became a speechwriter for Earl Graves, founder of *Black Enterprise* magazine. In 2010 Atwell began writing speeches for New York governor David Paterson.

Doug Blackburn was sports editor during the initial months of the *City Sun* and was succeeded at in 1984 by Tony Paige. Blackburn left the weekly to cover the NHL for the *New York Times*.

Abe Blashko was recruited from the Guardian newspaper to do *City Sun* political cartoons and continued as late as 1995. After the *City Sun* folded, he did illustrations for Black Star News, but ended the relationship when that paper lost one of his cartoons, Blashko said.

Ericka Blount-Danois freelanced for a number of publications including the *Baltimore Sun*, Crisis, *Heart and Soul*, and *Black Enterprise*. She continues to do freelance writing and editing while serving as a professor in the Communications Studies Department of Morgan State University.

Herb Boyd continued to write prolifically for the *Amsterdam News* and was managing editor of The Black World Today Web site (now called OurWorldToday.tv). Boyd is the author of seventeen books, including *Pound for Pound: The Life and Times of Sugar Ray Robinson*, *The Harlem Reader*, and *Autobiography of a People: Three Centuries of African American History Told by Those Who Lived It*.

Angela Briggins left the *City Sun* in 1993 and wrote mostly fiction under various pen names. She credited the *City Sun* with giving her dexterity to write film and music reviews.

Karen Carrillo was a contributor to arts, culture, and news site SeeingBlack.com. In 2010 she worked as a writer for the International Oil Working Group.

Clinton Cox left the *City Sun* at the end of 1992 to write youth-oriented books on African American history and the role of blacks in the military. Cox moved to Denver from upstate New York. He died in February 2011.

Jerry Craft reinvented his comic strip *Moma's Boyz* for several picture books, including contributions to *Chicken Soup for the African American Soul*. Craft's work appears on Web sites including comicspace.com/jerrycraft and momasboyz.com.

Raoul Dennis is publisher and editor in chief of *Prince George's Suite* magazine, an award-winning bimonthly lifestyle publication serving Prince George's County, Maryland, outside Washington, D.C.

Paul Edwards was the "For Real" op-ed cartoonist. At the time of this book's writing, his status was unknown.

Peter Essick has worked as a freelance photographer for the past twenty-three years. His showcase client is *National Geographic*, where he has done thirty stories. Essick lives in Stone Mountain, Georgia.

Fern E. Gillespie wrote the "Culture and Flash" column in the early years of the *City Sun* and is now a full-time public relations practitioner.

Thomas Green Jr. is based in Atlanta and is an author and publisher of urban romance novels including *Change for a Dyme* and *Larry's Girls*.

Jay Gwamba started out covering sports for Tony Paige in late 1991 or early 1992. In 1993 he wrote some news stories when Paige served as executive editor. Gwamba also covered soccer for the *Irish Echo* newspaper.

Hugh Hamilton left the *City Sun* in 1993 to serve as legislative aide to city councilwoman Una Clarke, and later councilman Lloyd Henry. Hamilton succeeded Utrice Leid in the twenty-first century as host of WBAI-FM's *Talkback!*

Farhan Haq left the *City Sun* in April 1993 and wrote dispatches for Inter Press Service. He was a spokesman at the United Nations.

Cecil Harris left the *City Sun* at the end of 1992 to join Gannett Westchester Newspapers. From there he covered the expansion Carolina Hurricanes for the *News and Observer* of Raleigh, North Carolina. Harris has written three books, *Breaking the Ice*, on blacks in hockey; *Call the Yankees My Daddy*, on baseball; and *Charging the Net*, a history of blacks in tennis.

Simone Joye followed her stint at the *City Sun* by volunteering with the Salvation Army and then got hooked on grant writing. She went to Yonkers-based Leake and Watts and later became executive director of the Boys and Girls Clubs of Newark, New Jersey. Joye founded her grant-writing company in New Jersey in 1992, and it was the first minority-owned company of its kind in the state, she said. In 2002 she moved to Atlanta. Her All Write Communications does grant writing, and 30 Plus Classics promotes soul music.

Kenton Kirby was editor of the *Caribbean News* and also did work for CUNY-TV.

Andrew Lichtenstein received his first real photo assignment from the *City Sun* when he persuaded Leid and Cooper to send him to Haiti to cover President Aristide. Lichtenstein's work appeared in the *Atlantic Monthly*.

Utrice C. Leid was host and executive producer of *Talkback!* on WBAI-FM from the mid- to late 1990s and was a sought-after public speaker. In 2001 she was named general manager of WBAI and was the force behind a bruising reorganization of personnel that opponents called a lockout or coup. Leid was accused of physically assaulting *Democracy Now!* host Amy Goodman and was also accused of pulling the plug on congressman Major Owens of Brooklyn when he began to criticize the alleged lockout on the air. Leid left the tumult in New York after less than a year for south Florida, where she became executive editor of the *Broward Times*, a black weekly. In 2007, Leid edited Peter Noel's book about Rudy Giuliani, *Why Blacks Fear "America's Mayor."*

Errol Louis left the *City Sun* four months after its 1984 launch. He freelanced, then went to Yale for graduate studies. He was a writer with the *New York Sun*, a conservative daily newspaper, before joining the *Daily News* in 2004 as an op-ed columnist. In February 2010 Louis was named the Jack Newfield Professor of Journalism at Hunter College in New York.

Rhea Mandulo After the *City Sun* shutdown, Mandulo wrote for *Black Enterprise* and other publications, according to an Internet search. She was listed in 2009 as a high school English teacher in Brooklyn.

Farai Philemon Makotsi returned to his native Zimbabwe after news that his brother had died. On February 4, 2007, the *Standard* newspaper of Zimbabwe reported that Makotsi, forty-eight, had died at home after complaining of having difficulty breathing. Two sons and a daughter survived.

Peter Noel wrote in-depth pieces for the *City Sun* in the late 1980s, moved on to write for the *Village Voice*, and resumed writing again for the *City Sun* in the early 1990s. In 2008 he published *Why Blacks Fear "America's Mayor,"* a book about New York mayor Rudy Giuliani's turbulent relationship with the city's blacks.

Vinette Pryce continued to write for the *Amsterdam News* and Caribbean-oriented *Everybody's* magazine, where she penned the "Pryce Is Right" column.

Anthony Carter Paige joined WFAN-AM in 1995. Initially there one day a week, he left to do public relations for a boxing organization. Paige's next move was to ESPN radio for six months. He returned to WFAN as only the fourth black sports journalist working full-time in twenty years.

Lucas Rivera wrote for the *New York Press*, an alternative weekly.

Malik Russell earned his master's degree in public administration and worked as director of communications for several nonprofits in the Washington, D.C., area. He also taught at Morgan State University.

Arlene Schulman wrote sports pieces for Paige's section in the 1980s. I located the writer in 2007 at ArlenesScratchPaper.blogspot.com

Joe Sexton left the *City Sun* in 1984 for the *New York Times*. He advanced from deputy metro editor to metro editor. Sexton's reply to my interview request was "Thanks for the note of interest. And it sounds like an interesting and challenging project you have undertaken. But I am going to decline your invitation to participate. I do so for a variety of reasons, and I thank you in advance for respecting them. Sorry and good luck.—Joe." Sexton was cited in Gerald Boyd's 2010 memoir, *My Times in Black and White: Race and Power at the New York Times*.

Joan Shepard joined the *City Sun* staff in the early 1990s. Shepard, fifty-six, died in April 1998.

Kimberleigh J. Smith served as chair of the policy committee for the Women's HIV Collaborative of New York from 1999 to 2005. She was also assistant director of policy, advocacy, and research for the Federation of Protestant Welfare Agencies. Smith is senior director, state and local policy, of Harlem United: Community AIDS Center, Inc.

Richard Torres (Status unknown).

Annette Walker worked at the *City Sun* from 1991 to 1995. She wrote her first article for the *Amsterdam News* in 1978 but did most of her work during the 1990s, when she also worked for WBAI-FM. Walker had the distinction of working for Cooper, Tatum, and Leid in two venues. Walker is a Denver-based freelance writer.

Armond White continued his career in journalism at the alternative *New York Press*. A decade (1985–95) of White's *City Sun* articles was compiled in *The Resistance*, an anthology. White also published *Rebel for the Hell of It: The Life of Tupac Shakur*.

Stephen John Williams found a new home for his "This Week in History" column at Allimadi's *Black Star News*.

Van Dora Williams interned at the *City Sun* in 1984 to 1985 and went on to become a journalist at WHRO-TV, a PBS station in Norfolk, Virginia. She reported the award-winning "Noble Desire," a report about a West African nation that acknowledged its role in the Middle Passage slave trade. Williams was a producer on several PBS documentaries including *Banished*, a story about African American homeowners who were violently forced off their land during the Jim Crow era. She co-produced "Voting Rights Northern Style," the multimedia online site about Andrew W. Cooper. She is a professor at Hampton University Scripps Howard School of Journalism and Communications.

Deborah P. Work left the *City Sun* for the *Fort Lauderdale Sun-Sentinel*. She moved with her husband to the *Orlando Sentinel*.

About the Author

Wayne Dawkins joined Trans Urban News service as a volunteer in June 1977. Weeks before, he graduated from Long Island University. In January 1978 he was hired as a reporter-researcher and stayed until the grant-funded project ended in summer 1979. That September he began studies at Columbia University Graduate School of Journalism. Upon graduation in May 1980, he began his twenty-three-year, four-daily-newspaper career at Gannett Westchester Newspapers in Mount Vernon, New York (now known as the *Journal News* of Westchester and Rockland counties). Dawkins was an instructor in the Trans Urban News Writers Workshop during 1981–82. He was a charter subscriber of the *City Sun* while living in southern New Jersey, where he was a reporter with the *Courier-Post* of Cherry Hill. Dawkins is author of *Black Journalists: The NABJ Story* and *Rugged Waters: Black Journalists Swim the Mainstream.* Since 2005 he has been an assistant professor at Hampton University Scripps Howard School of Journalism and Communications in Virginia. Dawkins is a 1990 Columbia University Distinguished Journalism Alumni award winner and a 2004 Columbia University Alumni Federation medal winner. In 2011 he received the Hampton University Edward L. Hamm Sr. Distinguished Teaching Award. Dawkins is founding editor of the *Black Alumni Network* (Columbia journalism) newsletter.

Notes

1. Boy to Man

1. Jocelyn A. Cooper, the youngest daughter and third-generation owner of 350 Grand Avenue, has the deed with the purchase price of the Cooper home.

2. Craig Steven Wilder, *A Covenant with Color: Race and Social Power in Brooklyn* (New York: Columbia University Press, 2000), 178.

3. Gilbert Osofsky, *Harlem: The Making of a Ghetto: Negro New York, 1890–1930* (New York: Harper and Row, 1971), ix; Herb Boyd, *The Harlem Reader* (New York: Random House, 2003).

4. Osofsky, *Harlem*, 128–29.

5. Henry Louis Gates Jr. and Nellie Y. McKay, *The Norton Anthology of African American Literature* (New York: W. W. Norton, 1997).

6. David Levering Lewis, *W. E. B. Du Bois: The Fight for Equality and the American Century, 1919–1963* (New York: Henry Holt, 2000), 153–82; Boyd, *The Harlem Reader*, 2003.

7. Lerone Bennett Jr., *Before the Mayflower: A History of Black America* (Chicago: Johnson Publishing, 2003), 554.

8. Robert Cooper, telephone interview by author, 2005.

9. Ibid.

10. Distance calculated at MapQuest.com.

11. Wilder, *A Covenant with Color*, 6.

12. Ibid., 12–14.

13. Edgar J. McManus, *A History of Negro Slavery in New York* (Syracuse, N.Y.: Syracuse University Press, 1966), 7.

14. Wilder, *A Covenant with Color*, 12. The Dutch West India Company opened trade with Brazil and the slave trade with Angola in 1648.

15. McManus, *History of Negro Slavery*.

16. Ibid. Brooklyn is the fourth-largest city in the United States, according to *National Geographic* 163, no. 5 (May 1983).

17. Wilder, *A Covenant with Color*, 178.

18. Osofsky, *Harlem*, 18, 28–29.

19. Bennett, *Before the Mayflower*, 2003.

20. Ibid., 561.

21. Ibid., 562.

22. Arthur M. Schlesinger Jr., *The Almanac of American History* (New York: G. P. Putnam's Sons, 1983).

23. Wilder, *A Covenant with Color*, 178.

24. Ibid., 143.

25. Ibid., 145.

26. Bliss Broyard, *One Drop: My Father's Hidden Life; A Story of Race and Family Secrets* (Boston: Little, Brown, 2007), 321.

27. Bennett, *Before the Mayflower*, 564.

28. Virginia Crawley Thomas, interview by author, summer 2005.

29. Jocelyn C. Cooper, interview by author, December 10, 2005.

30. Ibid.

31. Jocelyn C. Cooper interview, December 10, 2005; Dominga Cooper, interview by author, April 17, 2008.

32. Ibid.

33. Jocelyn C. Cooper interview, August 10, 2005.

34. Ibid.

35. Virginia Crawley Thomas interview, summer 2005.

36. Jocelyn C. Cooper interviews, December 10, 2005, and March 16, 2008.

37. Ronald T. Takaki, *A Different Mirror: A History of Multicultural America* (Boston: Little, Brown, 1993), 368–69; David Levering Lewis, *W. E. B. Du Bois, 1868–1919: Biography of a Race* (New York: Henry Holt, 1994), 336–37.

38. Jocelyn C. Cooper interview, December 10, 2005.

39. In 2008 Jocelyn C. Cooper found Andrew W. Cooper's PS 45 autograph album, dated June 24, 1941. Andy was thirteen. At the time, elementary schools customarily housed kindergarten through the eighth grade.

40. *National Geographic*, May 1983.

41. Jocelyn C. Cooper interviews, 2005 and 2006.

42. Robert Cooper, interview by author, August 2007.

43. Vincent Ragsdale, interview by author, February 15, 2007.

44. Robert Cooper interview, 2007.

45. Wilder, *A Covenant with Color*, 178.

46. Broyard, *One Drop*, 333.

47. Ibid.

48. Robert Caro, *The Power Broker: Robert Moses and the Fall of New York* (New York: Knopf, 1974), 510, 512.

49. Harold Connolly, *A Ghetto Grows in Brooklyn* (New York: New York University Press, 1977), 136–37.

50. Wilder, *A Covenant with Color*, 196.

51. Caro, *The Power Broker*, 512.

52. Wilder, *A Covenant with Color*, 196–97.

53. Caro, *The Power Broker*, 512.

54. Kevin Baker, "Jitterbug Days," *New York Times*, January 22, 2006.

55. Jocelyn C. Cooper interview, March 16, 2008; Dominga Cooper's family tree; Dominga and Robert Cooper, e-mail reply regarding several recipes, March 20, 2008.

56. "The Battle of Detroit," *Time*, March 23, 1942.

57. Robert Cooper interview, near Las Vegas, August 2007.

58. Jocelyn C. Cooper interview, December 9, 2005.

59. Ibid.

60. Ibid.

61. Ibid.

62. Jocelyn C. Cooper interview, March 16, 2008.

63. Ibid.

64. Wilder, *A Covenant with Color*, 125–36.

65. Ibid.

66. Armistead S. Pride and Clint C. Wilson II, *A History of the Black Press* (Washington, D.C.: Howard University Press, 1997), 188–89; George Sullivan, *Journalists at Risk: Reporting America's Wars* (New York: Twenty-first Century, 2004); Charles A. Simmons, *The African-American Press: A History of News Coverage during National Crises* (New York: McFarland, 1997).

67. Wilder, *A Covenant with Color*, 137.

68. Ibid., 136.

69. Jocelyn C. Cooper interview, March 16, 2008.

70. Connolly, *A Ghetto Grows in Brooklyn*, 129, 130.

71. Ibid.

72. Jocelyn C. Cooper interviews, July and August 2005.

73. Wilder, *A Covenant with Color*, 226.

2. Jim Crow Brooklyn

1. Bennett, *Before the Mayflower*, 576.

2. Wilder, *A Covenant with Color*, 205–7.

3. Wilder, *A Covenant with Color*, 178.

4. Harold Connolly, *A Ghetto Grows in Brooklyn* (New York: New York University Press, 1977), 166.

5. Bennett, *Before the Mayflower*, 579.

6. Ira Katznelson, *When Affirmative Action Was White: An Untold History of Racial Inequality in Twentieth Century America* (New York: W. W. Norton, 2005), 121, 123–24.

7. Ibid.

8. Henry Louis Gates Jr., "The Passing of Anatole Broyard," in *Thirteen Ways of Looking at a Black Man* (New York: Random House, 1997).

9. http://www.wenatcheewa.gov.

10. Bennett, *Before the Mayflower*, 582.

11. Jocelyn C. Cooper interview, March 25, 2008.

12. The official listing of St. Philip's is 265 Decatur Street, which is the parish hall. The church, however, fronts on 334 McDonough Street, as parishioner Leon Philips explained to me on October 19, 2008.

13. Ibid.

14. Ibid.

15. "Always a Pleasure," barrypopik.com.

16. David Freedlander, "Sylvia's Patrons Say O'Reilly's Out of Touch," *Newsday*, September 26, 2007.

17. Jocelyn C. Cooper interview, March 26, 2008.

18. In an interview in December 2005, Thomas Russell Jones called Andy's Coop in Brooklyn a candy store and ice cream parlor. Jocelyn Cooper that said sandwiches and hot food were served in addition to ice cream; 396 Gates is now a funeral home.

19. Jocelyn C. Cooper interview; Robert Cooper interview, August 2007.

20. Will Anderson, "Breweries of Brooklyn: An Informal History," 1976. Schaefer was also the last operating brewery, closing in 1976. Dennis Hevesi, "Something's Brewing in Bushwick," *New York Times*, June 29, 2003.

21. Anderson, "Breweries of Brooklyn."

22. Frederick M. Binder and David M. Reimers, *All the Nations under Heaven: An Ethnic and Racial History of New York City* (New York: Columbia University Press, 1995), 207.

23. http://www.socialexplorer.com.

24. Joceyln C. Cooper interview, May 2008.

25. Andrew W. Cooper's brothers did not serve in the same branch of the service, explained Robert and Ming Cooper in March 2008. Palma was a World War II veteran and served in the army in Berlin. Milton was in World War II too and served in the merchant marine. He was not allowed to graduate with the class because of his race; navy officers informed his parents they were not to attend the ceremony. Robert entered the air force in 1954 and served for more than twenty-five years, retiring in 1979 with the rank of captain. He spent fifteen years enlisted and achieved the rank of master sergeant while attending officer training school.

26. In 1972 the Coopers sold the Decatur Street house to Chris Rock's parents. Rock references the house in his sitcom *Everybody Hates Chris*.

27. Andrea Cooper Andrews, interview by author, February 9, 2008.

28. Ibid.

29. Bennett, *Before the Mayflower*, 585.

30. Ibid., 586.

31. Ibid., 588.

32. Ibid.

33. Jocelyn C. Cooper interview, May 2008.

34. Shirley Chisholm, *Unbought and Unbossed* (New York: Avon Books, 1970), 42.

35. Ibid.

36. Ibid., 46–47.

37. Ibid., 47.

38. Jocelyn C. Cooper interview.

39. Wilder, *A Covenant with Color*, p. 206, table 9.7.

40. Connolly, *A Ghetto Grows in Brooklyn*, 151, 130, 132; Wilder, *A Covenant with Color*, 177–78.

41. Jocelyn C. Cooper interview, May 22, 2006.

42. Wilder, *A Covenant with Color*, 214.

43. Ibid., 210.

44. Ibid., 227–30, 213.

45. "Negotiations Ended in Sale of *Eagle*," *New York Times*, June 11, 1955.

46. "The Press: Negro Timesman," *Time*, December 3, 1945.

47. Richard Sandomir, "In Print, Cheerleading and Indifference," *New York Times*, April 13, 1997.

48. Dennis McDougal, *Privileged Son: Otis Chandler and the Rise and Fall of the L.A. Times Dynasty* (Cambridge, Mass.: Perseus, 2001).

49. Andrea Cooper Andrews interview, February 9, 2007.

50. Wilder, *A Covenant with Color*, 214.

51. Ibid.

3. Political Awakening

1. Bennett, *Before the Mayflower*, 595.

2. Jacob Javits, "Integration from the Top Down," *Esquire*, December 1958.

3. Schlesinger, *The Almanac of American History*, 554.

4. The T. R. Jones–Berman race occurred in 1960.

5. Sewell Chan, "Thomas R. Jones, 93, a Judge Who Agitated for Urban Renewal, Dies," *New York Times*, November 1, 2006.

6. Chisholm, *Unbought and Unbossed*, 59.

7. Jacqueline McMickens spoke of Emory O. Jackson in a December 2005 interview.

8. Gene Roberts and Hank Klibanoff, *The Race Beat: The Press, the Civil Rights Struggle, and the Awakening of a Nation* (New York: Vintage Books, 2007), 50, 51, 52, 249, 305, 311.

9. Ibid.

10. Jocelyn C. Cooper interviews, August 2006 and November 2008.

11. Andrea Cooper Andrews interview, February 9, 2007.

12. Enoch Williams was a future assemblyman; Earl Graves was a future official in JFK's administration and founding publisher of *Black Enterprise* magazine.

13. Chisholm, *Unbought and Unbossed*, 60–61.

14. *Unity Democrat*, Fall holiday edition, 1961.

15. Sheffield Farms dairy (not to be confused with Ebinger's bakery). The home office was located in Norwich, New York. Bedford-Stuyvesant Restoration is based at the former Sheffield site.

16. Andrea C. Andrews interviews, winter 2007.

17. *Unity Democrat*, Fall election edition, 1961.

18. *Unity Democrat*, Fall holiday edition 1961.

19. Andrew W. Cooper, "Ebingers STILL Discriminates," *Unity Democrat*, February 1962.

20. Ibid.

21. George Stolz, "If You're Thinking of Living in New Rochelle," *New York Times*, May 24, 1987.

22. Bennett, *Before the Mayflower*, 603.

23. Ibid.

24. Ibid.

25. Joan Bacchus, cartoon, *Unity Democrat*, September 1961, special primary issue; Jonathan Kandell, "Carmine De Sapio, Political Kingmaker and Last Tammany Hall Boss, Dies at 95," *New York Times*, July 28, 2004.

26. *Unity Democrat*, Fall 1961.

27. Ibid.

28. *Unity Democrat*, December 1961.

29. Ibid.

30. *Unity Democrat*, February 1962.

31. Handwritten notes from Joan Bacchus Maynard to Wayne Dawkins, June 29, 2005. "When the federal agents arrested Marcus Garvey," Maynard wrote, "they said, 'we have caged the lion.' Garvey said, 'but my cubs are free!'"

32. Layhmond Robinson, "Democrats Press Brooklyn Fight; but Disputing Factions Are Waging a Genteel War," *New York Times*, May 26, 1964.

33. Chisholm, *Unbought and Unbossed*, 62.

34. Bennett, *Before the Mayflower*, 606.

35. Ibid.

36. Bennett, *Before the Mayflower*, 600.

37. Ibid., 598, 600–602.

38. C. Gerald Fraser, interview by author, 2007.

39. Bennett, *Before the Mayflower*, 607–8, 368–69.

4. Civil Rights, Brooklyn Style

1. Jocelyn C. Cooper interview, April 25, 2009.

2. Jocelyn C. Cooper interviews, May 2008.

3. Jocelyn C. Cooper interview, August 27, 2008.

4. Carlos Russell, "Perspectives on Politics: A Black Community Looks at Itself," 1978, Union Graduate School, 245 and 255.

5. Douglas Martin, "William Epton, 70, Is Dead; Tested Free-Speech Limits," *New York Times*, February 3, 2002; Kwame Anthony Appiah and Henry Louis Gates Jr., "Harlem Riot of 1964," in *Africana: Civil Rights; An A–Z Reference of the Movement That Changed America* (Philadelphia: Running Press, 2005).

6. Wilder, *A Covenant with Color*, 176.

7. Ibid.

8. Vincent Cannato, *The Ungovernable City: John Lindsay and His Struggle to Save New York* (New York: Basic Books, 2001).

9. Bennett, *Before the Mayflower*, 610.

10. Andrea Cooper Andrews interview, February 2007.

11. Mamie Locke, African American National Biography profile of Hamer, 2008.

12. Jocelyn C. Cooper interview.

13. Cooper and Carter wrote that they "led the caucus to seat the Mississippi Freedom Democrats at last year's National Democratic Convention," in their "We're Backing John Lindsay for Mayor," undated literature, 1965.

14. In the Steering Committee meeting notice of April 15, 1965, Martin P. (Pat) Carter and Andrew W. Cooper are listed as chairman and co-chairman. In the Rally for Freedom flier, June 20, 1965, James Baldwin, Ossie Davis, and Dick Gregory were listed along with elected officials and religious leaders.

15. Francis X. Clines, "Paul O'Dwyer, New York's Liberal Battler for Underdogs and Outsiders, Dies at 90," *New York Times*, June 25, 1998.

16. Bennett, *Before the Mayflower*, 610; John Dittmer, *Local People: The Struggle for City Rights in Mississippi* (Urbana: University of Illinois Press, 1994), 297, 298, 301–2.

17. Chisholm, *Unbought and Unbossed*, 63–64.

18. Raanan Geberer, "Brooklyn Pays Tribute to Justice Thomas R. Jones," *Brooklyn Daily Eagle*, November 3, 2006.

19. Erin Einhorn, "Thomp Will 'Surprise Awful Lot of People,'" *New York Daily News*, April 12, 2009; "R. Risley Dent Jr., Brooklyn Lawyer, Democratic Primary Victor for State Senator, Dies," *New York Times*, June 8, 1964. R. Risley Dent Jr. was the first black state senator elected during the spring primary; however, he died in June before taking office, and William C. Thompson replaced him.

20. Cannato, *Ungovernable City*, 22; Binder and Reimers, *All the Nations under Heaven*.

21. Cannato, *Ungovernable City*, 22–23.

22. Bennett, *Before the Mayflower*, 612.

23. Cannato, *Ungovernable City*, 21.

24. "We're Backing John Lindsay for Mayor," four-page campaign promotion, Cooper family archives.

25. Ibid.

26. Cannato, *Ungovernable City*, 31.

27. Ibid., 35.

28. Ibid., 37.

29. Ibid., 38–39.

30. Ibid., 40–41.

31. Ibid., 43.

32. Paul Kerrigan interviews, April 24–25, 2009, New York, N.Y.

33. Ronald W. Walters, *Freedom Is Not Enough: Black Voters, Black Candidates, and American Presidential Politics* (Lanham, Md.: Rowman and Littlefield, 2005).

34. These are my conservative approximations of the Bedford-Stuyvesant boundaries. I lived in the community from 1956 to 1975 and in East New York, then Crown Heights, from 1975 to 1979.

35. Thomas A. Johnson, "Negro Teachers Give School Plan; Say Black Community Must Have Control in Own Area," *New York Times*, September 20, 1967.

36. Robert Conot, *Rivers of Blood, Years of Darkness* (New York: Morrow, 1968).

37. Don Terry, "Sam Yorty, Maverick Mayor of Los Angeles, Dies at 88," *New York Times*, June 6, 1998.

38. Jocelyn C. Cooper and Constance Carter interviews.

39. Cannato, *Ungovernable City*, 47.

40. Ibid.

41. Ibid., 50.

42. Sam Tanenhaus, "The Buckley Effect," *New York Times Magazine*, October 2, 2005.

43. Cannato, *Ungovernable City*, 44.

44. Ibid., 52.

45. Ibid., 41.

46. Ibid., 55.

47. Ibid., 66.

48. Ibid., 67.

49. Jocelyn C. Cooper interview, July 16, 2008.

50. Jocelyn C. Cooper interview, May 2008.

51. Wilder, *A Covenant with Color*, chap. 10.

52. Reggie Butts interview.

53. Jocelyn A. "Jo-An" Cooper interview, October 8, 2005.

54. Wayne Dawkins, "Andrew W. Cooper, Brooklyn's City Son," *African Voices*, Winter 2006–7.

5. Cooper versus Power

1. Arthur M. Schlesinger Jr., *Robert Kennedy and His Times*, vol. 2 (Boston: Houghton Mifflin, 1978), 786.

2. Ibid.

3. Ibid.

4. Ibid.

5. Ibid.

6. Connolly, *A Ghetto Grows in Brooklyn*, 156–57.

7. Ibid.

8. Ibid.

9. Observation by Jocelyn C. Cooper. Restoration headquarters was built on the former Sheffield site.

10. New York State Constitutional Convention: AlbanyLaw.edu and library.rochester.edu.

11. Butts interview and May 2007 comment at ceremony.

12. *New York Times*, June 24, 1966, August 11, 1966.

13. Wayne Dawkins, *African Voices*, Winter 2006–7; National Black Programming Consortium Web site.

14. Wilder, *A Covenant with Color*, 178.

15. Ibid.

16. *New York Times*, June 24, 1966.

17. http://blackpublicmedia.org/Hampton. Joan Bacchus Maynard (1928–2006) was a longtime advocate for the preservation of Weeksville, the nineteenth-century Free African community in Brooklyn.

18. "Files Suit against Rocky, Boro Leaders: Would Stop Elections," *New York Amsterdam News*, June 25, 1966.

19. Ibid. Forty years later, at a ceremony in May 2007 honoring Cooper's activism, Basil Paterson (a former New York secretary of state and before that New York City deputy mayor) explained the absurdity of the boundaries: "Andrew Cooper's court papers declared that almost 400,000 blacks had been partitioned among five Congressional districts in 'so tortuous, artificial and labyrinthine a manner that the lines are irrational and unrelated to any proper purpose.'"

20. Full names of Brooklyn congressmen confirmed in the Eighty-eighth Congress roster: Emanuel Cellar (10th), Eugene J. Keough (11th), Edna F. Kelley (12th), John J. Rooney (14th), Hugh L. Carey (15th).

21. At the Cooper forty-year tribute in 2007, Paterson told well-wishers at St. Francis College of Brooklyn: "When [Andrew W. Cooper] filed the complaint in the U.S. District Court, he was well aware that he was launching a missile at the powerful political forces in the city and the state, Republican and Democratic. Clearly, he was bold and bodacious!"

22. Jocelyn C. Cooper interviews.

23. Jocelyn C. Cooper interview, 2007.

24. "Federal Court Rules That 3-Judge Panel Should Hear Cooper Petition," *New York Times*, August 11, 1966.

25. Andrew W. Cooper and Wayne Barrett, "Chisholm's Compromise," *Village Voice*, October 30, 1978.

26. Jocelyn C. Cooper interview, January 2, 2009.

27. "Protest Governor's Insult to Bedford-Stuyvesant," *New York Courier*, June 25, 1966.

28. "Federal Court Rules That 3-Judge Panel Should Hear Cooper Petition," *New York Times*, August 11, 1966.

29. "James M. Power, Ex-president of Board of Elections, 86, Dies," *New York Times*, November 23, 1971.

30. Ibid.

31. *Cooper vs. Power*, 102-page onionskin court document, reviewed July 13, 2008, at Jocelyn C. Cooper's home.

32. Ibid.

33. Ibid.

34. "Judges: '61 Apportionment Violated Constitution," *New York Times*, May 11, 1967.

35. Connolly, *A Ghetto Grows in Brooklyn*, 174.

36. "Judges: Reapportion by '68 election," *New York Times*, December 19, 1967; *New York Times*, December 24, 1967.

37. Chisholm, *Unbought and Unbossed*, 79, 81.

38. Connolly, *A Ghetto Grows in Brooklyn*, 174.

39. Cooper and Barrett, "Chisholm's Compromise."

40. Thomas Russell Jones interview, December 2005.

41. Chisholm, *Unbought and Unbossed*, 79.

42. Ibid.

43. Cooper and Barrett, "Chisholm's Compromise."

44. Thomas Russell Jones interview, December 2005; Connolly, *A Ghetto Grows in Brooklyn*, 174.

45. Thomas Russell Jones interview, December 2005.

46. Constance Carter interview, July 2005.

47. Ibid.

48. Connolly, *A Ghetto Grows in Brooklyn*, 174.

49. Chisholm, *Unbought and Unbossed*, 81.

50. Ibid., 51.

51. Ibid., 81.

52. Thomas A. Johnson, *New York Times*, April 5, 1972.

53. Ibid.

54. Martin Arnold, "Brooklyn Is Expected to Elect Its First Negro to the House If Redistricting Bill Passes," *New York Times*, February 23, 1968.

55. Chisholm, *Unbought and Unbossed*, 78.

56. Sydney H. Schanberg, "State Reshapes House Districts; Court Fight Due," *New York Times*, March 27, 1968.

57. Paul Kerrigan interviews, March 26, 2009, and April 24–25, 2009.

58. Robert Cooper interview, summer 2007, near Las Vegas.

59. Chisholm, *Unbought and Unbossed*, 82.

60. Cooper and Barrett, "Chisholm's Compromise."

61. Schlesinger, *The Almanac of American History*.

62. Bennett, *Before the Mayflower*, 621.

63. Chisholm, *Unbought and Unbossed*, 83.

64. Andrew W. Cooper lost the three-candidate state Senate primary.

65. Connolly, *A Ghetto Grows in Brooklyn*, 175.

66. Chisholm, *Unbought and Unbossed*, 84.

67. Ibid.

68. Chisholm, *Unbought and Unbossed*, 85.

69. Ibid., 88.

70. James Barron, "Shirley Chisholm, 'Unbossed' Pioneer in Congress, Is Dead at 80," *New York Times*, January 3, 2005.

6. Schaefer Suds

1. Andrew "Andy" William Stanfield (December 1927–June 1985). Walter Carlson, "Advertising: On Social Action and Business," *New York Times*, April 20, 1965. Stanfield won gold and silver medals at the 1952 and 1956 Olympic Games.

2. Jocelyn C. Cooper interviews. Stanfield's wife was the matron of honor at the Cooper's wedding, said Cooper in December 2008.

3. In a January 13, 2006, interview, Brewery heir Rudy Schaefer said that Cooper was a very good public relations man who was frequently out of the office. Schaefer spoke via telephone from Key Largo, Florida.

4. Undated announcement with headshots and captions of Andy Cooper and Holton.

5. Gloria Thomas Williams interview, December 2005.

6. Jocelyn C. Cooper interview, July 13, 2008. Thomas ran the Jersey City YMCA where young Jocelyn was crowned "Miss High- Y." Through her mother Lina, Jocelyn Cooper in the late 1950s was reintroduced to Thomas, an ordained AME Zion minister who was dean of students at Wilberforce College when Floyd Flake, a future congressman and ordained minister, was a student. Thomas was artistic and notoriously gay. When he died in the 1960s, a neighbor of Mrs. Cooper winked and said, "Sorry about the death of your sister."

7. Jocelyn Cooper, a longtime member of the Links, said she joined the group when Andy Cooper and Gloria Thomas Williams initiated the "Show of Stars" campaign.

8. *Schaefer Scene* 1, no. 1 (Spring 1969).

9. "Schaefer Programs Generate $75,650 for Charity," *Schaefer Scene* 1, no. 1 (Spring 1969): 3.

10. Clarence Irving interview, December 24, 2005.

11. Harold Jackson and Jim Haskins, *The House that Jack Built* (Colossus Books, 2003).

12. Neil Strauss, "At Work with Ron Delsener, Rock's Mr. In-Between," *New York Times*, August 11, 1994.

13. "Schaefer Rescues Park Jazz Series; Rheingold Is Out," *New York Times*, May 29, 1968.

14. Ibid.

15. F&M Schaefer Corporation 1970 Annual Report.

16. Schaefer concerts at Brooklyn Academy of Music. Jocelyn C. Cooper interview, March 10, 2009.

17. Ron Anderson interview, March 11, 2009.

18. Jocelyn C. Cooper interviews, March 10–11, 2009.

19. Andy Cooper's Schaefer report, 1970.

20. State Division of Human Rights, February 7, 1969, correspondence.

21. Lynda Richardson, "Public Lives: A Firm New Boss at an Old Voice of the Left," *New York Times*, January 17, 2001.

22. Utrice C. Leid and age fifteen.

23. Andy Logan, "Mayoral Follies: The 1969 Election," *New York Times*, January 25, 1998.

24. Rudolph Schaefer III interview, January 13, 2006.

25. Horace Shuman, my best friend and neighbor on Kosciusko Street, and I were die-hard Mets fans as boys and watched many Schaefer TV commercials. Shuman said that whenever the ice block commercial aired, he would feel so thirsty that he went to get ice water from his refrigerator. As a grownup today, Shuman does not drink beer or other alcoholic beverages.

26. "Schaefer Went Public and Thrived Briefly," *New York Times*, April 21, 1968, March 15, 1970.

27. One-third of Schaefer sales in New York City area: 1979 trade cases, *F&M Schaefer Brewing Co. v. C. Schmidt and Sons Inc. and Citibank, N.A.*, U.S. Court of Appeals, Second Circuit.

28. Urban Affairs statement from Cooper to H. H. Jones, January 19, 1971.

29. "Schaefer Plant, Last Brewery in Brooklyn, Closes in 1976," *New York Times*, January 21, 1976.

30. "Rival Says Stewart Bought Realty in Atlantic Ave. Area," *New York Daily News*, April 8, 1970.

31. Cooper family documents.

32. "Assembly Junks Atlantic Ave. Bill as 1,000 Picket," *New York Daily News*, April 9, 1970.

33. *New York Magazine*, May 4, 1970, 8.

34. "Atlantic Avenue 'Development,'" editorial, *New York Times*, April 7, 1970.

35. "Atlantic Ave. Bill Is Dead for Now," *New York Times*, April 1, 1970.

36. Andy Cooper correspondence, April 1, 1970.

37. *New York Daily News*, May 6, 1970.

38. "Property Stewart Bought Is Issue in Brooklyn Race," *New York Times*, June 20, 1970.

39. Ibid.

40. Jocelyn C. Cooper interview, March 11, 2009.

41. Bennett, *Before the Mayflower*, 628–29.

42. Ibid., 632–33.

43. Ibid.

44. Internet Movie Database, imdb.com.

45. Andrea Cooper Andrews interview, February 2007.

7. One Man's Opinion

1. Schlesinger, *The Almanac of American History*.

2. Bennett, *Before the Mayflower*, 636.

3. "The First Black Woman to Run for President," *All Things Considered*, NPR, October 17, 2008.

4. *Chisholm '72: Unbought and Unbossed*, DVD, 2004.

5. Jo Freeman, "Shirley Chisholm's 1972 Presidential Campaign," February 2005, http://uic.edu.

6. Bennett, *Before the Mayflower*, 634–35.

7. Andrea S. Cooper Andrews interview, New York, February 9, 2007.

8. *Local Level* (newsletter) 2, no. 1 (1973).

9. Basil Wilson and Charles Green, *The Struggle for Black Empowerment in New York City: Beyond the Politics of Pigmentation* (New York: Praeger, 1989).

10. Major Owens and Twelfth (then the Eleventh) Congressional District. The *West Wing* (NBC) character is believed to be based on Owens. The real-life congressman is the father of Geoffrey Owens, the character Elvin on *The Cosby Show*.

11. Sam Roberts, "Rethinking the Runoff," *New York Times*, September 18, 2005.

12. With 2.6 million residents, Brooklyn, a.k.a. Kings County, was the nation's fourth most-populated county in 1970 after Los Angeles (city and suburbs, 7 million), Cook (Chicago and suburbs, 5.5 million), and Wayne (Detroit and suburbs, 2.7 million). By 1979, Brooklyn–Kings County had shrunk to 2.2 million residents and slipped to number five because of the emergence of Harris County (Houston and suburbs). "Preliminary Estimate of Intercensal Population of Counties," 1970–79, http://census.gov.

13. http://brooklyn.com/population.html.

14. *Community Training News* (an NYCTI publication) 1, no. 2 (February 1974).

15. Hazel Smith, "Edging toward the New Millennium," *New York Beacon*, November 6, 1996.

16. Jocelyn Cooper said that Ernesta Procope persuaded her husband John, the publisher, to hire Cooper. Procope declined to be interviewed for this project and said she did not want to participate.

17. Cooper, "One Man's Opinion," August 17, 1974.

18. Ibid., August 24, 1974.

19. Adelphi University's main campus was in Garden City, Long Island, N.Y.

20. Philip Coltoff interview, January 2008.

21. Ibid.

22. Ibid.

23. Procope/Bowman Co. letters, from the estate of Andrew W. Cooper.

24. Sam Roberts, "When the City's Bankruptcy Was Just a Few Words Away," *New York Times*, December 31, 2006.

25. Gretchen Morgenson, "Big Rescues Can Work, Just Ask New York," *New York Times*, May 11, 2008.

26. *New York Amsterdam News*, Saturday, January 17, 2008.

27. Ibid.

28. Cooper, "One Man's Opinion," February 14, 1976.

29. Dinkins, Paterson, Rangel, and Sutton were known, either endearingly or pejoratively, as the "Gang of Four." In 2009, Rangel was in Democratic leadership in Congress. Dinkins was the city's first black mayor. Paterson's son is governor of New York. Rangel lost his bid for mayor, but the former Manhattan borough president was a broadcast radio mogul.

30. Lynda Richardson, "Firm New Boss at an Old Voice of the Left," *New York Times*, January 17, 2001.

31. Leid's Saturday-night interrogations in Trinidad: my memory of stories Utrice C. Leid told the Trans Urban News Service staff, circa 1978–79. There are stories in which Leid references TNS and possibly Cooper's "One Man's Opinion" columns that were rejected.

32. Cooper, "One Man's Opinion," March 6, 1976.

33. Ibid., March 20, 1976.

34. Ibid., March 27, 1976.

35. Ibid., April 10, 1976.

36. Ibid., May 1, 1976.

37. Howard Hurwitz, *The Last Angry Principal* (Portland, Ore.: Halcyon House, 1988); Leonard Buder, "Champion of School Discipline, Howard Lawrence Hurwitz," *New York Times*, March 26, 1976.

38. Cooper, "One Man's Opinion," May 8 and May 15, 1976.

39. Ibid.

40. Ibid., May 22, 1976.

41. David N. Dinkins, "Dinkins on Chisholm, and the Changing Political Scene," *Columbia* magazine, Spring 2005.

42. Cooper, "One Man's Opinion," May 29, 1976.

43. Ibid., June 5, 1976.

44. Ibid.

45. Jerome Krase and Ray Hutchison, *Race and Ethnicity in New York City* (Emerald Group, 2005), 227.

46. Cooper, "One Man's Opinion," July 3, 1976.

47. Schlesinger, *The Almanac of American History*, 604.

48. Andy Cooper, "Barbara Jordan—Another look," *New York Amsterdam News*, August 24, 1976.

49. Monte Williams, "Samuel D. Wright, 73, Assemblyman," *New York Times*, February 1, 1998.

50. Jocelyn C. Cooper interview, May 20, 2009.

51. Lynda Richardson, "Firm New Boss at an Old Voice of the Left," *New York Times*, January 17, 2001.

8. Trans Urban News Service

1. Betty Winston Baye, "Trans-Urban News First Graduates," *New York Amsterdam News*, November 8, 1980.

2. The phrase "Summer of Sam" is borrowed from Brooklynite Spike Lee's 1999 movie title. Corky Siemaszko, "Son of Sam: New York's Summer of Terror, 30 Years Later," *New York Daily News*, 2007, nydailynews.com.

3. Robert Curvin and Bruce Porter, *Blackout Looting* (New York: John Wiley and Sons, 1979).

4. Blackout History Project, Center for History and New Media, George Mason University, Fairfax, Va.

5. Jennifer Lee, "John L. Procope, 82, Publisher of Black Newspaper in Harlem," *New York Times*, July 18, 2005.

6. "Cities: How New York City Lurched to the Brink," *Time*, June 16, 1975.

7. Corky Siemaszko, "The Politics of Turmoil," *New York Daily News*, summer 2007, nydailynews.com.

8. Betsy Leondar-Wright, "Black Job Loss Déjà Vu," *Dollars and Sense*, May 5, 2004.

9. Wilbur C. Rich, *David Dinkins and New York City Politics: Race, Images, and the Media* (Albany: State University of New York Press, 2007).

10. Corky Siemaszko, "The Politics of Turmoil," *New York Daily News*, summer 2007.

11. Marc Eliot, *Down 42nd Street: Sex, Money, Culture, and Politics at the Crossroads of the World* (New York: Warner Books, 1991).

12. Rich, *David Dinkins*, 32–33.

13. Wolfgang Saxon, "Mobil Plans to Keep Its Base in New York: Koch Calls Decision Breakthrough for City Economy; Company Will Shift 1,300 to Virginia," *New York Times*, January 18, 1978.

14. Rich, *David Dinkins*.

15. Ibid.

16. Siemaszko, "The Politics of Turmoil."

17. Frank Lombardi, "Koch Wins It in a Landslide: Gets Nod by 75,000, Takes 4 Boroughs," "Bronx Is Burning," nydailynews.com, 2007.

18. Eliot, *Down 42nd Street*.

19. Rich, *David Dinkins*.

20. Siemaszko, "The Politics of Turmoil"; "Bronx Is Burning," nydailynews.com, summer 2007.

21. Jocelyn C. Cooper interviews, 2005, 2006, 2007.

22. Jocelyn Cooper interview; interview with Jocelyn A. "Jo-An" Cooper, a recording industry executive. Jocelyn A. Cooper and Rock are friends.

23. Interview with Robert and Dominga Cooper, Henderson, Nevada, August 7, 2007.

24. The pugnacious but civically engaged Beny Primm died in 2002, according to online obituaries.

25. Robert Cooper interview, 2007; author's personal observations, 1978–79.

26. William Miles's documentary *Men of Bronze* was recognized by the New York Club, a CINE Golden Eagle award, and the American Association for State and Local History, all in 1978.

27. Community News Service and Annette Samuels.

28. The grant was from the federal Comprehensive Employment and Training Act (CETA) and was managed by Colony South Brooklyn Houses. A Bloomberg administration deputy mayor who attended the May 2007 memorial was familiar with the grant details.

29. U.S. representative John Conyers, D-Mich., told Michael Moore in *Fahrenheit 911* that if politicians actually took the time to read the legislation they voted on, government would be paralyzed.

30. Wayne Dawkins, "The Black United Front: Out of Police-Community Tensions, a Movement," M.S. thesis, Columbia University Journalism School, 8–13.

31. The blizzard of February 5–7, 1978, dumped eighteen inches of snow over thirty-six hours with near-hurricane-strength winds. "Weather 2000 Forecast Research: Historical Snowstorms Impacting New York City," http://www.weather2000.com/NY_Snowstorms .html.

32. Notes from author's 1978 UNICEF daybook.

33. Morris McKoy interview, November 3, 2007.

34. Wise wrote a book about the Torsney case, according to Morris McKoy.

35. According to the *New York Daily News*, the city was $1 billion in debt.

36. "Cities of the United States," City-Data.com, http://city-data.com/us-cities.

37. Bruce Lambert, "Roger Starr, New York Planning Official, Author, and Editorial Writer, Is Dead at 83," *New York Times*, September 11, 2001.

38. Arthur Browne, Dan Collins, and Michael Goodwin, *I, Koch: A Decidedly Unauthorized Biography of the Mayor of New York City, Edward I. Koch* (New York: Dodd, Mead, 1988).

39. At that time, one out of eight New Yorkers was receiving welfare. *Village Voice*, 1981.

40. Wayne Barrett and Andy Cooper, "Koch's War on the Poor," *Village Voice*, May 29, 1978.

41. Ibid.

42. Ibid.

43. Ibid.

44. Ibid.

45. Ibid.

46. In 1978, Health and Human Services was called Health Education and Welfare (HEW).

47. Barrett and Cooper, "Koch's War on the Poor."

48. "Not one brick was laid in Harlem," widow Jocelyn Cooper said repeatedly about the Model Cities antipoverty program that functioned in Brooklyn but seemed nonexistent uptown in Harlem. She attributed the quote to Bruce Llewelyn, who died in 2010. The term "Gang of Four" used by Koch and Andrew W. Cooper for Dinkins, Rangel, Sutton, and Patterson was used alternately as a term of endearment or disdain.

49. Jack Newfield, "AM News Sells Out Harlem," *Village Voice*, April 10, 1978.

50. "Crown Heights' Demographics: An Explosion Waiting to Happen," Trans Urban News Service special report, published in the *New York Amsterdam News* in 1978.

51. Trans Urban News Service special report, May 19, 1978, July 3, 1978; "Who Controls Crown Heights?" *Village Voice*, July 24, 1978; "Showdown at Crown Heights," *Village Voice*, 1978.

52. Martin Gottlieb, "Bubble and Trouble in New York's Venerable Melting Pot," *New York Times*, August 29, 1991. Arthur Miller's death in 1978 and Victor Rhodes's beat-down are

referenced in the twenty-second paragraph of a twenty-four-paragraph account in the *New York Times* in 1991. Trans Urban News Service Special report, *New York Amsterdam News*, May 19, 1979.

53. Dawkins, "The Black United Front."

54. Geoffrey Stokes, "Buying Brooklyn: Richmond Runs for His Life," *Village Voice*, June 19, 1978. Edolphus Towns inherited Richmond's Fourteenth Congressional District seat. In 1978, Shirley Chisholm's district was the Twelfth.

55. *Village Voice*, August 21, August 28, September 18, and October 2, 1978.

56. Andrew W. Cooper and Wayne Barrett, "Chisholm's Compromise," *Village Voice*, October 30, 1978. The editor's note on the first jump page read: "This is a personal memoir by Andrew W. Cooper, a political writer and director of Trans Urban News Service, a wire service that supplies minority news to print and broadcast media. Wayne Barrett, frequent *Voice* contributor, collaborated with Cooper on this article. Gabrielle Patrick provided research assistance."

57. Ibid.

58. Ibid.

59. Ibid.

60. Ibid.

9. TNS Shuts Down

1. Wayne Dawkins, "Deputy Mayor Ward Quits over Hospitals Issue," *New York Amsterdam News*, August 25, 1979; Wayne Dawkins and Constance Dvorkin, "Resurgence of KKK in the Northeast Worries Leaders," *New York Amsterdam News*, December 29, 1979; Wayne Dawkins, "200-Foot Steel Tower Collapses in Bed-Stuy," *New York Amsterdam News*, January 12, 1980.

2. Cooper famously dismissed the black students at Columbia University Journalism School as know-it-alls with suspect news judgment and also dismissed graduate school as a waste of time. Yet he wrote an enthusiastic recommendation letter for me, far superior to the recommendation from the chairman of Long Island University's journalism department, who should have known a lot about a three-semester dean's list student and associate editor of the weekly student newspaper. An admissions officer at Columbia University privately told me years later that Cooper's letter convinced the selection committee to choose me for the elite program.

3. Morris McKoy interview, November 3, 2007.

4. "Urban Journalism Trainees Show Program's Worth," *New York Daily News*, June 22, 1980.

5. Betty Winston Baye and Wayne Dawkins, "Harlem: 1920's Mecca for West Indians," *New York Amsterdam News*, September 6, 1980; Baye and Dawkins, "Jamaicans at Home and Abroad Eye Coming Elections with Concern," *New York Amsterdam News*, October 4, 1980.

6. Betty Winston Baye, "Trans Urban News First Graduates," *New York Amsterdam News*, November 8, 1980.

7. Ibid.

8. Vinette Pryce interview, June 18, 2007. In 1995 Shabazz was charged with contracting a hit man to try and assassinate minister Louis Farrakhan. In 1994 Shabazz's mother, Betty, suggested that the minister was involved in the murder of her husband Malcolm. Charges against Qubilah Shabazz were dropped on the condition she undergo alcohol abuse treatment and psychiatric treatment.

9. Ibid.

10. Baye, "Trans Urban News First Graduates."

11. Ibid.

12. Wayne Barrett and Andrew W. Cooper, "Koch's 99 Attacks against the Other New York," *Village Voice*, April 15–21, 1981. The credit line read: "Many thanks for research assistance by Ken Thorbourne, Matt Tallmer, Judy Wessler and staff students of the Trans Urban News Service."

13. Wayne Barrett and Andrew W. Cooper, "Koch's War on the Poor," *Village Voice*, May 29, 1978.

14. Barrett and Cooper, "Koch's 99 Attacks."

15. Ibid.

16. Ibid.

17. Ibid.

18. Ibid.

19. Ibid.

20. *TNS Reports* 1, no. 4 (1981).

21. From an online biography of Utrice C. Leid published at dorsai.org, May 27, 2000: "Stories generated by TUNS were authoritatively written and of superior quality (indeed, TUNS won several coveted awards for reporting), but it soon also became a pattern that mainstream news organizations subscribing to the service found its editorial offerings to hot politically or too black. Although they were paying for the service, many mainstream clients would not carry or use TUNS's stories. It was tantamount to censorship, and it effectively nullified the existence of TUNS by 1981." Some biographers incorrectly identified Trans Urban News Service as TUNS. The business self-identified as TNS on second reference.

22. During a May 2, 2007, radio interview with Hugh Hamilton on WBAI-FM, New York, Hamilton, a native of Guyana, asked me why "black newspaper" was often a pejorative term in the late 1900s. My reply: "In fairness to the *Amsterdam News* and some other black weeklies, these papers did not own their printing presses, so they were at the mercy of printers that gave them limited time to print their editions. The *Amsterdam News* was printed by a company in Northern Westchester. Numerous typographical errors and sloppy layouts could be attributed to the long distances traveled to produce the paper, and the short window of time to proofread the content. Simply put, human error."

23. "Black and Blue: Transit Guardians v. TA Police Dept," *TNS Reports* 1, no. 4 (1981).

24. Ibid.

25. Ibid.

26. Ibid.

27. Ibid.

28. Ibid.

29. Lawson, a spokesman for the Harlem numbers racket, wrote harsh words about Dutch Schultz, the Jewish gangster who shot his way into Harlem and took over the lucrative numbers business until he was gunned down. Weaver, the great-great grandson of Frederick Douglass, was quoted saying undiplomatic things about Jewish Americans, but as Cooper wrote, "That's a problem that belongs to Fred Weaver, and the editors of the *Amsterdam News*, not David Dinkins."

30. Andrew W. Cooper, "One Man's Opinion: The *New York Post* as Political Lynch Mob," *TNS Reports* 1, no. 4 (1981).

31. Edward V. Schneier and Brian Murtaugh, *New York Politics: A Tale of Two States* (New York: M. E. Sharpe, 2001), 103; Clyde Haberman, "For Koch, the Real Problems Now Begin," *New York Times*, September 27, 1981.

32. Arthur Schlesinger Jr., "I Am the Greatest," review of *Mayor*, *New York Review of Books*, April 12, 1984.

33. Lou Cannon, *President Reagan: The Role of a Lifetime* (New York: Simon and Schuster, 1991), 90–92, 109.

34. David A. Thomas and John J. Gabarro, *Breaking Through: The Making of Minority Executives in Corporate America* (Cambridge: Harvard Business Press, 1999), 55–56.

35. Trans Urban News Service Annual Report, January 1–December 31, 1981; correspondence from Cooper to author, March 18, 1982.

36. Trans Urban News Service Annual Report, January 1–December 31, 1981.

37. Ibid.

38. Ibid.

39. The author and the *Daily Argus*. My former paper was merged with other Westchester, N.Y., dailies and renamed the *Journal News* of Westchester and Rockland counties.

40. Trans Urban News Service Annual Report, January 1–December 31, 1981; correspondence from Cooper to author, March 18, 1982.

41. Trans Urban News Service Annual Report, January 1–December 31, 1981.

42. Ibid.

43. Ibid.

44. Ibid.

45. Correspondence from Cooper to author, June 2, 1982.

46. Clayton Riley, first D. Parke Gibson winner. "Cooper Wins Journalism Award," TNS news release, September 27, 1981.

47. Ibid.

10. Rising Sun

1. Correspondence from Virgil H. Hodges to Utrice C. Leid, April 25, 1983. "Since 1980, when the program started," wrote the state deputy commissioner of labor, "your success in

training 100 men and women, and job placement in the media or media-related jobs have been outstanding. I can say, after receiving the monitor's reports, that your program is truly one of New York State's most outstanding."

2. An extension and specialized training and placement for interns: correspondence from Utrice C. Leid to author, October 4, 1982.

3. "Plans for the immediate future" was the label for a closing two-paragraph item in the eight-page annual report that detailed performance from January 1 to December 31, 1982. "My staff and I are planning to produce a badly needed, quality weekly newspaper," Cooper wrote. "You will hear more from us about this exciting venture in the weeks and months to come." Cooper signed his statement below at an ascending forty-five-degree angle with a felt-tip pen.

4. Madison Research was contracted to perform the demographic compilation and analysis.

5. Correspondence from Cooper to author, January 11, 1983.

6. Ibid.

7. Ibid.

8. Ibid.

9. Ibid.

10. Ibid.

11. Harlem was no longer center of black universe; according to an issue of *American Heritage* magazine in 2005, Brooklyn had the largest black community in North America.

12. *Black Alumni Network* newsletter, March 1983, 2.

13. Correspondence from Cooper to author, January 11, 1983.

14. Correspondence from Cooper to author, May 2, 1983.

15. Correspondence from Utrice Leid to author, June 28, 1983.

16. Correspondence from Cooper to author, May 3, 1983.

17. Correspondence from Utrice C. Leid to Betty Winston Baye and author, May 10, 1983. Baye and I were both reporters at the *Daily Argus* of Mount Vernon, New York. We were also editors of the monthly *Black Alumni Network* newsletter for graduates of the Columbia University Journalism School. Leid asked us to place the following item in the newsletter: "New Black Weekly looking for committed, energetic and capable reporters to cover New York City. Starting salary low, but excellent opportunity for learning and advancement."

18. Correspondence of May 3, 1983.

19. Ibid.

20. Correspondence from Leid, May 10, 1983.

21. "Bitter Struggle at *Daily News*," *Black Alumni Network* newsletter, October 1983.

22. Wayne Dawkins, "Ex-editor Speaks Out," *Black Alumni Network* newsletter, December 1983.

23. Errol Louis interview, November 2006, Nashville, Tenn. Dow Jones is the parent company of the *Wall Street Journal*. It owned a chain of small newspapers and news services.

24. Ibid.

25. Ibid.

26. Errol Louis, "Death of a Generation," *City Sun*, vol. 1, no. 1, June 6, 1984.

27. Errol Louis reported that although the numbers did not break down by race, high schools with the highest dropout rates were in black communities: Roosevelt in the Bronx, Brandeis in Manhattan, Boys and Girls in Brooklyn, and Andrew Jackson in Queens.

28. Beny Primm.

29. Freedom's Journal opening.

30. Wayne Dawkins, "Why Did the *City Sun* Matter?" *NABJ Journal*, winter 2006–7.

31. *City Sun*, June 20–26, 1984.

32. "Radio Cacophony," editorial, *City Sun*, July 18–24, 1984; "Imitation Is One Thing, Piracy Is Another," *City Sun*, July 10–17, 1984.

33. *City Sun*, June 20–26, 1984.

34. "Beatty's Legacy to Brooklyn," editorial, *City Sun*, August 1–7, 1984.

35. Clinton Cox interviews, summer 2007.

36. Larry J. Sabato, "Jesse Jackson's 'Hymietown' Remark," *Washington Post*, July 21, 1988.

37. Isaiah Poole, "Frisco's Winners and Losers," *City Sun*, July 25–31, 1984.

38. Dawkins, "Why Did the *City Sun* Matter?"

39. Ramon Jimenez, "The Game Is On," *City Sun*, October 31–November 6, 1984. Jimenez was identified immediately below his byline as a South Bronx activist and one of the founding members of the Bronx Rainbow Club. He wrote the article from the perspective of a participant in the anti-Reagan campaign in the Bronx.

40. Cannon, *President Reagan*, 493–94.

11. Bright, Shining Years

1. "Groups Rally for Justice in Bumpurs Killing" and "A Thorough Report on the Bumpurs Killing, or a Whitewash?" editorial, *City Sun*, November 21–27, 1984.

2. Victor Garcia, "Eyewitness: It Was like a War," *City Sun*, November 7–13, 1984.

3. Jim Bellows, *The Last Editor: How I Saved the New York Times, the Washington Post, and the Los Angeles Times from Dullness and Complacency* (Kansas City: Andrews and McMeel, 2002).

4. The "This Week in History" feature did not have a headline but did feature a caricature of Bumpurs and twenty-one lines of fourteen-point type. In Baumann's cartoon "That's a Good Boy," a suit leans against shabby buildings. Money bags are on the street. The man is patting the head of a cop who is on his knees and has a bleeding corpse between his razor-sharp jaws.

5. *City Sun*, November 7–13, 1984.

6. *City Sun*, November 14–20, 1984.

7. *City Sun*, November 21–27, 1984.

8. *City Sun*, November 28–December 4, 1984.

9. Ibid.

10. Van Dora Williams interview, June 19, 2009.

11. Phil Makotsi, "Living with the New FBI" and "Charge Feds with 'Legal Terror,'" *City Sun*, December 5–11, 1984.

12. Jack Newfield, "A response to the Mayor," *City Sun*, December 5–11.

13. Wayne Barrett, "Tales of the Other New York," *City Sun*, November 7–13, 1984.

14. Phil Makotsi, "New Yorkers Denounce Apartheid," *City Sun*, December 12–18, 1985.

15. "Some Kind—and Unkind—Words . . . ," *City Sun*, December 19–25, 1984.

16. Benjamin Ward, "Disputes *City Sun*'s Editorial on Bumpurs Killing," *City Sun*, January 9–15, 1985.

17. "Bumpurs Kin: Not Satisfied with Cop Indictment," *City Sun*, February 6–12, 1985.

18. "Thousands of Cops Protest Bumpurs, 66, Indictment," *City Sun*, February 13–19, 1985.

19. "Do New York's Finest Scare Mayor Koch?" and editorial, "Scandal at the 106th and 108th precincts," *City Sun*, May 8–14, 1985.

20. Voluntary petition for reorganization, March 11, 1985. Documents revealing the bankruptcy filing were mailed anonymously to me in October 2007.

21. Statement of Financial Affairs filed with U.S. Bankruptcy Court, Eastern District, April 25, 1985. Plan of Reorganization, the City Sun Publishing Co., March 25, 1986.

22. Errol Louis interview, November 7, 2005.

23. Farhan Haq interview, July 25, 2007.

24. Ken Auletta, "The Mayor," *New Yorker*, September 17, 1979.

25. Colin A. Moore, "Is the Joke on Koch or on Us?" *City Sun*, July 31, 1985.

26. "The Crisis in Black Leadership," *City Sun*, January 23, 1985.

27. "A Small Tribute to a Great Man," editorial, *City Sun*, March 13, 1985.

28. Ibid.

29. "A Farce of a Mayoral Campaign," editorial, *City Sun*, May 29, 1985; "Brooklyn Pols Back Away from Farrell Campaign," *City Sun*, June 12, 1985.

30. Ibid.

31. House advertisement: "The Farrell Candidacy . . . How Did It Really Happen?" *City Sun*, July 24, 1985.

32. "Koch to Seek Third Term," *New York Times*, July 1, 1985.

33. Kenton Kirby and Utrice Leid, "Black Transit Cops: The Battle's on the Inside," *City Sun*, July 24–30, 1985.

34. Ibid.

35. Ibid.

36. Frederick Kennedy, letter to *City Sun*, September 4–10, 1985.

37. *City Sun*, December 18–24, 1985.

38. "Koch's 3–1 November Win," *New York Times*, November 6, 1986.

39. Phil Makotsi, "Stewart Lawyer Charges D.A. with Sabotage," *City Sun*, July 31–August 6, 1985.

40. Ibid.

41. "Stewart Case Takes Yet Another Turn as Medical Examiner Flip-Flops on the Cause of Artist's Death," *City Sun*, October 16–22, 1985.

42. Utrice C. Leid and Phil Makotsi, "Who Killed Michael Stewart?" *City Sun*, August 7–13, 1985; "Stewart Lawyer: 'Sloppy' Case by D.A. Will Net Cops' Acquittal," *City Sun*, September 18–24, 1985.

43. "The Stewart Case: It's Over Even Before It Ends," *City Sun*, November 13–19, 1985.

44. "Outrage over Stewart Verdict," *City Sun*, November 27–December 3, 1985.

45. "After the Verdict, Now What?" editorial, *City Sun*, December 4–10, 1985.

46. "Stewart Case Has Healed the Community," *City Sun*, December 11–17, 1985.

12. Nineteen Eighty-Six

1. Moe Foner, "Notable New Yorkers," Columbia University Oral History, 293–95.

2. Ibid.

3. "1199: A Union in Turmoil," editorial, *City Sun*, January, 9, 1985.

4. Rebecca Brown, "The Origins of SEIU 1199NW," June 2002, http://depts.washington.edu/labhist/uwunions/brown-1199.htm; Sam Roberts, "Turmoil at 1199: Union Wrestles with Its Demons," *New York Times*, October 26, 1987; Frank J. Prial, "Infighting Seen as Hurting Hospital Union's Image," *New York Times*, October 11, 1987; Fox Butterfield, "Union Seeking to End Strife Readies Accord," *New York Times*, November 30, 1987.

5. Utrice C. Leid, "Union Head Target of New Probe," *City Sun*, February 5, 1986; Leid, "Dissidents Audit Union's Books; Find Irregularities," *City Sun*, March 26, 1986; Moe Foner, "Notable New Yorkers," Columbia University Oral History.

6. Utrice C. Leid, "Union Leader Is Booted Out," *City Sun*, June 25, 1986.

7. Jack Newfield and Wayne Barrett, *City for Sale: Ed Koch and the Betrayal of New York* (New York: Harper and Row, 1988).

8. Ibid., 83, 85.

9. Ibid., 86.

10. Ibid., 66.

11. *City Sun*, March 12–18, 1986.

12. Newfield and Barrett, *City for Sale*, 99–101.

13. *City Sun*, March 26–April 1, 1986.

14. "No Tears for Donald Manes, Only for His Victims," *City Sun*, March 19–25, 1986.

15. Ronal Smothers, "Addabbo's Changing District," *New York Times*, April 12, 1986.

16. Ibid.

17. Ibid.

18. "Frontrunners Emerge in Race for Addabbo's Seat," *City Sun*, May 14–20, 1986.

19. Editorial, *City Sun*, June 4–10, 1986.

20. "Queens: Congressional Race Still Mired in Legal Battles," *City Sun*, July 16–22, 1986.

21. "The Battle for the 6th Congressional District: There's More to It Than Meets the Eye," editorial, *City Sun*, July 16–22, 1986.

22. Christopher Atwell, "Raw Power Gave Flake the Edge, Waldron Says," *City Sun*, September 3–9, 1986.

23. "Roy Innis Stakes His Claim in Brooklyn," *City Sun*, July 2–8, 1986; Frank Lynn, "Innis, CORE Leader, Enters Brooklyn Race for Congress," *New York Times*, June 19, 1986.

24. Phil Makotsi, "Owens-Innis Showdown Shows Up Hidden Agenda," *City Sun*, June 25–July 1, 1986, 4–5.

25. Phil Makotsi, "Former CORE Exec Charges 'Innis Ordered Me Killed,'" *City Sun*, August 27–September 2, 1986.

26. "Innis Ducks Debate," *City Sun*, September 3–9, 1986. Innis lost by a 3:1 ratio to Major Owens in 1986.

27. "Assemblyman 'Buries the Hatchet' with County Organization to Save His Seat," *City Sun*, August 20–26, 1986.

28. "Now Is the Time to Help Ourselves," *City Sun*, November 26–December 2, 1986.

29. The *Beacon*, Education Opportunity Program newsletter, fall 2007, Buffalo State, State University of New York.

30. "Instead of a Bloc Vote, We Get Blockheads," *City Sun*, December 10–16, 1986.

31. "Felon Friedman Appoints Successor; No Black Political Opposition," *City Sun*, December 10–16, 1986.

32. Nelson Mandela, *Long Walk to Freedom* (Boston: Little, Brown, 1994), 296–97.

33. "Those Are Sanctions?" editorial, *City Sun*, August 20–26, 1986.

34. "Mugabe Defiant," plus editorial, *City Sun*, September 10–16, 1986; "Mugabe Denounces S. Africa Collaboration," *City Sun*, October 8–14, 1986.

35. *City Sun*, September 23–29, 1986.

36. Bruce W. Nelan, "Mozambique Anger over a Plane Crash," *Time*, November 3, 1986.

37. "Who Is This Unmasked Man?" *City Sun*, November 26–December 2, 1986.

38. "CORE Exec Makes Secret Trip to S. Africa," *City Sun*, December 10–16, 1986.

39. *City Sun*, December 17–23, 1986, year-end wrap-up.

40. "Judge Sentences New York 8," *City Sun*, January 22–28, 1987.

41. "Mutulu Shakur, the Alleged 'Mastermind' of the 1981 Brinks Armored Car Holdup Attempt in Nanuet, NY, States His Own Case," *City Sun*, April 9–15, 1986.

42. "Case Not Proved," *Time*, February 3, 1986.

43. Who's Next? & Enough Is Enough," *City Sun*, April 30–May 6, 1986.

44. "Federal Probe Yields No Justice in [Michael] Stewart Death," and "The Federal Probe of the Michael Stewart Case Is Another Lethal Blow to Justice," editorial, *City Sun*, July 9, 1986.

45. "Who's in Charge Here?" editorial and illustration, *City Sun*, November 19, 1986.

46. "The More Things Change, the More They Stay the Same," editorial, *City Sun*, November 12, 1986; and "Koch, Ward Give NY the Fast Shuffle."

47. "PBA to City: We Don't Want a Civilian Review Board," *City Sun*, November 5–11, 1986.

48. "The Year That Put Us All to the Test" was the headline for the *City Sun* edition of December 17–23, 1986, which closed the publishing year.

13. Howard Beach

1. Vincent Canby, "*Goodfellas*: A Cold-Eyed Look at the Mob's Inner Workings," *New York Times*, September 19, 1990. Coincidentally, the Brooklyn meatpacking scene from *Goodfellas* was filmed in Howard Beach.

2. M. A. Farber, "The Howard Beach Case: Puzzling Picture of a Racial Attack," *New York Times*, January 5, 1987.

3. Ibid.

4. Ibid.

5. Walter C. Rucker and James M. Upton, *Encyclopedia of American Race Riots* (Greenwood, 2006).

6. Farber, "The Howard Beach Case."

7. wcbstv.com/classic.

8. Joseph P. Fried, "Witness in Howard Beach Case Erupts during Relentless Cross Examination," *New York Times*, October 20, 1987.

9. Carlyle C. Douglas and Mary Connelly, "A New Version of Events at Howard Beach," *New York Times*, February 8, 1987.

10. Farber, "The Howard Beach Case."

11. Ibid.

12. Charles Hynes and Bob Drury, *Incident at Howard Beach* (New York: Putnam, 1990), 53.

13. Ibid.

14. Ibid.

15. Joseph P. Fried, "Cedric Sandiford, 41, a Victim of the Howard Beach Attack," *New York Times*, November 21, 1991.

16. Farber, "The Howard Beach Case."

17. "Howard Beach Wrap-Up," *City Sun*, January 14–20, 1987, 5.

18. Hynes and Drury, *Incident at Howard Beach*, 95.

19. Ibid., 96.

20. Howard Kurtz, "State Calls Sharpton Group a Façade," *Washington Post*, March 30, 1990.

21. Q&A interview with Maddox and Mason, *City Sun*, January 7–13, 1987, 2.

22. Ibid.

23. Hynes and Drury, *Incident at Howard Beach*, 55.

24. "Howard Beach Wrap-Up," *City Sun*, January 14–20, 1987, 5.

25. Ibid.

26. Gloria J. Browne-Marshall, "The U.S. Constitution: An African-American Context," 2009, http://lawandpolicygroup.org.

27. "Two of Three Suspects Released," Howard Beach Wrap-Up, *City Sun*, January 14–20, 1987.

28. Ibid.

29. Ibid.

30. Ibid.

31. Hynes and Drury, *Incident at Howard Beach*, 51.

32. Ibid., 96.

33. Ibid.

34. Ibid.

35. Hynes and Drury, *Incident at Howard Beach*, 74.

36. Joanne Reitano, *The Restless City: A Short History of New York from Colonial Times to the Present* (New York: Routledge, 2006), 196.

37. *Washington Post*, February 10, 1987, and December 27, 1989 (reversal); December 26, 1987 (Blum sues); May 22, 1987 (Blum cleared); October 9, 1987 (witness); July 16, 1988 (verdicts); February 4, 1987 (indictments considered).

14. Arts Beat

1. Jo-An Cooper interview, October 8, 2005.

2. Armond White, *City Sun*, August 6–12, 1986.

3. Larry Rohter, "Spike Lee Makes His Movie," *New York Times*, August 10, 1986.

4. Armond White, "The Man Who Lost His Roots!" in *The Resistance: Ten Years of Pop Culture That Shook the World* (New York: Overlook Press, 1995), 94–97.

5. Esther Iverem, *We Gotta Have It: Twenty Years of Seeing Black at the Movies, 1986–2006* (New York: Thunder's Mouth Press, 2007), 19.

6. White, *The Resistance*, 95.

7. That *City Sun* edition carried 8.67 ad pages. Twenty-seven percent of all space in the edition was advertising, less than the ideal 65:35 news-advertising ratio.

8. White, *City Sun*, August 3, 1988.

9. "Paramount Settles Buchwald's Compensation Suit," *New York Times*, September 12, 1996. Murphy took offense at Armond White's 1988 critique, but audiences learned eight years after the fact that the original idea for the movie was not Murphy's. The humorist Art Buchwald (1925–2007) and his coproducer Alain Bernheim complained that Murphy had stolen Buchwald's idea, a two-page treatment he sold to Paramount Studios in 1983. In 1992 the courts awarded Buchwald $900,000.

10. Howard French, "New Picture Emerges in Case of Larry Davis," *New York Times*, October 18, 1987.

11. Peter Noel, *City Sun*, August 3–9, 1988.

15. Journalist of the Year

1. Pamela Newkirk, *Within the Veil: Black Journalists, White Media* (New York: New York University Press, 2000), 115.

2. Wayne Dawkins, *Black Journalists: The NABJ Story* (Merrillville, Ind.: August Press, 1997), 180.

3. Newkirk, *Within the Veil*, 119.

4. "Bitter Struggle at *Daily News*," *Black Alumni Network* newsletter, October 1983. At the New York Association of Black Journalists meeting, Dave Hardy said that half of the *Daily News* readership was nonwhite, but only 5 percent of the editorial staff was black. The newspaper management at that time resisted settling the lawsuit. Earl Caldwell quashed rumors that he was fired. His thrice-weekly column was missing for a month. Caldwell said, "I've been on strike for a month" because of a salary dispute and the decision of push his column from page 4 to the back of the paper.

5. Danny Alterman interview, December 2005.

6. Newkirk, *Within the Veil*, 98–99.

7. *City Sun*, March 11–17, 1987.

8. Ibid.

9. Newkirk, *Within the Veil*, 114.

10. Molly Ivins, "Coppeeee!" *Washington Journalism Review*, April 1987.

11. Newkirk, *Within the Veil*, 101.

12. Ben Johnson and Mary Bullard-Johnson, *Who's What and Where* (Columbia, Mo., 1988); Newkirk, *Within the Veil*, 120.

13. Newkirk, *Within the Veil*, 121, 104–6, 108.

14. Ibid., 103–4, 104–6.

15. Ibid., 108–9.

16. Ibid., 109, 110.

17. Clinton Cox, "Life in the Belly of the Beast," *City Sun*, March 11, 1987.

18. *Columbia Journalism Review*, November–December 1987.

19. Caldwell Q&A, *City Sun*, March 18, 1987; Newkirk, *Within the Veil*, 121.

20. Caldwell Q&A, *City Sun*, March 18, 1987.

21. *Black Alumni Network* newsletter, June 1987.

22. Ibid.

23. "For Black Reporters at the *Daily News*, It's a Matter of Honor," *City Sun*, March 11, 1987, "Hardy Becomes Focal Point of Courtroom Combat," *City Sun*, March 25, 1987.

24. Newkirk, *Within the Veil*, 123–24.

25. Makotsi, "*Daily News* Reporters Torpedo Racism at the Paper," *City Sun*, April 22, 1987.

26. Ibid.

27. Wayne Dawkins, "*Daily News* Improves Climate for Minority Journalists," *Black Alumni Network* newsletter, October 1987.

28. June 16, 1987, at U.S. Bankruptcy Court in Westbury, New York, motion to convert Chapter 11 case to a Chapter 7 case. Signed May 4, 1987.

29. The *New York Post*, founded by Alexander Hamilton in 1801 and the oldest newspaper still publishing in New York City, was acquired by Murdoch in 1976 from the liberal

Schiff family, who employed black journalists who included Tom Poston, Earl Caldwell, Joel Dreyfuss, and Dorothy Hicks (Maynard).

30. Newkirk, *Within the Veil*, 124.

31. Wilbert Tatum oral history at Columbia University, 65, 66.

32. Ibid., 69, 12, 38.

33. Jonathan P. Hicks, "*Amsterdam News*' Blunt Publisher Still Has Visions of Running the *Post*," *New York Times*, March 22, 1993.

34. Ibid.

35. Lincoln Anderson, "Wilbert Tatum, 76, Publisher, Longtime East Villager," *Villager*, March 11–17, 2009.

36. Ibid.

37. Tatum oral history, 51.

38. Ibid., 56.

39. Ken Smikle interview, 2009.

40. Ibid.

41. Tatum oral history, 67.

42. Ibid., 72.

43. Alex Jones, "Black Papers: Businesses with a Mission," *New York Times*, August 17, 1987.

44. Ibid.

45. Wayne Dawkins, "Why Did the *City Sun* Matter," *NABJ Journal*, winter 2007.

46. Ibid.

47. Yanick Rice Lamb interview, June 16, 2007.

48. Dawkins, "Why Did the *City Sun* Matter?"

49. Phil Makotsi, *City Sun*, July 29, 1987.

50. Peter Noel, *City Sun*, August 19–25; *City Sun*, September 2–8.

51. "Koch Calls the *City Sun* 'Vile,' 'Racist,'" *City Sun*, September 16–22, 1987.

52. "Three in Howard Beach Attack Are Guilty of Manslaughter; A Year of Tension and Waiting for the Verdict," *New York Times*, December 22, 1987.

53. Joseph P. Fried, "Two Girls Do Not Support State on Howard Beach Incident," *New York Times*, October 15, 1987.

54. Joseph P. Fried, "Witness in Howard Beach Case Erupts during Relentless Cross Examination," *New York Times*, October 20, 1987.

55. *New York Times*, December 22, 1987.

56. Joseph P. Fried, "Defendants in the 2nd Howard Beach Trial, Citing Verdict, Will Seek Dismissals," *New York Times*, December 23, 1987.

16. Tawana Brawley

1. Mike Taibbi and Anna Sims-Phillips, *Unholy Alliances: Working the Tawana Brawley Story* (New York: Harcourt Brace Jovanovich, 1989), 12–15.

2. Ibid., 17.

3. Ibid., 19.

4. Ibid.

5. Ibid., 22.

6. Ibid., 32.

7. Ibid., 29.

8. Ibid., 47.

9. Utrice C. Leid, "Upstate Race Case Is the 'Last Straw,' Say Activists," *City Sun*, December 9–15, 1987.

10. Taibbi and Sims-Phillips, *Unholy Alliances*, 39.

11. Ibid., 40.

12. "Farrakhan Issues Warning on Upstate Race Case," *City Sun*, December 16–22, 1987.

13. Taibbi and Sims-Phillips, *Unholy Alliances*, 49.

14. Ibid., 128–29.

15. Ibid., 74–77, 81–83, 96–97.

16. Ibid., 173, 194–95, 200–207.

17. Ibid., 146–47, 93.

18. Ibid., 103, 104, 200.

19. Ibid., 141, 116–17.

20. Ibid., 142–43.

21. Ibid., 114–15, 110, 112, 152, 168, 174–75.

22. Ibid., 65.

23. Ibid.

24. Ed Diamond, "The Soundbite and the Fury: The Art of Instant Spokesmanship," *New York*, March 28, 1988.

25. Jim Sleeper, *The Closest of Strangers: Liberalism and the Politics of Race in New York* (New York: W. W. Norton, 1991), 204.

26. Taibbi and Sims-Phillips, *Unholy Alliances*, 66–67.

27. Ibid., 138–39.

28. Ibid., 116–17.

29. Ibid., 141.

30. Ibid., 142–43.

31. "Jesse, Say It Ain't So," editorial, *City Sun*, April 13–19, 1988.

32. Todd Steven Burroughs interview, July 22, 2010. After Seton Hall, Burroughs earned a Ph.D. in history from the University of Maryland and now teaches at Morgan State University.

33. The Rev. Jimmy Swaggart, a leading televangelist of that period, was undone by a sex scandal with a Louisiana prostitute in winter 1988.

34. Utrice C. Leid, "Flake Is Target of 2 Federal Probes," *City Sun*, May 19–24, 1988.

35. "Meshing the Sacred and the Secular; Floyd Flake Offers Community Development via Church and State," *New York Times*, November 23, 1995.

36. Floyd Flake and his wife were indicted in August 1988 and 1990. Josh Barbanel, "Congressman Flake's Indictment: Good Works or Greed?" *New York Times*, August 6, 1990.

37. "Glenda Brawley Moves to a Brooklyn Church," *New York Times*, June 11, 1988.

38. Sleeper, "The Closest of Strangers," 206–7.

39. Ibid.

40. Robert D. McFadden et al., *Outrage: The Story behind the Tawana Brawley Hoax* (New York: Bantam, 1990), 317–19; Taibbi and Sims-Phillips, *Unholy Alliances*, 358–59.

41. McFadden et al., *Outrage*, 320.

42. Ibid., 323; Taibbi and Sims-Phillips, *Unholy Alliances*, 366.

43. Michael H. Cottman, "Brawley Story Splits Black Reporters in New York," *NABJ Journal*, November–December 1988.

44. Ibid.

45. "The Victims of the Brawley Case," editorial, *New York Times*, September 28, 1988.

46. McFadden et al., *Outrage*, 380, 381, 384.

47. Ibid., 385.

48. Martha A. Miles and Richard L. Madden, "After the Grand Jury: What Happened to Tawana Brawley's Case—and to Attitudes about Race and Justice," *New York Times*, October 9, 1988.

49. Ibid.

17. Mayoral Race

1. Wilbur Rich, *David Dinkins and New York City Politics: Race, Images, and the Media* (Albany: State University of New York Press, 2007), 29.

2. Ibid., 34.

3. Ibid., 36–37.

4. Ibid., 29.

5. Ibid., 39.

6. *City Sun*, September 11–17, 1985.

7. Rich, *David Dinkins*, 38.

8. Earl Caldwell, *Black American Witness: Reports from the Front* (Washington, D.C.: Lion House, 1994), 187–88.

9. Ibid.

10. Ibid., 189.

11. Hugh Hamilton, "Reversing the Science of Exclusion," *City Sun*, March 22–28, 1989.

12. George H. W. Bush, *All the Best, George Bush: My Life in Letters and Other Writings* (New York: Simon and Schuster, 1999), 104.

13. *City Sun*, June 6–12, 1984.

14. Robert R. Taylor network at MIT, http://rrtn.org.

15. McFadden et al., *Outrage*, 370.

16. "Anatomy of a Horror," *New York Magazine*, May 15, 1989.

17. Patrice O'Shaunessey, "Central Park Jogger Case Forever Changed Innocent Victims and the City," *New York Daily News*, April 12, 2009.

18. Helen Benedict, *Virgin or Vamp: How the Press Covers Sex Crimes* (New York: Oxford University Press, 1992).

19. Ibid., 215.

20. "Time to Show Your Face, Dave," editorial, *City Sun*, July 12–18, 1989.

21. Logan Hill, "How I Made It: Spike Lee on 'Do the Right Thing,'" *New York Magazine*, April 7, 2008; "Spike Lee Replies, 'Say it ain't so, Joe,'" *New York Magazine*, letters, July 17, 1989.

22. Armond White, "Exiles on Catfish Row," *City Sun*, July 12–18, 1989.

23. Tony Chapelle, "*Daily News* Case Update," *Black Enterprise*, August 1989.

24. Ibid.

25. Ibid.; and *City Sun*, August 9–15, 1989.

26. Wayne Dawkins, *Black Journalists: The NABJ Story* (Merrillville, Ind.: August Press, 1997), 196.

27. Ibid., 200.

28. Ibid.

29. Ibid., 196–202.

30. Esther Iverem's *New York Newsday* article, reprinted in the Black Alumni Network newsletter.

31. Sleeper, *The Closest of Strangers*, 193.

32. Ibid.

33. Leonard Buder, *New York Times*, November 14, 1989.

34. Nick Ravo, "Marchers and Brooklyn Youths Trade Racial Jeers," *New York Times*, August 27, 1989.

35. Rich, *David Dinkins*, 42–43.

36. Richard Lacayo, Janice C. Simpson, and James Willwerth, "Hope, Not Fear," *Time*, September 25, 1989.

37. Utrice C. Leid, *City Sun*, July 26–August 1, 1989.

38. Frank Macchiarola interview, February 10, 2006.

39. Ibid.

40. Rich, *David Dinkins*, 46–47.

41. Charles S. Isaacs, "The Hands That Didn't Reach Back: Dinkins and the White Vote," *City Sun*, November 15–21, 1989, 1, 4, 8.

42. Rich, *David Dinkins*, 44, 65.

18. Dinkins's First Months

1. "The Decline of New York," *Time*, September 17, 1990.

2. Rich, *David Dinkins*, 107–8.

3. Claire Jean Kim, *Bitter Fruit: The Politics of Black-Korean Conflict in New York City* (New Haven, Conn.: Yale University Press, 2003), 21.

4. Ibid.

5. Ibid., 22.

6. Rich, *David Dinkins*, 108.

7. Ibid.

8. "The Decline of New York," *Time*, September 17, 1990.

9. Kim, *Bitter Fruit*, 26.

10. Ibid., 34.

11. Ibid.

12. Russell W. Baker, "New York's Korean Grocery Turmoil Rooted in Cultural and Economic Conditions," *Christian Science Monitor*, May 31, 1990, 7.

13. Kim, *Bitter Fruit*, 24.

14. Rich, *David Dinkins*, 113.

15. Patrice O'Shaughnessy, "Seventeen Years Don't Diminish Fire Tragedy," *New York Daily News*, March 2007.

16. Editorial, *City Sun*, March 28–April 3, 1990, 1, 28.

17. Hugh Hamilton and Peter Essick, "Hidden Exiles No More," special report, *City Sun*, June 6–12, 1990.

18. Donatella Lorch, "Haitians' Outrage Brings Solidarity," *New York Times*, April 22, 1990.

19. Hugh Hamilton interview, May 16, 2010.

20. Ronald Segal, *The Black Diaspora: Five Centuries of the Black Experience outside Africa* (New York: Farrar, Straus and Giroux, 1995).

21. Peter Essick, "El Batey," *City Sun*, June 6–12, 1990, 13, 16.

22. Ibid.

23. Hugh Hamilton, "Big Dreams in Little Haiti: New Realities and the Fight for Respect in Strife-Torn Miami," *City Sun*, June 6–12, 1990, 25–26.

24. Ibid.

25. Hugh Hamilton, "Toughing It Out in the Big City," *City Sun*, June 6–12, 1990.

26. Ibid.

27. Ibid.

28. Raymond Burrows interview, June 10, 2006.

29. Ibid., plus a follow-up interview, April 26, 2010.

30. Arnold Lubasch, "Court Suspends Maddox for Refusal to Testify at Grievance Hearing," *New York Times*, May 22, 1990.

31. Clinton Cox, "Mandela's Visit and the 'Game of Nations,'" *City Sun*, June 20–26, 1990; Nelson Mandela, *Long Walk to Freedom: The Autobiography of Nelson Mandela* (Boston: Little, Brown, 1994), 507–8.

32. *City Sun*, June 20–26, 1990, 42–43. The letter was reprinted from Nelson Mandela, *Speeches: Intensifying the Struggle to Abolish Apartheid* (Pathfinder Press, June 1990).

33. Arnold Lubasch, "Indictment Names Queens Lawmaker in Misuse of Funds," *New York Times*, August 3, 1990; Josh Barbanel, "Congressman Flake's Indictment: Good Works or Greed," *New York Times*, August 6, 1990; M. A. Farber, "Demise of Flake Case: Choice of Tactic at Issue," *New York Times*, April 5, 1991.

34. "Woman Who Accused Flake Is Killed in an Auto Accident," *New York Times*, October 16, 1990.

35. Abe Blashko interview, at his Manhattan home, March 10, 2010.

36. Richard Vigilante, *Strike: The Daily News War and the Future of American Labor* (New York: Simon and Schuster, 1994); Wayne Dawkins, *Rugged Waters: Black Journalists Swim the Mainstream* (Newport News, Va.: August Press, 2003), 24–25.

37. Vigilante, *Strike*, 67–68, 112; Sleeper, *The Closest of Strangers*, 316.

38. Vigilante, *Strike*, 62–64, 65–66.

39. Ibid.

40. James Ledbetter, "Crisis at the *City Sun*: A Militant Black Paper Loses a Soldier," *Village Voice*, December 1, 1992.

41. "The Decline of New York," *Time*, September 17, 1990.

42. Hugh Hamilton, "City Rallies to Fight Census Undercount," *City Sun*, September 5–11, 1990.

43. Rich, *David Dinkins*, 65.

44. Ibid.

19. Crown Heights Riot

1. Sam Roberts, "Metro Matters: Three Who Inspired Political Change Now Embody It," *New York Times*, September 16, 1991.

2. *Board of Estimate of City of New York v. Morris* (1989), case summary, http://infoplease.com.

3. Hugh Hamilton interview, May 2010. After the *City Sun*, Hamilton worked as a communications and legislative aide for Clarke, then Henry, for a combined ten years.

4. Ibid.

5. Ibid.

6. Hugh Hamilton, "A Foreign-Policy Agenda Dinkins Should Pursue," *City Sun*, February 13–19, 1991.

7. Hugh Hamilton, "Cheap Street: Bargain Days on the Fulton Mall," *City Sun*, March 27–April 2, 1991.

8. Ibid.

9. Hugh Hamilton, "Uptown Eco Blues: Environmental Woes in Harlem," *City Sun*, June 5–11, 1991.

10. Evelyn Nieves, "Malcolm X: A Firestorm over a Film Script," *New York Times*, August 9, 1991.

11. Andy Logan, "Low Hopes," *New Yorker*, August 26, 1991.

12. James C. McKinley Jr., "On That Chat with Dinkins: Make It Almost Everybody," *New York Times*, August 1, 1991.

13. The *New Yorker*, a weekly, was dated August 26, but the normal conventions of major American magazine publishing meant that the issue was released in the previous week.

14. Edward S. Shapiro, *Crown Heights: Blacks, Jews, and the 1991 Brooklyn Riot* (Hanover, N.H.: Brandeis University Press, 2003), 4, 37.

15. "Watching Dr. Jeffries Self-Destruct," editorial, *New York Times*, August 25, 1991.

16. Shapiro, *Crown Heights*, 4–5.

17. Shapiro, *Crown Heights*, 6–7.

18. Utrice C. Leid, "Yankel Rosenbaum and Annie Winston: Victims of Negligence, Not Wound, Killed Hasid, Says Doctor," *City Sun*, September 4–10, 1991.

19. Shapiro, *Crown Heights*, 193. In 2002 the city paid a $400,000 settlement to the Cato family to drop a lawsuit alleging Emergency Medical Service negligence in treating Gavin Cato's wounds.

20. Shapiro, *Crown Heights*.

21. Vinette Pryce interview, June 18, 2007.

22. Ibid.

23. Shapiro, *Crown Heights*, 37–38.

24. Ibid., 40–41.

25. Carlos Russell, "Perspectives on Politics: A Black Community Looks at Itself" (Ph.D. diss., Union Graduate School, 1978), 245, 255.

26. Daniel Patrick Moynihan and Nathan Glazer, *Beyond the Melting Pot: The Negroes, Puerto Ricans, Jews, Italians, and Irish of New York City* (Cambridge, Mass.: MIT Press, 1970); Shapiro, *Crown Heights*, 148.

27. Shapiro, *Crown Heights*, 146–47, 148, 150–51; Andrew W. Cooper, "The Two Nations of Crown Heights," *New York Times*, January 6, 1993.

28. "Gavin's Death Must Spark a Beginning," *City Sun*, August 28–September 3, 1991; Felicia Lee, "Bitterness Pervades Funeral for Crown Heights Boy," *New York Times*, August 27, 1991.

29. Joe Conason and Ianthe Thomas, "Crown Heights: Who Controls the Streets" (July 3, 1978), in *The Village Voice Anthology (1956–1980): Twenty-five Years of Writing from The Village Voice*, ed. Geoffrey Stokes (New York: Quill, 1982).

30. Ibid.

31. Shapiro, *Crown Heights*.

32. Andrew W. Cooper, "The Two Nations of Crown Heights," *New York Times*, January 6, 1993.

33. Ibid.

34. Shapiro, *Crown Heights*, 17–18.

35. Ibid., 20–21.

36. Colin Moore, "Unequal Justice under the Law: Charles Hynes and the Hasidim," *City Sun*, December 16–22, 1992; Charles Hynes, "Hynes Answers Colin Moore," *City Sun*, January 13–19, 1993.

37. Shapiro, *Crown Heights*, 20; Robert D. McFadden, "Black Marchers in Protest at Hynes' Summer Home," *New York Times*, September 8, 1991.

38. Shapiro, *Crown Heights*, 16–17.

39. Ibid., 21.

40. Ibid., 142–43.

41. "Ya Me? Ya You!" *City Sun*, September 25–October 1, 1991; Andy Logan, "Around City Hall: 'Ya Me, Ya You!'" *New Yorker*, November 4, 1991.

20. The Breakup

1. Farhan Haq interview, July 25, 2007.

2. Farhan Haq, "'New World Order' Brings New Challenges to the Caribbean," *City Sun*, October 23–29, 1991; "Palestinians Fear 'Autonomy' of Bantustans as Madrid Peace Talks Begin," *City Sun*, October 30–November 5, 1991; "An Egyptian Is Named to Top UN Post," *City Sun*, November 27–December 3, 1991.

3. Farhan Haq, "One Year after Aristide's Inauguration, 2,500 Protest Coup," *City Sun*, February 12–18, 1992.

4. Vigilante, *Strike*.

5. "Clarence Thomas or Anita Hill? It's Bad News Either Way," editorial, *City Sun*, October 16–22, 1991.

6. Stephen E. Davis, "The Man Who Killed the Presidential Debate," *City Sun*, April 15–21, 1992.

7. Robert McNatt, "Battle to Win Black Readers Turns Bitter," *Crain's New York Business*, May 18–24, 1992; Gabe Pressman, "The Twilight of the Gang of Four," nbcnewyork.com, March 2010.

8. McNatt, "Battle."

9. Dawkins, *Rugged Waters*, 53.

10. Bennett, *Before the Mayflower*, 696.

11. Dawkins, *Rugged Waters*, 54.

12. Bennett, *Before the Mayflower*, 696.

13. Anthony Carter Paige interview, April 14, 2006.

14. Farhan Haq interview, July 25, 2010.

15. Clinton Cox interview, circa 2007.

16. Gerald M. Boyd with Robin D. Stone, *My Times in Black and White: Race and Power at the New York Times* (Chicago: Lawrence Hill Books, 2010).

17. Herbert Daughtry, *No Monopoly on Suffering: Blacks and Jews in Crown Heights (and Elsewhere)* (Trenton, N.J.: Africa World Press, 1997).

18. Boyd, *My Times in Black and White*.

19. Dawkins, *Rugged Waters*, 24, 37, 74.

20. Bryan Monroe, "Newsroom Diversity: "Truth vs. Fiction," *Nieman Reports*, Fall 2003.

21. Robert F. Keeler, *Newsday: A Candid History of a Respectable Tabloid* (New York: Morrow, 1990).

22. Shapiro, *Crown Heights*, 172–73; Noel, "Crown Heights Verdict Saved Lives."

23. Clinton Cox, "Democracy or Mobocracy?" *City Sun*, September 30–October 6, 1992; Associated Press, *City Sun*, October 28–November 3, 1992; "Cops Won't Like These Pictures," *City Sun*, November 18–24, 1992.

24. "Mr. Mayor, Act Like It," editorial, *City Sun*, September 23–29, 1992.

25. Farhan Haq interview.

26. James Ledbetter, "Crisis at the *City Sun*: A Militant Black Paper Loses a Soldier," *Village Voice*, December 1, 1992.

27. Ibid.

28. Annette Walker interview, March 6, 2007.

29. Anthony Carter Paige interview, April 14, 2006.

30. Clinton Cox interview, June 22, 2007.

31. Richard Prince, "Clouds over 'City Sun,'" *NABJ Journal*, January 1993.

32. Bennett, *Before the Mayflower*, 698.

33. Hugh Hamilton interview, November 2010.

34. Cecil Harris interview, April 2006.

35. Stephen E. Davis, "The Agony of Interfaith: Under Its $400,000-a-Year Boss, the Only Hospital in Crown Heights Is Still Losing Millions," *City Sun*, December 2–8, 1992; and Stephen E. Davis and Peter Noel, "Who's Responsible for the Mess at Interfaith?" *City Sun*, December 16–22, 1992.

21. Setting Sun

1. Leid's dismissal of Simone Joye was not isolated. The managing editor was dismissive and closed-minded on more than one occasion: According to Annette Walker, Leid told Yvette Moore, a member of the New York Association of Black Journalists and a journalist with a church publication (Methodist), "You're an advocacy journalist," with no apparent hint of irony as the managing editor of an unapologetically militant black weekly. And regarding New York ABJ president Yanick Rice Lamb, Walker said that Leid asked, "Why is she president? She's a paste-up girl." Lamb was a copy editor who designed pages at the *New York Times*. She later became Connecticut editor and deputy style editor. Walker wrote for the *City Sun* and later served at WBAI-FM. Leid would not consent to an interview.

2. Simone Joye, "Black Man, White Justice: Did the PBA and Brooklyn D.A. Railroad Darryl King as a Death Penalty Case?" *City Sun*, February 3–9, 1993.

3. Simone Joye interview, May 22, 2007; Anthony Carter Paige interview, April 14, 2006.

4. Ericka Blount interview, September 15, 2007.

5. Ericka Blount interview, August 4, 2010.

6. Milton Alimadi interview, January 6, 2006.

7. Thomas Green interview, October 6, 2008.

8. *New Yorker*, February 15, 1993.

9. Carroll Carey Howard, "Disrespect of the Black Woman," *City Sun*, February 17–23, 1993.

10. "The Black Community vs. the *Daily News*," editorial, *City Sun*, February 3–9, 1993; "Bonfire of Racism at the *Daily News*," *City Sun*, January 20–26, 1993.

11. Jocelyn C. Cooper interview, November 11, 2007.

12. Dawkins, *Rugged Waters*, 77; Jeanie Kasindorf, "Whose *Post* Is It Anyway? A Capraesque Tragicomedy Starring Hirschfeld, Tatum, Hoffenberg, Kalikow—and a Working-Class Hero Named Hamill," *New York Magazine*, March 29, 1993.

13. Jonathan P. Hicks, "*Amsterdam News*' Blunt Publisher Still Has Visions of Running the *Post*," *New York Times*, March 23, 1993.

14. Lucas Rivera, "The Thorn in the *Amsterdam News*," *City Sun*, March 24–30, 1993.

15. John Taylor, "Defining Moments," *New York Magazine*, August 30, 1993. In a revealing moment in 2010, when Dinkins received a "Speaking Truth to Power" award named for Andrew W. Cooper, the former mayor said as little as possible about Cooper to the St. Francis College audience, except "That man gave me hell."

16. Catherine S. Manegold, "The Games Dinkins and Giuliani Play," *New York Times*, September 6, 1993.

17. Todd S. Purdum, "Buttoned Up," *New York Times Magazine*, September 12, 1993.

18. Todd S. Purdum, "Giuliani Ousts Dinkins by a Thin Margin," *New York Times*, November 3, 1993; Charles Isaacs, "Why Dinkins Lost: An Analysis," *City Sun*, November 10–16, 1993.

19. Jonathan P. Hicks, "For Black Politicians, a Debate of Strategy and Leadership; After Dinkins's Defeat, Can a New Group of Leaders with New Concerns Achieve the Old Unity?" *New York Times*, February 2, 1994; Andy Logan, "In the Spirit of LaGuardia," *New Yorker*, February 21, 1994.

20. Lois Smith Brady, "Jocelyn A. Cooper, John J. Gilstrap," *New York Times*, November 14, 1993.

21. Copy of the 36-page "The *City Sun* on the Air" business and marketing plan.

22. Jonathan Mark, "Jews and the Juice: *City Sun* Editorial Condemning O.J. Praises Jews for Never Forgetting Their Past," *Jewish Week*, July 14, 1994.

23. Jocelyn C. Cooper interview, January 4, 2010.

24. "Hate Radio Creed: Let Us Prey," *City Sun*, February 22–28, 1995; and "The White Goddess of Hate Radio: Beth Gilinsky's Unholy Alliance," *City Sun*, January 24–30, 1996.

25. Malik Russell, *City Sun*, January 25–31, 1995; March 22–28, 1995; May 3–9, 1995; July 5–11, 1995; August 2–8, 1995; October 11–17, 1995; November 1–7, 1995; February 28–March 5, 1996.

26. Maitefa Angaza interview, August 21, 2007.

27. Lisa W. Foderaro, "Black Weekly's Survival Is in Question," *New York Times*, November 9, 1996; James Ledbetter, "Can the *Sun* Rise Again?" *Village Voice*, November 19, 1996.

28. Danny Alterman interview, December 2005.

22. Dusk

1. Valerie Burgher, "Not Necessarily the News: The Black Press Revisited," *Village Voice*, February 25, 1997.

2. Ibid.

3. Angela G. King, "Black Weekly Plans Comeback," *New York Daily News*, May 1997.

4. Leslie Cauley, "Internet Use Triples in a Decade; Broadband Surges," *USA Today*, June 4, 2009.

5. Wayne Dawkins, "Is Anybody Out There? *Black Issues Book Review*, May–June 2005.

6. Metro *City Sun* editorials, 1997. The unpublished pieces were printed on hard copy and also saved on PC floppy disk.

7. Abigail Pogrebin, "A Publishing Odd Couple," *Brill's Content*, February 2001.

8. E. R. Shipp and Utrice Leid on Amy Goodman's "Democracy Now."

9. Amy Waldman, "*Amsterdam News*' New Generation: Owner's Daughter Tries to Rebuild Famous Paper for Blacks," *New York Times*, February 13, 1998.

10. Alterman interview, December 21, 2005.

11. During Jocelyn A. Cooper's twelve-year tenure as a senior-level executive in the music industry from the early 1990s through the first years of the new century, she generated over $160 million in record sales, according to the citation on her Outstanding Twenty-Year Alumna award at Hampton University's 136th commencement in 2006. Shawn E. Rhea, "Turning Melodies into Royalties: The Real Revenue in the Music Business Lies in the Ownership Rights to the Hits; Here's How to Publish and Not Perish," *Black Enterprise*, December 1997.

12. Andrea Andrews interview, January 2007.

13. Lynn Nottage interview, March 3, 2010; Joe Dziemianowicz, "Brooklyn Writer Lynn Nottage Wins Pulitzer," *New York Daily News*, April 21, 2009.

14. Jocelyn C. Cooper interview, August 2009.

15. Ron Howell, "Andrew Cooper, Published *City Sun*," Newsday.com, January 30, 2002; Vinette Pryce, "Sun Sets on Brooklyn's City Scribe," *New York Amsterdam News*, January 31, 2002; Thomas J. Lueck, "Andrew W. Cooper, 74, Pioneering Journalist, Is Dead," *New York Times*, January 30, 2002; "Journalist-Activist Andrew Cooper, 74," *New York Daily News*, February 13, 2002; James Barron, "Shirley Chisholm, 'Unbossed' Pioneer in Congress, Is Dead at 80," *New York Times*, January 3, 2005.

16. A. Philip Randolph Campus High School. The mission said in part: "The school will graduate students who possess the academic, social, cultural and technical background and curiosity to live successful productive lives in the 21st century." A. Philip Randolph is a magnet school located near City College and Andy Cooper's childhood church, St. Mark's Episcopal.

17. Young Journalists in Training Program, stfraniciscollege.edu.

18. John Riley, "$3.25M in Bell Killing," *Newsday*, July 28, 2010.

19. A. G. Sulzberger, "After a Delay, the New Atlantic Pavilion I Is Open," *New York Times*, January 5, 2010.

Bibliography

Books

Appiah, Kwame Anthony, and Henry Louis Gates Jr. *Africana: Civil Rights: An A–Z Reference of the Movement That Changed America*. Philadelphia: Running Press, 2005.

Barrett, Wayne, and Jack Newfield. *City for Sale: Ed Koch and the Betrayal of New York*. New York: Harper and Row, 1987.

Benedict, Helen. *Virgin or Vamp: How the Press Covers Sex Crimes*. New York: Oxford University Press, 1992.

Bennett, Lerone, Jr. *Before the Mayflower: A History of Black America*. Chicago: Johnson Publishing, 2003.

Binder, Frederick M., and David M. Reimers. *All the Nations under Heaven: An Ethnic and Racial History of New York City*. New York: Columbia University Press, 1995.

Biondi, Martha. *To Stand and Fight: The Struggle for Civil Rights in Postwar New York City*. Cambridge, Mass.: Harvard University Press, 2003.

Boyd, Herb. *The Harlem Reader*. New York: Random House, 2003.

Broyard, Bliss. *One Drop: My Father's Life—A Story of Race and Family Secrets*. Boston: Little, Brown, 2007.

Bush, George H. W. *All the Best, George Bush: My Life in Letters and Other Writings*. New York: Simon and Schuster, 1999.

Caldwell, Earl. *Black American Witness: Reports from the Front*. Washington, D.C.: Lion House, 1994.

Cannato, Vincent. *The Ungovernable City: John Lindsay and His Struggle to Save New York*. New York: Basic Books, 2001.

Chisholm, Shirley. *The Good Fight*. New York: Harper and Row, 1973.

———. *Unbought and Unbossed*. New York: Avon Books, 1970.

Cohen, Cathy J. *Boundaries of Blackness: AIDS and the Breakdown of Black Politics*. Chicago: University of Chicago Press, 1999.

Connolly, Harold X. *A Ghetto Grows in Brooklyn*. New York: New York University Press, 1977.

Cross, June. *Secret Daughter: A Mixed-Race Daughter and the Mother Who Gave Her Away*. New York: Viking, 2007.

Curvin, Robert, and Bruce Porter. *Blackout Looting*. New York: John Wiley and Sons, 1979.

Daughtry, Herbert, Sr. *No Monopoly on Suffering: Blacks and Jews in Crown Heights (And Elsewhere)*. Trenton, N.J.: Africa World Press, 1997.

Dawkins, Wayne. *Black Journalists: The NABJ Story*. Merrillville, Ind.: August Press, 1997.

———. *Rugged Waters: Black Journalists Swim the Mainstream.* Newport News, Va.: August Press, 2003.

Dittmer, John. *Local People: The Struggle for Civil Rights in Mississippi.* Urbana and Chicago: University of Illinois Press, 1994.

Eig, Jonathan. *Opening Day: The Story of Jackie Robinson's Season.* New York: Simon and Schuster, 2007.

Eliot, Marc. *Down 42nd Street: Sex, Money, Culture, and Politics at the Crossroads of the World.* New York: Warner Books, 1991.

Freeman, Joshua Benjamin. *In Transit: The Transport Workers Union in New York City, 1933–1966.* New York: Oxford University Press, 2001.

George, Nelson. *Buppies, B-Boys, Baps, and Bohos: Notes on Post-soul Black Culture.* New York: HarperCollins, 1992.

Glazer, Nathan, and Daniel Patrick Moynihan. *Beyond the Melting Pot: The Negroes, Puerto Ricans, Jews, Italians, and Irish of New York City.* 2nd ed. Cambridge, Mass.: MIT Press, 1970.

Goldschmidt, Henry. *Race and Religion: Among the Chosen Peoples of Crown Heights.* Piscataway, N.J.: Rutgers University Press, 2006.

Greenberg, Cheryl Lynn. *Or Does It Explode: Black Harlem in the Great Depression.* New York: Oxford University Press, 1991.

Iverem, Esther. *We Gotta Have It: Twenty Years of Seeing Black at the Movies, 1986–2006.* New York: Thunder's Mouth Press, 2007.

Harris, Cecil. *Call the Yankees My Daddy: Reflections on Baseball, Race, and Family.* Guilford, Conn.: Lyons Press, 2006.

Hynes, Charles, and Bob Drury. *Incident at Howard Beach.* New York: Putnam, 1990.

Jacobs, James B., and Kimberly Potter. *Hate Crimes, Criminal Law, and Identity Politics.* New York: Oxford University Press, 1998.

Johnson, Ben, and Mary Bullard-Johnson. *Who's What and Where: A Directory and Reference Book of America's Minority Journalists.* Columbia, Mo.,1988.

Katznelson, Ira. *When Affirmative Action Was White: An Untold Story of Racial Inequality in Twentieth Century America.* New York: W. W. Norton, 2005.

Kelley, Norman. *The Big Mango.* New York: Akashic Books, 2000.

Kim, Claire Jean. *Bitter Fruit: The Politics of Black-Korean Conflict in New York City.* New Haven, Conn.: Yale University Press, 2003.

Kurtz, Howard. *Media Circus: The Trouble with America's Newspapers.* New York: Times Books, 1993.

Lewis, David Levering. *W. E. B. Du Bois: The Fight for Equality and the American Century, 1919–1963.* New York: Henry Holt, 2000.

Lincoln, Charles Eric, and Lawrence H. Mamiya. *The Black Church in the African American Experience.* Durham, N.C.: Duke University Press, 1990.

Mandela, Nelson. *Long Walk to Freedom: The Autobiography of Nelson Mandela.* Boston: Little, Brown, 1994.

McFadden, Robert D., et al. *Outrage: The Story behind the Tawana Brawley Hoax.* New York: Bantam, 1990.

McManus, Edgar J. *A History of Negro Slavery in New York.* Syracuse, N.Y.: Syracuse University Press, 2001.

Mills, Kay. *This Little Light of Mine: The Life of Fannie Lou Hamer.* New York: Dutton, 1993.

Newkirk, Pamela. *Within the Veil: Black Journalists, White Media.* New York: New York University Press, 2000.

Njeri, Itabari. *The Last Plantation: Color, Conflict, and Identity; Reflections of a New World Black.* Boston: Houghton Mifflin, 1997.

Osofsky, Gilbert. *Harlem: The Making of a Ghetto; Negro New York, 1890–1930.* New York: Harper and Row, 1971.

Parmet, Herbert S. *George Bush: The Life of a Lone Star Yankee.* New York: Scribner, 1997.

Peirce, Neal R., and Jerry Hagstrom. *The Book of America: Inside Fifty States Today.* New York: W. W. Norton, 1983.

Pride, Armistead S., and Clint C. Wilson II. *A History of the Black Press.* Washington, D.C.: Howard University Press, 1997.

Rainer, Peter. *Love and Hisses: The National Society of Film Critics Sound Off on the Hottest Movie Controversies.* San Francisco: Mercury House, 1992.

Reitano, Joanne. *The Restless City: A Short History of New York from Colonial Times to the Present.* New York: Routledge, 2006.

Rich, Wilbur C. *David Dinkins and New York City Politics: Race, Images, and the Media.* Albany, N.Y.: State University of New York Press, 2007.

Roberts, Eugene, Jr., and Hank Klibanoff. *The Race Beat: The Press, the Civil Rights Struggle, and the Awakening of a Nation.* New York: Vintage, 2007.

Schlesinger, Arthur M., Jr. *The Almanac of American History.* New York: G. P. Putnam's Sons, 1983.

Segal, Ronald. *The Black Diaspora: Five Centuries of the Black Experience outside Africa.* New York: Farrar, Straus and Giroux, 1995.

Shapiro, Edward S. *Crown Heights: Blacks, Jews, and the 1991 Brooklyn Riot.* Hanover, N.H.: Brandeis University Press, 2006.

Schneier, Edward V., and Brian Murtaugh. *New York Politics: A Tale of Two States.* New York: M. E. Sharpe, 2001.

Sleeper, Jim. *The Closest of Strangers: Liberalism and the Politics of Race in New York.* New York: W. W. Norton, 1991.

Stokes, Geoffrey. *The Village Voice Anthology (1956–1980): Twenty-five Years of Writing from the Village Voice.* New York: Morrow, 1982.

Takaki, Ronald. *A Different Mirror: A History of Multicultural America.* Boston: Little, Brown, 1994.

Taibbi, Mike, and Anna Sims-Phillips. *Unholy Alliances: Working the Tawana Brawley Story.* San Diego: Harcourt Brace Jovanovich, 1989.

Teaford, Jon. *Rough Road to Renaissance: Urban Revitalization in America, 1940–1985.* Baltimore: Johns Hopkins University Press, 1990.

Thomas, Andrew Peyton. *Crime and the Sacking of America: The Roots of Chaos.* Dulles, Va.: Brassey's, 1994.

Thomas, David A., and John J. Gabarro. *Breaking Through: The Making of Minority Executives in Corporate America*. Cambridge, Mass.: Harvard Business Press, 1999.

Vigilante, Richard. *Strike: The Daily News War and the Future of American Labor*. New York: Simon and Schuster, 1994.

Walters, Ronald. *Freedom Is Not Enough*. Lanham, Md.: Rowman and Littlefield, 2005.

White, Armond. *The Resistance: Ten Years of Pop Culture That Shook the World*. Woodstock, N.Y.: Overlook Press, 1995.

Wilder, Craig Steven. *A Covenant with Color: Race and Social Power in Brooklyn*. New York: Columbia University Press, 2000.

Williams, Juan. *Eyes on the Prize: America's Civil Rights Years*. New York: Viking Penguin, 1987.

Magazines and Journals

African Voices
American Heritage
American Journalism Review
Black Alumni Network newsletter
Black Enterprise
Black Issues Book Review
Brill's Content
Columbia Journalism Review
Crain's New York Business
Dollars and Sense
Ebony
Esquire
Jewish Week
NABJ Journal
New York
New York Times Magazine
New Yorker
St. Louis Journalism Review
Schaefer Scene
Time
TNS Reports
Unity Democrat

Newspapers

Brooklyn Eagle
Christian Science Monitor

City Sun
Los Angeles Times
New York Amsterdam News
New York Beacon
New York Courier
New York Daily News
New York Press
New York Times
Newsday
San Francisco Chronicle
USA Today
Village Voice
Villager
Washington Post

Oral Histories, Theses, and Dissertations

Bundy, Kissette. Oral history interview with Wilbert Tatum. Columbia University Oral History Project, 1987.

Dawkins, Wayne. "Black United Front." Master's project, Columbia University Graduate School of Journalism, 1980.

Masters, Robert, and Dan North. Oral history interviews with Moe Foner. Columbia University Oral History Project, 1985, 1986, 2001.

Russell, Carlos. "Perspectives on Politics: A Black Community Looks at Itself." Ph.D. diss., Union Graduate School, 1978.

Video and Digital Media

Dawkins, Wayne (producer), and Van Dora Williams (director). *Voting Rights Northern Style.* Hampton University, 2007.

Friendly, Fred. *The Other Side of the News: Tawana Brawley and the Press.* Columbia University Media and Society Seminars Collection, PBS Video, 1988.

Sparrow, Jim. Blackout History Project. George Mason University, Center for History and New Media, 2000.

Lynch, Shola. *Chisholm '72: Unbought and Unbossed.* Lantern Lane Entertainment DVD, 2004.

Index